Lecture Notes in Computer Science   10867

Commenced Publication in 1973
Founding and Former Series Editors:
Gerhard Goos, Juris Hartmanis, and Jan van Leeuwen

More information about this series at http://www.springer.com/series/7407

Susan Stepney · Sergey Verlan (Eds.)

Unconventional Computation and Natural Computation

17th International Conference, UCNC 2018
Fontainebleau, France, June 25–29, 2018
Proceedings

Springer

Editors
Susan Stepney 🆔
University of York
Heslington, York
UK

Sergey Verlan 🆔
Université Paris-Est Créteil
Créteil
France

ISSN 0302-9743   ISSN 1611-3349   (electronic)
Lecture Notes in Computer Science
ISBN 978-3-319-92434-2   ISBN 978-3-319-92435-9   (eBook)
https://doi.org/10.1007/978-3-319-92435-9

Library of Congress Control Number: 2018944401

LNCS Sublibrary: SL1 – Theoretical Computer Science and General Issues

Printed on acid-free paper

This Springer imprint is published by the registered company Springer International Publishing AG part of Springer Nature
The registered company address is: Gewerbestrasse 11, 6330 Cham, Switzerland

Preface

The 17th International Conference on Unconventional Computation and Natural Computation (UCNC 2018) was held June 25–29, 2018, on the campus of the IUT de Fontainebleau at the University of Paris-Est Créteil – Val de Marne, Fontainebleau, France. The UCNC series of international conferences is genuinely interdisciplinary and it covers theory as well as experiments and applications. It is concerned with various proposals for computation that go beyond the Turing model, with human-designed computation inspired by nature, and with the computational nature of processes taking place in nature. Typical, but not exclusive, topics are: hypercomputation; chaos and dynamical systems-based computing; granular, fuzzy, and rough computing; mechanical computing; cellular, evolutionary, molecular, neural, and quantum computing; membrane computing; amorphous computing, swarm intelligence; artificial immune systems; physics of computation; chemical computation; evolving hardware; the computational nature of self-assembly, developmental processes, bacterial communication, and brain processes.

More information about this conference series and its full history can be found on the following website: https://www.cs.auckland.ac.nz/research/groups/CDMTCS/conferences/uc/uc.html

Submissions to UCNC 2018 comprised 22 full papers across a wide variety of topics, including (but not limited to) quantum computing, algorithmic self-assembly, and chemical reaction networks. Of these, 15 were accepted for presentation at the conference and publication in these proceedings. Each submission was reviewed by at least three, and on average 3.2, Program Committee members. Beyond the contributed papers and associated talks, UCNC 2018 was greatly enhanced by the plenary talks and tutorials provided by several prestigious speakers. Satoshi Murata from Tohoku University, Japan, gave a plenary talk entitled "Molecular Robotics Project." Julian Miller from the University of York, UK, presented his plenary talk "The Alchemy of Computation: How to Use the Unknown." Lee Cronin from the University of Glasgow, UK, gave a plenary talk titled "Exploring Computation in Chemical Systems with Programmable Chemical Arrays." A tutorial titled "Rule-Based Modeling in Systems Biology: A Kappa Tutorial" was provided by Jean Krivine from CNRS and University of Paris Didérot, France.

The conference was accompanied by four workshops, which were partially included in the conference program. The Workshop on Membrane Computing was organized by Rudolf Freund from the Technical University of Vienna, Austria, and Sergiu Ivanov from the University of Évry, France. The invited speaker for that workshop was Artiom Alhazov from the Academy of Sciences of Moldova, Moldova.

The Decision Making in Nature Workshop was organized by Makoto Naruse from the National Institute of Information and Communications Technology, Japan, and Matteo Cavaliere from Manchester Metropolitan University, UK. The invited speakers for this workshop were Taiki Takahasi from Hokkaido University, Japan, and Hirokazu Hori from the University of Yamanashi, Japan.

The 9th International Workshop on Physics and Computation was organized by Michael Cuffaro and Philippos Papayannopoulos from the University of Western Ontario, Canada. The invited speakers for this workshop were Judit X. Madarász from the Hungarian Academy of Sciences, Hungary, and Oron Shagrir from the Hebrew University of Jerusalem, Israel.

The Self-Assembly Workshop was organized by Damien Woods from Inria, France, and it had the following invited speakers: Matt Patitz from the University of Arkansas, USA, Pierre-Étienne Meunier from Inria, France, and Nicolas Schabanel from CNRS and ENS Lyon, France.

UCNC 2018 was also co-located with the Machines, Computations, and Universality Conference (MCU 2018). A joint session was held on June 28 featuring an invited talk by Damien Woods from Inria, France, entitled "Molecular Computation with DNA Self-Assembly."

UCNC 2018 brought together researchers from all over the world to share and discuss ideas on forms of computation inspired by natural systems and unconventional methods. Its success as the 17th conference in the series is owed to the great amount of help from many people and organizations. First and foremost, we would like to thank the Steering Committee co-chairs, Nataša Jonoska and Jarkko Kari, whose expert guidance and invaluable advice helped to shape all aspects of the conference. Next, a huge debt of gratitude is owed to the Program Committee members and external reviewers, who carefully reviewed all submissions and provided important feedback to help decide which papers to accept.

Partial financial support for the conference was provided by IUT de Sénart-Fontainebleau, the University of Paris-Est Créteil, Laboratoire d'Algorithmique Complexité et Logique, Faculté des Sciences et Technologies of the University of Paris-Est Créteil, and Institut national de recherche en informatique et en automatique (Inria). We also thank the administration of IUT de Fontainebleau for the perfect infrastructure made available to UCNC 2018. Finally, we would like to thank our secretaries, Nathalie Gillet and Flore Tsila, for their extensive assistance in organizing the event and for smoothly running the conference.

Special thanks are due to Springer for the efficient cooperation in the timely production of this volume, as well as for the financial sponsorship supporting the best student paper award and some student travel grants.

June 2018

Susan Stepney
Sergey Verlan

Organization

Steering Committee

Thomas Back	Leiden University, The Netherlands
Cristian S. Calude (Founding Chair)	University of Auckland, New Zealand
Lov K. Grover	Bell Labs, USA
Natasha Jonoska (Co-chair)	University of South Florida, USA
Jarkko Kari (Co-chair)	University of Turku, Finland
Lila Kari	University of Western Ontario, Canada
Seth Lloyd	Massachusetts Institute of Technology, USA
Giancarlo Mauri	Università degli Studi di Milano-Bicocca, Italy
Gheorghe Păun	Institue of Mathematics of the Romanian Academy, Romania
Grzegorz Rozenberg (Emeritus Chair)	Leiden University, The Netherlands
Arto Salomaa	Univeresity of Turku, Finland
Tommaso Toffoli	Boston University, USA
Carme Torras	Institute of Robotics and Industrial Informatics, Spain
Jan van Leeuwen	Utrecht University, The Netherlands

Program Committee

Andy Adamatzky	University of the West of England, UK
Selim G. Akl	Queens University, Canada
Martyn Amos	Manchester Metropolitan University, UK
Pablo Arrighi	University of Marseille, France
Olivier Bournez	LIX and Ecole Polytechnique, France
Cristian Calude	University of Auckland, New Zealand
Matteo Cavaliere	University of Edinburgh, UK
Erzsébet Csuhaj-Varjú	Eötvös Loránd University, Hungary
Alberto Dennunzio	University of Milano-Bicocca, Italy
Michael J. Dinneen	University of Auckland, New Zealand
Rudolf Freund	Vienna University of Technology, Austria
Angel Goni-Moreno	Newcastle University, UK
Masami Hagiya	University of Tokyo, Japan
Kazuo Iwama	Kyoto University, Japan
Natasha Jonoska	University of South Florida, USA
Jarkko Kari	University of Turku, Finland
Lila Kari	University of Waterloo, Canada
Viv Kendon	Durham University, UK
Giancarlo Mauri	University of Milano-Bicocca, Italy

Ian McQuillan   University of Saskatchewan, Canada
Niall Murphy   University of Cambridge, UK
Turlough Neary   University of Zurich/ETH Zurich, Switzerland
Pekka Orponen   Aalto University, Finland
Matthew Patitz   University of Arkansas, USA
Mario J. Pérez-Jiménez   University of Seville, Spain
Ion Petre   Åbo Akademi University, Finland
Kai Salomaa   Queen's University, Canada
Shinnosuke Seki   University of Electro-Communications, Tokyo, Japan
Oron Shagrir   Hebrew University of Jerusalem, Israel
Hava Siegelmann   University of Massachusetts Amherst, USA
Susan Stepney (Co-chair)   University of York, UK
Sergey Verlan (Co-chair)   University of Paris-Est Créteil, France
Damien Woods   Inria, France

Organizing Committee

Patrick Cégielski (Co-chair)   University of Paris-Est Créteil
Julien Cervelle   University of Paris-Est Créteil
Luidnel Maignan   University of Paris-Est Créteil
Antoine Spicher   University of Paris-Est Créteil
Pierre Valarcher   University of Paris-Est Créteil
Pascal Vanier   University of Paris-Est Créteil
Sergey Verlan (Co-chair)   University of Paris-Est Créteil

Additional Reviewers

Sepinoud Azimi   Luca Manzoni
Da-Jung Cho   Antonio E. Porreca
Hwee Kim   Luis Valencia Cabrera
Marco S. Nobile   Hendrik Jan Hoogeboom
Daniel Terno   Timothy Ng
Jason Bernard   Chiu-Wing Sham
Daniel Cruz

Sponsoring Institutions

IUT de Sénart-Fontainebleau
University of Paris-Est Créteil (UPEC)
Laboratoire d'Algorithmique Complexité et Logique (LACL)
Faculté des Sciences et Technologies of the University of Paris-Est Créteil
Institut National de Recherche en Informatique et en Automatique (Inria)
Springer

Abstracts of Invited Talks

Exploring Computation in Chemical Systems With Programmable Chemical Arrays

Abhishek Sharma, Juan Manuel Parrilla Gutierrez, and Leroy Cronin

Department of Algorithms and Their Applications, School of Chemistry,
University of Glasgow, Glasgow, G12 8QQ, UK
Lee.Cronin@glasgow.ac.uk

Complex physicochemical processes occurring in nature such as evolution, biological neural networks, self-assembly have inspired the development of unconventional computation architectures such as DNA computing, swarm intelligence, evolutionary algorithms. Molecular computation such as DNA computing utilized information processing capabilities of DNA base pairs and have shown to solve the Hamiltonian path problem and 20-variable 3-SAT problem. On the other hand, reaction-diffusion computers based on excitation media such as Belousov-Zhabotinsky reaction have shown to have potential for computation arising from demonstrating logic gates, and solving a Voronoi diagram. The former computation architecture relies on data storage information processing via molecular recognition principles and latter depends on interactions between spatiotemporal excitation patterns.

In this talk I will describe a new approach to a computational architecture that interfaces addressable and programmable grids that connect to a chemical system. The proposed architecture uses a hybrid approach by combining macroscale reaction-diffusion and molecular computation capabilities to enhance the information processing and ease of input-output (I/O) capabilities. The architectures consist of an array of addressable chemicals either in a phase partitioned physically e.g. droplets or using reaction diffusion. By addressing the array using either a localized mechanical, electrical, or optical input and then reading out via a camera the dynamics and computational abilities of the system will be probed. The control over the array allows us to define macroscale I/O and process control as a "physical firmware". However, the information processing occurs at molecular scale via complex molecular reaction networks within the chemical substrate. Preliminary results from our initial investigations will be presented that explore the encoding, information processing, and decoding process. The abilities of these systems to solve a particular subset of computational problems will also be presented.

The Alchemy of Computation:
How to Use the Unknown

Julian F. Miller

Department of Electronic Engineering, University of York,
Heslington, York, YO10 5DD, UK
julian.miller@york.ac.uk

The traditional way of solving many kinds of problems is to utilise a small number of well-understood components and through analysis and logic assemble a larger system that satisfies the user requirements. It is undeniable that this approach has enabled us to create extraordinary artefacts and technologies. However, such an approach explores and utilises only a tiny fraction of the problem solving capabilities of systems. This issue was highlighted by Michael Conrad's "price of programmability" which asserts that conventional programming and design excludes many of the processes that may lead to us solving the problem.

Biological organisms however have never been designed at all and the various forms have arisen through a process of natural evolution. It is undeniable that although this process has not created the technological marvels of today, it has created extraordinary solutions of survival in a complex world. In doing so, natural evolution has exploited and utilised a vast number of physical effects and interactions.

In recent years it has become apparent that it is possible to utilise conventional technology and computing to build unconventional computational systems that do not pay the price of programmability. These are arrived at through a form of computational alchemy, in which many possible systems are assembled and assessed without an understanding of how the parts interact or even the physics of their interaction.

Two techniques are presented that illustrate this. One is called Cartesian Genetic Programming. In this, graph-based computational structures are evolved to solve many kinds of problems including electronic circuits, image feature detectors and neural networks. The other technique, called evolution in materio, applies artificial evolution to the manipulation of materials to solve computational problems.

Molecular Robotics Project

Satoshi Murata

Tohoku University, 6-6-01 Aobayama, Sendai, Miyagi 980-8579, Japan
murata@molbot.mech.tohoku.ac.jp

Abstract. This talk introduces the molecular robotics project in Japan. This project was conducted from 2012 to 2017 by 70 laboratories in Japan supported by Grant- in-Aid for Scientific Research on Innovative Areas, MEXT, Japan. The purpose of this project is to develop a methodology for constructing a robot composed of molecular level elements, such as sensors, processors, ac-tuators and a structure containing them.

Keywords: Molecular robotics project · Amoeba-type molecular robot Gel automaton

A "robot" is defined as an "autonomous system" that acquires information from the external environment with a sensor, processes the information, and exerts an effect on the environment according to the result. There is also a need for a body (structure) to distinguish the system from the environment and to integrate these components. In the molecular robotics project, we worked on the design, production and integration/control technologies for molecular robotic system [1, 2].

As a prototype, we developed an amoeba type molecular robot [3, 4]. The amoeba robot is a micro-sized liposome enclosing molecular sensors, molecular actuators driven by kinesin and microtubules, and a molecular computer. In this robot, the mechanism called DNA clutch is activated by an input of light signal, and the sliding movement of microtubule/kinesin is transformed into amoeba-like liposomal defor-mation. For fabrication of this prototype, the technique of enclosing various molecular devices in a high density in liposomes, a protocol to drive many different molecular devices in the same solution have been developed. Another challenge in the project is to design and fabricate a millimeter scale reaction fields. For this purpose, we propose a model called "gel automaton" in which an array of gel capsules/beads acting as an automaton [5]. Theoretical studies of its computational capability and experimental studies of molecular implementation of the model have been conducted. Along with these prototypes, various element technologies/tools for molecular robotics have been developed throughout the project. Some examples are: an RNA nanostructure device capable of controlling the fate of cancer cell [6], method to accelerate DNA reaction (toe-hold exchange) speed, method to amplify DNA signal, realizing orthogonal reaction system in the same solution [7], and etc.

Through this project, we have established a molecular robotics community in Japan consisting of researchers from various fields of expertise. In addition, we are engaged in educational activities for young people such as undergraduate students and high school students to disseminate the awareness of molecular robotics.

References

1. Murata, S., Konagaya, A., Kobayashi, S., Saito, H., Hagiya, M.: Molecular robotics: a new paradigm for artifacts. New Gener. Comput. **31**, 27–45 (2013). (Ohmsha, Ltd. and Springer)
2. Hagiya, M., Konagaya, A., Kobayashi, S., Saito, H., Murata, S.: Molecular robots with sensors and intelligence. Acc. Chem. Res. **47**(6), 1681–1690 (2014)
3. Sato, Y., Hiratsuka, Y., Kawamata, I., Murata, S., Nomura, S.M.: Micrometer-sized molecular robot changes its shape in response to signal molecules, Sci. Robot. **2**(4), eaal3735 (2017)
4. Keya, J.J., Suzuki, R., Kabir, A.M.R., Inoue, D., Asanuma, H., Sada, D., Hess, H., Kuzuya, A., Kakugo, A.: DNA-assisted swarm control in a biomolecular motor system, Nature Commun. **9**, 453 (2018)
5. Hagiya, M., et al.: On DNA-based gellular automata. In: Ibarra, O., Kari, L., Kopecki, S. (eds.) UCNC 2014. LNCS, vol. 8553, pp. 177–189. Springer, Cham (2014)
6. Osada, E., Suzuki, Y., Hidaka, K., Ohno, H., Sugiyama, H., Endo, M., Saito, H.: Engineering RNA-protein complexes with different shapes for imaging and therapeutic applications. ACS Nano. **8**(8), 8130–8140 (2014)
7. Murayama, K., Kashida, H., Asanuma, H.: Acyclic L-Threoninol nucleic acid (LaTNA) with suitable structural rigidity cross-pairs with DNA and RNA. Chem. Commun. **51**, 6500–6503 (2015)

Molecular Computation with DNA Self-assembly

Damien Woods

Inria, Paris, France

The field of algorithmic self-assembly is concerned with the theory and practice of having molecules stick together to grow computational structures in an autonomous bottom-up fashion. Theoretical work focuses on characterising the computational expressiveness of self-assembly models. Practice is concerned with using molecules, such as DNA, to implement algorithmic self-assembly programs in the wet-lab. The presentation will cover both topics. First, there will be an introduction to what it means to compute during a self-assembly process, an overview of some computational models, as well as basic mathematical results. Attendees will then hear about how one goes about designing and experimentally implementing algorithmic self-assembling DNA tiles in the wet lab, and will see some of our latest results from recent joint work with David Doty, Cameron Myhrvold, Joy Hui, Felix Zhou, Peng Yin and Erik Winfree.

Contents

P Systems with Activation
and Blocking of Rules

Artiom Alhazov[1], Rudolf Freund[2(✉)], and Sergiu Ivanov[3]

[1] Institute of Mathematics and Computer Science, Academy of Sciences of Moldova,
Academiei 5, 2028 Chişinău, Moldova
artiom@math.md
[2] Faculty of Informatics, TU Wien, Favoritenstraße 9–11, 1040 Vienna, Austria
rudi@emcc.at
[3] IBISC, Université Évry, Université Paris-Saclay,
23 Boulevard de France, 91025 Évry, France
sergiu.ivanov@univ-evry.fr

Abstract. We introduce new possibilities to control the application of
rules based on the preceding applications, which can be defined in a
general way for (hierarchical) P systems and the main known derivation modes. Computational completeness can be obtained even with
non-cooperative rules and using both activation and blocking of rules,
especially for the set modes of derivation. When we allow the application of rules to influence the application of rules in previous derivation
steps, applying a non-conservative semantics for what we consider to be
a derivation step, we can even "go beyond Turing".

1 Introduction

Originally founded by Gheorghe Păun in 1998, see [30], membrane systems, now
known as P systems, are a model of computing based on the abstract notion of a
membrane which can be seen as a container delimiting a region containing objects
which are acted upon by the rewriting rules associated with the membranes.
Quite often, the objects are plain symbols coming from a finite alphabet, i.e.,
multisets (for basic results on multiset computing, for example, see [27]), but
P systems operating on more complex objects (e.g., strings, arrays) are often
considered, too, for instance, see [18].

A comprehensive overview of different flavors of membrane systems and their
expressive power is given in the handbook which appeared in 2010, see [31]. For
a state of the art snapshot of the domain, we refer the reader to the P systems
website [34] as well as to the Bulletin of the International Membrane Computing
Society [33].

The work is supported by National Natural Science Foundation of China
(61320106005, 61033003, and 61772214) and the Innovation Scientists and Tech-
nicians Troop Construction Projects of Henan Province (154200510012).

Nearly thirty years ago, the monograph on regulated rewriting by Jürgen Dassow and Gheorghe Păun [15] already gave a first comprehensive overview on many concepts of regulated rewriting, especially for the string case. Yet as it turned out later, many of the mechanisms considered there for guiding the application of productions/rules can also be applied to other objects than strings, e.g., to n-dimensional arrays [16]. As exhibited in [22], for comparing the generating power of grammars working in the sequential derivation mode, many relations between various regulating mechanisms can be established in a very general setting without any reference to the underlying objects the rules are working on, using a general model for graph-controlled, programmed, random-context, and ordered grammars of arbitrary type based on the applicability of rules. Also in the field of P systems [31,34] where mainly multisets have been considered, such regulating mechanisms were used, e.g., see [12].

Dynamic evolution of the set of available rules has been considered from the very beginning of membrane computing. Already in 1999, generalized P systems were introduced in [17]; in these systems the membranes, alongside the objects, contain *operators* which act on these objects, while the P system itself acts on the operators, thereby modifying the transformations which will be carried out on the objects in the subsequent steps. Among further ideas on dynamic rules, one may list rule creation [9], activators [1], inhibiting/deinhibiting rules [14], and symport/antiport *of rules* [13]. One of the more recent developments in this direction are *polymorphic P systems* [5,7,26], in which rules are defined by pairs of membranes, whose contents may be modified by moving objects in or out, as well as P systems with randomized right-hand sides of rules [2,3], where the right-hand sides are chosen randomly and in different ways from the given set of rules.

We here follow an approach started to be elaborated in [4], where in the general framework of sequential systems the applicability of rules is controlled by the application of rules in the preceding derivation step(s). The application of a rule in one derivation step may either activate some rules to be applied in the next derivation step(s) or may block their application. We immediately observe that the application of a rule requires its activation in a preceding step. A computation may also take derivation steps without applying a rule as long as there are some rules activated for future derivation steps. In contrast to the general framework for control mechanisms as described in [22], we here are not dealing with the applicability of rules itself but with the possible activation or blocking of rules by the effective application of rules in preceding steps.

In the following we will establish computational completeness results for various kinds of one-membrane P systems (resembling multiset grammars) and several derivation modes, using activation and blocking of rules to be applied in succeeding derivation steps. We may even allow the application of rules to influence previous derivation steps, but using a conservative semantics that considers derivations to be consistent when such backwards activations or blockings of rules are not changing the correctness of the derivation, we cannot "go beyond Turing", which on the other hand can be achieved by allowing such backwards information to change past configurations by triggering the applications of newly activated rules and by using a less conservative semantics looking at infinite computations on finite multisets as in red-green "P automata"(for instance, see [19]).

Various possibilities of how one may "go beyond Turing" are discussed in [28], for example, the definitions and results for red-green Turing machines can be found there. In [8] the notion of red-green automata for register machines with input strings given on an input tape (often also called *counter automata*) is introduced and the concept of *red-green P automata* for several specific models of membrane systems is explained. Via red-green counter automata, the results for acceptance and recognizability of finite strings by red-green Turing machines are carried over to red-green P automata. The basic idea of red-green automata is to distinguish between two different sets of states (red and green states) and to consider infinite runs of the automaton on finite input objects (strings, multisets); allowed to change between red and green states more than once, red-green automata can recognize more than the recursively enumerable sets (of strings, multisets), i.e., in that way one can "go beyond Turing". In the area of P systems, first attempts to do that can be found in [11,32]. Computations with infinite words by P automata were investigated in [24].

In [20,21], infinite runs of P automata are considered, taking into account the existence/non-existence of a recursive feature of the current sequence of configurations. In that way, infinite sequences over $\{0,1\}$, called "observer languages", are obtained where 1 indicates that the specific feature is fulfilled by the current configuration and 0 indicates that this specific feature is not fulfilled. The recognizing runs of red-green automata then correspond with ω-regular languages over $\{0,1\}$ of a specific form ending with 1^ω as observer languages. The special observer language $\{0,1\}^* \{1\}^\omega$ corresponds with the acceptance condition for P automata called "partial adult halting". This special acceptance variant for P automata with infinite runs on finite multisets is motivated by an observation made for the evolution of time lines described by P systems – at some moment, a specific part (a succession of configurations) of the evolving time lines, for example, the part describing time 0, shall not change any more.

We now may also consider variants of P systems with activation and blocking of rules as well as infinite computations on a given finite multiset. Such an infinite computation is called *valid* if each prefix of the computation becomes stable, i.e., neither the configuration itself nor the set of applicable rules changes any more. This less conservative semantics for activating and/or blocking the rules in preceding derivation steps allows us to take the infinite sequence of stable configurations obtained in this way as the final computation on the given input and – provided it exists – we may just consider the result of the first computation step and thus the second configuration to see whether the input has been accepted. Again this can be seen as looking at a specific part of the evolving time lines, now the part describing time 1, requiring that it should not change any more, but now also requesting that the whole computation should converge.

In the following section, we recall some notions from formal language theory as well as the main definitions of the general framework for P systems working under different derivation modes, see [25]. Then we define the new concept of activation and blocking of rules based on the applicability of rules within this general framework of static P systems. In Sect. 4 we prove first results only using activation of rules. Computational completeness results using both activation and blocking of rules are established in Sect. 5. Then we extend our systems by allowing activation and blocking of rules in previous derivation steps in Sect. 6, and finally even discuss how to "go beyond Turing" in Sect. 7. A summary of the results obtained in this paper and some future research topics extending the notions and results considered in this paper are given in Sect. 8.

2   Definitions

After some preliminaries from formal language theory, we define our model for hierarchical P systems in the general setting of this paper as well as the main derivation modes considered in the area of membrane systems, see [25]. Then we define the new variant of controlling rule applications in P systems by activation and blocking of rules induced by the application of rules in a derivation step.

2.1   Preliminaries

The set of integers is denoted by $\mathbb{Z}$, the set of non-negative integers by $\mathbb{N}_0$, and the set of positive integers (natural numbers) by $\mathbb{N}$. An *alphabet* V is a finite non-empty set of abstract *symbols*. Given V, the free monoid generated by V under the operation of concatenation is denoted by V^*; the elements of V^* are called strings, and the *empty string* is denoted by λ; $V^* \setminus \{\lambda\}$ is denoted by V^+. Let $\{a_1, \ldots, a_n\}$ be an arbitrary alphabet; the number of occurrences of a symbol a_i in x is denoted by $|x|_{a_i}$; the *Parikh vector* associated with x with respect to $a_1, \ldots a_n$ is $\left(|x|_{a_1}, \ldots, |x|_{a_n}\right)$. The *Parikh image* of a language L over $\{a_1, \ldots, a_n\}$ is the set of all Parikh vectors of strings in L, and we denote it by $Ps(L)$. For a family of languages FL, the family of Parikh images of languages in FL is denoted by $PsFL$. The families of regular and recursively enumerable string languages are denoted by REG and RE, respectively.

A (finite) multiset over the (finite) alphabet V, $V = \{a_1, \ldots, a_n\}$, is a mapping $f : V \longrightarrow \mathbb{N}_0$ and can be represented by any string x the Parikh vector of which with respect to $a_1, \ldots, a_n$ is $(f(a_1), \ldots, f(a_n))$. The set of all finite multisets over an alphabet V is denoted by V°.

For more details of formal language theory the reader is referred to the monographs and handbooks in this area [15, 31].

2.2   Register Machines

As a computationally complete model able to generate (accept) all sets in $PsRE$ we will use register machines:

A *register machine* is a construct $M = (n, H, R_M, p_0, h)$ where n, $n \geq 1$, is the number of registers, H is the set of instruction labels, p_0 is the start label, h is the halting label (only used for the HALT instruction), and R_M is a set of (labeled) instructions being of one of the following forms:

- $p : (\text{ADD}(r), q, s)$ increments the value in register r and in a non-deterministic way chooses to continue either with the instruction labeled by q or with the instruction labeled by s,
- $p : (\text{SUB}(r), q, s)$ decrements the value in register r and continues the computation with the instruction labeled by q if the register was non-empty, otherwise it continues with the instruction labeled by s;
- $h : \text{HALT}$ halts the machine.

M is called deterministic if in all ADD-instructions $p : (\text{ADD}(r), q, s)$, it holds that $q = s$; in this case we write $p : (\text{ADD}(r), q)$. Deterministic register machines can accept all recursively enumerable sets of vectors of natural numbers with k components using precisely $k + 2$ registers, see [29].

2.3 A General Model for Hierarchical P Systems

We first recall the main definitions of the general model for hierarchical P systems and the basic derivation modes as defined, for example, in [25].

A *(hierarchical) P system (with rules of type X)* working in the derivation mode δ is a construct

$$\Pi = (V, T, \mu, w_1, \ldots, w_m, R_1, \ldots, R_m, f, \Longrightarrow_{\Pi, \delta}) \text{ where}$$

- V is the alphabet of *objects*;
- $T \subseteq V$ is the alphabet of *terminal objects*;
- μ is the hierarchical membrane structure (a rooted tree of membranes) with the membranes uniquely labeled by the numbers from 1 to m;
- $w_i \in V^*$, $1 \leq i \leq m$, is the *initial multiset* in membrane i;
- R_i, $1 \leq i \leq m$, is a finite set of *rules of type X* assigned to membrane i;
- f is the label of the membrane from which the result of a computation has to be taken from (in the generative case) or into which the initial multiset has to be given in addition to w_f (in the accepting case),
- $\Longrightarrow_{\Pi, \delta}$ is the derivation relation under the derivation mode δ.

The symbol X in "rules of type X" may stand for "evolution", "communication", "membrane evolution", etc.

A configuration is a list of the contents of each cell; a sequence of configurations $C_1, \ldots, C_k$ is called a *computation* in the derivation mode δ if $C_i \Longrightarrow_{\Pi, \delta} C_{i+1}$ for $1 \leq i < k$. The derivation relation $\Longrightarrow_{\Pi, \delta}$ is defined by the set of rules in Π and the given derivation mode which determines the multiset of rules to be applied to the multisets contained in each membrane.

The *language generated by* Π is the set of all terminal multisets which can be obtained in the output membrane f starting from the initial configuration $C_1 = (w_1, \ldots, w_m)$ using the derivation mode δ in a halting computation, i.e.,

$$L_{gen,\delta}(\Pi) = \left\{ C(f) \in T^\circ \mid C_1 \overset{*}{\Longrightarrow}_{\Pi,\delta} C \wedge \neg \exists C' : C \Longrightarrow_{\Pi,\delta} C' \right\},$$

where $C(f)$ stands for the multiset contained in the output membrane f of the configuration C. The configuration C is halting, i.e., no further configuration C' can be derived from it.

The family of languages of multisets generated by P systems of type X with at most n membranes in the derivation mode δ is denoted by $Ps_{gen,\delta}OP_n(X)$.

We also consider P systems as accepting mechanisms: in membrane f, we add the input multiset w_0 to w_f in the initial configuration $C_1 = (w_1, \ldots, w_m)$ thus obtaining $C_1[w_0] = (w_1, \ldots, w_f w_0, \ldots, w_m)$; the input multiset w_0 is accepted if there exists a halting computation in the derivation mode δ starting from $C_1[w_0]$, i.e.,

$$L_{acc,\delta}(\Pi) = \left\{ w_0 \in T^\circ \mid \exists C : \left(C_1[w_0] \overset{*}{\Longrightarrow}_{\Pi,\delta} C \wedge \neg \exists C' : C \Longrightarrow_{\Pi,\delta} C' \right) \right\}.$$

The family of languages of multisets accepted by P systems of type X with at most n membranes in the derivation mode δ is denoted by $Ps_{acc,\delta}OP_n(X)$.

The set of all multisets of rules applicable in each membrane to a given configuration can be restricted by imposing specific conditions, thus yielding the following basic derivation modes (for example, see [25] for formal definitions):

- asynchronous mode (abbreviated *asyn*): at least one rule is applied;
- sequential mode (*sequ*): only one rule is applied;
- maximally parallel mode (*max*): a non-extendable multiset of rules is applied;
- maximally parallel mode with maximal number of rules (*max_{rules}*): a non-extendable multiset of rules of maximal possible cardinality is applied;
- maximally parallel mode with maximal number of objects (*max_{objects}*): a non-extendable multiset of rules affecting as many objects as possible is applied.

In [6], these derivation modes are restricted in such a way that each rule can be applied at most once, thus yielding the set modes *sasyn*, *smax*, *smax_{rules}*, and *smax_{objects}* (the sequential mode is already a set mode by definition).

As many variants of P systems can be *flattened* to only one membrane, see [23], throughout the paper we will assume the simplest membrane structure of only one membrane which in effect reduces the P system to a multiset processing mechanism, and, observing that $f = 1$, in what follows we will use the reduced notation

$$\Pi = (V, T, w_1, R, \Longrightarrow_{\Pi,\delta}).$$

3   P Systems with Activation and Blocking of Rules

We now define our new concept of regulating the application of rules at a specific moment by activation and blocking relations for (generating) P systems.

A *P system with activation and blocking of rules* (an *AB-P system* for short) of type X working in the derivation mode δ is a construct

$$\Pi_{AB} = (\Pi, L, f_L, A, B, L_1, \Longrightarrow_{\Pi_{AB}, \delta})$$

where $\Pi = (V, T, w, R, \Longrightarrow_{\Pi, \delta})$ is a P system of type X, L is a finite set of labels with each label having assigned one rule from R by the function f_L, A, B are finite subsets of $L \times L \times 2^{\mathbb{N}}$, and $L_1 \subseteq L$ describes the set of rules which may be used in the first derivation step. The elements of A and B are of the form (p, q, T) with $p, q \in L$ and T being a finite subset of $\mathbb{N}$; the elements of T indicate how many steps in the future the application of p activates (for A) or blocks (for B) the application of the rule q.

Now let $\Longrightarrow_{\Pi/P, \delta}$, for any set of rules P, $P \subseteq R$, denote the derivation relation obtained from $\Longrightarrow_{\Pi, \delta}$ by reducing the set of available rules from R to P. Then a sequence of multisets $w_i \in O$, $0 \leq i \leq n$, with $w_0 = w$ is called a *valid derivation* of $z = w_n$ – we also write $w_0 \Longrightarrow_{\Pi_{AB}, \delta} w_1 \Longrightarrow_{\Pi_{AB}, \delta} \ldots w_n$ – if and only if, with R_k denoting the set of rules applied to w_k in the k-th derivation step, for every i, $0 \leq i < n$, the following conditions hold true:

- either $w_i \Longrightarrow_{\Pi/P_i, \delta} w_{i+1}$, where P_i is the set of all rules r (identified by their labels) such that there is a relation $(r_j, r, T) \in A$ with $i - j \in T$, which means that the application of a rule r_j in the j-th derivation step has activated rule r probably to be applied in the i-th derivation step, and there is no rule relation $(r_j, r, T) \in B$ such that $i - j \in T$, which means that the application of the rule r_j in the j-th derivation step would block rule r to be applied in the i-th derivation step, **or**
- P_i is empty, i.e., no rule r is activated to be applied i-th derivation step or every activated rule is blocked, too; in this case we take $w_i = w_{i-1}$ provided there is still some rule activated to be applied later.

With this interpretation we see that A can be called the set of *activating rule relations* and B the set of *blocking rule relations*. The role of L_1 is to get a derivation started by defining the rules to be applied in the first derivation step.

In the same way as for the original model of P systems we can define the language generated/accepted by the AB-P system Π_{AB}, now using the derivation relation $\Longrightarrow_{\Pi_{AB}, \delta}$ instead of $\Longrightarrow_{\Pi, \delta}$.

The families of languages of multisets generated/accepted by AB-P systems of type X in the derivation mode δ (in only one membrane) is denoted by $Ps_{\gamma, \delta}OP(X, AB)$, $\gamma \in \{gen, acc\}$.

If the set B of blocking rules is empty, then the AB-P system is said to be a *P system with activation of rules* (an *A-P system* for short) of type X; the corresponding sets of multisets generated/ accepted as well as the respective families of languages of multisets are denoted in the same way as for AB-P system by just omitting the B. In this case we will usually not allow the second case in a derivation of the A-P system that in a derivation step no rule is activated to be applied. Moreover, an A-P system is called an *A1-P system* if for all $(p, q, T) \in A$ we have $T = \{1\}$, which means that the rules applied in one derivation step activate only the rules which can be applied in the next step; in this case we only write (p, q) instead of (p, q, T).

4   Results Below $PsRE$

It is folklore that sequential P systems with non-cooperative rules (i.e., rules with exactly one symbol in their left-hand side) can only generate semilinear sets, i.e., $PsREG$. Our first example shows that using sequential A1-P systems with non-cooperative rules we can generate non-semilinear sets.

Example 1. The non-semilinear set $\{a^n b^m \mid 1 \leq n, 1 \leq m \leq 2^n\}$ can be generated by a sequential A1-P systems with non-cooperative rules (this type of rules is abbreviated *ncoo*):

$$\Pi = (V = \{a, b, A, B\}, T = \{a, b\}, w = Ab, R, \Longrightarrow_{\Pi, sequ}),$$
$$R = \{A \rightarrow a, b \rightarrow BB, A \rightarrow AA, B \rightarrow b\},$$
$$\Pi_{AB} = (\Pi, L, f_L, A, B = \emptyset, L_1, \Longrightarrow_{\Pi_{AB}, sequ}),$$
$$L = \{p_a, p_b, p_A, p_B\},$$
$$L_1 = \{p_a, p_A, p_B\},$$
$$f_L = \{(p_a, A \rightarrow a), (p_b, b \rightarrow BB), (p_A, A \rightarrow AA), (p_B, B \rightarrow b)\},$$
$$A = \{(p_a, p_a), (p_b, p_a), (p_b, p_b), (p_b, p_A), (p_A, p_B), (p_B, p_b), (p_B, p_B)\}.$$

The set A of activating rule relations is graphically illustrated in the following figure which shows that this construction is rather similar to using graph control:

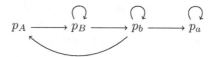

With every adding of one symbol A we may at most double the current number of symbols b using the rules labeled p_B and p_b. At some moment instead of activating p_A by p_b we may switch to p_a whereafter only p_a can be applied any more, yielding a terminal multiset provided all symbols B have been derived to the terminal symbol b before switching from p_b to p_a.   □

In the following proofs we will simplify the notation for AB-P systems by writing labeled rules as $p : r$ instead of first listing all rules r in the underlying P system Π and then in Π_{AB} listing the labels p as well as finally defining the function f_L by listing all pairs (p, r). In a shorter way, the whole AB-P system then can be written as $\Pi_{AB} = (V, T, w, R, A, B, L_1, \Longrightarrow_{\Pi_{AB}, \delta})$ with R already containing the labeled rules.

Corollary 1. $PsREG \subsetneq Ps_{gen, sequ}OP(ncoo, A1)$

Using the maximally parallel derivation mode, we can at least simulate ET0L-systems:

Theorem 1. $PsET0L \subseteq Ps_{gen,max}OP(ncoo, A1)$

Proof (Sketch). Like in P systems with states, see [5], we can use new symbols t_k representing the n tables T_k of the extended tabled Lindenmayer system to be simulated. Using a rule $t_{i,j} : t_i \to t_j$ then indicates that after the application of table T_i the table T_j is to be used; hence, all rules in T_j as well as all rules $t_{j,k} : t_j \to t_k$ for all k and $t_{j,e} : t_j \to \lambda$ are activated by corresponding rule relations in A. The rules $t_{j,e} : t_j \to \lambda$ do not activate any rule, which means that after having applied this rule the computation in the A1-P system ends.

In order to start correctly, we use an initial symbol t_0 and define $L_1 = \{t_{0,k} : t_0 \to t_k \mid 1 \leq k \leq n\}$ which allows us to activate the rules for simulating any table T_k. □

5 Computational Completeness Results

In this section we show that several simple variants of P systems become computationally complete when using the control of activation and blocking of rules.

5.1 Sequential P Systems with Non-cooperative Rules

Theorem 2. $PsRE = Ps_{\gamma,sequ}OP(ncoo, AB)$ *for* $\gamma \in \{gen, acc\}$.

Proof. The proof idea is to show how to simulate register machines. For a given register machine $M = (n, H, R_M, p_0, h)$ we construct an equivalent AB-P system

$$\Pi_{AB} = (V, T, w, R, A, B, L_1, \Longrightarrow_{\Pi_{AB},sequ})$$

in the following way: For every label $p \in H \setminus \{h\}$ we use labels $\left\{l_p, \hat{l}_p, \tilde{l}_p\right\}$ for an ADD-instruction and labels $\left\{l_p, l'_p, l''_p, \hat{l}_p, \tilde{l}_p, \bar{l}_p,\right\}$ for a SUB-instruction; for the final instruction $h : \mathtt{HALT}$ we only use the rule $l_h : h \to \lambda$. For any p, we also use the symbols p, p', and for each register r its contents is described by the number of symbols a_r in (the configurations of) Π_{AB}. The starting rule is given by $L_1 = \{l_{p_0}\}$.

An ADD-instruction $p : (\mathtt{ADD}(r), q, s)$ is simulated by the following labeled rules in R and rule relations in A:

1. $l_p : p \to p' a_r$ and $(l_p, \bar{l}_p), (l_p, \tilde{l}_p) \in A$;
2. $\bar{l}_p : p' \to q, \tilde{l}_p : p' \to s$ and $(\bar{l}_p, l_q), (\tilde{l}_p, l_s) \in A$.

A SUB-instruction $p : (\mathtt{SUB}(r), q, s)$ is simulated by the following labeled rules in R and rule relations in A and B:

1. $l_p : p \to p'$ and $(l_p, \hat{l}_p), (l_p, \tilde{l}_p, 3) \in A$;
2. $\hat{l}_p : a_r \to a_{r,p}$ and $(\hat{l}_p, l''_p), (\hat{l}_p, \tilde{l}_p, 2) \in A$, $(\hat{l}_p, \tilde{l}_p, 2) \in B$;
3. $l''_p : a_{r,p} \to \lambda$;
4. $\bar{l}_p : p' \to q, \tilde{l}_p : p' \to s$ and $(\bar{l}_p, l_q), (\tilde{l}_p, l_s) \in A$.

If the rule $\hat{l}_p : a_r \rightarrow a_{r,p}$ can be applied in the second step, two steps afterwards it activates $\bar{l}_p$ and at the same time blocks $\tilde{l}_p$, which has been activated in the first simulation step and thus will be applied if the register is empty, i.e., if $\hat{l}_p$ cannot be applied.   □

5.2   P Systems Working in the $smax$-Mode

Theorem 3. $PsRE = Ps_{\gamma,\delta}OP(ncoo, AB)$ *for* $\gamma \in \{gen, acc\}$ *and any set derivation mode* δ *from* $\{smax, smax_{rules}, smax_{objects}\}$.

Proof. Again we show how to simulate a register machine $M = (n, H, R_M, p_0, h)$. The equivalent AB-P system $\Pi_{AB} = (V, T, w, R, A, B, L_1, \Longrightarrow_{\Pi_{AB},\delta})$ contains similar ingredients as the one constructed in the proof of Theorem 2; yet the simulation of SUB-instructions now allows us to only use activation and blocking of rules for the next step using the possibility of having several rules applied in parallel:

1. $l_p : p \rightarrow \bar{p}$ and $(l_p, l'_p), (l_p, \hat{l}_p) \in A$;
2. $l'_p : \bar{p} \rightarrow p'$, $\hat{l}_p : a_r \rightarrow a_{r,p}$ and $(l'_p, \tilde{l}_p), (\hat{l}_p, \bar{l}_p), (\hat{l}_p, l''_p) \in A$; $(\hat{l}_p, \tilde{l}_p) \in B$;
3. $l''_p : a_{r,p} \rightarrow \lambda$, $\bar{l}_p : p' \rightarrow q$, $\tilde{l}_p : p' \rightarrow s$ and $(\bar{l}_p, l_q), (\tilde{l}_p, l_s) \in A$.

If register r is empty, in the second step only $\tilde{l}_p$ is activated to be applied in the third step; otherwise, the application of $\hat{l}_p$ activates $\bar{l}_p$ and at the same time blocks $\tilde{l}_p$.   □

5.3   (Purely) Catalytic P Systems Working in the max-Mode

A typical variant of rules in P systems are so-called catalytic rules of the form $ca \rightarrow cv$, where c is a catalyst, a symbol which never evolves itself, but helps another symbol a to evolve into a multiset v. The type of P systems using only catalytic rules is called purely catalytic (abbreviated $pcat$); if both catalytic rules and non-cooperative rules are allowed, we speak of a catalytic P system (abbreviated cat). In the description of the families of sets of multisets generated/accepted by such (purely) catalytic P systems the maximal number of catalysts to be used is indicated as a subscript, i.e., we write $pcat_n$ and cat_n.

The following result then is a consequence of the preceding proofs:

Corollary 2. *For* $\gamma \in \{gen, acc\}$ *and* $\delta \in \{max, max_{rules}, max_{objects}\}$,
$$PsRE = Ps_{\gamma,\delta}OP(pcat_2, AB) \text{ and}$$
$$PsRE = Ps_{\gamma,\delta}OP(cat_1, AB).$$

Proof. Looking carefully into the proof of Theorem 3, we see that the only rules where the set mode is needed are those of the form $\hat{l}_p : a_r \rightarrow a_{r,p}$. Using one catalyst c_1, we can use the rules $\hat{l}_p : c_1 a_r \rightarrow c_1 a_{r,p}$ instead. The remaining details of the proof of Theorem 3 can remain as they are for the *catalytic* case.

For the *purely catalytic* case, we need a second catalyst c_2 for all the other rules, e.g., we take $l_p : c_2 p \rightarrow c_2 p'$ instead of $l_p : p \rightarrow p'$. These observations complete the proof.   □

6 P Systems Using Backwards Activation and Blocking of Rules

The definition of AB-P systems given in Sect. 3 can be extended by allowing the relations in A and B to be of the form (r_j, r, T) with the finite set T also containing negative integers. In that way rules can be activated or blocked in previous steps.

A conservative semantics for this extension is calling a derivation $w_0 \Longrightarrow_{\Pi_{AB},\delta} w_1 \Longrightarrow_{\Pi_{AB},\delta} \ldots w_n$ to be *consistent* if and only if the available sets of rules for previous steps are not changed by having rules activated or blocked backwards in time.

In that way, at least for computationally complete AB-P systems, no increase in the computational power is obtained.

7 Going Beyond Turing

We are now discussing how to "go beyond Turing" by using a less conservative semantics for activating and/or blocking the rules in preceding derivation steps.

The main idea is to consider infinite computations on given finite multisets – compare this with the idea of red-green Turing machines, see [28], and of red-green register machines, see [8] – and call such an infinite computation valid if each prefix of the computation becomes stable, i.e., neither the configuration itself nor the set of applicable rules changes any more. We consider the infinite sequence of stable configurations obtained in this way as the final computation on the given input; then – provided it exists – we just consider the stable first configuration to see whether the input has been accepted. This idea can be used for all the computationally complete variants of P systems with activation and blocking of rules considered in this paper.

There are several ways to look at these infinite computations and the development of the configurations, yet we have in mind the following, based on the ideas elaborated in [20]: we consider the time line of evolutions of the configurations where in each step every configuration evolves again according to the actual activations and blockings of rules including the backwards signals.

One interesting construction principle which may be applied for simulating red-green P systems/automata (starting in red) in all these variants can be the following:

- in order to even capture sequential P systems with activation and blocking of rules, we expand the times in the rule relations by a factor of two, hence, the original computations will happen in each odd derivation step;
- we use two new symbols YES and NO; in the initial configuration we add the new symbol NO;
- each rule p changing the color from red to green activates the rule $p_Y : NO \to YES$ by the backwards activation $(p, p_Y, -1)$ (no such rule is allowed to be activated in L_1);

- each rule p changing the color from green to red activates the rule p_N : $YES \to NO$ by the backwards activation $(p, p_N, -1)$ (no such rule is allowed to be activated in L_1);
- the mind change (change of color) is propagated backwards by using the backwards activation relations $(p_N, p_N, -2)$ and $(p_Y, p_Y, -2)$, respectively;
- these rules p_N and p_Y then are used "backwards" in every even derivation step; the backwards propagation stops when one of these rules is applied in the second derivation step (as a convention, backwards activation rules have no effect any more if they activate a rule before time 1);
- if the computation of a red-green P automaton stabilizes in green, i.e., no mind (color) change from green to red takes place any more, then, of course, no changes in the second configuration occur any more, i.e., it has become stable and therefore available for "reading out" the result of the computation.

We conclude that with every kind of P systems with activation and blocking of rules which allows for the *deterministic* simulation of register machines we can simulate the corresponding variant of red-green P automata which characterize the Σ_2-sets in the Arithmetical Hierarchy (see [10]), i.e., with such systems we at least get Σ_2; compare this with the results obtained in [20, 21].

It is interesting to mention that only "backwards " rule activations are used in the algorithm described above, but no "backwards" rule blockings.

8 Conclusion

We have considered the concept of regulating the applicability of rules based on the application of rules in the preceding step(s) within a very general model for hierarchical P systems and for the main derivation modes. These concepts of activation and blocking of rules can also be extended in a natural way to the many variants of tissue P systems, i.e., networks of cells where a rule to be applied can affect multiple cells at the same time.

Especially for the set modes of derivation, the resulting computational power already reaches computational completeness even with non-cooperative rules and using both activation and blocking of rules. Using a special semantics for activating and/or blocking the rules in preceding derivation steps, we could even show how to "go beyond Turing" with activating rules in preceding derivation steps. An interesting topic for future research is to investigate how powerful such AB-P systems are in generating ω-strings.

Acknowledgements. The authors are very grateful for the useful comments of the referees.

References

1. Alhazov, A.: A note on P systems with activators. In: Păun, Gh., Riscos-Núñez, A., Romero-Jiménez, A., Sancho-Caparrini, F. (eds.) Second Brainstorming Week on Membrane Computing, Sevilla, Spain, 2–7 February 2004, pp. 16–19 (2004)
2. Alhazov, A., Freund, R., Ivanov, S.: P systems with randomized right-hand sides of rules. In: 15th Brainstorming Week on Membrane Computing, Sevilla, Spain, January 31–February 5 2017 (2017)
3. Alhazov, A., Freund, R., Ivanov, S.: Hierarchical P systems with randomized right-hand sides of rules. In: Gheorghe, M., Rozenberg, G., Salomaa, A., Zandron, C. (eds.) CMC 2017. LNCS, vol. 10725, pp. 15–39. Springer, Cham (2018). https://doi.org/10.1007/978-3-319-73359-3_2
4. Alhazov, A., Freund, R., Ivanov, S.: Systems with activation and blocking of rules (2018)
5. Alhazov, A., Freund, R., Ivanov, S., Oswald, M.: Observations on P systems with states. In: Gheorghe, M., Petre, I., Pérez-Jiménez, M.J., Rozenberg, G., Salomaa, A. (eds.) Multidisciplinary Creativity. Hommage to Gheorghe Păun on His 65th Birthday, Spandugino (2015)
6. Alhazov, A., Freund, R., Verlan, S.: P systems working in maximal variants of the set derivation mode. In: Leporati, A., Rozenberg, G., Salomaa, A., Zandron, C. (eds.) CMC 2016. LNCS, vol. 10105, pp. 83–102. Springer, Cham (2017). https://doi.org/10.1007/978-3-319-54072-6_6
7. Alhazov, A., Ivanov, S., Rogozhin, Yu.: Polymorphic P systems. In: Gheorghe, M., Hinze, T., Păun, Gh., Rozenberg, G., Salomaa, A. (eds.) CMC 2010. LNCS, vol. 6501, pp. 81–94. Springer, Heidelberg (2010). https://doi.org/10.1007/978-3-642-18123-8_9
8. Aman, B., Csuhaj-Varjú, E., Freund, R.: Red–Green P automata. In: Gheorghe, M., Rozenberg, G., Salomaa, A., Sosík, P., Zandron, C. (eds.) CMC 2014. LNCS, vol. 8961, pp. 139–157. Springer, Cham (2014). https://doi.org/10.1007/978-3-319-14370-5_9
9. Arroyo, F., Baranda, A.V., Castellanos, J., Păun, Gh.: Membrane computing: the power of (rule) creation. J. Univ. Comput. Sci. 8, 369–381 (2002)
10. Budnik, P.: What Is and What Will Be. Mountain Math Software (2006)
11. Calude, C.S., Păun, Gh.: Bio-steps beyond turing. Biosystems 77(1–3), 175–194 (2004)
12. Cavaliere, M., Freund, R., Oswald, M., Sburlan, D.: Multiset random context grammars, checkers, and transducers. Theor. Comput. Sci. 372(2–3), 136–151 (2007)
13. Cavaliere, M., Genova, D.: P systems with symport/antiport of rules. In: Păun, Gh., Riscos-Núñez, A., Romero-Jiménez, A., Sancho-Caparrini, F. (eds.) Second Brainstorming Week on Membrane Computing, Sevilla, Spain, 2–7 February 2004, pp. 102–116 (2004)
14. Cavaliere, M., Ionescu, M., Ishdorj, T.O.: Inhibiting/de-inhibiting rules in P systems. In: Pre-proceedings of the Fifth Workshop on Membrane Computing (WMC5), Milano, Italy, June 2004, pp. 174–183 (2004)
15. Dassow, J., Păun, Gh.: Regulated Rewriting in Formal Language Theory. Springer, Berlin (1989)
16. Freund, R.: Control mechanisms on #-context-free array grammars. In: Păun, Gh. (ed.) Mathematical Aspects of Natural and Formal Languages, pp. 97–137. World Scientific Publishing, Singapore (1994)

17. Freund, R.: Generalized P-systems. In: Ciobanu, G., Păun, Gh. (eds.) FCT 1999. LNCS, vol. 1684, pp. 281–292. Springer, Heidelberg (1999). https://doi.org/10. 1007/3-540-48321-7_23

18. Freund, R.: P systems working in the sequential mode on arrays and strings. Int. J. Found. Comput. Sci. **16**(4), 663–682 (2005). https://doi.org/10.1142/ S0129054105003224

19. Freund, R.: P automata: new ideas and results. In: Bordihn, H., Freund, R., Nagy, B., Vaszil, Gy. (eds.) Eighth Workshop on Non-Classical Models of Automata and Applications, NCMA 2016, Debrecen, Hungary, 29–30 August 2016. Proceedings, books@cg.at, vol. 321, pp. 13–40. ÖsterreichischeComputer Gesellschaft (2016)

20. Freund, R., Ivanov, S., Staiger, L.: Going beyond turing with P automata: partial adult halting and regular observer ω-languages. In: Calude, C.S., Dinneen, M.J. (eds.) UCNC 2015. LNCS, vol. 9252, pp. 169–180. Springer, Cham (2015). https:// doi.org/10.1007/978-3-319-21819-9_12

21. Freund, R., Ivanov, S., Staiger, L.: Going beyond Turing with P automata: regular observer ω-languages and partial adult halting. IJUC **12**(1), 51–69 (2016)

22. Freund, R., Kogler, M., Oswald, M.: A general framework for regulated rewriting based on the applicability of rules. In: Kelemen, J., Kelemenová, A. (eds.) Computation, Cooperation, and Life. LNCS, vol. 6610, pp. 35–53. Springer, Heidelberg (2011). https://doi.org/10.1007/978-3-642-20000-7_5

23. Freund, R., Leporati, A., Mauri, G., Porreca, A.E., Verlan, S., Zandron, C.: Flattening in (Tissue) P systems. In: Alhazov, A., Cojocaru, S., Gheorghe, M., Rogozhin, Yu., Rozenberg, G., Salomaa, A. (eds.) CMC 2013. LNCS, vol. 8340, pp. 173–188. Springer, Heidelberg (2014). https://doi.org/10.1007/978-3-642-54239-8_13

24. Freund, R., Oswald, M., Staiger, L.: ω-P automata with communication rules. In: Martín-Vide, C., Mauri, G., Păun, Gh., Rozenberg, G., Salomaa, A. (eds.) WMC 2003. LNCS, vol. 2933, pp. 203–217. Springer, Heidelberg (2004). https://doi.org/ 10.1007/978-3-540-24619-0_15

25. Freund, R., Verlan, S.: A formal framework for static (Tissue) P systems. In: Eleftherakis, G., Kefalas, P., Păun, Gh., Rozenberg, G., Salomaa, A. (eds.) WMC 2007. LNCS, vol. 4860, pp. 271–284. Springer, Heidelberg (2007). https://doi.org/10. 1007/978-3-540-77312-2_17

26. Ivanov, S.: Polymorphic P systems with non-cooperative rules and no ingredients. In: Gheorghe, M., Rozenberg, G., Salomaa, A., Sosík, P., Zandron, C. (eds.) CMC 2014. LNCS, vol. 8961, pp. 258–273. Springer, Cham (2014). https://doi.org/10. 1007/978-3-319-14370-5_16

27. Kudlek, M., Martín-Vide, C., Păun, Gh.: Toward a formal macroset theory. In: Calude, C.S., Păun, Gh., Rozenberg, G., Salomaa, A. (eds.) WMC 2000. LNCS, vol. 2235, pp. 123–133. Springer, Heidelberg (2001). https://doi.org/10.1007/3-540-45523-X_7

28. van Leeuwen, J., Wiedermann, J.: Computation as an unbounded process. Theor. Comput. Sci. **429**, 202–212 (2012). https://doi.org/10.1016/j.tcs.2011.12.040

29. Minsky, M.L.: Computation: Finite and Infinite Machines. Prentice-Hall Inc, Upper Saddle River (1967)

30. Păun, Gh.: Computing with membranes. J. Comput. Syst. Sci. **61**, 108–143 (1998)

31. Păun, Gh., Rozenberg, G., Salomaa, A.: The Oxford Handbook of Membrane Computing. Oxford University Press Inc, New York (2010)
32. Sosík, P., Valík, O.: On evolutionary lineages of membrane systems. In: Freund, R., Păun, Gh., Rozenberg, G., Salomaa, A. (eds.) WMC 2005. LNCS, vol. 3850, pp. 67–78. Springer, Heidelberg (2006). https://doi.org/10.1007/11603047_5
33. Bulletin of the International Membrane Computing Society (IMCS). http://membranecomputing.net/IMCSBulletin/index.php
34. The P Systems Website. http://ppage.psystems.eu/

Thermodynamically Favorable Computation via Tile Self-assembly

Cameron Chalk[1], Jacob Hendricks[2], Matthew J. Patitz[3(✉)], and Michael Sharp[3]

[1] Department of Electrical and Computer Engineering,
University of Texas at Austin, Austin, TX, USA
ctchalk@utexas.edu
[2] Department of Computer Science and Information Systems,
University of Wisconsin - River Falls, River Falls, WI, USA
jacob.hendricks@uwrf.edu
[3] Department of Computer Science and Computer Engineering,
University of Arkansas, Fayetteville, AR, USA
{patitz,mrs018}@uark.edu

Abstract. The recently introduced Thermodynamic Binding Networks (TBN) model was developed with the purpose of studying self-assembling systems by focusing on their thermodynamically favorable final states, and ignoring the kinetic pathways through which they evolve. The model was intentionally developed to abstract away not only the notion of time, but also the constraints of geometry. Collections of monomers with binding domains which allow them to form polymers via complementary bonds are analyzed to determine their final, stable configurations, which are those which maximize the number of bonds formed (i.e. enthalpy) and the number of independent components (i.e. entropy). In this paper, we first develop a definition of what it means for a TBN to perform a computation, and then present a set of constructions which are capable of performing computations by simulating the behaviors of space-bounded Turing machines and boolean circuits. In contrast to previous TBN results, these constructions are robust to great variability in the counts of monomers existing in the systems and the numbers of polymers that form in parallel. Although the Turing machine simulating TBNs are inefficient in terms of the numbers of unique monomer types required, as compared to algorithmic self-assembling systems in the abstract Tile Assembly Model (aTAM), we then show that a general strategy of porting those aTAM system designs to TBNs produces TBNs which incorrectly simulate computations. Finally, we present a refinement of the TBN model which we call the Geometric Thermodynamic Binding Networks (GTBN) model in which monomers are defined with rigid geometries and form rigid bonds. Utilizing the constraints

C. Chalk—This author's research was supported in part by National Science Foundation Grants CCF-1618895 and CCF-1652824.

M.J. Patitz and M. Sharp—This author's research was supported in part by National Science Foundation Grants CCF-1422152 and CAREER-1553166.

S. Stepney and S. Verlan (Eds.): UCNC 2018, LNCS 10867, pp. 16–31, 2018.
https://doi.org/10.1007/978-3-319-92435-9_2

imposed by geometry, we then provide a GTBN construction capable of
simulating Turing machines as efficiently as in the aTAM.

1   Introduction

The study of self-assembling systems has resulted in a wide range of theoretical
models and results, showing powers and limitations of such systems across a large
landscape of variation in component structures, dynamics, and other important
system properties [3,5,7,11,13,14,16,18,19]. Theoretical studies have also given
rise to experimental implementations in which artificial self-assembling systems
are being developed and demonstrated in laboratories [10,21,22]. While at times
theoretical studies are intended solely to explore the mathematical boundaries
between the possible and impossible, at other times they are geared toward
informing researchers on the behaviors of existing physical systems. Toward that
end, theoretical models of self-assembly have been developed which seek to elu-
cidate errors observed in experimental implementations (e.g. the kinetic Tile
Assembly Model [24]), and among these is the Thermodynamic Binding Network (TBN) model [9]. Although such models are generally intended to abstract
away many of the details of physical systems, they are often designed to highlight certain important aspects and isolate them for study. For the TBN model
in particular, the desire is to focus on thermodynamically favored end states of
systems while ignoring the kinetic pathways through which they evolve, in the
hopes of being able to better design systems whose "sink states" will be those we
desire, *and avoid those we don't*, regardless of intermediate states which may be
traversed along the way. Preliminary work with the TBN model [2,9] has provided initial tools to begin working with self-assembling systems in this model,
and the goal of this paper is to extend them to TBN systems capable of performing a larger class of computations. Since the notion of what it means to compute
in such a model is not obvious, we provide a definition of computing with TBNs.
We then present a result showing that for any space-bounded Turing machine
there exists a TBN which can simulate it on any input. However, the size of the
set of monomers required for the construction is on the order of the amount of
space used multiplied by the number of time steps of the machine, making it less
efficient than typical algorithmic self-assembling systems. Nonetheless, the construction is robust to the system containing multiple copies of the computation
simulation self-assembling in parallel, and also to large ranges of the numbers of
monomers of each type, which is in contrast to the previous results. We further
extend our construction to the simulation of arbitrary fan-in fan-out Boolean
circuits.

Next, we present results which relate the simulation of computations within
the abstract Tile Assembly Model (aTAM) [24] to TBNs, as there are many
results related to computation in the aTAM (e.g. [6,8,12,15,20,23,25]), which
has been shown to be computationally universal [24]. Along this line, we first
consider a standard class of aTAM systems which are used to simulate Turing
machines (i.e. "zig-zag" systems) and consider what happens if the tiles of those

systems are interpreted as monomers of a TBN (in a straightforward manner). We present a set of criteria which are relatively natural and likely to be met by the computations performed by many Turing machines and which, if true for a particular Turing machine, demonstrate why a TBN created in such a way would not correctly simulate the Turing machine's computations, and would be capable of outputting incorrect answers. Notably, the argument presented pertains to all of our currently known approaches to simulating computations using TBNs which are more monomer-efficient than those of our first result, leaving an open question of whether or not more efficient simulation is possible in the TBN model. For our final result, we present a refinement to the TBN model which we call the Geometric Thermodynamic Binding Networks (GTBN) model, in which monomers and bonds between them are restricted by geometric constraints (unlike in the TBN model, but similar to the aTAM), and show how GTBNs can efficiently simulate arbitrary Turing machines for decidable languages. Please note that due to space constraints, many technical details can be found online in [4].

2   Preliminaries

In this section we provide definitions for the TBN model. Due to space constraints, definitions for the abstract Tile Assembly Model and zig-zag assembly systems can be found in [4].

2.1   TBN Model

We use the definitions from [9], the majority of which we repeat here, but please see [9] for more details and examples.

Let $\mathbb{N}, \mathbb{Z}, \mathbb{Z}^+$ denote the set of nonnegative integers, integers, and positive integers, respectively. A key type of object in our definitions is a multiset, which we define in a few different ways as convenient. Let $\mathcal{A}$ be a finite set. We can define a multiset over $\mathcal{A}$ using the standard set notion, e.g., $\mathbf{c} = \{a, a, c\}$, where $a, c \in \mathcal{A}$. Formally, we view multiset $\mathbf{c}$ as a vector assigning counts to $\mathcal{A}$. Letting $\mathbb{N}^{\mathcal{A}}$ denote the set of functions $f : \mathcal{A} \to \mathbb{N}$, we have $\mathbf{c} \in \mathbb{N}^{\mathcal{A}}$. We index entries by elements of $a \in \mathcal{A}$, calling $\mathbf{c}(a) \in \mathbb{N}$ the *count of a in $\mathbf{c}$*.

Molecular bonds with precise binding specificity are modeled abstractly as binding "domains", designed to bind only to other specific binding domains. Formally, consider a finite set $\mathcal{D}$ of *primary domain types*. Each primary domain type $a \in \mathcal{D}$ is mapped to a *complementary domain type* (a.k.a., *codomain type*) denoted a^*. Let $\mathcal{D}^* = \{a^* \mid a \in \mathcal{D}\}$ denote the set of codomain types of $\mathcal{D}$. The mapping is assumed 1-1, so $|\mathcal{D}^*| = |\mathcal{D}|$. We assume that a domain of primary type $a \in \mathcal{D}$ binds only to its corresponding complementary type $a^* \in \mathcal{D}^*$, and vice versa. The set $\mathcal{D} \cup \mathcal{D}^*$ is the set of *domain types*.

We assume a finite set $\mathcal{M}$ of *monomer types*, where a monomer type $\mathbf{m} \in \mathbb{N}^{\mathcal{D} \cup \mathcal{D}^*}$ is a non-empty multiset of domain types, e.g., $\mathbf{m} = \{a, b, b, c^*, a^*\}$. A *thermodynamic binding network* (TBN) is a pair $\mathcal{T} = (\mathcal{D}, \mathcal{M})$ consisting of a finite set $\mathcal{D}$ of primary domain types and a finite set $\mathcal{M} \subset \mathbb{N}^{\mathcal{D} \cup \mathcal{D}^*}$ of monomer types. A *monomer collection* $\vec{c} \in \mathbb{N}^{\mathcal{M}}$ of $\mathcal{T}$ is multiset of monomer types; intuitively, $\vec{c}$ indicates how many of each monomer type from $\mathcal{M}$ there are, but not how they are bound. Since one monomer collection usually contains more than one copy of the same domain type, we use the term *domain* to refer to each copy separately. We similarly reserve the term *monomer* to refer to a particular instance of a monomer type if a monomer collection has multiple copies of the same monomer type.

A single monomer collection $\vec{c}$ can take on different configurations depending on how domains in monomers are bound to each other. To formally model configurations, we first need the notion of a bond assignment. Let (U, V, E) be the bipartite graph describing all possible bonds, where U is the multiset of all primary domains in all monomers in $\vec{c}$, V is the multiset of all codomains in all monomers in $\vec{c}$, and E is the set of edges between primary domains and their complementary codomains $\{\{u, v\} \mid u \in U, v \in V, v = u^*\}$. A *bond assignment* M is a matching on (U, V, E). Then, a *configuration* α of monomer collection $\vec{c}$ is the (multi)graph $(U \cup V, E_M)$, where the edges E_M include both the edges in the matching M and an edge between each pair of domains within the same monomer. Specifically, for each pair of domains $d_i, d_j \in \mathcal{D} \cup \mathcal{D}^*$ that are part of the same monomer in $\vec{c}$, let $\{d_i, d_j\} \in E_M$, calling this a *monomer edge*, and for each edge $\{d_i, d_i^*\}$ in the bond assignment M, let $\{d_i, d_i^*\} \in E_M$, calling this a *binding edge*. Let $[\vec{c}]$ be the set of all configurations of a monomer collection $\vec{c}$. For a configuration α, we say the size of a configuration, written $|\alpha|$, is simply the number of monomers in it.[1] Each connected component in α is called a *polymer*. Note that a polymer is itself a configuration, but of a smaller monomer collection $\vec{c}' \subseteq \vec{c}$ (as $\vec{c}'$ and $\vec{c}$ are multisets). As with all configurations, the size of a polymer is the number of monomers in it.

Which configurations are thermodynamically favored over others depends on two properties of a configuration: its bond count and entropy. The *enthalpy* $H(\alpha)$ of a configuration is the number of binding edges (i.e., the cardinality of the matching M). The *entropy* $S(\alpha)$ of a configuration is the number of polymers (connected components) of α.

As in [9], we study the particularly interesting limiting case in which enthalpy is *infinitely* more favorable than entropy — the other limiting case, with entropy infinitely more favorable, is degenerate since only configurations with each monomer unbound to any other are favorable. We say a configuration α is *saturated* if it has no pair of domains d and d^* that are both unbound; this is equivalent to stating that α has maximal bonding among all configurations in $[\vec{c}]$. We say a configuration $\alpha \in [\vec{c}]$ is *stable* (aka thermodynamically favored) if it is saturated and maximizes the entropy among all saturated configurations,

---

[1] We define the size of a configuration as in [9]. One may consider the size of a configuration instead as the number of domains in it, which may capture more subtle characteristics since some monomers may have many more domains than others. However, this distinction does not effectively alter any results in this work.

i.e., every saturated configuration $\alpha' \in [\vec{\mathbf{c}}]$ obeys $S(\alpha') \leq S(\alpha)$. Let $[\vec{\mathbf{c}}]_\square$ denote the set of stable configurations of monomer collection $\vec{\mathbf{c}}$.

2.2   Zig-Zag Simulation of Turing Machines

Due to space constraints, we only briefly mention what it means for a "zig-zag" aTAM system to simulate a Turing machine M. Essentially, the tape of M at each time step is represented by a single column of tiles. The columns form from left to right, with each column completing (by growing one tile at a time in the upward or downward direction) before the column to its right begins. Each tile represents one cell of the tape, with one cell also representing the state of the machine during that computation step (and thus also the head position). An partial example can be seen in Fig. 1. Therefore, the computation proceeds from left to right until the machine enters a halting state.

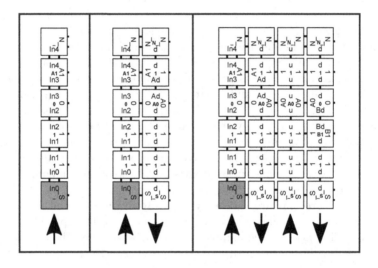

Fig. 1. An example of zig-zag growth in the aTAM.

3   Simulating Space-Bounded Turing Machines

Our first result proves that for any Turing machine M such that M requires no more than s tape cells and t time steps (we mention time bound t for efficiency of monomer types and polymer size, but the result also holds if we assume the worst case where $t = O(2^s)$), there exists a TBN which simulates M. We provide definitions of what it means for a TBN to simulate a Turing machine, then formally state our Theorem and give our proof, which is by construction.

For the remainder of the section, let M be an arbitrary s space-bounded and t time-bounded Turing machine. Let i be an arbitrary input bit string to M, noting that $0 \leq |i| \leq s$.

Definition 1 uses the following notation.

1. Let $T = (D, M)$ be a TBN with D a finite set of primary domain types and M a finite set of monomer types.
2. Let O and I be subsets of M. We call O the set of *output monomer types*, and call I the set of *input monomer types*.
3. Let $\vec{c}$ be a monomer collection of T.
4. Let E_{input} be a function from finite sets of input monomers (i.e. monomers of types in I) to binary strings of length s. Let S be a finite set of input monomers and let i be a binary string of length s. If $E_{input}(S) = i$, then we say that S *encodes* i.
5. Let E_{output} be a map from a finite set of output monomers (i.e. monomers of types in O) to binary strings of length s. If S is a finite set of monomers and $o \in \{0,1\}^s$ are such that $E_{output}(S) = o$, then we say that S *encodes* o.

Definition 1 says that a monomer collection for a TBN *simulates* a Turing machine M on some input i if every stable configuration of the monomer collection is such that every polymer p that contains a set of monomers with input monomer type which encodes i also contains the set of monomers with output monomer type that encodes $M(i)$.[2]

Definition 1. *A monomer collection $\vec{c}$ for the TBN T simulates an s space-bounded Turing machine M on input i if and only if there exist encodings E_{input} and E_{output} such that for every stable configuration α in $[\vec{c}]_\square$, if α contains a polymer that contains a monomer with type in I, then*

1. *letting S_{in} be the set of monomers in α with types in I, $E_{input}(S_{in}) = i$,*
2. *letting S_{out} be the set of monomers in α with types in O, $E_{output}(S_{out}) = M(i)$, where $M(i)$ is the output of the Turing machine M on input i.*

Theorem 1. *For any s space-bounded, t time-bounded Turing machine M, there exists a set of primary domain types D, and sets of monomer types M, M_{seed}, and $O \subset M$ consisting of monomers with binding domains in $D \cup D^*$ such that, for any valid input i to M, the following properties hold.*

1. *there exists a monomer type $m_i \in M_{seed}$ such that m_i encodes i,*
2. *for $M_i = M \cup \{m_i\}$, there exists a monomer collection $\vec{c}$ for TBN $T_i = (D, M_i)$ such that $\vec{c}$ simulates M on input i, and*
3. *the set of output monomer types for the simulation is equal to O.*

---

[2] Under some reasonable representation of monomers as binary strings, one might require that the encoding is sufficiently weak, in FAC^0 for example [1,17]. However, in this paper we do not require such restrictions on encodings in the definition of "simulation". We do note that the encodings E_{input} and E_{ouput} that we use are straightforward encodings which require checking $O(\log s)$ domains in order to determine the input i. Moreover, we note that to translate M and i to a TBN, we first translate M and i to an aTAM system via a standard technique and then translate this aTAM system to a TBN using a straightforward approach whose details can be found in [4].

3.1 Overview of the Proof of Theorem 1

In this section we give a brief overview of the construction used to prove Theorem 1. We first note the complexities of the construction. The input monomer $\mathcal{M}_i$ must contain a domain for each input bit, and this is bounded by the amount of space used by M and thus $\mathcal{M}_i$ contains $O(s)$ domains. Since $\mathcal{O}$ needs to contain two monomers for each position in the output, which is the amount of space used by the machine, $|\mathcal{O}| = O(s)$ (and each has 4 domains). Since unique domains and monomers must be created for each point in time t and space s of the computation (each with 4 domains), as well as capping monomers for each of those monomers (with 2 domains each), plus a single input monomer (with s domains), and the output monomers of $\mathcal{O}$, the sizes of $\mathcal{D}$ and $\mathcal{M}$ are $O(st|Q||\Gamma|)$, where Q is the set of states of M and Γ is its tape library.

The abstract Tile Assembly Model has been shown to be computationally universal [24], and many aTAM results utilize a construction technique in which a Turing machine is simulated as a series of columns self-assemble in a zig-zag manner, with each successive column representing the contents of the tape, the state of the machine, and the location of the read-write head at successive steps in time. Despite the fact that the TBN model does not incorporate any geometry or any notion of time, we are still able to leverage the ideas of an aTAM zig-zag system simulating a Turing machine to design the domains and monomers of a TBN.

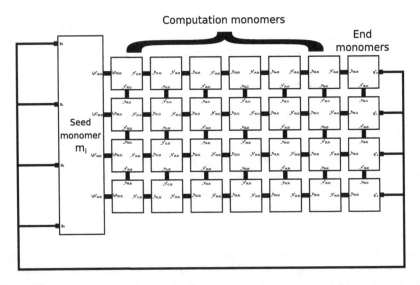

Fig. 2. A schematic example of a polymer encoding a Turing machine simulation. The rectangle and squares represent monomers and black lines represent bound domains.

Essentially, for each tile type of the aTAM system, we first design a monomer with 4 domains roughly equivalent to the tile's glue labels. Then, using the time and space bounds of the Turing machine to determine the height of each column and the number of columns, we make a copy of each of those monomers (and their domains) specific for each row and column location. The other main components are the *seed monomer* which has a domain for each bit of input to the Turing machine, *end monomers* which bind to the monomers representing the last column of the computation as well as to the seed monomer, and finally the *cap monomers*. There is a cap monomer specific to every monomer type m (except the seed monomers), which has exactly one complementary domain for each primary domain type on m — e.g., if $m = \{\_h_{(1,1)}, \_v_{(1,2)}, \_h^*_{(2,1)}, \_v^*_{(1,1)}\}$, the corresponding cap monomer is $\{\_h^*_{(1,1)}, \_v^*_{(1,2)}\}$. The purpose of cap monomers is to make the attachment of a monomer onto the large TM simulating polymer "entropy-neutral": without capping monomers, binding a monomer to the large polymer reduces entropy by one; with capping monomers, the binding of the monomer to the large polymer implies the cap monomer is free, resulting in 0 net entropy gain/loss. Additionally, s end monomers must be bound to the seed monomer in order to maximize enthalpy, where s is the space used by the TM simulation. The complete TM simulating polymer —by virtue of binding its end monomers to the matching computation monomers as well as the seed— implies a number of free end cap monomers equal to s, creating a net entropy gain of s, causing the correct simulating polymer to be in the stable configuration.

Although the number of unique monomer types for this construction is high, an important aspect of it is that, unlike previous results in the TBN model, the construction is robust to inexact counts of monomer types. In fact, the only requirements for the counts of monomer types in a collection which correctly simulates the Turing machine is that the number of input monomers present is less than or equal to the number of any of the computation monomer or end monomer types, and that the number of each of the cap monomer types is greater than the number of any of the other monomer types. Given any collection in which the counts of monomer types respect these ratios, that collection correctly simulates the Turing machine (following Definition 1) with $\mathcal{I}$ equal to the input monomer type and $\mathcal{O}$ equal to the end monomer types. The single stable configuration of any such collection will include (1) a polymer for every copy of the input monomer which contains that input monomer as well as a full set of computation monomers which represent the entire computation and the output encoded by the end monomers (see Fig. 2 for an example), (2) the leftover, unused computation and end monomers each in a polymer of size 2 which also includes its unique cap monomer, and (3) the singleton cap monomers whose computation or end monomers are incorporated in the computation-simulating polymers. Such a configuration is saturated and maximizes entropy over all saturated configurations, and thus is stable.

4 Simulation of Arbitrary Boolean Circuits via TBN Without a Tile Assembly Pathway

Under the TBN model —with no consideration of a corresponding tile assembly system— the TM simulation discussed in Sect. 3 is easily generalized to arbitrary fan-in fan-out Boolean circuits, mainly via the removal of planarity constraints imposed by the bonds of the aTAM. One may suspect the removal of an accompanying aTAM system also removes the argument for a plausible kinetic pathway, yet the construction described here is similar enough to the system described in Sect. 3 to argue that a similar "monomer-by-monomer attachment to a growing assembly" pathway exists for this construction as well.

An overview of the construction is given here in an explicit example shown in Fig. 3. The use of seed monomers, capping monomers, and end monomers are effectively identical to the construction given in Sect. 3. The main difference in this construction is the construction of the computation monomers: for each gate g of fan-in i and fan-out o which computes $f_g : \{0,1\}^i \to \{0,1\}^o$, we construct 2^i computation monomers — one for each possible input to the gate. The monomer corresponding to a particular input s to the gate exposes domains corresponding to $f_g(s)$ which are complementary with the gate monomers for the gates in C take input from g.

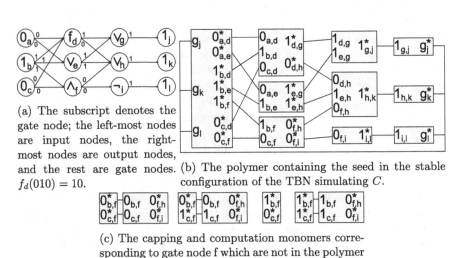

(a) The subscript denotes the gate node; the left-most nodes are input nodes, the right-most nodes are output nodes, and the rest are gate nodes. $f_d(010) = 10$.

(b) The polymer containing the seed in the stable configuration of the TBN simulating C.

(c) The capping and computation monomers corresponding to gate node f which are not in the polymer containing the seed.

Fig. 3. An example simulation of an arbitrary Boolean circuit C. (a) shows the circuit represented as a directed acyclic graph with edges corresponding to the input/outputs of the gate. (b) shows the TBN polymer which effectively simulates the circuit. (c) shows an example of the monomer set constructed for each gate in the circuit.

5 A Negative Result on Porting Computing Systems from the aTAM to the TBN Model

In this section we provide very high-level details of an argument which shows what occurs when standard aTAM systems which are designed to simulate Turing machines are treated as TBNs. This is similar to the TBN designed for the proof of Theorem 1 but without creating unique, hard-coded monomer types for each location.

Let M be an s-space-bounded Turing machine and T_M be a standard zigzag aTAM tile set which simulates M. (Note that this argument will also apply when M is not space-bounded.) For $n \in N$ where n is a valid input to M, let T_n be the set of "input" tile types which assemble the binary representation of n as a vertical column to serve as the input to T_M. Then the aTAM system $T_{M(n)} = (T_M \cup T_n, \sigma_n, 2)$, where σ_n is simply the first tile of T_n at the origin, simulates $M(n)$. We refer to the unique terminal assembly of $T_{M(n)}$ as S_n (i.e. simulation n). Additionally, if X is a set of coordinate locations, by $S_n(X)$ we refer to the subassembly of S_n contained at the locations of X. Let $i \neq j \neq k$ be valid inputs to M, and S_i, S_j and S_k be the terminal assemblies of $T_{M(i)}$, $T_{M(j)}$, and $T_{M(k)}$, respectively, such that the following conditions hold:

1. The outputs $M(i) \neq M(k)$
2. There exist columns (i.e. sets of all tile locations in a given column) c_1 and c_2, and individual tile locations l_1 and l_2 in c_1 and c_2, respectively, such that:
   (a) $S_i(c_1) = S_j(c_1)$ (i.e. both columns have the exact same tile types in each location) except at location l_1, where they have differing tile types with different glues on their west sides (which would represent different cell values for the respective simulated tape cells of M)
   (b) $S_j(c_2) = S_k(c_2)$ except at location l_2 where they have tile types which differ in their west glues
   (c) $S_i(l_1) = S_k(l_2)$
   (d) $S_j(l_1) = S_j(l_2)$
   (e) $S_i(c_2) \neq S_k(c_2)$

If a TBN is created to simulate M using the same techniques as for the proof of Theorem 1 which skip the blow-up performed to make hard-coded monomers for each location, these conditions of the computation being simulated on input i allow "splicing" to occur between polymers which could represent computations on inputs i, j, and k and still retain a polymer in which all domains are bound, and a configuration with maximum enthalpy and entropy which does not simulate $M(i)$. The intuitive reason here is that in the hard-coded construction for Theorem 1, a set of unique monomer types exists for every row and column of the simulated computation and thus each monomer type occurs no more than one time in the polymer representing the computation, but in this system the same monomer types may be reused many times. (See Fig. 4 for a schematic depiction.) The conditions required by this argument are also relatively natural and likely to occur for sets of three inputs for a large number of computations, as they only require that across two pairs of three different inputs there are points at which the computations have nearly identical tape contents, and also a tape cell location whose value is changed at one point and then changed back to the former value later and the rest of the configuration matches across another pair of the two inputs. While this result does not show the impossibility of so-called efficient Turing machine simulation, it implies that, if possible, more innovative techniques will be required. This leads us to our next result, in which we consider a variant of the TBN model which imposes geometry on the monomers and their bonds, and we demonstrate efficient Turing machine simulation.

6 Geometric Thermodynamic Binding Networks

The result of Sect. 3 demonstrates that computation can be simulated by TBNs when they are composed of location-specific monomers for every location within the computation, which is quite inefficient compared to, for instance, the number of unique tile types required to simulate computations within the aTAM. However, Sect. 5 shows that treating aTAM tiles of computation-simulating systems directly as monomers of a TBN results in systems with many fewer monomer types, but which incorrectly simulate computations. Intuitively, the reason for the failure of such systems is due to the lack of geometry included within the TBN model, which allows for the domains of any monomer to bind to complementary domains of any other monomers, independent of the patterns of connections, which would not be the case if the monomers had to conform to geometric constraints on their sizes and locations. In order to address this issue, in this section we introduce a refinement to the TBN model which includes such geometric constraints.

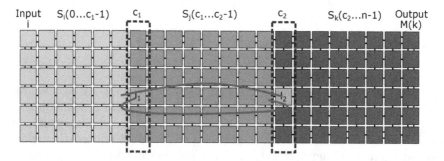

Fig. 4. Schematic view of how portions of three computation-simulating polymers could be connected together to yield a polymer representing an invalid computation.

6.1 GTBN Model Definition

We define the *Geometric Thermodynamic Binding Networks* (GTBN) model to be an extension of the TBN model, with a few notable differences which restrict the ways in which polymers can form. A GTBN is a pair $\mathcal{T} = (\mathcal{D}, \mathcal{M})$ consisting of a finite set $\mathcal{D}$ of primary domain types and a finite set $\mathcal{M}$ of monomer types. But, rather than a monomer simply being defined as a multiset of domains, a *geometric monomer type* $m \in \mathcal{M}$ is instead defined as a polygon p, along with a set of pairs (d, l) where $d \in \mathcal{D} \cup \mathcal{D}^*$ and $l \in \mathbb{R}^2$ is the point on the perimeter of p where d is located.[3] Geometric monomers are taken to be rigid polygons, and given a pair of geometric monomers, m_1 and m_2 where $(d_i, l_i) \in m_1$ and $(d_i^*, l_j) \in m_2$, if m_1 and m_2 can be positioned in the plane so that they do not overlap but the locations l_i and l_j on m_1 and m_2, respectively, are adjacent to each other, then those domains can bind. Bonds are rigid and therefore so are polymers formed by their binding. Geometric monomers and polymers can be translated and rotated (but not reflected), and can bind together if they can be positioned such that they do not overlap and complementary domains on their perimeters are adjacent. In this paper, we will only consider geometric monomers which are unit squares with at most a single domain on any face, located in the center of the face. (Note that this is similar to tiles in the aTAM, but while the aTAM prevents tiles from rotating through two dimensional space, geometric monomers are allowed to within the GTBN.) Thus, each monomer in a geometric polymer can be represented by a pair (p, m) where $p \in \mathbb{N}^2$ represents the coordinates of the center of the geometric monomer and $m \in \mathcal{M}$ the monomer type, and a geometric polymer is a set of such pairs, and the *geometric monomer binding graph* contains edges representing complementary domains which are adjacent to each other in some polymer.

A major difference between TBNs and GTBNs is that, due to geometric constraints, it is possible to have a configuration in a GTBN in which there exists an unbound domain d on some monomer and an unbound domain d^* on either that or another monomer, but d and d^* cannot bind together. That is, it may be impossible for the monomers (or the polymers containing them) to be validly positioned so that the domains are adjacent. Therefore, we define a condition of a GTBN configuration called *effectively saturated* which occurs when the configuration either (1) is saturated, or (2) for all pairs of domains d and d^* such that both are unbound, there is no valid positioning of the monomers or polymers containing them such that d and d^* can be placed adjacent to each other (i.e. they are geometrically prevented from binding).

6.2   Efficient Simulation of Turing Machines in GTBNs

With the definition of the GTBN model, we are now able to prove that the geometric constraints of the model allow for efficient, accurate simulation of Turing machines. In this section we present the theorem statement and a high-level overview of the proof, which is by construction.

Theorem 2. *Let $L \in DTIME(f(n))$ be a decidable language for arbitrary function f, and M be a Turing machine which decides L. There exists a set of primary domain types $\mathcal{D}$, and sets of geometric monomer types $\mathcal{M}$, $\mathcal{M}_{seed}$, and*

---

[3] Note that the definitions can naturally be extended to 3D polyhedra.

$\mathcal{O} \subset \mathcal{M}$ consisting of geometric monomers with binding domains $\mathcal{D} \cup \mathcal{D}^*$ such that, for any valid input i to M, the following properties hold:

1. there exists a set of geometric monomer types $m_i \subset \mathcal{M}_{seed}$ such that m_i collectively encodes i,
2. for $\mathcal{M}_i = \mathcal{M} \cup m_i$, there exists a geometric monomer collection $\vec{c}$ for GTBN $\mathcal{T}_i = (\mathcal{D}, \mathcal{M}_i)$ such that $\vec{c}$ simulates M on input i, and
3. the set of output geometric monomer types for the simulation is equal to $\mathcal{O}$.

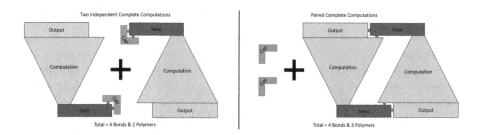

Fig. 5. This illustrates the pairing of two complete computations. The dislodging of the seed caps creates an entropy bonus of one. This bonus is what makes the final complete paired construction favorable.

The proof of Theorem 2 is by construction, and begins similarly to the construction for the proof of Theorem 1, with the creation of domains and (geometric) monomers of a GTBN $\mathcal{T}$ based off of the definition of a zig-zag aTAM system $\mathcal{T}_M$ which simulates the Turing machine M, with a few notable differences. Mainly, it does not require increasing the size of the domain and monomer sets by creating copies hard-coded for each position in the simulation.

We now note the complexity of this construction. The seed requires $O(n)$ unique domains and monomers to make the seed, where n is the number of input bits. The number of computation/end domains and monomers is $O(|Q||\Gamma|)$, where Q is the set of states in M and Γ is the tape alphabet. The number of tape extension monomers is constant. The capping monomers only scale the current complexity and can be ignored asymptotically. Therefore, the overall bound on the number of domains and monomers is $O(n + |Q||\Gamma|)$.

We first note that the geometric monomers are all designed to simply be unit squares like the aTAM tiles, with single domains located in the center of faces to represent the tiles' glues. Since this construction doesn't require monomers hard-coded to locations, and in fact doesn't require a fixed number of rows or columns, it is able to simulate a tape of steadily increasing length and so utilizes collections of monomers that combine to extend the length of the tape.

It is ensured that the deterministic path followed by the zig-zag aTAM system which simulates the same Turing machine is faithfully encoded by the resulting "computation" polymer of the single stable configuration by the geometric constraints placed on the positioning of geometric monomers and the rigidity of their bonds, which prevents erroneous "re-wiring" to occur as it could in the regular TBN example of Sect. 5. However, in order to create an entropy gap which makes the configuration containing the correct computation simulations the single stable configuration, since we can no longer have bound domains which span the full distance of the polymer (as they do from the seed to end monomers in the proof of Theorem 1), we instead provide an analogous method of freeing additional caps —thus gaining entropy— by designing the monomers so that polymers encoding the computation combine in pairs (as seen in Fig. 5).

Thus, an arbitrary halting Turing machine computation can be simulated efficiently in terms of domain and monomer type counts, both of which are $O(|Q||\Gamma|)$ (where Q is the state set and Γ is the tape alphabet). As with the construction for the proof of Theorem 1, this construction is robust over a class of configurations in which relationships exist between the counts of different categories of monomers. The inclusion of the fact that the language being decided $L \in DTIME(f(n))$ is simply to specify the count of computation monomers which must be included in the collection, relative to input seeds, to ensure that the computation can be completely represented without running out of monomers, i.e. $O(f(n)^2)$ copies of the computation monomers must be available per copy of the seed monomer.

Acknowledgements. The authors would like to thank David Doty, Pierre-Étienne Meunier, David Soloveichik, Chris Thachuk, and Damien Woods for much help in developing these results.

References

1. Barrington, D.A.M., Immerman, N., Straubing, H.: On uniformity within NC1. J. Comput. Syst. Sci. **41**(3), 274–306 (1990). https://doi.org/10.1016/0022-0000(90)90022-D. http://www.sciencedirect.com/science/article/pii/002200009090022D
2. Breik, K., Prakash, L., Thachuk, C., Heule, M., Soloveichik, D.: Computing properties of stable configurations of thermodynamic binding networks. CoRR abs/1709.08731 (2017). http://arxiv.org/abs/1709.08731
3. Cannon, S., Demaine, E.D., Demaine, M.L., Eisenstat, S., Patitz, M.J., Schweller, R.T., Summers, S.M., Winslow, A.: Two hands are better than one (up to constant factors): self-assembly in the 2HAM vs. aTAM. In: Portier, N., Wilke, T. (eds.) STACS. LIPIcs, vol. 20, pp. 172–184. Schloss Dagstuhl - Leibniz-Zentrum fuer Informatik (2013). http://dblp.uni-trier.de/db/conf/stacs/stacs2013.html#CannonDDEPSSW13
4. Chalk, C., Hendricks, J., Patitz, M.J., Sharp, M.: Thermodynamically favorable computation via tile self-assembly. Technical report 1802.02686, Computing Research Repository (2018). http://arxiv.org/abs/1802.02686
5. Cheng, Q., Aggarwal, G., Goldwasser, M.H., Kao, M.Y., Schweller, R.T., de Espanés, P.M.: Complexities for generalized models of self-assembly. SIAM J. Comput. **34**, 1493–1515 (2005)
6. Cook, M., Fu, Y., Schweller, R.T.: Temperature 1 self-assembly: deterministic assembly in 3D and probabilistic assembly in 2D. In: Proceedings of the 22nd Annual ACM-SIAM Symposium on Discrete Algorithms, SODA 2011. SIAM (2011)

7. Doty, D.: Theory of algorithmic self-assembly. Commun. ACM **55**(12), 78–88 (2012)
8. Doty, D., Patitz, M.J., Summers, S.M.: Limitations of self-assembly at temperature 1. Theor. Comput. Sci. **412**, 145–158 (2011)
9. Doty, D., Rogers, T.A., Soloveichik, D., Thachuk, C., Woods, D.: Thermodynamic binding networks. In: Brijder, R., Qian, L. (eds.) DNA 2017. LNCS, vol. 10467, pp. 249–266. Springer, Cham (2017). https://doi.org/10.1007/978-3-319-66799-7_16
10. Evans, C.G.: Crystals that count! Physical principles and experimental investigations of DNA tile self-assembly. Ph.D. thesis, California Institute of Technology (2014)
11. Fekete, S.P., Hendricks, J., Patitz, M.J., Rogers, T.A., Schweller, R.T.: Universal computation with arbitrary polyomino tiles in non-cooperative self-assembly. In: Proceedings of the Twenty-Sixth Annual ACM-SIAM Symposium on Discrete Algorithms (SODA 2015), San Diego, CA, USA 4–6 January 2015, pp. 148–167 (2015). https://doi.org/10.1137/1.9781611973730.12. http://epubs.siam.org/doi/abs/10.1137/1.9781611973730.12
12. Furcy, D., Micka, S., Summers, S.M.: Optimal program-size complexity for self-assembly at temperature 1 in 3D. In: Phillips, A., Yin, P. (eds.) DNA 2015. LNCS, vol. 9211, pp. 71–86. Springer, Cham (2015). https://doi.org/10.1007/978-3-319-21999-8_5
13. Gilber, O., Hendricks, J., Patitz, M.J., Rogers, T.A.: Computing in continuous space with self-assembling polygonal tiles. In: Proceedings of the Twenty-Seventh Annual ACM-SIAM Symposium on Discrete Algorithms (SODA 2016), Arlington, VA, USA, 10–12 January 2016, pp. 937–956 (2016)
14. Jonoska, N., McColm, G.L.: Flexible versus rigid tile assembly. In: Calude, C.S., Dinneen, M.J., Păun, Gh., Rozenberg, G., Stepney, S. (eds.) UC 2006. LNCS, vol. 4135, pp. 139–151. Springer, Heidelberg (2006). https://doi.org/10.1007/11839132_12
15. Lathrop, J.I., Lutz, J.H., Patitz, M.J., Summers, S.M.: Computability and complexity in self-assembly. Theory Comput. Syst. **48**(3), 617–647 (2011)
16. Meunier, P., Woods, D.: The non-cooperative tile assembly model is not intrinsically universal or capable of bounded turing machine simulation. In: Proceedings of the 49th Annual ACM SIGACT Symposium on Theory of Computing, STOC 2017, Montreal, QC, Canada, 19–23 June 2017, pp. 328–341 (2017). https://doi.org/10.1145/3055399.3055446
17. Murphy, N.: Uniformity conditions for membrane systems: uncovering complexity below P. Ph.D. thesis, National University of Ireland Maynooth (2010)
18. Padilla, J.E., Patitz, M.J., Schweller, R.T., Seeman, N.C., Summers, S.M., Zhong, X.: Asynchronous signal passing for tile self-assembly: fuel efficient computation and efficient assembly of shapes. Int. J. Found. Comput. Sci. **25**(4), 459–488 (2014)
19. Patitz, M.J.: An introduction to tile-based self-assembly and a survey of recent results. Nat. Comput. **13**(2), 195–224 (2014). https://doi.org/10.1007/s11047-013-9379-4
20. Patitz, M.J., Summers, S.M.: Self-assembly of decidable sets. Nat. Comput. **10**(2), 853–877 (2011)
21. Schulman, R., Winfree, E.: Programmable control of nucleation for algorithmic self-assembly. SIAM J. Comput. **39**(4), 1581–1616 (2009). https://doi.org/10.1137/070680266
22. Schulman, R., Winfree, E.: Synthesis of crystals with a programmable kinetic barrier to nucleation. Proc. Natl Acad. Sci. **104**(39), 15236–15241 (2007)

23. Soloveichik, D., Winfree, E.: Complexity of self-assembled shapes. SIAM J. Comput. **36**(6), 1544–1569 (2007)
24. Winfree, E.: Algorithmic self-assembly of DNA. Ph.D. thesis, California Institute of Technology, June 1998
25. Woods, D.: Intrinsic universality and the computational power of self-assembly. In: MCU: Proceedings of Machines, Computations and Universality, Univ. of Zürich, Switzerland, 9–12 September, vol. 128, pp. 16–22. Open Publishing Association (2013)

Optimal Staged Self-assembly of Linear Assemblies

Cameron Chalk[1](✉), Eric Martinez[2], Robert Schweller[2], Luis Vega[2],
Andrew Winslow[2], and Tim Wylie[2]

[1] Department of Electrical and Computer Engineering,
University of Texas at Austin, Austin, USA
ctchalk@utexas.edu

[2] Department of Computer Science, University of Texas - Rio Grande Valley,
Edinburg, USA
{eric.m.martinez02,robert.schweller,luis.a.vega01,andrew.winslow,
timothy.wylie}@utrgv.edu

Abstract. We analyze the complexity of building linear assemblies, sets of linear assemblies, and $\mathcal{O}(1)$-scale general shapes in the staged tile assembly model. For systems with at most b bins and t tile types, we prove that the minimum number of stages to uniquely assemble a $1 \times n$ *line* is $\Theta(\log_t n + \log_b \frac{n}{t} + 1)$. Generalizing to $\mathcal{O}(1) \times n$ lines, we prove the minimum number of stages is $\mathcal{O}(\frac{\log n - tb - t\log t}{b^2} + \frac{\log\log b}{\log t})$ and $\Omega(\frac{\log n - tb - t\log t}{b^2})$.

Next, we consider assembling sets of lines and general shapes using $t = \mathcal{O}(1)$ tile types. We prove that the minimum number of stages needed to assemble a set of k lines of size at most $\mathcal{O}(1) \times n$ is $\mathcal{O}(\frac{k\log n}{b^2} + \frac{k\sqrt{\log n}}{b} + \log\log n)$ and $\Omega(\frac{k\log n}{b^2})$. In the case that $b = \mathcal{O}(\sqrt{k})$, the minimum number of stages is $\Theta(\log n)$. The upper bound in this special case is then used to assemble "hefty" shapes of at least logarithmic edge-length-to-edge-count ratio at $\mathcal{O}(1)$-scale using $\mathcal{O}(\sqrt{k})$ bins and optimal $\mathcal{O}(\log n)$ stages.

Keywords: Tile self-assembly · Staged self-assembly
DNA computing · Biocomputing

1 Introduction

Modern technology applications increasingly involve precise design and manufacture of materials and devices at the nanoscale. One approach to nanoscale design is to use *self-assembly*: local interaction rules that direct the aggregation of large numbers of simple units. Seeman [15] discovered that short strands of DNA whose interactions are controlled by attraction between their base sequences can be programmed to carry out such self-assembly. This approach was subsequently

This research was supported in part by National Science Foundation Grants CCF-1117672 and CCF-1555626.

extended both experimentally and theoretically by Winfree [16], who introduced the *abstract Tile Assembly Model (aTAM)* to describe systems of four-sided planar *tiles* which randomly collide and attach if abutting sides have matching *glues* of sufficient bonding strength. This simple model is computationally universal [16] and experimentally capable of complex algorithmic behaviors [12].

Staged Tile Assembly. Here we study a tile assembly model introduced by Demaine et al. [9] that permits carrying out assembly in multiple *bins* whose products can be mixed together later, capturing the common experimental technique of decomposing a complex reaction into *stages* of simpler reactions. This model generalizes the *two-handed* [4] or *hierarchical* [7] *tile self-assembly model (2HAM)*. Unlike the aTAM, in which single tiles attach to a multi-tile seed *assembly*, the 2HAM permits arbitrary pairs of assemblies to attach provided they do so via glues of sufficient strength. Growth without a seed occurs naturally in experimental DNA tile systems [3,14], motivating the study of two-handed models.

Efficient Assembly. One of the fundamental goals of self-assembly is the design of *efficient* systems that assemble given shapes or patterns. Staged systems have three combinatorial measures of efficiency: the number of tile types (*tile complexity*), the maximum number of bins used in any stage (*bin complexity*), and the number of stages of the system (*stage complexity*). Numerous constructions of efficient staged systems that assemble given shapes [9,11] and patterns [10,17] have been given. Here, we give new, more efficient constructions for assembling height-1 and height-$\mathcal{O}(1)$ rectangles called *lines*, sets of such lines, and *hefty* general shapes of sufficient edge-length-to-edge-count ratio. The results are summarized in Table 1 and described below.

Assembling $1 \times n$ Lines. The construction of lines is often used as a subroutine in the assembly of more complex shapes [9,11] or as a simple benchmark [1,6]. In the 2HAM, assembling $1 \times n$ lines requires n tile types; as a corollary, staged systems with 1 bin, 1 stage, and n tile types assemble $1 \times n$ lines.

If $\mathcal{O}(1)$ bins and $\mathcal{O}(\log n)$ stages are permitted, then $\mathcal{O}(1)$ tile types suffice [9], demonstrating a trade-off between two measures of staged system complexity. However, no general trade-off relating all three complexity measures were known prior to this work for assembling $1 \times n$ lines. Here we obtain tight upper and lower bounds that completely characterize the trade-off: for systems of at most t tile types and b bins, the minimum number of stages needed to assemble any $1 \times n$ line is $\Theta(\log_t n + \log_b \frac{n}{t} + 1)$ (Theorems 1 and 2).

A precursor to the upper bound construction was used to generate a set of gadgets to achieve the primary results in [5]. The lower bound approach (Theorem 2) is novel and is not information-theoretic. As a result, it holds for all n rather than almost all n, a common limitation of information-theoretic lower bounds in tile self-assembly.

Assembling $\mathcal{O}(1) \times n$ **Lines.** In the 2HAM, $\mathcal{O}(1) \times n$ lines can be assembled using $n^{\mathcal{O}(1)}$ tile types [8],[1] but a lower bound exceeding $\Omega(\frac{\log n}{\log \log n})$ remains open. The assembly of $\mathcal{O}(1) \times n$ lines has not been studied explicitly in the staged model, however some constructions of Demaine et al. [11] utilize $\mathcal{O}(1) \times n$ line construction as a subroutine.

We give staged systems that use t tile types and b bins that assemble $\mathcal{O}(1) \times n$ lines in $\mathcal{O}(\frac{\log n - tb - t \log t}{b^2} + \frac{\log \log b}{\log t})$ stages (Theorem 4) and prove that for almost all n, $\Omega(\frac{\log n - tb - t \log t}{b^2})$ stages are required (Theorem 5). The upper bound implies a number of new results, including the assembly of $\mathcal{O}(1) \times n$ lines by systems with $\mathcal{O}(1)$ bins, $\mathcal{O}(1)$ stages, and $\mathcal{O}(\frac{\log n}{\log \log n})$ tile types, beating our lower bound of $\Omega(\log n)$ tile types for $1 \times n$ lines (Theorem 2).

This result utilizes the *bit-pad* gadget of [5], and the construction of this pad is the bottleneck for the complexity we achieve. Used naively, this bit-pad gadget can be used to assemble $\mathcal{O}(\log n) \times n$ rectangles within the stated complexity.

Here, we combine with bit-pad gadget with a a novel "sideways" counter to reduce the rectangle height from $\mathcal{O}(\log n)$ to $\mathcal{O}(1)$. This counter involves a non-deterministic guessing strategy for copying sets of $\log n$ bits though a $\mathcal{O}(1)$-height regions, "deactivating" incorrect copies. This technique solves a common difficulty in assembling shapes with narrow regions of low "geometric bandwidth" [2,8] and may have other applications in two-handed self-assembly.

Assembling $\mathcal{O}(1) \times n$ **Line Sets and General Shapes.** Finally, we consider constructing a set of k $\mathcal{O}(1)$-height lines of differing lengths up to n, in service of general shape construction. The first result is a b-bin, $\mathcal{O}(\frac{k \log n}{b^2} + \frac{k \sqrt{\log n}}{b} + \log \log n)$-stage, $\mathcal{O}(1)$-tile system for assembling any such set of lines (Theorem 6). This is complemented by a lower bound of $\Omega(\frac{k \log n}{b^2})$ (Theorem 7), optimal within an additive $\mathcal{O}(\log \log n)$ factor for small b.

In the special case of systems with $\mathcal{O}(\sqrt{k})$ bins and $\mathcal{O}(1)$ tile types, we give a tight bound of $\Theta(\log n)$ stages (Theorem 8 and Corollary 1). We then use the upper bound to efficiently assemble *hefty* shapes whose edge lengths are at least logarithmic in the number of edges with a $\mathcal{O}(1)$ scale factor increase. This small scale factor contrasts with the results of [5], where more efficient assembly of shapes is obtained, but with unbounded scale factor.

We also prove that any such shape can be assembled by a system with $\mathcal{O}(1)$ tile types, $\mathcal{O}(\sqrt{k})$ bins, and $\mathcal{O}(\log n)$ stages (Theorem 9), optimal for nearly every choice of k and n (Theorem 10) and giving an affirmative answer to a question of [11].

2 The Staged Self-assembly Model

Here, we give a technical introduction to the two-handed tile assembly model (2HAM) and the staged self-assembly model. The *two-handed tile assembly model*

---

[1] The result is given for the aTAM in [8] but the same tile set at temperature 2 in the 2HAM behaves identically.

Table 1. An overview of old and new results on problems considered in this paper. Variables t and b denote resource constraints on tile types and bins, respectively. For line sets, k denotes the number of lines in the set, while n denotes the length of the longest line. For general shapes, k denotes the number of edges in the shape, while n denotes the edge length of the minimum-diameter bounding square of the shape. A hefty shape is a shape whose edges are all length at least logarithmic in the number of edges.

Bins	Tiles	Upper bound	Lower bound	Reference
$1 \times n$ *lines*				
$\mathcal{O}(1)$	$\mathcal{O}(1)$	$\Theta(\log n)$		Corollary 1, Theorem 3 of [9]
b	t	$\Theta(\log_t n + \log_b \frac{n}{t} + 1)$		Theorems 1 and 2
$\mathcal{O}(1) \times n$ *lines (standard glues)*				
1	$n^{\mathcal{O}(1)}$	1		Theorem 3.2 of [8]
b	t	$\mathcal{O}(\frac{\log n - t \log t - tb}{b^2} + \frac{\log \log b}{\log t})$	$\Omega(\frac{\log n - t \log t - tb}{b^2})$	Theorems 4 and 5
Line sets				
b	$\mathcal{O}(1)$	$\mathcal{O}(\frac{k\sqrt{\log n}}{b} + \frac{k \log n}{b^2} + \log \log n)$	$\Omega(\frac{k \log n}{b^2})$	Theorems 6 and 7
$\mathcal{O}(\sqrt{k})$		$\Theta(\log n)$		Theorem 8 and Corollary 1
Hefty hole-free shapes				
$\mathcal{O}(k)$	$\mathcal{O}(1)$	$\mathcal{O}(\log n)$	$\Omega(\frac{\log n}{k})$	Corollary 1 of [11], Theorem 3 of [9]
$\mathcal{O}(\sqrt{k})$		$\Theta(\log n)$		Theorems 9 and 10

is a model of tile-based assembly processes in which large assemblies can combine freely, in contrast to the well-studied aTAM that limits assembly to single-tile addition to a growing seed assembly. An example system is shown in Fig. 1a.

The *staged self-assembly model* is a generalization of the 2HAM in which the terminal assemblies of one 2HAM system can be used, in place of single tiles, as the input assemblies of another 2HAM system. Each system exists in a separate *bin*, and the terminal assemblies of a set of bins can be combined as the input assemblies to another bin in the subsequent *stage*. A staged system then consists of a mixing "graph" that defines which bins' contents are mixed into each bin in the subsequent stage. Figure 1b shows a small example system.

Tiles. A *tile* is a non-rotatable unit square with each edge labeled with a *glue* from a set Σ. Each pair of glues $g_1, g_2 \in \Sigma$ has a non-negative integer *strength* $\text{str}(g_1, g_2)$. Each pair of glues $g_1, g_2 \in \Sigma$ has a non-negative integer *strength* $\text{str}(g_1, g_2)$, with $\text{str}(g_1, g_2) = 0$ unless $g_1 = g_2$. Every set Σ contains a special *null glue* whose strength with every other glue is 0.

Configurations, Bond Graphs, and Stability. A *configuration* is a partial function $A : \mathbb{Z}^2 \to T$ for some set of tiles T, i.e. an arrangement of tiles on a square grid. For a given configuration A, define the *bond graph* G_A to be the

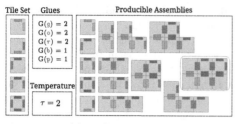
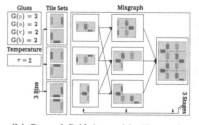

(a) 2HAM Example   (b) Staged Self-Assembly Example

Fig. 1. (a) A 2HAM example that uniquely builds a 2×3 rectangle. The top 4 tiles in the tile set all combine with strength-2 glues building the 'L' shape. The tile with blue and purple glues needs two tiles to cooperatively bind to the assembly with strength 2. All possible producibles are shown with the terminal assembly highlighted. (b) A simple staged self-assembly example. The system has 3 bins and 3 stages, as shown in the mixgraph. There are six tiles in our system that we assign to bins as desired. From each stage only the terminal assemblies are added to the next stage. The result of this system is the assembly shown in the output bin in stage 3.

weighted grid graph in which each element of $\mathrm{dom}(A)$ is a vertex, and the weight of the edge between a pair of tiles is equal to the strength of the coincident glue pair. A configuration is said to be τ-*stable* for positive integer τ if every edge cut of G_A has strength at least τ, and is τ-*unstable* otherwise.

Assemblies. For a configuration A and vector $\boldsymbol{u} = \langle u_x, u_y \rangle$ with $u_x, u_y \in \mathbb{Z}^2$, $A + \boldsymbol{u}$ denotes the configuration $A \circ f$, where $f(x,y) = (x + u_x, y + u_y)$. For two configurations A and B, B is a *translation* of A, written $B \simeq A$, provided that $B = A + \boldsymbol{u}$ for some vector $\boldsymbol{u}$. For a configuration A, the *assembly* of A is the set $\tilde{A} = \{B : B \simeq A\}$. An assembly $\tilde{A}$ is a *subassembly* of an assembly $\tilde{B}$, denoted $\tilde{A} \sqsubseteq \tilde{B}$, provided that there exists an $A \in \tilde{A}$ and $B \in \tilde{B}$ such that $A \subseteq B$. An assembly is τ-*stable* provided the configurations it contains are τ-stable. Assemblies $\tilde{A}$ and $\tilde{B}$ are τ-*combinable* into an assembly $\tilde{C}$ provided there exist $A \in \tilde{A}$, $B \in \tilde{B}$, and $C \in \tilde{C}$ such that $A \cup B = C$, $A \cap B = \varnothing$, and $\tilde{C}$ is τ-stable.

Two-Handed Assembly and Bins. We define the assembly process in terms of bins. A *bin* is an ordered tuple (S, τ) where S is a set of *initial* assemblies and τ is a positive integer parameter called the *temperature*. For a bin (S, τ), the set of *produced* assemblies $P'_{(S,\tau)}$ is defined recursively as follows:

1. $S \subseteq P'_{(S,\tau)}$.
2. If $A, B \in P'_{(S,\tau)}$ are τ-combinable into C, then $C \in P'_{(S,\tau)}$.

A produced assembly is *terminal* provided it is not τ-combinable with any other producible assembly, and the set of all terminal assemblies of a bin (S, τ) is denoted $P_{(S,\tau)}$. Intuitively, $P'_{(S,\tau)}$ represents the set of all possible supertiles that can self-assemble from the initial set S, whereas $P_{(S,\tau)}$ represents only the set of supertiles that cannot grow any further.

The assemblies in $P_{(S,\tau)}$ are *uniquely produced* iff for each $x \in P'_{(S,\tau)}$ there exists a corresponding $y \in P_{(S,\tau)}$ such that $x \sqsubseteq y$. Thus unique production implies that every producible assembly can be repeatedly combined with others to form an assembly in $P_{(S,\tau)}$.

Staged Assembly Systems. An *r-stage b-bin mix graph* M is an acyclic r-partite digraph consisting of rb vertices $m_{i,j}$ for $1 \leq i \leq r$ and $1 \leq j \leq b$, and edges of the form $(m_{i,j}, m_{i+1,j'})$ for some i, j, j'. A *staged assembly system* is a 3-tuple $\langle M_{r,b}, \{T_1, T_2, \ldots, T_b\}, \tau \rangle$ where $M_{r,b}$ is an r-stage b-bin mix graph, T_i is a set of tile types, and τ is an integer temperature parameter.

Given a staged assembly system, for each $1 \leq i \leq r$, $1 \leq j \leq b$, we define a corresponding bin $(R_{i,j}, \tau)$ where $R_{i,j}$ is defined as follows:

1. $R_{1,j} = T_j$ (this is a bin in the first stage);
2. For $i \geq 2$, $R_{i,j} = \left(\bigcup_{k:\ (m_{i-1,k}, m_{i,j}) \in M_{r,b}} P_{(R_{(i-1,k)}, \tau)} \right)$.

Thus, the jth bin in stage 1 is provided with the initial tile set T_j, and each bin in any subsequent stage receives an initial set of assemblies consisting of the terminally produced assemblies from a subset of the bins in the previous stage as dictated by the edges of the mix graph.[2] The *output* of the staged system is simply the union of all terminal assemblies from each of the bins in the final stage.[3] We say that this set of output assemblies is *uniquely produced* if each bin in the staged system uniquely produces its respective set of terminal assemblies.

Shapes. The *shape* of an assembly is the polyomino defined by the tile locations, i.e. dom(A), and is *scaled by a factor* c by replacing each cell of the polyomino with a $c \times c$ block of cells. A shape is *hole-free* provided it is simply connected.

Since every shape is a polyomino, its boundary consists of unit-length horizontal and vertical line segments. An *edge* of a shape is a maximal contiguous parallel sequence of such segments. A shape with k edges is *hefty* provided each edge has length at least $\frac{4 \log_2 k + 4}{26} = \Omega(\log k)$. A shape S is an $h \times w$ *line* provided $S = \{y+1, y+2, \ldots, y+h\} \times \{x+1, x+2, \ldots x+w\}$ for some $x, y \in \mathbb{Z}^2$.

3   Assembling $1 \times n$ Lines

We start by analyzing the parameterized staged complexity of assembling $1 \times n$ lines using systems with t tile types and b bins. The following upper bound follows immediately from combining the construction of Lemmas 1 and 2.[4]

---

[2] The original staged model [9] only considered $\mathcal{O}(1)$ distinct tile types, and thus for simplicity allowed tiles to be added at any stage. Because systems here may have super-constant tile complexity, we restrict tiles to only be added at the initial stage.

[3] This is a slight modification of the original staged model [9] in that the final stage may have multiple bins. However, all of our results apply to both variants of the model.

[4] The "+1" implies the trivial requirement of at least one stage.

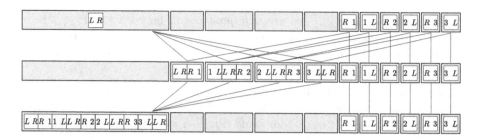

Fig. 2. A high level example using $t = 7$ tile types and 11 bins. Note that the growing assembly in the third stage's leftmost bin maintains the property that L and R glues are exposed on the left and right identical to the single tile in the first stage's leftmost bin. This two-stage mixing process repeats, each time increasing the length of the assembly in the leftmost bin by a factor of $\Theta(t)$.

Theorem 1. *There exists a constant c such that for any $b, t, n \in \mathbb{N}$ with $b, t > c$ there exists a staged assembly system with b bins and t tile types whose uniquely produced output is a $1 \times n$ line using $\mathcal{O}(\log_t n + \log_b \frac{n}{t} + 1)$ stages.*

Lemma 1. *For any $b, t, n \in \mathbb{N}$ with $t \geq 5$ and $b \geq \frac{3}{2}t + \frac{5}{2}$, there exists a staged assembly system with b bins and t tile types whose uniquely produced output is a $1 \times n$ line using $\mathcal{O}(\log_t n + 1)$ stages.*

Lemma 2. *For any $b, t, n \in \mathbb{N}$ with $b > 11$ and $\frac{3}{2}t + \frac{5}{2} > b$, there exists a staged assembly system with b bins and t tile types whose uniquely produced output is a $1 \times n$ line using $\mathcal{O}(\log_b \frac{n}{t-b} + 1)$ stages.*

Detailed proofs are omitted due to space constraints. We instead give a brief overview of the constructions here. Both constructions consider constant fractions t', b' of t, b, respectively.

In the case of Lemma 1 (when $b \geq \frac{3}{2}t + \frac{5}{2}$), t' copies of a $1 \times \ell$ assembly are assembled into a $1 \times \ell t'$ assembly in two stages (initially, $\ell = 1$). An example of this technique for a specific t and b can be seen in Fig. 2. Growing by a factor of t' in $\mathcal{O}(1)$ stages implies $\mathcal{O}(\log_t n)$ stages suffice to assemble $1 \times n$ lines, where n is a power of t'. Since this system generates all powers of t' in intermediate stages, values of n that are not powers of two are handled by keeping a *partial growth bin* where k distinct $1 \times (t')^i$ assemblies are concatenated to a growing assembly each time the ith digit in the base t' expansion of n is k. If Lemma 1 does not apply but $b \geq \frac{t}{2}$, then shrinking t by a factor of 3 and applying Lemma 1 implies $\mathcal{O}(\log_{t/3} n + 1) = \mathcal{O}(\log_t n + 1)$ stages suffice.

Otherwise, $t/2 > b$ and Lemma 2 applies. In this case, the above technique fails because there are too few bins for the t' tiles used to connect t' copies of a $1 \times \ell$ assembly. Instead, the assembly is grown by factors of b' (rather than t') using b' tile types as connectors. The $t' - b'$ tiles not used as connectors create a $1 \times (t' - b')$ assembly that is assigned in the first stage to each of the connector tiles' bins, increasing the length of connectors in the first stage. Growing by a factor of b' in $\mathcal{O}(1)$ stages using assemblies which start at length

$t' - b'$ implies $\mathcal{O}(\log_b \frac{n}{t-b} + 1)$ stage complexity. Lengths that are not powers of b' are handled identically as in Lemma 1, but utilizing the base b' (rather than base t') expansion of n. Since $\frac{t}{2} > b$, $\mathcal{O}(\log_b \frac{n}{t-b}) = \mathcal{O}(\log_b \frac{n}{t})$.

3.1 Lower Bound

A lower bound can also be shown for assembling $1 \times n$ lines by proving an equivalent statement: that a system with s stages, b bins, and t tile types can uniquely assemble only lines of length $\mathcal{O}(\min(t^s, tb^s))$.

Theorem 2. *For any $b, t, n \in \mathbb{N}$, a staged system with b bins and t tile types whose uniquely produced output is a $1 \times n$ line must use $\Omega(\log_t n + \log_b \frac{n}{t} + 1)$ stages.*

4 Assembling $\mathcal{O}(1) \times n$ Lines

We now turn our attention to assembling $\mathcal{O}(1) \times n$ lines. Theorem 4 assembles a $\mathcal{O}(1) \times n$ line using a staged system with t tile types, b bins, and $\mathcal{O}(\frac{\log n - tb - t \log t}{b^2} + \frac{\log \log b}{\log t})$ stages, breaking the $\Omega(\log_t n + \log_b \frac{n}{t} + 1)$ lower bound for $1 \times n$ lines.[5] A complementary lower bound of $\Omega(\frac{\log n - tb - t \log t}{b^2})$ for any constant height is given by Theorem 5.

4.1 Special Class of $\mathcal{O}(1) \times n$ Lines

As a warmup, we describe a simpler construction restricted to an infinite set (but not all) of $\mathcal{O}(1) \times n$ lines. This simpler construction already beats the trivial lower bound of n for $1 \times n$ lines in the aTAM. Details of fine-tuning the termination of the counting, yielding the desired result for all n (Theorem 4), is omitted due to space constraints.

Theorem 3. *For any $t, b, n = \Omega(1)$ with $n \in \{i : i = 2^m(2m+3), m \in \mathbb{N}\}$, there exists a temperature-2 staged assembly system with b bins and t tile types whose uniquely produced output is a $\mathcal{O}(1) \times n$ line using $\mathcal{O}(\log \log n)$ stages.*

The construction has four phases:

1. *Counter gadgets* assemble a horizontal counter that counts from 0 to $2^m - 1$ for some $m \in \mathbb{N}$ with $n = 2^m(2m + 3)$. Nondeterminism enables efficiently building all such counter gadgets, but creates many unwanted counter gadgets.
2. *Deactivator gadgets* are assembled. They attach to and *deactivate* unwanted counter gadgets for later disposal.

---

[5] Note that the first bound is missing the additive constant to ensure at least one stage. There is still a requirement of at least one stage, but '+1' may be insufficient as the term could be negative.

3. The remaining desired counter gadgets assemble with each other with the help of *gum pads*. The horizontal counter of desired length is assembled.
4. Deactivated counter gadgets are "disposed" by attaching to the bottom of the resulting linear assembly, and the assembly is completed into a rectangle.

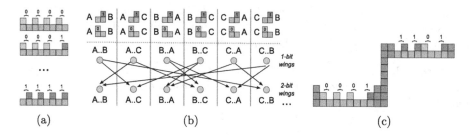

Fig. 3. (a) An example of how 4-bit wing gadgets geometrically encode binary strings. (b) Using $\mathcal{O}(1)$ bins and tile types, the number of bits represented on counter gadgets is doubled every stage. (c) Using vertical lines built from $\mathcal{O}(1)$ tile types, left and right wings are nondeterministically brought together to form a counter gadget.

Phase 1: Assembling Counter Gadgets

- *Wing gadgets* are rectangular assemblies with geometric bumps on their north surface, where the bumps geometrically encode an *index* in binary using m bits (Fig. 3a).
- A wing gadget *has index i* provided it geometrically encodes a binary string representing i, and all m-*bit* wing gadgets are nondeterministically built using $\mathcal{O}(1)$ tiles, $\mathcal{O}(1)$ bins, and $\mathcal{O}(\log m)$ stages using the mix-graph shown in Fig. 3b.
- Two wing gadgets are nondeterministically brought together with $\mathcal{O}(1)$-size assemblies to form *counter gadgets*, as shown in Fig. 3c.

Phase 2: Deactivating Bad Counter Gadgets

- A *deactivator gadget* detects counter gadgets whose left and right wings do not have the same index and *deactivates* them, preventing their assembly with other counter gadgets in a later stage (Fig. 4c). A deactivator gadget is built by assembling an *error checker* and a *deactivator base*.
- Error checkers (Fig. 4a) are assemblies of $\mathcal{O}(1)$ width and $2m+3$ length that, given an m-bit left wing and right wing gadget, can bind to those gadgets if the binary strings represented by those gadgets differ at any of their m bit locations. These gadgets are built using $\mathcal{O}(1)$ tiles, $\mathcal{O}(1)$ bins, and $\mathcal{O}(\log m)$ stages.

- Alone, error checkers cannot completely guarantee that a counter gadget will not interact with the glues of other assemblies. To deactivate the counter gadgets, error checkers are combined with a *deactivator base* to create our deactivator gadgets (Fig. 4b). The deactivator base is built $\mathcal{O}(1)$ tiles, $\mathcal{O}(1)$ bins, and $\mathcal{O}(\log m)$ stages.
- Deactivator gadgets are mixed with counter gadgets to deactivate *mismatched* counter gadgets encoding different values on east and west wings (Fig. 4c). Deactivated counter gadgets are "disposed" later.

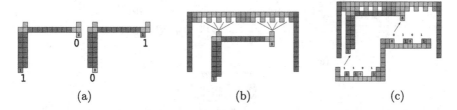

(a)   (b)   (c)

Fig. 4. (a) The two different kinds of error checkers. These attached non-deterministically to the deactivator base using their northern geometric teeth. (b) The error checker attaching to the base, nondeterministically choosing a location, completing our deactivator gadget. Through nondeterminism, deactivator gadgets can be created to detect mismatches at every possible bit location. (c) A deactivator gadget attaching to a mismatched counter gadget.

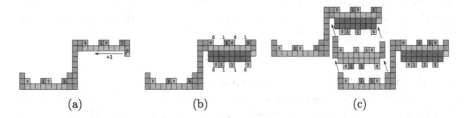

(a)   (b)   (c)

Fig. 5. (a) Increment tiles begin adding *geometric teeth* on the underside of the right wing. (b) The geometric teeth on the underside of the right wing. They represent the same number as the top of the right wing after being incremented by one. (c) A gum pad detects matching geometric teeth and adheres two counter gadgets together.

Phase 3: Line Formation

- Counter gadgets that have not been deactivated are mixed with $\mathcal{O}(1)$ *increment tiles* that bind to their right wings, exposing a geometric representation of each wing's binary string, incremented by 1 (Figs. 5a and b).
- *Gum pads* allow a pair of left and right wings on two counter gadgets to attach side-by-side if the indices of the two wings are identical (Fig. 5c). Gum pads are built using $\mathcal{O}(1)$ tile types, $\mathcal{O}(1)$ bins, and $\mathcal{O}(\log m)$ stages.
- Gum pads are mixed with the counter gadgets, allowing them to self-assemble into a linear assembly of length n that counts horizontally from 0 to $2^m - 1$.

Phase 4: Disposal and Finishing

- Deactivated counter gadgets are disposed by attaching to the bottom of the linear assembly, increasing the assembly's width by $\mathcal{O}(1)$, as shown in Fig. 6a.
- A final bin has $\mathcal{O}(1)$ tile types that finish the line by filling any gaps or jagged edges, so that the end result is a rectangle.

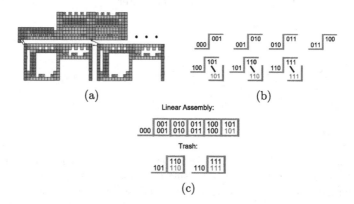

(a)   (b)

(c)

Fig. 6. (a) Disposing of trash assemblies. $\mathcal{O}(1)$ tiles are added to the westmost edge of the counter. Using these tiles, deactivators can attach to the bottom of the counter. The empty space is filled with $\mathcal{O}(1)$ filler tile types. (b) Stopper gadgets for every number at least 5 assembled and mixed with the counter gadgets. (c) Mixed with gum pads, the counter gadgets assemble, a horizontal counter counting from 0 to 5; with stopped counter gadgets as trash.

Complexity. Counter gadgets, deactivator gadgets, and gum pads are all assembled using a common technique borrowed from [9] that uses $\mathcal{O}(1)$ tile types and $\mathcal{O}(\log m)$ stages to assemble $\Theta(m)$ assemblies (in $\mathcal{O}(1)$ bins). The same technique is also used to assemble the $\Theta(m)$ lines used in the deactivator gadgets and toothed gum and counter gadget "pads", starting with $\mathcal{O}(1)$ bit gadgets and also using $\mathcal{O}(1)$ bins and $\mathcal{O}(\log m)$ stages. Thus, all aforementioned gadgets can be assembled in parallel using $\mathcal{O}(1)$ tile types, $\mathcal{O}(1)$ bins, and $\mathcal{O}(\log m)$ stages. Since $n = 2^m(2m + 3)$, $m = \Theta(\log n)$, and $\mathcal{O}(\log m) = \mathcal{O}(\log \log n)$.

4.2   Generalizing to All n

The construction of Theorem 3 builds counter gadgets using a horizontal counting method to count from 0 to $2^m - 1$ for any $m \in \mathbb{N}$, yielding assemblies of length $n = 2^m(2m + 3)$ for all $m \in \mathbb{N}$. General values of n are achieved by fine-tuning length at two scales: "large scale" via terminating the counter early at a specific value before the desired n and "small scale" via attaching a smaller assembly to reach exactly n from where the counter terminated.

Terminating the counter early is achieved by deactivating "high-value" counter gadgets with values larger than a specified value using *stopper gadgets*, as shown in Fig. 6. Encoding the counter termination value dominates the stage complexity, giving the following result:

Theorem 4. *For any* $t, b, n \in \mathbb{N}$ *with* $t, b = \Omega(1)$, *there exists a temperature-2 staged system with* b *bins and* t *tile types that assembles a* $\mathcal{O}(1) \times n$ *line using* $\mathcal{O}(\frac{\log n - tb - t \log t}{b^2} + \frac{\log \log b}{\log t})$ *stages.*

4.3   Lower Bounds for $\mathcal{O}(1) \times n$ Lines

Lower bounds for assembling $\mathcal{O}(1) \times n$ lines are obtained using information-theoretic arguments based on combining the bound on information content from [5] with the lower bound of $\lceil \log_2 n \rceil$ on the number of bits needed to specify n for almost all n:

Theorem 5. *For any* $b, t \in \mathbb{N}$ *and almost all* $n \in \mathbb{N}$, *any staged self-assembly system with* b *bins and* t *tile types and uniquely assembles a* $\mathcal{O}(1) \times n$ *line must use* $\Omega(\frac{\log n - tb - t \log t}{b^2})$ *stages.*

5   Assembling $\mathcal{O}(1) \times n$ Line Sets

Now we consider extending the construction of a $\mathcal{O}(1) \times n$ line to a set of k such lines, working towards the construction of hefty shapes in Sect. 6. The first upper bound construction uses parallel instances of the Theorem 4 construction to assemble multiple lines in parallel with a comparable number of stages.

Theorem 6. *Let* $L = \{n_1, \ldots, n_k\} \subseteq \mathbb{N}$ *with* $n = \max(L)$. *There exists a staged assembly system with* $\mathcal{O}(1)$ *tile types,* b *bins, and* $\mathcal{O}(\frac{k\sqrt{\log n}}{b} + \frac{k \log n}{b^2} + \log \log n)$ *stages whose uniquely produced output is a set of* $\mathcal{O}(1) \times n_i$ *lines for all* $n_i \in L$.

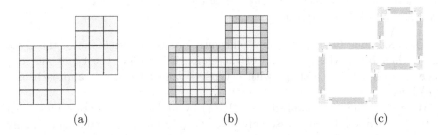

(a)   (b)   (c)

Fig. 7. (a) A hefty hole-free shape to be constructed. (b) The shape scaled by factor 2 with backbone (green) and vertices (blue). (c) The decomposition of the backbone into vertices and lines. (Color figure online)

Theorem 7. *Let $L = \{n_1, \ldots, n_k\} \subseteq \mathbb{N}$ with $n = \max(L)$. For almost all L, any staged self-assembly system with $\mathcal{O}(1)$ tile types and b bins that assembles $\mathcal{O}(1) \times n_i$ lines for all $n_i \in L$ has $\Omega(\frac{k \log n}{b^2})$ stages.*

In the case that $b = \mathcal{O}(\sqrt{\log n})$, the prior two theorems are tight up to additive terms. However, as b increases, the "crazy mixing" approach [9] used in the modular construction of Theorem 6 fails to utilize the growing number of possible mix graphs. The next construction achieves optimal stage complexity for large bin counts, specifically bin counts scaling with k:

Theorem 8. *Let $L = \{n_1, \ldots, n_k\} \subseteq \mathbb{N}$ with $n = \max(L)$. There exists a staged self-assembly system with $\mathcal{O}(1)$ tile types, $\mathcal{O}(\sqrt{k})$ bins, and $\mathcal{O}(\log n)$ stages that assembles $\mathcal{O}(1) \times n_i$ lines for all $n_i \in L$.*

The following lower bound matches this construction and follows directly from Theorem 7.

Corollary 1. *Let $L = \{n_1, \ldots, n_k\} \subseteq \mathbb{N}$ with $n = \max(L)$. For almost all L, any staged self-assembly system with $\mathcal{O}(1)$ tile types and $\mathcal{O}(\sqrt{k})$ bins that assembles $\mathcal{O}(1) \times n_i$ lines for all $n_i \in L$ has $\Omega(\log n)$ stages.*

6   Assembling Hefty Shapes

The efficient line set assembly result of Theorem 8 can be combined with a technique of [11] to assemble general shapes optimally:

Theorem 9. *Let S be a hefty hole-free shape with k vertices and minimum-diameter bounding square of edge length n. There exists a $\tau = 2$ staged system with $\mathcal{O}(\sqrt{k})$ bins, $\mathcal{O}(1)$ tile types, and $\mathcal{O}(\log n)$ stages that uniquely produces S scaled by a factor $\mathcal{O}(1)$.*

Theorem 10. *Let S be a hefty shape with k edges and minimum-diameter bounding square of edge length n with $k = \mathcal{O}(n^{2-\varepsilon})$ for some $\varepsilon > 0$. For almost all S, any staged self-assembly system with $\mathcal{O}(1)$ tile types and $\mathcal{O}(\sqrt{k})$ bins that assembles S has $\Omega(\log n)$ stages.*

The technique of [11] is to first efficiently create the *backbone* of the given shape, then fill in the backbone of the shape using $\mathcal{O}(1)$ tile types and one stage (see Fig. 7). For a shape with k vertices (and edges), this approach uses $\mathcal{O}(k)$ bins.

We reduce the bin complexity to $\mathcal{O}(\sqrt{k})$ by replacing k separate bins, each containing a different edge assembly, with $\mathcal{O}(\sqrt{k})$ bins, each containing many edge assemblies each labeled with geometric teeth, similar to the construction of Theorem 8. In exchange, $\mathcal{O}(\log n)$ additional stages must be used to assemble these edge assemblies.

References

1. Adleman, L., Cheng, Q., Goel, A., Huang, M.D., Wasserman, H.: Linear self-assemblies: equilibria, entropy and convergence rates. In: 6th International Conference on Difference Equations and Applications (2001)
2. Adleman, L.M., Cheng, Q., Goel, A., Huang, M.D.A., Kempe, D., de Espanés, P.M., Rothemund, P.W.K.: Combinatorial optimization problems in self-assembly. SIAM J. Comput. **38**(6), 2356–2381 (2009)
3. Barish, R.D., Schulman, R., Rothemund, P.W.K., Winfree, E.: An information-bearing seed for nucleating algorithmic self-assembly. Proc. Natl. Acad. Sci. **106**(15), 6054–6059 (2009)
4. Cannon, S., Demaine, E.D., Demaine, M.L., Eisenstat, S., Patitz, M.J., Schweller, R.T., Summers, S.M., Winslow, A.: Two hands are better than one (up to constant factors): Self-assembly in the 2HAM vs. aTAM. In: STACS 2013, LIPIcs, vol. 20, pp. 172–184. Schloss Dagstuhl (2013)
5. Chalk, C., Martinez, E., Schweller, R., Vega, L., Winslow, A., Wylie, T.: Optimal staged self-assembly of general shapes. Algorithmica **80**, 1383–1409 (2017)
6. Chandran, H., Gopalkrishnan, N., Reif, J.: Tile complexity of linear assemblies. SIAM J. Comput. **41**(4), 1051–1073 (2012)
7. Chen, H.L., Doty, D.: Parallelism and time in hierarchical self-assembly. In: 23rd Annual ACM-SIAM Symposium on Discrete Algorithms (SODA), pp. 1163–1182. SIAM (2012)
8. Cheng, Q., Aggarwal, G., Goldwasser, M.H., Kao, M.Y., Schweller, R.T., de Espanés, P.M.: Complexities for generalized models of self-assembly. SIAM J. Comput. **34**, 1493–1515 (2005)
9. Demaine, E.D., Demaine, M.L., Fekete, S.P., Ishaque, M., Rafalin, E., Schweller, R.T., Souvaine, D.L.: Staged self-assembly: nanomanufacture of arbitrary shapes with $O(1)$ glues. Nat. Comput. **7**(3), 347–370 (2008)
10. Demaine, E.D., Eisenstat, S., Ishaque, M., Winslow, A.: One-dimensional staged self-assembly. Nat. Comput. **12**(2), 247–258 (2013)
11. Demaine, E.D., Fekete, S.P., Scheffer, C., Schmidt, A.: New geometric algorithms for fully connected staged self-assembly. In: Phillips, A., Yin, P. (eds.) DNA 2015. LNCS, vol. 9211, pp. 104–116. Springer, Cham (2015). https://doi.org/10.1007/978-3-319-21999-8_7
12. Evans, C.: Crystals that count! Physical principles and experimental investigations of DNA tile self-assembly. Ph.D. thesis, Caltech (2014)
13. Rothemund, P.W.K., Winfree, E.: The program-size complexity of self-assembled squares (extended abstract). In: Proceedings of the 32nd ACM Symposium on Theory of Computing, STOC 2000, pp. 459–468 (2000)
14. Schulman, R., Winfree, E.: Synthesis of crystals with a programmable kinetic barrier to nucleation. Proc. Natl. Acad. Sci. **104**(39), 15236–15241 (2007)
15. Seeman, N.C.: Nucleic-acid junctions and lattices. J. Theoret. Biol. **99**, 237–247 (1982)
16. Winfree, E.: Algorithmic self-assembly of DNA. Ph.D. thesis, Caltech (1998)
17. Winslow, A.: Staged self-assembly and polyomino context-free grammars. Nat. Comput. **14**(2), 293–302 (2015)

The Scope of a Relativistic Quantum Process with Spin-Momentum Entanglement

Tanner Crowder$^{(\boxtimes)}$ and Marco Lanzagorta

The Naval Research Laboratory, Washington DC 20375, USA
{tanner.crowder,marco.lanzagorta}@nrl.navy.mil

Abstract. Using an imperfectly prepared state, we show that under a Lorentz transformation, the evolution of a massive spin-1/2 particle violates many standard assumptions made in quantum information theory, including complete positivity. Unlike other recent endeavors in relativistic quantum information, we are able to quantify and maximize how much information can be transferred through such a quantum process by calculating the scope. We show that, surprisingly, in many instances the relativistic noise increases the amount of information that can be transferred, and in fact, even if the initial state is arbitrarily close to the completely mixed state, information can still be transferred perfectly.

Keywords: Quantum information · Relativity · Channel capacity

1 Introduction

The study of transmitting spin-momentum entangled particles through relativistic noise was initiated by [1]. However, it is fairly standard to assume that a quantum system and its environment are in a pure product state [2,3]. The consequences of this assumption are far reaching and are often taken for granted. For example, from this assumption, one can show that the local dynamics of a quantum system must not decrease entropy, not increase purity, and not increase the informatic content of a message. We will not foray into the debate about when this assumption is good enough or valid, but instead consider an example of a spin-1/2 particle whose spin is entangled with its momentum.

We will use somewhat of a toy model and assume the initial state is in a superposition of only two definite momentum states, but one could use states like those described in [1] to generalize our model. In contrast to [1,4], the local dynamics of our model are linear, which allows us to calculate the maximal amount of information that can be transferred in a quantum process undergoing a Lorentz transformation. Although we have taken a simplified approach, the

© Springer International Publishing AG, part of Springer Nature (outside the US) 2018
S. Stepney and S. Verlan (Eds.): UCNC 2018, LNCS 10867, pp. 46–58, 2018.
https://doi.org/10.1007/978-3-319-92435-9_4

reduced dynamics contradict many standard assumptions made about quantum processes, including all of the ones listed above.

When one sends classical information through a quantum channel, one chooses a basis of the state space to represent the classical bits. This choice of basis induces a classical channel with a classical capacity, and each choice of basis generates a potentially new channel with its own capacity; for a discussion on capacity see [5]. As we range over every basis of the state space, we get an interval of capacities which is the *scope* of that channel [6]. Martin's procedure for calculating scope explicitly uses the fact that the channel is non-expansive in the Bloch representation, and he assumes the information is encoded in to pure states. As we will show, our maps are expansive, and we do not have access to the entire state space, so we will modify Martin's approach and show how to maximize the information transfer. With our model, we show that even with an arbitrarily noisy preparation procedure, information can be sent perfectly through the process by choosing an appropriate communication basis. The advantage to calculating the scope of a quantum channel is that it not only gives a procedure for maximizing the capacity, but it does so without any additional error correcting codes [7]. In some of the examples we use, one of the communication bases appears not to suffer the effects of relativistic noise. So the naive approach would be to use that basis to encode information. However, as we will show, that is not always the optimal communication basis.

Although most of this manuscript is framed in the language of a general quantum communication problem, the topics discussed are directly related to computation. For instance, in [8], they showed that relativistic effects can increase computational complexity when running algorithms on a quantum computer. Specifically, they showed that in the presence of enough relativistic noise, Grover's search algorithm turns linear, negating the computational speed up given by quantum phenomena.

2   Wigner Angles in Relativity

Consider a massive spin-1/2 quantum elementary particle described by the Dirac equation. In this case, the relativistic effects on a Dirac spinor are given through the Wigner rotation [9, 10]. That is, the net effect of a Lorentz transformation can be described by the unitary transformation $\delta\hat{U}$, which represents the infinitesimal Lorentz transformation $\delta\Lambda(x)$ in the inertial frame at x. Thus, the effect of an infinitesimal Lorentz transformation on a spinor $\psi_{p,\sigma}$ of momentum p and spin projection σ has the following form [9]:

$$\delta\hat{U} \, \psi_{p,\sigma} = N(p, \delta\Lambda p) \sum_{\alpha} \delta D_{\sigma\alpha} \, \psi_{\delta\Lambda p,\alpha}, \tag{1}$$

where $N(p, \delta\Lambda p)$ is a normalization factor, and the matrix $(\delta D_{\sigma\alpha})_{\sigma\alpha}$ provides a representation of the little group. Physically, this matrix is associated with the spin-1/2 representation of an infinitesimal Wigner rotation.

We shall mainly concern ourselves with one-particle (positive energy) states that are in a superposition of states with definite momentum and spin: $|p, 0\rangle$ and

$|q, 1\rangle$; for convenience we omit the indices of the 4-momentum of the particle, and use the computational basis $\{|0\rangle, |1\rangle\}$ to label the spin states. Throughout this manuscript, we use a treatment similar to that of [1,11] and note that the expression $|p, s\rangle$ denotes a state of definite spin projection s and momentum p. However, in contrast to massless particles, one can choose a single arbitrary quantization axis to describe the (potentially non-definite) spin states of massive particles with different momenta. Lastly, we will take the combined system to be $\mathcal{H}_p \otimes \mathcal{H}_s$, where $\mathcal{H}_p$ and $\mathcal{H}_s$ are the momentum and spin state Hilbert spaces, respectively.

In situations where the Wigner rotation takes place along a single direction (e.g. around the y-axis), the corresponding 2-level unitary transformation is given by the unitary matrix

$$D = e^{i\sigma_y \Omega_p/2} = \begin{pmatrix} \cos\left(\Omega_p/2\right) & \sin\left(\Omega_p/2\right) \\ -\sin\left(\Omega_p/2\right) & \cos\left(\Omega_p/2\right) \end{pmatrix}, \tag{2}$$

where Ω_p is the *Wigner angle*, which in general depends on the momentum p and the Lorentz transformation Λ.

Taking the quantization axis parallel to the z-direction (i.e. eigenvectors of the σ_z spin operator), the effect of the Lorentz transformation on the two positive energy Dirac states (spin up and spin down) is given by:

$$\hat{U}|p, 0\rangle = \cos\left(\frac{\Omega_p}{2}\right)|\Lambda p, 0\rangle - \sin\left(\frac{\Omega_p}{2}\right)|\Lambda p, 1\rangle, \tag{3}$$

$$\hat{U}|p, 1\rangle = \sin\left(\frac{\Omega_p}{2}\right)|\Lambda p, 0\rangle + \cos\left(\frac{\Omega_p}{2}\right)|\Lambda p, 1\rangle. \tag{4}$$

Note that the concept of the Wigner rotation can be easily generalized for the study of Dirac states in the presence of classical gravitational fields described by Einstein's General Relativity [10,12]. Finally, there have been questions about the whether or not the linear application of Wigner rotations is problematic. However, in [15], it was shown there is no problem with the application.

3   The Reduced Density Matrix in Relativity

Recently, there have been discussions about the reduced density matrix and the appropriate measurement observables related to relativistic spin-1/2 particles [13,14,16–18]. Specifically, how much information can be ascribed to the reduced density matrix when the particle has relativistic momentum. In [14], they argue that since after a Lorentz transformation the measurement statistics of a massive spin-1/2 particle can depend on the momentum, the spin and momentum are not independent variables, and therefore the reduced density matrix is meaningless. Their argument hinges on the fact one cannot compute the expectation value of $|p, 0\rangle$ from its reduced density matrix in every inertial frame, but this revelation should not come as a surprise. In fact, if one were to prepare the state $|p, 0\rangle$ in one inertial frame, in a different inertial frame it can transform to $|\Lambda p, 1\rangle$ under a Wigner rotation as seen in Eq. (3). This effect is due to the way the Wigner rotation mixes the spin and momentum, even when the particle is initially in a momentum eigenstate.

However, in the reference frame of the observer, the state $|p, 0\rangle$ transforms under the Wigner rotation to the state described in Eq. (3), for which the reduced density matrix is

$$\mathrm{tr}_p(U|p, 0\rangle\langle p, 0|U^\dagger) = \begin{pmatrix} \cos^2 \Omega_p/2 & 0 \\ 0 & \sin^2 \Omega_p/2 \end{pmatrix}. \tag{5}$$

Although that density matrix cannot predict the measurement statistics in every frame of reference, it correctly predicts the expectation values when using the standard Pauli spin operators in the measurement device's frame of reference. Note this happens even though the spin-measurement depends on the momentum, which manifests as the Wigner angle Ω_p.

It is our contention that the results in [14] are more of a commentary on the observables associated with a relativistic Stern-Gerlach device, rather than the usefulness of the reduced density matrix. As long as one computes the reduced density matrix in the measurement device's frame of reference by properly transforming the initial state with a Wigner rotation, and one uses the correct observables, there is no ambiguity about the measurement statistics predicted by the reduced density matrix [13,16,17]. Even though there is no local transformation rule for the reduced density matrix, it still provides the ability to calculate informatic quantities like scope, capacity, and entropy. As [18] discusses, there are at least seven candidates for relativistic spin observables, and none are universally accepted/rejected as *the* relativistic spin observable. Since it is still an open question of how to reconcile a measurement procedure with the mathematical construction of a relativistic spin observable [18], in the following, we will not constrain ourselves to a particular preparation or measurement device, like the Stern-Gerlach, and instead, operate with the most general rules of quantum mechanics. That being said, we conjecture that no matter what observable one uses, a Lorentz transformation can increase the information content of a relativistic particle.

4   Quantum Information in Relativity

To analyze the effect of a Lorentz transformation on quantum information, we will assume there is a black box that produces the state

$$|\Psi\rangle = r|p, 0\rangle + s|q, 1\rangle, \tag{6}$$

with $|r|^2 > |s|^2$. To be clear, when writing the state $|m, n\rangle$, we are describing a particle with momentum m and spin n in reference to a fixed axis in the laboratory's frame of reference. We are also assuming that the sender and receiver have a shared knowledge of this fixed axis.

When tracing out the momentum, the reduced state is

$$\rho = \begin{pmatrix} |r|^2 & 0 \\ 0 & |s|^2 \end{pmatrix}. \tag{7}$$

To an observer, ρ might resemble an imperfectly prepared state in a communication protocol; i.e., for sufficiently large $|r|$, ρ might be an adequate approximation of $|0\rangle\langle0|$, so that we might attempt to communicate with it. To completely characterize the channel, we must be able to prepare an arbitrary spin state $|\phi\rangle$. To do so, we perform a local unitary transformation V of the spin state $|0\rangle$ so that $V|0\rangle = |\phi\rangle$. Globally, the preparation is

$$I \otimes V|\Psi\rangle = r|p, \phi\rangle + s|q, \phi^\perp\rangle, \tag{8}$$

where $|\phi^\perp\rangle = V|1\rangle$; the reduced state of that system is

$$|r|^2|\phi\rangle\langle\phi| + |s|^2|\phi^\perp\rangle\langle\phi^\perp|. \tag{9}$$

There are many unitary matrices that will map $|0\rangle$ to $|\phi\rangle$, so it's natural to wonder if the preparation procedure is well-defined; the answer is yes. The global state $I \otimes V|\Psi\rangle$ will pick up a phase from V and thus depends on V; however, that phase gets traced out. Explicitly, if we want to prepare the arbitrary spin state $|\phi\rangle = (a\ b)^t$ (with $|a|^2 + |b|^2 = 1$), then the unitary matrix V must be of the form

$$V = \begin{pmatrix} a & -e^{i\theta}b^* \\ b & e^{i\theta}a^* \end{pmatrix}. \tag{10}$$

However, $\mathrm{tr}_p(I \otimes V|\Psi\rangle\langle\Psi|I \otimes V)$ computes to

$$\begin{pmatrix} |a|^2|r|^2 + |b|^2|s|^2 & ab^*(|r|^2 - |s|^2) \\ a^*b(|r|^2 - |s|^2) & |a|^2|s|^2 + |b|^2|r|^2 \end{pmatrix}, \tag{11}$$

where tr_p is the partial trace over the momentum. The phase $e^{i\theta}$ does not appear in the reduced state, and thus the choice of V is inconsequential to the observer.

On a state of the form

$$\omega = |r|^2|\phi\rangle\langle\phi| + |s|^2|\phi^\perp\rangle\langle\phi^\perp|, \tag{12}$$

we define the map

$$\varepsilon(\omega) = \mathrm{tr}_p(\hat{U}(I \otimes V)|\Psi\rangle\langle\Psi|(I \otimes V)^\dagger\hat{U}^\dagger), \tag{13}$$

which describes the local dynamics under a global Lorentz transformation. Again, any phase picked up by the choice of V is lost in the partial trace, and the map is well-defined on such states. Generally, the state space is the convex hull of the pure states. Since there is no way to generate a pure state with the black box, it would be meaningless to ask what $\varepsilon(|\phi\rangle\langle\phi|)$ is. However, we can form all convex combinations of states like ω, and ask how ε operates on them;

that convex hull is the state space. Since the partial trace and conjugation by $\hat{U}$ are linear operators, ε has a well-defined convex-linear extension,

$$\varepsilon(p_1\omega_1 + p_2\omega_2) = \text{tr}_p(\hat{U}[I \otimes (p_1V_1 + p_2V_2)]|\Psi\rangle\langle\Psi|[I \otimes (p_1V_1 + p_2V_2)]^\dagger\hat{U}^\dagger), \quad (14)$$

to that convex subspace of density matrices. In fact, ε has a linear extension to the set of all 2×2 matrices, which we will make use of subsequently in our analysis; however, we do so with the understanding that this is of mathematical convenience and that we cannot generate every state.

In order to calculate information flow through the relativistic channel, we will employ the *Bloch* representation. Each qubit can be written as a 2×2 positive semi-definite Hermitian matrix:

$$\rho = \frac{I + x \cdot \sigma}{2} \quad (15)$$

$$= \frac{1}{2}\begin{pmatrix} 1 + x_3 & x_1 - ix_2 \\ x_1 + ix_2 & 1 - x_3 \end{pmatrix}, \quad (16)$$

where σ is a vector whose entries are the Pauli spin matrices. The vector $x = [x_1\ x_2\ x_3]^t$ is the Bloch vector. Generally, the state space of Bloch vectors is the ball of radius 1, but in our case, the state space is the ball of radius $|r|^2 - |s|^2$. Each state is represented by a unique Bloch vector, and every channel induces a unique map on the Bloch vector:

$$\varepsilon\left(\frac{I + x \cdot \sigma}{2}\right) = \frac{I + f(x) \cdot \sigma}{2}. \quad (17)$$

When the channel ε is linear and has the completely mixed state as a fixed point, the induced map is a matrix called the Bloch matrix. The Bloch matrix for ε is

$$f = \frac{1}{|r|^2 - |s|^2}\begin{pmatrix} |r|^2\cos\Omega_p - |s|^2\cos\Omega_q & 0 & -|r|^2\sin\Omega_p + |s|^2\sin\Omega_q \\ 0 & |r|^2 - |s|^2 & 0 \\ |r|^2\sin\Omega_p - |s|^2\sin\Omega_q & 0 & |r|^2\cos\Omega_p - |s|^2\cos\Omega_q \end{pmatrix}. \quad (18)$$

Although f has the appearance of a standard Bloch matrix, f is an expansive map, so it does not map the unit ball to itself, and thus it does not always map states to states. To be more precise,

$$||fx||^2 = ||x||^2 + \frac{4|r|^2|s|^2(||x||^2 - x_3^2)\sin^2(\Omega_p/2 - \Omega_q/2)}{(|r|^2 - |s|^2)^2} \quad (19)$$

$$\geq ||x||^2.$$

Eq. (19) is not surprising since the process does not make sense on the whole state space. One can check though that for $||x|| \leq |r|^2 - |s|^2$, $||fx|| \leq 1$; that is, f maps our state space to valid states. The *purity* of a quantum state is a measure of how mixed it is. If ρ has the Bloch vector x, then its purity is calculated as

$$\text{tr}(\rho^2) = 1/2(1 + ||x||^2). \quad (20)$$

Generally, a quantum process must decrease purity; however, as shown in Eq. (19), when $|x_2| \neq ||x||$, the purity of the state undergoing a Lorentz transformation always increases (except for very specific values of Ω_p and Ω_q).

Since f is expansive, it will not increase the *von Neumann entropy*,

$$S(\rho) = -\lambda_+ \log_2(\lambda_+) - \lambda_- \log_2(\lambda_-), \tag{21}$$

where $\lambda_\pm$ are the eigenvalues of ρ. We can also express the eigenvalues and entropy in terms of the Bloch vector: if x is the Bloch vector for ρ, then

$$\lambda_\pm = 1/2(1 \pm ||x||) \text{ and} \tag{22}$$

$$S(\rho) = H((1 + ||x||)/2); \tag{23}$$

here, H is the base two Shannon entropy (for a discussion on Shannon entropy see [5]). Since H is strictly decreasing on $[1/2, 1]$ and f is expansive, from the observer's prospective, f decreases the entropy of the spin state. If one were to have $\Omega_p = 2\pi$ and $\Omega_q = \pi$, then f maps the mixed state $[|r|^2 - |s|^2 \ 0 \ 0]^t$ to the pure state $[1 \ 0 \ 0]^t$. In Fig. 1, we have included a plot of the von Neumann entropy for the specific case of $r = \sqrt{9/10}$ and $s = \sqrt{1/10}$.

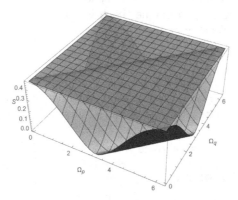

Fig. 1. Plot of the entropy pre- and post-evolution for the state in Eq. (7) with $r = \sqrt{9/10}$ and $s = \sqrt{1/10}$. The plane gives reference to the entropy pre-evolution, whereas the entropy post-evolution varies with Ω_p and Ω_q.

Since the states are getting more pure, it is reasonable to ask how that affects the amount of information that can be transferred with such a system. Similar to [4], one can show that the states are becoming more distinguishable by calculating the probability of error function [19]. However, the calculation for distinguishability employs an ideal measurement procedure. Generally though, when classical information is sent through a quantum process, states are prepared and measured in the same basis, and in general, a positive information flow using an ideal measurement procedure does not correspond to positive information flow using a fixed basis [20,21]. To represent classical information with quantum states, one usually chooses a basis of the state space to represent a 0 and 1. With each choice of basis, we are implicitly defining a classical channel, each with its own classical capacity. The *scope* of a quantum channel is the range of classical capacities as one varies over every basis in the state space [6]. In contrast to [4], the local dynamics of ε are linear, so with a little finesse there is a mechanism to calculate the scope (in [6], Martin specifically uses the fact that the map is non-expansive; however, that proof can be modified to work in this case).

In the Bloch representation, the communication bases correspond to antipodal points on the unit 3-sphere $\partial \mathbb{B}$: if $u \in \partial \mathbb{B}$, then u represents 0 and $-u$ represents 1. However, we cannot generate pure states and therefore cannot generate points on $\partial \mathbb{B}$. Instead, we let

$$u \cdot (|r|^2 - |s|^2) \tag{24}$$

represent 0 and its antipode represent 1. Even though our state preparation is imperfect, our measurement procedure is not affected by the same shortcomings, and we can measure with $\{u, -u\}$. So, in the following, when we say 'using the $\{u, -u\}$ basis to transmit information,' we mean preparing states with the Bloch vectors $\pm u \cdot (|r|^2 - |s|^2)$, and measuring with $\pm u$. Then, the probability that a 0 is received when a 0 is sent is

$$P(0|0) = 1/2[1 + (|r|^2 - |s|^2)(u, fu)]; \tag{25}$$

note that since the process is unital, the induced classical channel is binary symmetric and $P(1|1) = P(0|0)$. As we range over every communication basis, we generate a range of channels, each with a classical capacity. The scope $s(f) \subseteq [0, 1]$ is that interval of capacities, and each value in that interval is an achievable capacity when using the corresponding choice of communication basis. Employing techniques similar to those in [6], the minimal and maximal capacities are given by (respectively)

$$1 - H\left(\frac{1 + m^-}{2}\right) \text{ and } 1 - H\left(\frac{1 + m^+}{2}\right), \text{ where} \tag{26}$$

$$m^- = \inf_{|u|=1} \left[(|r|^2 - |s|^2)|(u, fu)|\right] \text{ and}$$

$$m^+ = \sup_{|u|=1} \left[(|r|^2 - |s|^2)|(u, fu)|\right].$$

As shown in [6], the channels f and $(f + f^t)/2$ have the same scope, so we will calculate the scope of the latter. In this case, $\sup[|(u, \frac{f+f^t}{2}u)|]$ is the absolute value of the eigenvalue of largest magnitude, and $\inf[|(u, \frac{f+f^t}{2}u)|]$ is the absolute value of the eigenvalue of smallest magnitude when all of the eigenvalues have the same sign and is 0 otherwise. Then to calculate the scope, first assume that

$$|r|^2 \cos \Omega_p - |s|^2 \cos \Omega_q > 0. \tag{27}$$

Since we initially assumed that $|r|^2 - |s|^2 > 0$, if

$$\left||r|^2 \cos \Omega_p - |s|^2 \cos \Omega_q\right| \geq |r|^2 - |s|^2, \tag{28}$$

the scope is

$$s(f) = \left[1 - H\left(\frac{1 + |r|^2 - |s|^2}{2}\right), 1 - H\left(\frac{1 + ||r|^2 \cos \Omega_p - |s|^2 \cos \Omega_q|}{2}\right)\right]; \quad (29)$$

otherwise, the endpoints are flipped, and the scope is

$$s(f) = \left[1 - H\left(\frac{1 + ||r|^2 \cos \Omega_p - |s|^2 \cos \Omega_q|}{2}\right), 1 - H\left(\frac{1 + |r|^2 - |s|^2}{2}\right)\right]. \quad (30)$$

If instead of Eq. (27),

$$|r|^2 \cos \Omega_p - |s|^2 \cos \Omega_q \leq 0, \quad (31)$$

then the lower endpoint of the scope interval would be replaced with 0, but the analysis for the upper endpoint would remain the same. The scope calculation tells us that if the relativistic effects are large enough (see Eq. (29)), the naive choice of basis is not the optimal one to transmit information. In addition, one choice of basis could lead to a channel with 0 capacity, while information could still be transferred with a different choice of basis.

To study a specific example, let us take $r = \sqrt{9/10}$ and $s = \sqrt{1/10}$. Then if

$$|9/10 \cos(\Omega_p) - 1/10 \cos(\Omega_q)| \geq 8/10, \quad (32)$$

the optimal bases to transmit information are $\{e_1, -e_1\}$ and $\{e_3, -e_3\}$ (the e_i are the standard basis elements for $\mathbb{R}^3$). Consequently, the process has a higher capacity than if the effects of relativity were not present. This fact goes against our natural intuition since $fe_2 = e_2$, and thus $(8/10)e_2$ would not suffer the effects of the channel's noise. So shockingly, when Eq. (32) is satisfied, the noise is beneficial to the transmission of information. In fact, in the special case where $\Omega_p = 2\pi$ and $\Omega_q = \pi$, the channel has perfect capacity when using $\{e_3, -e_3\}$ to transmit information, whereas one would not achieve perfect capacity if the sender and receiver shared the same reference frame. In Fig. 2, we have plotted the channel capacity when using the $\{e_3, -e_3\}$ basis versus the $\{e_2, -e_2\}$ basis as we vary over Ω_p and Ω_q. For a more extreme example, the initial reduced state can be made arbitrarily close to the completely mixed state, i.e.,

$$|r|^2 = 1/2 + \varepsilon \text{ and } |s|^2 = 1/2 - \varepsilon \quad (33)$$

with $0 < \varepsilon << 1$, and the observer could still receive a copy of the message, assuming the sender used the correct basis. Even though it would look like a noisy signal before the Lorentz transformation, when $\Omega_p = 2\pi$ and $\Omega_q = \pi$, information can be transmitted perfectly using $\{e_3, -e_3\}$ without any error correction. In this example, for all but small intervals of Ω_p and Ω_q, it would be advantageous to communicate using $\{e_1, -e_1\}$ or $\{e_3, -e_3\}$ over the "noiseless" $\{e_2, -e_2\}$ basis.

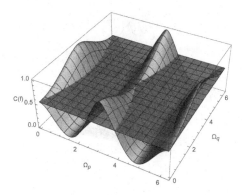

Fig. 2. The channel capacity when transmitting in the $\{\pm e_3\}$ basis (which varies over Ω_p and Ω_q) and the $\{\pm e_2\}$ basis (constant plane).

From what we have shown thus far, one can conclude that, in general, this process is not completely positive. But because this process is linear, we will calculate its Choi matrix [22],

$$C = \sum_{ij} I \otimes \varepsilon(E_{ij} \otimes E_{ij}), \tag{34}$$

and use C to obtain conditions for when the process is completely positive. For an arbitrary choice of r and s, (when $\Omega_p - \Omega_q \neq n\pi$) there will always be an eigenvalue of C that is negative, but so that the calculations do not get out of hand, let's continue with $r = \sqrt{9/10}$ and $s = \sqrt{1/10}$. In this case, the Choi matrix is

$$\frac{1}{8} \begin{pmatrix} 9\cos^2\frac{\Omega_p}{2} - \cos^2\frac{\Omega_q}{2} & \frac{1}{2}(\sin\Omega_q - 9\sin\Omega_p) & \frac{1}{2}(9\sin\Omega_p - \sin\Omega_q) & 9\cos^2\frac{\Omega_p}{2} - \cos^2\frac{\Omega_q}{2} \\ \frac{1}{2}(\sin\Omega_q - 9\sin\Omega_p) & 9\sin^2\frac{\Omega_p}{2} - \sin^2\frac{\Omega_q}{2} & \sin^2\frac{\Omega_q}{2} - 9\sin^2\frac{\Omega_p}{2} & \frac{1}{2}(\sin\Omega_q - 9\sin\Omega_p) \\ \frac{1}{2}(9\sin\Omega_p - \sin\Omega_q) & \sin^2\frac{\Omega_q}{2} - 9\sin^2\frac{\Omega_p}{2} & 9\sin^2\frac{\Omega_p}{2} - \sin^2\frac{\Omega_q}{2} & \frac{1}{2}(9\sin\Omega_p - \sin\Omega_q) \\ 9\cos^2\frac{\Omega_p}{2} - \cos^2\frac{\Omega_q}{2} & \frac{1}{2}(\sin\Omega_q - 9\sin\Omega_p) & \frac{1}{2}(9\sin\Omega_p - \sin\Omega_q) & 9\cos^2\frac{\Omega_p}{2} - \cos^2\frac{\Omega_q}{2} \end{pmatrix}. \tag{35}$$

Then ε is completely positive if and only if C is positive semi-definite [22]. However, the eigenvalues of C are 0, 0, and

$$1 \pm \frac{\sqrt{9\sin^2(\Omega_p/2 - \Omega_q/2) + 1}}{4}. \tag{36}$$

Since

$$1 - \frac{\sqrt{9\sin^2(\Omega_p/2 - \Omega_q/2) + 16}}{4} \in [-1/4, 0], \tag{37}$$

this process cannot be completely positive unless $\Omega_p - \Omega_q = 2n\pi$, in which case f is just a rotation of the Bloch sphere. Figure 3 plots the negative eigenvalue of

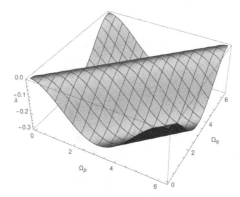

Fig. 3. The negative eigenvalue of C plotted with respect to Ω_p and Ω_q.

Choi's matrix as we range over Ω_p and Ω_q. It is well known that if the system and environment are in a pure product state, then the dynamics are completely positive; however, the converse is not necessarily true. Here the process is almost never completely positive, and there is an added degree of subtlety: instead of system-environment entanglement, the entanglement occurs across internal degrees of freedom.

5   Conclusion

In summary, using fairly basic assumptions, we showed that relativistic quantum processes violate many standard assumptions made in quantum informatics by only assuming an imperfectly prepared state. As shown in Fig. 3, the process is only completely positive on a set of measure zero. In addition, these processes are not exotic: preparing the state $|\Psi\rangle = r|p,0\rangle + s|q,1\rangle$ in the presence of a gravitational field would produce non-trivial Wigner rotations. Therefore (off that set of measure zero) the simple act of preparing and measuring the spin of such a state on Earth or an orbiting satellite is not a completely positive process; albeit, this effect would be small and difficult to measure. This unique behavior can be attributed to the way the Wigner rotation mixes the spin and momentum. By only measuring the spin state, the information about how the spin and momentum are mixed is destroyed.

The advantage of using this toy model with a small number of degrees of freedom is that we can perform analytical computations, such as maximizing capacity, which would be extremely difficult, if not impossible, had we used a more realistic model. Nonetheless, we expect that this behavior will also be relevant in those models. In future papers, we will address these challenges. As another avenue of further research, we wonder if one could employ a steganographic procedure to transmit information to someone in a different reference frame. By taking a state similar to the one in Eq. (33), in the preparer's frame of reference, the state is "close" to the completely mixed state. But as we showed, it can be used to send information perfectly to other frames of reference. Then using a state like Eq. (33), we could send hidden information from one frame to another. We plan on exploring the steganographic applications of relativistic effects in the future. Finally, we wonder if we can use the natural extension to the Bloch representation described in [23–25] and techniques similar to these to quantify the information flow of multi-qubit systems undergoing relativistic effects. Such an analysis might yield insights on the effect of a Lorentz transformation on a quantum computation.

Acknowledgements. We are grateful to C. Fuchs, K. Martin, and D. Terno for their helpful discussions during the preparation of this manuscript.

References

1. Peres, A., Scudo, P.F., Terno, D.R.: Quantum entropy and special relativity. Phys. Rev. Lett. **88**, 230402 (2002)
2. Nielsen, M., Chuang, I.L.: Quantum Computation and Quantum Information. Cambridge University Press, Cambridge (2000)
3. Breuer, H.-P., Petruccione, F.: The Theory of Open Quantum Systems. Oxford University Press, New York (2002)
4. Peres, A., Terno, D.R.: Relativistic doppler effect in quantum communication. J. Mod. Opt. **50**, 1165–1173 (2002)
5. Cover, T., Thomas, J.: Elements of Information Theory. Wiley, New Jersey (2006)
6. Martin, K.: The scope of a quantum channel. Proc. Symp. Appl. Math. **71**, 183–211 (2008)
7. Martin, K., Crowder, T., Feng, J.: Quantum error reduction without coding. In: Proceedings of Radar Sensor Technology XIX; and Active and Passive Signatures VI. 946114, vol. 9461 (2015)
8. Lanzagorta, M., Uhlmann, J.: Quantum computational complexity in curved spacetime. In: Burgin, M., Calude, C. (eds.) Information and Complexity, pp. 227–248. World Scientific (2016)
9. Weinberg, S.: The Quantum Theory of Fields. Cambridge University Press, New York (1995)
10. Lanzagorta, M.: Quantum Information in Gravitational Fields. Institute of Physics, California (2013)
11. Gingrich, R.M., Adami, C.: Quantum entanglement of moving bodies. Phys. Rev. Lett. **89**, 270402 (2002)
12. Lanzagorta, M., Salgado, M.: Detection of gravitational frame dragging using orbiting qubits. Class. Quantum Grav. **33**, 105013 (2016)
13. Céleri, L.C., Kiosses, V., Terno, D.R.: Spin and localization of relativistic fermions and uncertainty relations. Phys. Rev. A **94**, 062115 (2016)
14. Saldanha, P., Vedral, V.: Physical interpretation of the wigner rotations and its implications for relativistic quantum information. New J. Phys. **14**, 023041 (2012)
15. Lanzagorta, M., Crowder, T.: Comment on wigner rotations and an apparent paradox in relativistic quantum information. Phys. Rev. A **96**, 026101 (2017)
16. Taillebois, E.R.F., Avelar, A.T.: Spin-reduced density matrices for relativistic particles. Phys. Rev. A **88**, 060302 (2013)
17. Choi, T.: Relativistic spin operator and lorentz transformation of the spin state of a massive dirac particle. J. Korean Phys. Soc. **62**, 1085–1092 (2013)

18. Bauke, H., et. al.: Relativistic spin operators in various electromagnetic environments. Phys. Rev. A. **89** 052101 (2014)

19. Fuchs, C.A., van de Graaf, J.: Cryptographic distinguishability measures for quantum-mechanical states. IEEE Trans. Inf. Theory **45**, 1216–1227 (1999)

20. Crowder, T., Martin, K.: Classical representations of qubit channels. Electron. Notes Theor. Comp. Sci. **270**, 37–58 (2011)

21. Crowder, T., Martin, K.: Information theoretic representations of qubit channels. Found. Phys. **42**, 976–983 (2012)

22. Choi, M.D.: Completely positive linear maps on complex matrices. Linear Algebra Appl. **10**, 285–290 (1975)

23. Crowder, T.: Representations of Quantum Channels. Dissertation, Howard University (2013)

24. Crowder, T.: A quantum representation for involution groups. Electron. Notes Theor. Comput. Sci. **276**, 145–158 (2011)

25. Crowder, T.: A linearization of quantum channels. J. Geom. Phys. **92**, 157–166 (2015)

Mechanical Sequential Counting
with Liquid Marbles

Thomas C. Draper[1(✉)] (iD), Claire Fullarton[1] (iD), Neil Phillips[1] (iD),
Ben P. J. de Lacy Costello[2] (iD), and Andrew Adamatzky[1] (iD)

[1] Unconventional Computing Laboratory, University of the West of England,
Bristol BS16 1QY, UK
{tom.draper,claire.fullarton,neil.phillips,andrew.adamatzky}@uwe.ac.uk
[2] Institute of Biosensing Technology, Centre for Research in Biosciences,
University of the West of England, Bristol BS16 1QY, UK
ben.delacycostello@uwe.ac.uk

Abstract. Here we demonstrate the first working example of a liquid
marble-operated sequential binary counting device. We have designed a
lightweight gate that can be actuated by the low mass and momentum of
a liquid marble. By linking a number of these gates in series, we are able
to digitally count up to binary 1111 (upper limit only by our requirements). Using liquid marbles in such a system opens up new avenues of
research and design, by way of modifying the coating and/or core of the
liquid marbles, and thereby giving extra dimensions for calculation (e.g.
a calculation that takes into consideration the progress of a chemical
reaction inside a liquid marble). In addition, the new gate design has
multiple uses in liquid marble rerouting.

Keywords: Liquid marbles · Unconventional computing
Binary counter · Logic gate · Particle-coated droplets
Mechanical computing

1 Introduction

1.1 Liquid Marbles

Liquid marbles (LMs) were first reported by Aussillous and Quéré in 2001
[3], and have since become increasingly popular in chemistry, particularly con-
densed matter. They are composed of two parts: a microliter sized core of liquid
(usually water), surrounded by a powder coating. This gives them their other
name 'particle-coated droplets'. A typical volume of a LM is $10\,\mu L$, which results
in a typical diameter of $3\,mm$. A schematic of a LM is shown in Fig. 1. We shall
look at both the core and coating in turn.

The bulk of a LM is composed of the core. This microliter droplet is made
of water generally (because its high surface tension allows for the easiest LM
formation), though glycerol is quite common [4], and even petroleum has been
used [7]. This paper will focus on water-filled LMs.

© Springer International Publishing AG, part of Springer Nature 2018
S. Stepney and S. Verlan (Eds.): UCNC 2018, LNCS 10867, pp. 59–71, 2018.
https://doi.org/10.1007/978-3-319-92435-9_5

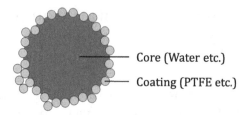

Core (Water etc.)

Coating (PTFE etc.)

Fig. 1. A schematic of a liquid marble. The core is generally comprised of water or glycerol, and the hydrophobic powder coating could be PTFE, PE, lycopodium grains, etc. A typical diameter of the entire LM is 3 mm, whilst the powder particle sizes could be 10 nm to 400 μm in diameter. Note the non-homogeneous coating.

The coating of a LM is comprised of a micro- or nano-sized powder, that (for water cores) is hydrophobic. 'Hydrophobic' comes from the Ancient Greek 'fear of water'. Chemically, hydrophobic powders are normally lacking in polar intramolecular bonds, which results in few intermolecular hydrogen-bonds forming between the water and the substrate. It is this shortage of attractive forces that is often (mistakenly) portrayed as a water-repelling repulsive force. Common examples of LM powder coatings include polytetrafluoroethylene (PTFE) [5], polyethylene (PE) [1] and modified-lycopodium grains [3]. A variety of possible powder coatings are demonstrated in Fig. 2. Note the difference in particle size, especially in the hybrid example shown in Fig. 2(d). This (in combination with the powders degree of hydrophobicity) gives rise to very different characteristics of LM lifetime, ruggedness and hysteresis. For a recent overview on these dependencies, see reference [11].

As can be seen in Figs. 1 and 2, the coating of LMs is not homogeneous. Rather, it is a mixture of single-layer and multilayer particles. Whether a single- or multilayer is formed is dependent on the identities of both the core and the coating. Particles with a very high surface contact angle (such as PTFE) tend to form single-layers. Conversely, less hydrophobic particles (such as the PE or nickel) tend to form a multilayer. It can be possible to convert a multilayer LM into a single-layer, by repeated rolling. The excess particles fall off the LM, leaving a single-layer.

There are often gaps in the particle coating, where the surface of the core is exposed to the atmosphere and therefore visible. As (perhaps) anticipated, this is more common in single-layered LMs. As a LM ages however, it looses some of its aqueous core to evaporation, which results in a slight contraction of the shell. This has the effect of closing these exposed sections. One would intuitively anticipate that this would, in turn, reduce the evaporation rate of the LM, however this is not the case [11]. The reasons behind this are still unclear, although a possibility is that the shrinking in pore size causes an increase in the capillary effect. This would result in the water core being closer to the surface, and therefore able to evaporate faster.

(a)   (b)

(c)   (d)

Fig. 2. Photographs of 10.0 μL liquid marbles. All examples have a diameter of 3 mm. The powder coatings portrayed are (a) PTFE (grain size: 6 μm to 10 μm), (b) PE (grain size: 100 μm), (c) Nickel (grain size: 4 μm to 7 μm) and (d) a Nickel-PE hybrid.

One of the main features of LMs, and one of the reasons for their use in this project, is that they roll with minimal resistance. On a typical surface (e.g. glass), a water droplet will adhere to the surface, causing resistance to its motion. Conversely, if a water droplet is placed on a hydrophobic surface (e.g. a non-stick frying pan), the water droplet will bead up and roll off with ease. A LM is literally coated in a hydrophobic powder, generating a very large contact angle, and therefore rolls with extreme ease. This gives LMs great merit in fields as diverse as glue delivery systems [8] and digital microfluidic bioassays [18].

Liquid marbles are a new, but strong, player in the field of digital microfluidics [17]. Microfluidics involves the formation, behavior, and ultimately the control of microliter quantities of fluid. It is a multidisciplinary area, with a large and growing interest in automation and high-throughput screening. *Digital* microfluidics is when the fluid is in discrete droplets, as oppose to in a continuous flow. There are a number of ways to manipulate these droplets, the most common of which are magnetic [21], electrowetting on dielectric (EWOD) [10], and surface acoustic wave (SAW) [13]. All of these techniques, however, require both a pre-treated surface and electricity. By encapsulating the droplet in a particle coating and forming a LM, there is the potential to remove both of these limitations. This would allow for the construction of cheap devices for point-of-care diagnostics in low-resource areas [20].

In order for the microfluidic LMs to increase in capability, there is a requirement for behavioral control. Control units will need to be able to route [19], merge [4], divide [6], and auto-generate [9] LMs. This work demonstrates a new re-routing technique for LMs, in the form of a mechanical computing device. This device does not require surface-pretreatment, and is powered by gravity: thereby removing the limitations of other digital microfluidic manipulation techniques.

1.2   Existing Computational Techniques with Liquid Marbles

Liquid marbles have recently been used experimentally for computation, in a collision-based interaction gate [9]. In the design, two LMs rolled down slopes towards each other and collided. The resulting change in vector was then interpreted as computation. In this LM interaction gate, the Boolean-determining signal was the presence (TRUE) or absence (FALSE) of a LM. It was noted that, due to the soft shell-like nature of the LMs, the collisions observed Margolus pathways [15], as shown in Fig. 3(a). These differ from the better-known billiard-ball pathways by allowing for the finite amount of time it takes for a soft-sphere to deform. This analogy could be broken, however, by increasing the kinetic energy of the impact above the effective surface tension of the LM. Above this threshold, the LMs would coalesce, and the system acted like the fusion gate shown in Fig. 3(b). In both instances the gate implemented AND and AND-NOT logical functions, based on the location of output LMs.

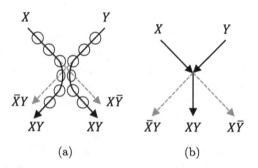

Fig. 3. Diagrams of interaction gates. (a) A Margolus gate, demonstrated using compressible spheres as signals. (b) A fusion gate, where the two signals coalesce to form one new signal.

The LM coating used in [9] was a mix of nickel (Ni) and PE, forming a hybrid LM that was ferromagnetic enough to be held by electromagnets. This feature was used to enable accurate timings on the interaction gate. Without this feature, ensuring timings and collisions was intractable.

Recent work [11] has shown that the impact survival time of PE LMs is far superior to Ni-PE hybrid LMs. Unfortunately, the non-magnetic nature of PE makes precise synchronization of the LMs arduous. It was decided, therefore, to develop a computing device that did not require such accurate timings, but could instead be run sequentially.

2   Liquid Marbles for Mechanical Counting

2.1   Mechanical Flip-Flop Gates

Mechanical flip-flops have been designed previously, though they have always been actuated by something relatively heavy, such as a coin [2], a ball [16], or even a can [14]. We have developed a distinct and notably different mechanical flip-flop, that is designed specifically to be actuated by the low mass and momentum of a single LM.

Shown in Fig. 4(a), the flip-flop is roughly shaped like an isosceles-triangle, with the top pointing to either 10 o'clock or 2 o'clock (its two bistable positions, when compared to the hour hand on the face of a clock). These are visualized in Fig. 4. When in use, LM #1 approaches the flip-flop from the top and follows the path guided to it by the flip-flop. As the LM moves along, its mass causes the flip-flop to 'flip'. As a result, when LM #2 approaches the flip-flop, it will both be guided in the other direction and reset the flip-flop to its original position. LM #3 will then follow the same path as LM #1, and so on. There are two overall consequences of this: as each LM passes through, the resting position of the flip-flop oscillates between the two bistable positions—10 o'clock and 2 o'clock; additionally, alternate LMs exit through alternate pathways. These pathways are demonstrated in Fig. 4(b).

This design acts like a traditional electronic flip-flop: it is a bistable multivibrator, and each of its two positions can be interpreted as binary 0 or 1. The rolling LMs act in a similar way to the electronic data signal pulses, changing the reading as they arrive. The LMs roll by converting their potential energy into kinetic energy, and so the system is powered by gravity instead of electricity. The LMs roll along guides, which act like the wires that guide electrons in an electronic system.

Each flip-flop has been laser cut from 3 mm thick cast acrylic. It has dimensions of 29 mm × 14 mm × 3 mm, and weighs 154 mg. The pivot point (diameter: 0.60 mm), easily seen in Fig. 4(a), has been engineered to be at the center of mass of the flip-flop.

2.2   Liquid Marble Actuated Mechanical Counter

By linking four of our flip-flop gates in series, we were able to design and construct a proof-of-principle logic device, capable of counting up to binary 1111 or

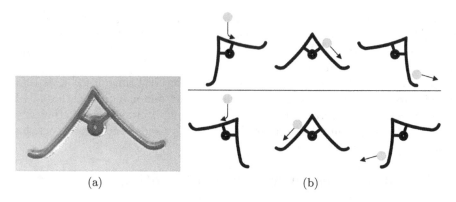

Fig. 4. (a) A photograph of our flip-flop gate. The front has been colored for visibility. The flip-flop is 29 mm across. (b) A diagram showing the motion that our mechanical flip-flop gate takes, when actuated using a LM. Starting at the 10 o'clock position, the LM enters the system and interacts with the flip-flip—rotating the flip-flop to the 2 o'clock position whilst the LM exits to the right. If at the 2 o'clock position when the LM enters, the flip-flop is rotated to the 10 o'clock position, and the LM exits to the left. A typical LM has a diameter of 3 mm.

decimal 15. The basic principle is similar to part of a 1965 patent [12]. Our design schematic is shown in Fig. 5(a) and a photograph of the constructed device is shown in Fig. 5(b). In this design, a flip-flop is considered to represent binary 0 when pointing to 10 o'clock, and binary 1 when pointing to 2 o'clock. The memory is read from the bottom up. So decimal 8 would be binary 1000, with the 1 physically situated at the bottom of the device.

To start, the system should have a clear memory, with all the flip-flops pointing to 10 o'clock, and the readout being 0000. When LM #1 enters the system from the top, it queries the first flip-flop and obeys the logic table shown in Table 1. On discovering that the first flip-flop reads 0, it changes it to a 1 and exits to the right (exiting the system). At this point the readout is 0001. One can consider that the LM has queried the memory, added one to its value, then rewritten the new value back to the memory: a destructive readout.

Table 1. Logic rules for the liquid marbles to observe, as they pass through the mechanical counting device and interact with flip-flop gates.

Flip-Flop	Bit	Action
Left	0	Change bit to 1, exit system
Right	1	Change bit to 0, query next bit (or OVERFLOW if none)

When LM #2 next enters the system, it queries the first flip-flop and reads a 1, so it changes it to a 0 and exits to the left towards the second flip-flip. Here

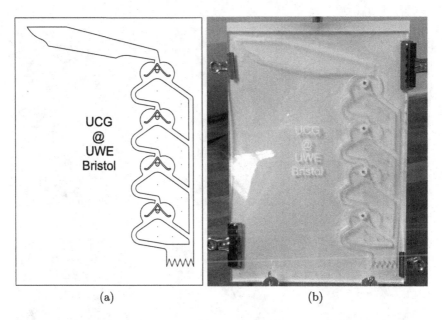

(a)   (b)

Fig. 5. The (a) CAD design file and (b) a photograph of the LM counting device. It measures 208 mm × 286 mm × 6 mm.

it reads a 0, so changes it to a 1 and exits to the right (exiting the system). At this point the readout is 0010. This continues in a similar manner until the system reads 1111 (decimal 15), at which point the next LM will cause a memory overflow and reset the readout to 0000. Stills from a video portraying operation of the device can be seen in Fig. 6. A more abstract view of the devices operation can be envisioned, where the two different bistable positions are indicated by a headless arrow. As a LM moves through the system it causes the flip-flop gates to alternate position, with 16 total possible states before overflow occurs ($2^4 = 16$). Such a schematic, with all possible states portrayed in order, reading from left to right & top to bottom, can be seen in Fig. 7.

As the LMs move through the device, it is worthy of note that they do not slide. Instead, the LMs demonstrate a superposition of both rotational and translational motion (i.e. rolling). This is in direct contrast to the motion expected of uncoated droplets. A side effect of this superposition is observed when two LMs are permitted to roll next to each other. Rather than running together like smooth ball bearings, they instead bounce off each other. This is caused by the approaching front of the chasing LM moving vertically down, in direct contrast to the rear of the leading LM moving vertically up. The clash causes both LM to temporally pause, and for the chasing LM to actually roll backwards. As such, the LMs must be timed so that they do not make contact with each other.

The LMs used in the counting device had a core of pure deionized water, with a volume of 15.0 μL. We found that this volume had the optimal mass to actuate our flip-flop gates. Heavier LMs often deformed or got stuck, whilst lighter LMs

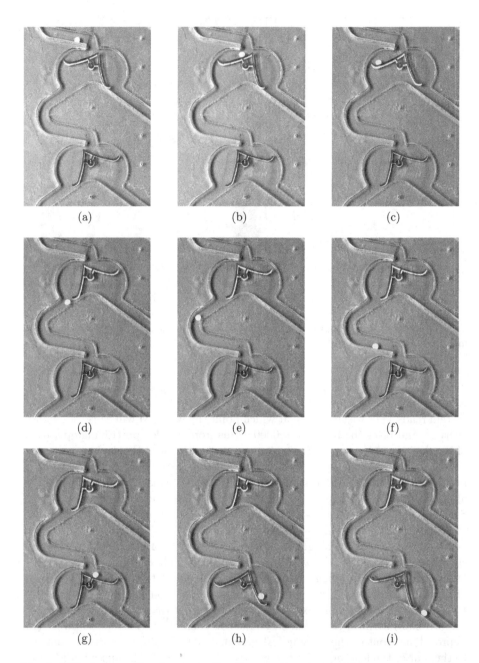

Fig. 6. Stills from a video demonstrating the counting device. These were restaged to improve clarity. Originals and video are available. The LM approaches from the top, flips the first gate from right to left, exits to the left, then flips the second gate from left to right, then exits to the right. The respective relative times of the frames are 0 ms, 99 ms, 233 ms, 466 ms, 533 ms, 633 ms, 733 ms, 1033 ms and 1199 ms.

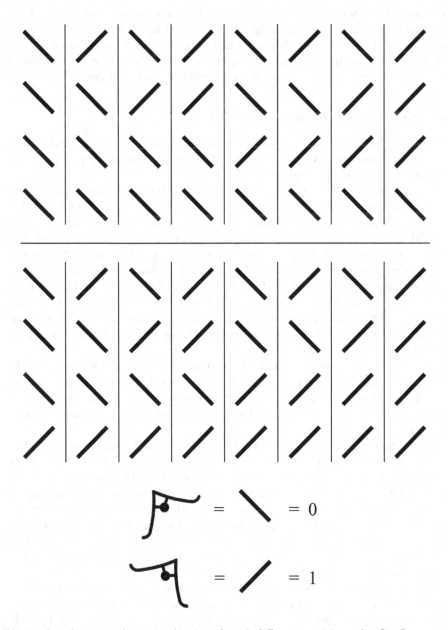

Fig. 7. An abstract schematic showing the 16 different positions the flip-flop gates take as each LM moves through the system. Read from left to right & top to bottom. Flip-flops are grouped in fours; each group represents the processing of a single LM. The least significant bit is at the top of a group, and the most significant bit is at the bottom of each group. On the 16th LM, the device overflows and assumes the first position (i.e. binary 0000).

were not able to actuate the gates. We used two different coatings for the LMs. The first was a Ni-PE coating, originally portrayed in reference [9]. The second was a pure PE coating, which has recently been shown to make stronger and longer-lasting LMs in collision-based activities [11]. LMs made from either of these coatings were able to successfully traverse our counting device.

2.3 Speed-Bumps in the Design Process

As with any R&D adventure, throughout the design of the counting device there were obstructions to overcome. We hope that this section will help anyone who intends to repeat or continue this work.

The main difficultly we had to overcome was the design and construction of a mechanical flip-flop that could be actuated by the small weight of a LM (~16 mg, less than two grains of sand). This was achieved over multiple iterations of constructing, testing and optimizing. During this process, we concentrated on minimizing the mass of the gate (while maintaining structural integrity), as this would reduce the moment of inertia. This had to be balanced with the limitations of the equipment available to us. The flip-flops were laser cut from 3 mm acrylic, and as such were limited by the both the melting of the acrylic and the Gaussian-style beam of the laser. Consequently, the absolute smallest arm-width we could cut was 0.8 mm, and the smallest we could reliably cut was 1.0 mm (which we used in the device).

The design also had to balance the increased moment of inertia caused by having long 'arms', with the increased pivoting ratio. This was achieved through testing a series of different sizes. During these tests, the pivot location was constantly updated to remain at the center of mass, therefore minimizing the force required to rotate the gate.

It was necessary to minimize the friction around the pivot. We initially used PTFE coated wire as the pivot (PTFE is regarded as one of the lowest-friction materials). However, the PTFE coating required a reduction in the diameter of the metal core of the wire. This had the unfortunate side effect of making the pivot too flexible. Instead, a steel pivot was used, which also has a low friction coefficient. However, this was insufficient, and so we laser-cut our own washers from 0.25 mm PTFE sheets (we were unable to source a supplier to provide them small enough). This proved to reduce the friction sufficiently to allow the flip-flop to rotate around the pivot.

The pitch of the device is critical to its successful operation. If the angle is too steep, then the LM will run too fast and either mis-actuate the flip-flop or come off the device entirely. Likewise, if the angle is too gentle, the LM will either not have enough momentum to actuate the flip-flop, or it will not roll at all. We discovered, using an in-house rig to adjust and accurately measure the pitch, that the ideal angle for our device is 52° from horizontal for 15 µL LMs.

2.4   Materials and Design

Both the flip-flop gates and the mechanical counting device were designed using the CAD software Autodesk AutoCAD 2018. They were then laser cut from 3 mm clear cast acrylic. The counting device was made up of a backboard and a front-board, which was itself composed of a large piece and several smaller pieces. The separate components of the counting device were held together by pins and clamps, before being affixed using RS Pro AB-3 Acrylic Adhesive (RS Components). Steel pins (0.50 mm diameter) were installed as pivots, and glued in position using epoxy resin. The PTFE washers were also CAD designed (outer diameter: 10.0 mm, inner diameter: 0.6 mm), before being laser cut from 0.25 mm sheet PTFE. The washers were then placed onto the steel pins before the flip-flop gates. For optimal performance, our device was tilted at 52° from horizontal.

3   Conclusions and Future Work

This paper demonstrates the first sequential logic device implemented using LMs. Through the careful design and construction of a light-weight and low-friction flip-flop gate, a simple proof-of-principle counting device has been constructed. This device counts upwards in integers, from binary 0000 to 1111 (decimal 0 to 15). This upper limit is only restricted by the size of the constructed device, leaving the possibility for much larger devices.

We have also reported on the design and construction of a new microfluidic LM router: the small mechanical LM-actuated flip-flop. By using gravity to power the device, and forgoing the traditional surface pre-treatment, development of low-resource devices is possible. There is also scope for using the LMs as cargo-carriers, and having the flip-flop gates act as path-directors.

A possible use for a device like this is in patient-care in challenging environments. If a spring-loaded syringe pump was injecting into a patient, then a small side-branch could be taken off the line. This spur (diverting less than 1%) could form LMs (using the set-up reported in reference [9]) which run through the counting system. This would provide a clear non-electrical digital readout of how much has been injected, compared to the analogue readout of the syringe. However, this set-up would obviously require pre-calibration.

There is much scope for continued worked in this field. We are already designing a larger and more complex arithmetic machine, to fully take advantage of the flip-flop gates. Additionally, the use of LMs allows for an entirely new dimension of programming: the LMs represent a combination of data signals and a clock pulse, and by varying the coating and/or core of the LM, each can be given a different purpose and identity. There is also scope for chemical reactions to be undertaken inside the LMs: for example a reaction that destroys a LM after a certain amount of time could be used to provide a time-limit on data signals.

In summary, we have produced a working model of a LM-actuated sequential binary counting device. This proof-of-principle device has enormous scope for continued development, and we anticipate a variety of designs in the future.

Acknowledgements. This research was supported by the EPSRC with grant EP/P016677/1 'Computing with Liquid Marbles'.

References

1. Asare-Asher, S., Connor, J.N., Sedev, R.: Elasticity of liquid marbles. J. Colloid Interface Sci. **449**, 341–346 (2015). https://doi.org/10.1016/j.jcis.2015.01.067
2. Asbury, W.: US Patent 957,135 (1909)
3. Aussillous, P., Quéré, D.: Liquid marbles. Nature **411**(6840), 924–927 (2001). https://doi.org/10.1038/35082026
4. Aussillous, P., Quéré, D.: Properties of liquid marbles. Proc. R. Soc. A Math. Phys. Eng. Sci. **462**(2067), 973–999 (2006). https://doi.org/10.1098/rspa.2005.1581
5. Bhosale, P.S., Panchagnula, M.V., Stretz, H.A.: Mechanically robust nanoparticle stabilized transparent liquid marbles. Appl. Phys. Lett. **93**(3), 034109 (2008). https://doi.org/10.1063/1.2959853
6. Bormashenko, E., Bormashenko, Y.: Non-stick droplet surgery with a superhydrophobic scalpel. Langmuir **27**(7), 3266–3270 (2011). https://doi.org/10.1021/la200258u
7. Bormashenko, E., Pogreb, R., Balter, R., Aharoni, H., Aurbach, D., Strelnikov, V.: Liquid marbles containing petroleum and their properties. Pet. Sci. **12**(2), 340–344 (2015). https://doi.org/10.1007/s12182-015-0016-y
8. Chandan, S., Ramakrishna, S., Sunitha, K., Satheesh Chandran, M., Santhosh Kumar, K.S., Mathew, D.: pH-responsive superomniphobic nanoparticles as versatile candidates for encapsulating adhesive liquidmarbles. J. Mater. Chem. A **5**(43), 22813–22823 (2017). https://doi.org/10.1039/C7TA07562F
9. Draper, T.C., Fullarton, C., Phillips, N., de Lacy Costello, B.P., Adamatzky, A.: Liquid marble interaction gate for collision-based computing. Mater. Today **20**(10), 561–568 (2017). https://doi.org/10.1016/j.mattod.2017.09.004
10. Fair, R.B.: Digital microfluidics: is a true lab-on-a-chip possible? Microfluid. Nanofluidics **3**(3), 245–281 (2007). https://doi.org/10.1007/s10404-007-0161-8
11. Fullarton, C., Draper, T.C., Phillips, N., Mayne, R., de Lacy Costello, B.P.J., Adamatzky, A.: Evaporation, lifetime, and robustness studies of liquid marbles for collision-based computing. Langmuir **34**(7), 2573–2580 (2018). https://doi.org/10.1021/acs.langmuir.7b04196
12. Godfrey, J.T.: US Patent 3,390,471 (1965)
13. Guttenberg, Z., Müller, H., Habermüller, H., Geisbauer, A., Pipper, J., Felbel, J., Kielpinski, M., Scriba, J., Wixforth, A.: Planar chip devicefor PCR and hybridization with surface acoustic wave pump. Lab Chip **5**(3), 308–317 (2005). https://doi.org/10.1039/B412712A
14. Kimball, W.D., Braren, C.I., Schaefer, G.P.: US Patent 2,052,513 (1930)
15. Margolus, N.: Universal cellular automata based on the collisions of soft spheres. In: Adamatzky, A. (ed.) Collision-Based Computing, pp. 107–134. Springer, London (2002). https://doi.org/10.1007/978-1-4471-0129-1_5
16. McEvoy, G.N.: US Patent 884,605 (1905)
17. Nguyen, N.T., Hejazian, M., Ooi, C., Kashaninejad, N.: Recent advances and future perspectives on microfluidic liquid handling. Micromachines **8**(6), 186 (2017). https://doi.org/10.3390/mi8060186
18. Oliveira, N.M., Reis, R.L., Mano, J.F.: The potential of liquid marbles for biomedical applications: a critical review. Adv. Healthc. Mater. **6**(19), 1700192 (2017). https://doi.org/10.1002/adhm.201700192

19. Ooi, C.H., Nguyen, N.T.: Manipulation of liquid marbles. Microfluid. Nanofluidics **19**(3), 483–495 (2015). https://doi.org/10.1007/s10404-015-1595-z
20. Zhang, Y., Nguyen, N.T.: Magnetic digital microfluidics a review. Lab Chip **17**(6), 994–1008 (2017). https://doi.org/10.1039/C7LC00025A
21. Zhang, Y., Park, S., Liu, K., Tsuan, J., Yang, S., Wang, T.H.: A surface topography assisted droplet manipulation platform for biomarker detection and pathogen identification. Lab Chip **11**(3), 398–406 (2011). https://doi.org/10.1039/C0LC00296H

Word Blending in Formal Languages: The Brangelina Effect

Srujan Kumar Enaganti[1], Lila Kari[2], Timothy Ng[2(✉)], and Zihao Wang[1]

[1] Department of Computer Science, The University of Western Ontario,
London, ON N6A 3K7, Canada
srujankumar@gmail.com, zwang688@uwo.ca
[2] School of Computer Science, University of Waterloo,
Waterloo, ON N2L 3GL, Canada
{lila,tim.ng}@uwaterloo.ca

Abstract. In this paper we define and investigate a binary word operation that formalizes an experimentally observed outcome of DNA computations, performed to generate a small gene library and implemented using a DNA recombination technique called Cross-pairing Polymerase Chain Reaction (XPCR). The *word blending* between two words xwy_1 and y_2wz that share a non-empty overlap w, results in xwz. We study closure properties of families in the Chomsky hierarchy under word blending, language equations involving this operation, and its descriptional state complexity when applied to regular languages. Interestingly, this phenomenon has been observed independently in linguistics, under the name "blend word" or "portmanteau", and is responsible for the creation of words in the English language such as smog (*smoke* + *fog*), labradoodle (*labrador* + *poodle*), and Brangelina (*Brad* + *Angelina*).

1 Introduction

Cross-pairing Polymerase Chain Reaction (XPCR) is an experimental DNA protocol introduced in [11] for extracting, from a heterogeneous pool of DNA strands, all the strands containing a given substrand. XPCR was then employed to implement several DNA recombination algorithms [13], for the creation of the solution space for a SAT problem [9], and for mutagenesis [12]. The combinatorial power of such a technique has been explained by logical-symbolic schemes in [23], while algorithms to create combinatorial libraries were improved and experimented in [10,12].

The formal language operation called *overlap assembly*, introduced in [5] under the name of self-assembly, and further investigated in [3,7,8], also models a special case of XPCR: The overlap assembly of two strings αx and $x\beta$ that share a non-empty overlap x, results in the string $\alpha x\beta$. A particular case of overlap assembly, called "chop operation", where the overlap consists of a single letter, was studied in [18,19], and generalized to an arbitrary length overlap in [20]. Other similar operations have been studied in the literature, such as the "short concatenation" [4], which uses only the maximum-length (possibly empty)

© Springer International Publishing AG, part of Springer Nature 2018
S. Stepney and S. Verlan (Eds.): UCNC 2018, LNCS 10867, pp. 72–85, 2018.
https://doi.org/10.1007/978-3-319-92435-9_6

overlap y between operands, the "Latin product" of words [14] where the overlap consists of only one letter, and the operation $\otimes$ which imposes the restriction that the non-overlapping part x is not empty [21]. Overlap assembly can also be considered as a particular case of "semantic shuffle on trajectories" with trajectory $0^*\sigma^+1^*$ or as a generalization of the operation $\odot_N$ from [6] which imposes the length of the overlap to be at least N. Many similar biological phenomena and operations can also be modelled using splicing systems [26, 27]. However, modeling these operations often does not require the full power of splicing. Properties of splicing languages under restrictions such as symmetry and reflexivity have been studied in [2, 15].

Returning to the biological process that motivated the study of overlap assembly, the XPCR procedure has been successfully used to join two different genes if they are attached to compatible primers [10]. Formally, $\alpha A\gamma$ and $\gamma D\beta$ were combined to produce $\alpha A\gamma D\beta$ (here A and D are gene sequences and α, γ and β are primers used). However, when $A = D$, that is, when two sequences containing the same gene were combined by XPCR, the result was not as expected. More specifically, when using XPCR with two strings $\alpha A\gamma$ and $\gamma A\beta$, instead of obtaining the expected $\alpha A\gamma A\beta$, the experiments repeatedly produced the result $\alpha A\beta$.

In this paper, we define and investigate a formal language operation called *word blending*, that formalizes this experimentally observed outcome of XPCR: The *word blending* of two words xAy_1 and y_2Az that share a non-empty overlap A results in xAz. Interestingly, this phenomenon has been observed independently in linguistics [16], under the name "blend word" or "portmanteau", and is responsible for the creation of words in the English language such as smog (*smoke* + *fog*), labradoodle (*labrador* + po*odle*), emoticon (*emotion* + *icon*), and Brangelina (*Brad* + *Angelina*).

The paper is organized as follows. Section 2 details the biological motivation behind the study of word blending, and introduces the main definitions and notations. Section 3 studies closure properties of the families in the Chomsky hierarchy under word blending, its right and left inverses, as well as iterated word blending. Section 4 investigates the decidability of existence of solutions to some language equations involving word blending, and Sect. 5 studies the descriptional state complexity of this operation when applied to regular languages.

2   Preliminaries

An alphabet Σ is a finite non-empty set of symbols. Σ^* denotes the set of all words over Σ, including the empty word λ, and Σ^+ denotes the set of all non-empty words over Σ. The length of the word w is denoted $lg(w)$. For words $w, x, y, z \in \Sigma^*$ such that $w = xyz$ we call the subwords x, y, and z *prefix*, *infix*, and *suffix* of w, respectively. The sets $\mathrm{pref}(w)$, $\mathrm{inf}(w)$, and $\mathrm{suff}(w)$ contain, respectively, all prefixes, infixes, and suffixes of w. This notation is extended to languages as $\mathrm{suff}(L) = \bigcup_{w \in L} \mathrm{suff}(w)$. The mirror image of a word $w \in \Sigma^*$ is defined as $\mathrm{mi}(\lambda) = \lambda$, and $\mathrm{mi}(w) = a_k \ldots a_2 a_1$ if $w = a_1 a_2 \ldots a_k$. The definition is extended to languages in the natural way, by $\mathrm{mi}(L) = \bigcup_{w \in L} \mathrm{mi}(w)$.

The complement of a language $L \subseteq \Sigma^*$ is $L^c = \Sigma^* \backslash L$. For two languages L_1 and L_2, the right quotient of L_1 by L_2 is defined as $L_1 L_2^{-1} = \{u \in \Sigma^* | \exists uv \in L_1, v \in L_2\}$, and the left quotient of L_1 by L_2 is defined as $L_2^{-1} L_1 = \{v \in \Sigma^* | \exists uv \in L_1, u \in L_2\}$.

The biological phenomenon we model in this paper was observed during the XPCR-based experiments, initially intended to achieve the catenation of two or more genes (genomic DNA strands). It was namely observed in [10] that, in the particular case where the two genes to be catenated were one and the same, that is, when the two input DNA strands were $\alpha A \gamma$ and $\gamma A \beta$ (here A represents a gene sequence), the output of a PCR-based amplification with primers α and β was $\alpha A \beta$. This output was different from the expected $\alpha A \gamma A \beta$, which had been the anticipated result. (Indeed, experiments using XPCR for the purpose of catenating two different genes A and D flanked by primers, that is, when the two input strands were $\alpha A \gamma$ and $\gamma D \beta$, had resulted in the output $\alpha A \gamma D \beta$. This "expected" output of XPCR was modelled by the previously mentioned operation of overlap assembly, given by $\alpha A \gamma + \gamma D \beta = \alpha A \gamma D \beta$).

Generalizing this experimentally newly-observed phenomenon to the case where the end words of the input strings are different, we model this string recombination as follows. Given two non-empty words x, y over an alphabet Σ, we define the *word blending*, or simply *blending*, of x with y as

$$x \bowtie y = \{z \in \Sigma^+ \mid \exists \alpha, \beta, \gamma_1, \gamma_2 \in \Sigma^*, \exists w \in \Sigma^+ : x = \alpha w \gamma_1, y = \gamma_2 w \beta, z = \alpha w \beta\}.$$

The definition of blending can be extended to languages L_1 and L_2 by

$$L_1 \bowtie L_2 = \bigcup_{x \in L_1, y \in L_2} x \bowtie y.$$

Note that, for a realistic model, we would need additional restrictions such as the fact that the w, γ_1 and γ_2 should be of a sufficient length and should not appear as a substring in the other strings involved.

We can also extend the blending operation to an iterated version on a language. Let $L \subseteq \Sigma^*$ be a language. We define the *iterated (word) blending* of L by $L^{\bowtie_0} = L$ and $L^{\bowtie_i} = L \bowtie L^{\bowtie_{i-1}}$. We define the iterated blending closure of L by

$$L^{\bowtie_*} = \bigcup_{i \geqslant 0} L^{\bowtie_i}.$$

We observe that the result of the iterated blending operation can be generated by a splicing system with null context splicing rules [17]. Splicing rules in [17] are of the form $(u_1, z, u_2; u_3, z, u_4)$. For such a rule, if we have strings $x = x_1 u_1 z u_2 x_2$ and $y = y_1 u_3 z u_4 y_2$, we obtain the word $x_1 u_1 z u_4 y_2$. A splicing rule is a null context rule when $u_1, u_2, u_3, u_4 = \lambda$. It is easy to see that the language $L^{\bowtie_*}$ can be generated from a splicing scheme with rules of the form $(\lambda, w, \lambda; \lambda, w, \lambda)$ for every word $w \in \Sigma^+$. The relationship between iterated blending and splicing will be discussed in greater detail in Sect. 3.

3   Closure Properties

In this section, we prove that the families of regular, context-free and recursively enumerable languages are closed under blending, and that the family of context-sensitive languages is not. The section also contains closure properties of Chomsky hierarchy families under the right and left inverse of word blending, as well as under iterated word blending.

The following lemma shows that word-blending is equivalent to a restricted version where only one-letter overlaps are utilized.

Lemma 1. *If x, y are non-empty words in Σ^+, then*

$$x \bowtie y = \{z \in \Sigma^+ \mid \exists \alpha, \beta, \gamma_1, \gamma_2 \in \Sigma^*, \exists a \in \Sigma : x = \alpha a \gamma_1, y = \gamma_2 a \beta, z = \alpha a \beta\}.$$

This result can be extended to languages in the natural way. Then from this lemma, we can show that the word blending of two languages can be obtained by combining the right quotient, catenation, left quotient and union operations, as follows.

Proposition 2. *Given languages $L_1, L_2 \subseteq \Sigma^+$,*

$$L_1 \bowtie L_2 = \bigcup_{a \in \Sigma} \left(L_1 (a\Sigma^*)^{-1} \right) a \left((\Sigma^* a)^{-1_l} L_2 \right).$$

Corollary 3. *Every full AFL is closed under word blending.*

We note that the families of regular languages, context-free languages and recursively enumerable languages are all full AFLs [28].

Proposition 4. *The family of context-sensitive languages is not closed under word blending.*

Proof. Let L_0 be a recursively enumerable language over Σ, that is not context-sensitive. It is known that a context-sensitive language L_1 over $\Sigma \cup \{a, b\}$ with $a, b \notin \Sigma$, can be constructed such that L_1 consists of words of the form Pba^i where $i \geqslant 0$ and $P \in L_0$ and, in addition, for every $P \in L_0$ there is an $i \geqslant 0$ such that $Pba^i \in L_1$ (see, e.g., [28]).

Since it is obvious that $L_1 \bowtie \{b\} = \{Pb \mid P \in L_0\}$, which is not context sensitive, it follows that the family of context sensitive languages is not closed under word blending with singleton words. $\square$

Recall that, given a binary word operation $\diamond$, the binary word operation $\square$ is called the *right-inverse of* $\diamond$ [22] if and only if for every triplet of words $u, y, w \in \Sigma^*$ the following relation holds: $w \in (u \diamond y)$ if and only if $y \in (u \square w)$. In other words, the operation $\square$ is called the right-inverse of $\diamond$ if it can be used to recover the right operand y in $u \diamond y$, from the other operand u and a word $w \in (u \diamond y)$ in the result. Define now the binary word operation $\bowtie^r$ as $u \bowtie^r w = \bigcup_{a \in \Sigma} \Sigma^* a \left(\left(u (a\Sigma^*)^{-1} a \right)^{-1_l} w \right)$. Informally, given a word $w = \alpha a \beta \in (\alpha a \gamma_1 \bowtie \gamma_2 a \beta)$, the operation $\bowtie^r$ outputs the right operand $y = \gamma_2 a \beta$ of word blending, if it is given as inputs the result $w = \alpha a \beta \in (u \bowtie y)$ and the left operand $u = \alpha a \gamma_1$. The definition of $\bowtie^r$ can be extended to languages naturally.

Proposition 5. *The operation $\bowtie^r$ is the right-inverse of $\bowtie$.*

Proof. If $w \in u \bowtie y$, there exist $\alpha, \beta, \gamma_1, \gamma_2 \in \Sigma^*, b \in \Sigma$ such that $w = \alpha b \beta, u = \alpha b \gamma_1, y = \gamma_2 b \beta$ by Lemma 1. Then, we have that $y = \gamma_2 b \beta \in \Sigma^* b \beta = \Sigma^* b \left((\alpha b)^{-1_l}(\alpha b \beta) \right) \subseteq \Sigma^* b \left(\left(((\alpha b \gamma_1)(b \Sigma^*)^{-1})b \right)^{-1_l} (\alpha b \beta) \right) \subseteq$
$\bigcup_{a \in \Sigma} \Sigma^* a \left(\left(((\alpha b \gamma_1)(a \Sigma^*)^{-1})a \right)^{-1_l}(\alpha b \beta) \right)$.

If $y \in u \bowtie^r w = \bigcup_{a \in \Sigma} \Sigma^* a \left(((u(a \Sigma^*)^{-1})a)^{-1_l} w \right)$, then there exist $b \in \Sigma$, and $\gamma_2 \in \Sigma^*, \gamma_3 \in (u(b \Sigma^*)^{-1})b$ such that $y = \gamma_2 b(\gamma_3^{-1_l} w)$. This implies that $w \in \left(u(b \Sigma^*)^{-1} \right) b (\gamma_3^{-1_l} w) = \left(u(b \Sigma^*)^{-1} \right) b \left((\gamma_2 b)^{-1_l}(\gamma_2 b(\gamma_3^{-1_l} w)) \right)$ which is included in $\left(u(b \Sigma^*)^{-1} \right) b \left((\Sigma^* b)^{-1_l} y \right) \subseteq \bigcup_{a \in \Sigma} \left(u(a \Sigma^*)^{-1} \right) a \left((\Sigma^* a)^{-1_l} y \right) = u \bowtie y$. □

Corollary 6. *The families of regular languages and recursively enumerable languages are closed under the right inverse of the blending. Moreover, if L_1 is an arbitrary language and L_2 is a regular language, then $L_1 \bowtie^r L_2$ is regular; if L_1 is a regular language and L_2 is a context-free language, then $L_1 \bowtie^r L_2$ is context-free.*

Proposition 7. *The family of context-free languages is not closed under the right inverse of blending.*

Proof. Consider the context-free languages $L_1 = \{a\$(b^{i_1} a^{i_1} \$) \cdots (b^{i_n} a^{i_n} \$) \mid n \geqslant 1, i_m \geqslant 1$ for $1 \leqslant m \leqslant n\}$, $L_2 = \{(a^{j_1} \$ b^{2j_1}) \cdots (a^{j_k} \$ b^{2j_k})(a^j \$ c^{2j}) \mid j \geqslant 1, k \geqslant 1, j_m \geqslant 1$ for $1 \leqslant m \leqslant k\}$ and the regular language $R = \{\$c^*\}$.

We now show that $(L_1 \bowtie^r L_2) \cap R = \{\$c^{2^n} \mid n \geqslant 2\}$. Since words in R start with $\$$ and contain only one symbol $\$$, the only cases in which the words in $L_1 \bowtie^r L_2$ have the pattern of the words in R are the cases of word pairs where the overlap letter is $\$$, and a prefix ending in $\$$ in the word from L_1 matches the prefix ending in the last occurrence of $\$$ in the word from L_2. More precisely, let $u = a\$b^{i_1} a^{i_1} \$ b^{i_2} a^{i_2} \$ \cdots b^{i_m} a^{i_m} \$ \cdots b^{i_n} a^{i_n} \$ \in L_1$ and $v = a^{j_1} \$ b^{2j_1} a^{j_2} \$ b^{2j_2} \cdots a^{j_m} \$ b^{2j_m} a^j \$ c^{2j} \in L_2$. For a word $w \in (L_1 \bowtie^r L_2)$ to belong to R, we must have

$$a\$b^{i_1} a^{i_1} \$ b^{i_2} a^{i_2} \$ \cdots b^{i_m} a^{i_m} \$ = a^{j_1} \$ b^{2j_1} a^{j_2} \$ b^{2j_2} \cdots a^{j_m} \$ b^{2j_m} a^j \$,$$

which implies $j_1 = 1, j_2 = i_1 = 2j_1 = 2, \ldots, j = i_m = 2j_m = 2^m$. Thus, $w = \$c^{2j} = \$c^{2^{m+1}}$, which implies $(L_1 \bowtie^r L_2) \cap R = \{\$c^{2^n} \mid n \geqslant 2\}$.

Since the family of context-free languages is closed under intersection with regular languages, it follows that it is not closed under the right inverse of blending. □

Proposition 8. *The family of context-sensitive languages is not closed under the right inverse of blending.*

Recall that given a binary word operation $\diamond$, the binary word operation $\square$ is called the *left-inverse of* $\diamond$ iff for every triplet of words $x, v, w \in \Sigma^*$ the following relation holds: $w \in (x \diamond v)$ if and only if $x \in (w \square v)$ [22].

Proposition 9. *The left inverse of blending can be expressed using the right inverse of blending, and mirror image as $w \bowtie^l v = mi(mi(v) \bowtie^r mi(w))$.*

Because all families of languages in the Chomsky hierarchy are closed under mirror image, their closure properties under the left-inverse of word blending are the same as their closure properties under the right-inverse of word blending.

We now consider the iterated blending operation $\bowtie_*$. Recall that, as mentioned in Sect. 2, for any language $L \subseteq \Sigma^*$, the language $L^{\bowtie_*}$ can be generated by a splicing system with null-context splicing rules defined as 6-tuples, as in [17]. As shown in [1], every splicing system where the rules are defined by 6-tuples, can also be implemented by a splicing system as defined in [27], which uses 4-tuple rules (see Definition 10). This connection, together with Proposition 2, allows us to express iterated word blending using so-called simple splicing systems [24], themselves a particular case of splicing systems based on 4-tuple splicing rules.

Definition 10 ([27]). *Let $\sigma = (\Sigma, R)$ be a splicing scheme, where Σ is the alphabet and R is a set of rules $R \subseteq \Sigma^* \# \Sigma^* \$ \Sigma^* \# \Sigma^*$. A rule $(u_1, u_2; u_3, u_4)$ is a word $u_1 \# u_2 \$ u_3 \# u_4 \in R$. For two strings $x, y \in \Sigma^*$, we have*

$$\sigma(x, y) = \{x_1 u_1 u_4 y_2 \mid x = x_1 u_1 u_2 x_2, y = y_1 u_3 u_4 y_2;$$

$$x_1, x_2, y_1, y_2 \in \Sigma^*, u_1 \# u_2 \$ u_3 \# u_4 \in R\}.$$

For a language L, we define $\sigma(L) = L \cup \bigcup_{x,y \in L} \sigma(x, y)$ and we define the iterated splicing of L by $\sigma^*(L) = \bigcup_{i \geqslant 0} \sigma^i(L)$ with $\sigma^0(L) = L$ and $\sigma^{i+1}(L) = \sigma(\sigma^i(L))$.

Simple splicing schemes are splicing schemes as above, but restricted to rules of the form $(a, \lambda; a, \lambda)$ for $a \in \Sigma$. Note that for two languages L_1 and L_2 over Σ, we now have that

$$L_1 \bowtie L_2 = \bigcup_{x \in L_1, y \in L_2} \sigma_{\bowtie}(x, y),$$

where $\sigma_{\bowtie}$ is the simple splicing scheme $\sigma_{\bowtie} = (\Sigma, R)$ with $R = \Sigma \# \lambda \$ \Sigma \# \lambda$. This observation together with Proposition 2 which showed that the word blending of two languages can be written $L_1 \bowtie L_2 = \bigcup_{a \in \Sigma} (L_1 (a\Sigma^*)^{-1}) a((\Sigma^* a)^{-1_l} L_2)$, gives us the following result.

Proposition 11. *For any language $L \subseteq \Sigma^*$, we have $\sigma_{\bowtie}(L) = L \bowtie L$ and $\sigma_{\bowtie}^*(L) = L^{\bowtie_*}$.*

We note that the splicing scheme $\sigma_{\bowtie}$ is finite, since the number of rules depends only on the number of symbols in Σ, and it is unary, since the rules use words of length at most 1. We also note that, even though in [24] consideration is restricted to the case when L is a finite language, the properties of the splicing systems obtained therein imply the following closure properties.

Proposition 12. *Every full AFL is closed under iterated word blending.*

Proof. Recall that $L^{\bowtie_*} = \sigma_{\bowtie}^*(L)$ and that $\sigma_{\bowtie}^*$ is finite and unary. For a splicing rule $u_1 \# u_2 \$ u_3 \# u_4$, the words u_1 and u_4 are called visible sites and u_2 and u_3 are invisible sites. In [26], it is shown that full AFLs are closed under regular splicing systems with finitely many visible sites. Since $\sigma_{\bowtie}^*$ is finite, the rules of $\sigma_{\bowtie}^*$ contain only finitely many visible sites. □

Now, we will give an explicit construction for $L^{\bowtie_*}$ when L is a regular language. We will require the following lemma concerning the structure of words generated by the iterated blending operation.

Lemma 13. *Let $L \subseteq \Sigma^+$ be a language. Then for each word $w \in L^{\bowtie_*}$, there exists $n \in \mathbb{N}$ such that there are words $u_i \in \inf(L), 1 \leqslant i \leqslant n$ and $\alpha_j \in \Sigma^*, 1 \leqslant j \leqslant n$ and symbols $a_k \in \Sigma, 1 \leqslant k \leqslant n-1$ where*

1. for $n > 1$,
    (a) $w = \alpha_1 a_1 \alpha_2 a_2 \cdots a_{n-1} \alpha_n$,
    (b) $u_i = a_{i-1} \alpha_i a_i \in \inf(L)$ for all $2 \leqslant i \leqslant n-1$,
    (c) $u_1 = \alpha_1 a_1 \in \pref(L)$ and $u_n = a_{n-1} \alpha_n \in \suff(L)$,
2. $u_1 = w \in L$ for $n = 1$.

Proposition 14. *Given an NFA A, there exists an NFA A' recognizing the language $L(A)^{\bowtie_*}$ which is effectively constructible.*

This construction gives us a way to test whether a regular language L is closed under iterated blending.

Proposition 15. *Let L be a regular language. It is decidable whether or not L is closed under $\bowtie_*$.*

Let $L, B \subseteq \Sigma^*$ be two languages. We say that B is a base of L (with respect to $\bowtie$) if $L = B^{\bowtie_*}$. In [24], it is shown that it is decidable whether or not a regular language is generated by a simple splicing scheme and a finite language base. Here, we extend the result to consider the case when the base need not be finite.

Theorem 16. *It is decidable whether or not a regular language has a base over $\bowtie_*$.*

As a consequence, we are able to not only decide whether a regular language is closed under $\bowtie_*$, but if it is, we know there always exists a finite base that generates it.

Corollary 17. *Let L be a regular language closed under $\bowtie_*$. Then L can be generated by a finite base.*

Note that in [24] languages generated by simple splicing schemes are assumed to have finite bases by definition. There it was also shown that the class of languages generated by these simple splicing schemes is a subclass of the family of regular languages. Here we do not have the finite base restriction, and Corollary 17 shows that allowing regular bases does not give simple splicing schemes and iterated word blending any more power than restricting bases to be finite.

4 Decision Problems

This section investigates the existence of solutions to language equations of the type $X \bowtie L = R$ and $L \bowtie Y = R$, where L, R are given known languages, X, Y are unknown languages, and $\bowtie$ is the word blending operation.

Proposition 18. *The existence of a solution Y to the equation $L \bowtie Y = R$ is decidable for given regular languages L and R.*

Proof. According to [22], since $\bowtie^r$ is the right-inverse of word blending, if there exists a solution Y to the given equation, then $Y' = (L \bowtie^r R^c)^c$ is also a solution. Moreover, in this case Y' is the maximal solution, in the sense that it includes all the other solutions to the equation. Since the family of regular languages is closed under $\bowtie^r$ and complement, the algorithm for deciding the existence of a solution starts with constructing $L \bowtie Y'$, which is also regular, and checking whether $L \bowtie Y'$ equals R. As equality of regular languages is decidable [25], if the answer to the question "Is $L \bowtie Y'$ equal to R?" is "yes", then a solution to the equation exists, and Y' is such a solution. If the answer is "no", then the equation has no solution. $\qquad\square$

Proposition 19. *The existence of a solution X to the equation $X \bowtie L = R$ is decidable for regular languages L and R.*

Proposition 20. *The existence of a singleton solution $\{w\}$ to the equation $L \bowtie \{w\} = R$ is decidable for regular languages L and R.*

Proof. If R is empty, a singleton solution $\{w\}$ to the equation $L \bowtie \{w\} = R$ exists if and only if L does not use all the letters from the alphabet Σ. The decision algorithm will check the emptiness of all regular languages $L \cap \Sigma^* a \Sigma^*$, where $a \in \Sigma$: If any of them is empty, then $\{w\} = \{a\}$ is a singleton solution, otherwise no singleton solution exists.

We now consider the case when R is not empty. If there is a singleton solution $\{w\}$ to the equation $L \bowtie \{w\} = R$, where $L, R \subseteq \Sigma^+, w \in \Sigma^+$ then there is a shortest singleton solution of length $k \geqslant 1$, denoted by $w_s = a_1 a_2 \cdots a_k$, with $a_1, a_2, \ldots, a_k \in \Sigma$. We now want to show that the number of states in any finite state automaton that accepts R is at least k.

If $lg(w_s) = 1$, then $\lambda \notin R$, so the number of states of any finite state machine that recognizes R is at least 2, which is greater than the length of w_s.

Suppose $k \geqslant 2$. Define $L_i = (L \bowtie a_i) a_{i+1} \cdots a_k$ for $1 \leqslant i < k$, and define $L_k = L \bowtie a_k$. Then, we have $R = \bigcup_{i=1}^{k} L_i$. Note that $L_1 \not\subseteq \bigcup_{i=2}^{k} L_i$, as otherwise $a_2 a_3 \cdots a_k$ would be a shorter singleton solution than w_s—a contradiction.

Let $\alpha \in L_1 \subseteq R$; α can be represented as $\alpha = \alpha_1 a_1 a_2 \cdots a_k$, where $\alpha_1 \in \Sigma^*$. Assume now that R is recognized by a DFA $M = (Q, \Sigma, \delta, q_0, F)$ with $n < k$ states. Then there is a derivation

$$q_0 \alpha_1 a_1 a_2 \cdots a_k \Longrightarrow^* q_{i_1} a_1 a_2 \cdots a_k \Longrightarrow q_{i_2} a_2 \cdots a_k \Longrightarrow \cdots \Longrightarrow q_{i_k} a_k \Longrightarrow q_{i_{k+1}}.$$

Because M has $n < k$ states, there is a state that occurs twice in the set $\{q_{i_2}, q_{i_3}, \ldots, q_{i_{k+1}}\}$.

If $q_{i_j} = q_{i_{k+1}}$ where $2 \leqslant j \leqslant k$, then $\alpha_1 a_1 \cdots a_{j-1}(a_j \cdots a_k)^+ \subseteq R$, and so there exists a word $\alpha_2 \in \Sigma^*$ such that $\alpha_1 a_1 \cdots a_{j-1}(a_j \cdots a_k)^+ \alpha_2 \subseteq L$. Thus, we have $\alpha \in \alpha_1 a_1 \cdots a_{j-1}(a_j \cdots a_k)^+ \alpha_2 \bowtie a_k \subseteq L_k \subseteq \bigcup_{i=2}^{k} L_i$.

If $q_{i_j} = q_{i_h}$ where $2 \leqslant j < h \leqslant k$, then $\alpha_1 a_1 \cdots a_{j-1}(a_j \cdots a_{h-1})^+ a_h \cdots a_k \subseteq R$, and so there exists a word $\alpha_2 \in \Sigma^*$ such that $\alpha_1 a_1 \cdots a_{j-1}(a_j \cdots a_{h-1})^+ \alpha_2 \subseteq L$. Then $\alpha \in (\alpha_1 a_1 \cdots a_{j-1}(a_j \cdots a_{h-1})^+ \alpha_2 \bowtie a_{h-1})a_h \cdots a_k \subseteq L_{h-1} \subseteq \bigcup_{i=2}^{k} L_i$.

In either case, for all words $\alpha \in L_1$, $\alpha \in \bigcup_{i=2}^{k} L_i$. Thus, we have that $L_1 \subseteq \bigcup_{i=2}^{k} L_i$, which is a contradiction.

For the equation $L \bowtie Y = R$, if there is a singleton solution, there is a singleton solution w_s of minimal length k, and the number of states in any finite state machine for R is at least k. If the minimal deterministic finite automaton that generates R has k states, the algorithm for deciding the existence of a singleton solution will check all the words β, where $lg(\beta) \leqslant k$. The answer is "yes" if this algorithm finds a string β such that $L \bowtie \{\beta\} = R$, and "no" otherwise. □

Proposition 21. *The existence of a singleton solution $\{w\}$ to the equation $\{w\} \bowtie L = R$ is decidable for regular languages L and R.*

Proposition 22. *The existence of a singleton solution $\{w\}$ to the equation $L \bowtie \{w\} = R$ is undecidable for regular languages R and context-free languages L.*

Proof. Assume, for the sake of contradiction, that the existence of a singleton solution $\{w\}$ to the equation $L \bowtie \{w\} = R$ is decidable for regular languages R and context-free languages L.

Given an arbitrary context-free language L' over an alphabet Σ, the context-free language $L_1 = \#\Sigma^+\# \cup L'\$$ can be constructed where $\#, \$ \notin \Sigma$. Note now that the equation $L_1 \bowtie \{w\} = \Sigma^*\$$ has a singleton solution $\{w\}$ if and only if $L' = \Sigma^*$ and the solution is $\{w\} = \{\$\}$. Thus, if we could decide the problem in the proposition, we would be able to decide whether or not $L' = \Sigma^*$ for arbitrary context-free languages L', which is impossible. □

Corollary 23. *The existence of a solution Y to the equation $L \bowtie Y = R$ is undecidable for regular languages R and context-free languages L.*

Proposition 24. *1. The existence of a singleton solution $\{w\}$ to the equation $\{w\} \bowtie L = R$ is undecidable for a regular language R and a context-free language L.*

2. The existence of a solution X to the equation $X \bowtie L = R$ is undecidable for a regular language R and a context-free language L.

5   State Complexity

By Proposition 2, the family of regular languages is closed under word blending. Thus, we can consider the state complexity of the blending operation on two regular languages. Recall from Proposition 2 that the blending of two languages can be expressed as a series of union, catenation, and quotient operations. While the state complexity of each of these operations is known, the state complexity of a combination of operations is not necessarily the same as the composition of the state complexities of the operations [29].

First, for illustrative purposes, we will construct an NFA that recognizes the blending of two languages given by DFAs. Let $A_m = (Q_m, \Sigma, \delta_m, s_m, F_m)$ be a DFA with $m \geqslant 1$ states that recognizes the language L_m and let $A_n = (Q_n, \Sigma, \delta_n, s_n, F_n)$ be a DFA with $n \geqslant 1$ states that recognizes the language L_n. We construct an NFA $B' = (Q', \Sigma, \delta', s', F')$, where $Q' = Q_m \cup Q_n$, $s' = s_m$, $F' = F_n$, and the transition function $\delta' : Q' \times \Sigma \to 2^{Q'}$ is defined for all $q \in Q'$ and $a \in \Sigma$ by

$$\delta'(q, a) = \begin{cases} \bigcup_{p \in Q_n} \delta_n(p, a) & \text{if } q \in Q_m \text{ and } \delta_m(q, a) \text{ is not the sink state,} \\ \delta_m(q, a) & \text{if } q \in Q_m \text{ and } \delta_m(q, a) \text{ is the sink state,} \\ \delta_n(q, a) & \text{if } q \in Q_n. \end{cases}$$

In Fig. 1, we define two DFAs A_m and A_n and show the NFA B' resulting from the construction described above. Intuitively, the machine B' operates by first reading the input word assuming that it is the prefix of some word recognized by A_m. Since the blending occurs on only one symbol, the machine guesses at which symbol the blend occurs. Once the blend occurs the machine continues and assumes the rest of the word is the suffix of some word recognized by A_n.

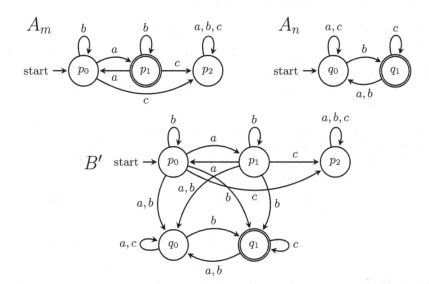

Fig. 1. The NFA B' recognizes the blend of the languages recognized by the DFAs A_m and A_n

Proposition 25. *The NFA B' recognizes the language $L_m \bowtie L_n$.*

Now, using the same basic idea, we will construct a DFA that recognizes the language of the blending of the two languages recognized by two given DFAs A_m and A_n. We construct a DFA $A' = (Q', \Sigma, \delta', s', F')$ where

- $Q' = Q_m \times 2^{Q_n}$,
- $s' = (s_m, \varnothing)$,
- $F' = \{(q, P) \in Q_m \times 2^{Q_n} \mid P \cap F_n \neq \varnothing\}$,
- $\delta'((q, P), a) = (\delta_m(q, a), P')$ for $a \in \Sigma$, where

$$P' = \begin{cases} \bigcup_{p \in P} \delta_n(p, a) & \text{if } \delta_m(q, a) \text{ is the sink state,} \\ \bigcup_{p \in Q_n} \delta_n(p, a) & \text{otherwise.} \end{cases}$$

Figure 2 shows the DFA A' that results from following the construction described above, where A_m and A_n are the DFAs shown in Fig. 1. Each state of A' is a pair consisting of a state of A_m and a subset of states of A_n. Informally, we can divide the computation of a word into two phases. In the first phase, states of the form (q, P) are reached where q is not the sink state of A_m. Here, the set P is determined solely by the input symbol as the machine tries to guess the symbol on which the blending occurs. In the second phase, the machine reaches states $(q_\varnothing, P)$, where $q_\varnothing$ is the sink state of A_m. The second phase only occurs when the blend occurs and the input that has been read is no longer a prefix of a word recognized by A_m. In this phase, the set P is determined by the transition function of A_n. We will show this formally in the following.

Proposition 26. *The DFA A' recognizes the language $L_m \bowtie L_n$.*

A simple count of the number of states in the state set of A' gives us as many as $m2^n$ states. We will show that, depending on the size of the alphabet, not all of these states are necessarily reachable. First, we consider the case where the alphabet is unary.

Theorem 27. *Let L_m and L_n be regular languages defined over a unary alphabet such that L_m is recognized by an m-state DFA and L_n is recognized by an n-state DFA. Then the state complexity of $L_m \bowtie L_n$ is $m + n - 1$ if both L_m and L_n are finite or 1 otherwise. Furthermore, this bound is reachable.*

Now, we will consider the state complexity when the languages are defined over alphabets of size greater than 1.

Lemma 28. *The DFA A' requires at most $(m-1) \cdot (k-1) + 2^n + 1$ states, where $k = |\Sigma| \leqslant 2^n$.*

Lemma 29. *Let $k \geqslant 3$ and $m, n \geqslant 2$. There exist families of DFAs A_m with m states and B_n with n states defined over an alphabet with k letters such that a DFA recognizing $A_m \bowtie B_n$ requires at least $(m-1) \cdot (k-1) + 2^n + 1$ states.*

These results together give us the following theorem.

A'

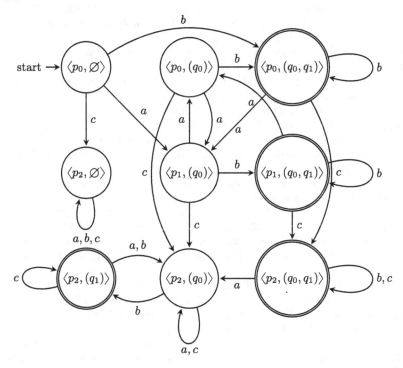

Fig. 2. The DFA A' recognizes the blend of the languages recognized by A_m and A_n from Fig. 1

Theorem 30. *Let A_m be a DFA with m states recognizing the language L_m and let A_n be a DFA with n states recognizing the language L_n, where L_m and L_n are defined over an alphabet Σ of size k. Then*

$$sc(L_m \bowtie L_n) \leqslant (m-1) \cdot (k-1) + 2^n + 1,$$

and this bound can be reached in the worst case.

Acknowledgements. We thank Giuditta Franco for fruitful discussions on modelling the outcomes of various XPCR experiments.

References

1. Bonizzoni, P., Ferretti, C., Mauri, G., Zizza, R.: Separating some splicing models. Inf. Process. Lett. **79**(6), 255–259 (2001)
2. Bonizzoni, P., Felice, C.D., Zizza, R.: The structure of reflexive regular splicing languages via Schützenberger constants. Theor. Comput. Sci. **334**(1), 71–98 (2005)
3. Brzozowski, J., Kari, L., Li, B., Szykuła, M.: State complexity of overlap assembly. arXiv preprint arXiv:1710.06000 (2017)

4. Carausu, A., Păun, Gh.: String intersection and short concatenation. Revue Roumaine de Mathématiques Pures et Appliquées **26**(5), 713–726 (1981)
5. Csuhaj-Varju, E., Petre, I., Vaszil, Gy.: Self-assembly of strings and languages. Theor. Comput. Sci. **374**(1), 74–81 (2007)
6. Domaratzki, M.: Minimality in template-guided recombination. Inf. Comput. **207**(11), 1209–1220 (2009)
7. Enaganti, S.K., Ibarra, O.H., Kari, L., Kopecki, S.: On the overlap assembly of strings and languages. Nat. Comput. **16**(1), 175–185 (2017)
8. Enaganti, S.K., Ibarra, O.H., Kari, L., Kopecki, S.: Further remarks on DNA overlap assembly. Inf. Comput. **253**, 143–154 (2017)
9. Franco, G.: A polymerase based algorithm for SAT. In: Coppo, M., Lodi, E., Pinna, G.M. (eds.) ICTCS 2005. LNCS, vol. 3701, pp. 237–250. Springer, Heidelberg (2005). https://doi.org/10.1007/11560586_20
10. Franco, G., Bellamoli, F., Lampis, S.: Experimental analysis of XPCR-based protocols. arXiv preprint arXiv:1712.05182 (2017)
11. Franco, G., Giagulli, C., Laudanna, C., Manca, V.: DNA extraction by XPCR. In: Ferretti, C., Mauri, G., Zandron, C. (eds.) DNA 2004. LNCS, vol. 3384, pp. 104–112. Springer, Heidelberg (2005). https://doi.org/10.1007/11493785_9
12. Franco, G., Manca, V.: Algorithmic applications of XPCR. Nat. Comput. **10**(2), 805–819 (2011)
13. Franco, G., Manca, V., Giagulli, C., Laudanna, C.: DNA recombination by XPCR. In: Carbone, A., Pierce, N.A. (eds.) DNA 2005. LNCS, vol. 3892, pp. 55–66. Springer, Heidelberg (2006). https://doi.org/10.1007/11753681_5
14. Golan, J.S.: The Theory of Semirings with Applications in Mathematics and Theoretical Computer Science. Addison-Wesley Longman Ltd., Reading (1992)
15. Goode, E., Pixton, D.: Recognizing splicing languages: syntactic monoids and simultaneous pumping. Discrete Appl. Math. **155**(8), 989–1006 (2007)
16. Gries, S.T.: Shouldn't it be breakfunch? A quantitative analysis of blend structure in English. Linguistics **42**(3), 639–667 (2004)
17. Head, T.: Formal language theory and DNA: an analysis of the generative capacity of specific recombinant behaviors. Bull. Math. Biol. **49**(6), 737–759 (1987)
18. Holzer, M., Jakobi, S.: Chop operations and expressions: descriptional complexity considerations. In: Mauri, G., Leporati, A. (eds.) DLT 2011. LNCS, vol. 6795, pp. 264–275. Springer, Heidelberg (2011). https://doi.org/10.1007/978-3-642-22321-1_23
19. Holzer, M., Jakobi, S.: State complexity of chop operations on unary and finite languages. In: Kutrib, M., Moreira, N., Reis, R. (eds.) DCFS 2012. LNCS, vol. 7386, pp. 169–182. Springer, Heidelberg (2012). https://doi.org/10.1007/978-3-642-31623-4_13
20. Holzer, M., Jakobi, S., Kutrib, M.: The chop of languages. In: Automata and Formal Languages, 13th International Conference, AFL 2011, Debrecen, pp. 197–210 (2011)
21. Ito, M., Lischke, G.: Generalized periodicity and primitivity for words. Math. Logic Q. **53**(1), 91–106 (2007)
22. Kari, L.: On language equations with invertible operations. Theor. Comput. Sci. **132**(1–2), 129–150 (1994)
23. Manca, V., Franco, G.: Computing by polymerase chain reaction. Math. Biosci. **211**(2), 282–298 (2008)
24. Mateescu, A., Păun, Gh., Rozenberg, G., Salomaa, A.: Simple splicing systems. Discrete Appl. Math. **84**(1–3), 145–163 (1998)

25. Mateescu, A., Salomaa, A.: Handbook of Formal Languages. Springer, New York (1997)
26. Pixton, D.: Splicing in abstract families of languages. Theor. Comput. Sci. **234**, 135–166 (2000)
27. Păun, Gh.: On the splicing operation. Discrete Appl. Math. **70**(1), 57–79 (1996)
28. Salomaa, A.: Formal Languages. Academic Press Inc., New York (1977)
29. Salomaa, K., Yu, S.: On the state complexity of combined operations and their estimation. Int. J. Found. Comput. Sci. **18**(4), 683–698 (2007)

Computational Completeness of Simple Semi-conditional Insertion-Deletion Systems

Henning Fernau[1,2,3], Lakshmanan Kuppusamy[1,2,3],
and Indhumathi Raman[1,2,3(✉)]

[1] Fachbereich 4 – Abteilung Informatikwissenschaften, CIRT,
Universität Trier, 54286 Trier, Germany
`fernau@uni-trier.de`
[2] School of Computer Science and Engineering, VIT, Vellore 632 014, India
`{klakshma,indhumathi.r}@vit.ac.in`
[3] School of Information Technology and Engineering, VIT, Vellore 632 014, India

Abstract. Insertion-deletion (or ins-del for short) systems are well studied in formal language theory, especially regarding their computational completeness. The need for many variants on ins-del systems was raised by the computational completeness result of ins-del system with (optimal) size $(1, 1, 1; 1, 1, 1)$. Several regulations like graph-control, matrix and semi-conditional have been imposed on ins-del systems. Typically, computational completeness are obtained as trade-off results, reducing the size, say, to $(1, 1, 0, 1, 1, 0)$ at the expense of increasing other measures of descriptional complexity. In this paper, we study *simple semi-conditional ins-del systems*, where an ins-del rule can be applied only in the presence or absence of substrings of the derivation string. We show that simple semi-conditional ins-del system, with maximum permitting string length 2 and maximum forbidden string length 1 and sizes $(2, 0, 0; 2, 0, 0)$, $(1, 1, 0; 2, 0, 0)$, or $(1, 1, 0; 1, 1, 1)$, are computationally complete. We also describe RE by a simple semi-conditional ins-del system of size $(1, 1, 0; 1, 1, 0)$ and with maximum permitting and forbidden string lengths 3 and 1, respectively. The obtained results complement the existing results available in the literature.

1 Introduction

Insertion-deletion systems are a computational model based on the operations of insertion and deletion of substrings in a string. Initially motivated on linguistic grounds, they more recently became quite popular as a theoretical model for DNA-based computations, as the basic operations fit well into this area. For further discussions on the history of this model, as well as giving insights into the rich literature of this area, we refer to [7,14,15].

In a nutshell, the rules of an insertion-deletion system (or ins-del system) can be of two types: insertion or deletion, i.e., either, a string is specified that may be inserted in a prescribed context within the current string, or it may be

© Springer International Publishing AG, part of Springer Nature 2018
S. Stepney and S. Verlan (Eds.): UCNC 2018, LNCS 10867, pp. 86–100, 2018.
https://doi.org/10.1007/978-3-319-92435-9_7

deleted relative to the context conditions. The potential biological meaning of such a rule should be clear. The main research question is under which restrictions can computational completeness results still be obtained. For instance, it is known [13] that for each recursively enumerable language (or RE language for short), there exists an ins-del system where only single symbols are inserted or deleted, and the allowed context conditions (to the left or to the right) are again (at most) single symbols. However, if we disallow checking contexts both to the left and to the right, then not all RE languages can be described; cf. [14]. In such situations, several regulation mechanisms have been studied and shown to achieve computational completeness results. From the viewpoint of biocomputing, let us only mention ins-del P systems [8,9], sometimes in disguise [4], tissue P systems with ins-del rules [10] and semi-conditional ins-del systems [6].

Meduna and Svec have reported on the use of several variants of context conditions in regulated rewriting in the textbook [11]. Here, (simple) semi-conditional rules are of particular importance. In the semi-conditional case, the conditions are sets of words and a rule can be applied if all words from its *permitting* condition are present and no word from the *forbidden* condition is present in the string. A semi-conditional grammar is said to be *simple* if each rule has only either a permitting condition or a forbidden condition. Let the maximum length of a string in the permitting and forbidden set be denoted by i and j, respectively; then the ordered pair (i, j) is called the *degree* of the semi-conditional grammar. From a biological point of view, these conditions can be interpreted as *global* context conditions, as opposed to the *local* context conditions traditionally represented within the ins-del rules themselves.

Ivanov and Verlan initiated the study of semi-conditional ins-del systems in [6]. They proved that with degree $(2, 2)$, inserting and deleting single symbols without any local context is sufficient to describe any RE language. Conversely, extending previous computational incompleteness results on non-regulated ins-del systems, it was shown in the same paper that ins-del systems that may insert or delete single symbols in one-sided single-symbol context are not able to describe the regular language $\{ab\}^+$, assuming that these systems can also globally check for single symbols only, i.e., if they are of degree $(1, 1)$.

No previous computational completeness results have been known for other degrees. This motivates the present study. We think that it might be possible to also globally check for the presence or absence of short molecular parts (strings) within biocomputational devices. Furthermore, we managed to cope with the already mentioned *simple* restriction on semi-conditional rules. Clearly, this additional restriction is a technical challenge. More specifically, we prove that simple semi-conditional ins-del systems of degree $(2, 1)$ are computationally complete if (i) strings of length two may either be inserted or deleted without any local conditions, or (ii) only single symbols (with one-sided single-symbol local context) may be inserted, but strings of length two may be deleted without any local conditions, or (iii) only single symbols (with one-sided single-symbol local context) may be inserted and single symbols (with two-sided single-symbol local context) may be deleted. We finally present a trade-off result for systems of degree $(3, 1)$.

2   Preliminaries

Let $\mathbb{N}$ denote the set of non-negative integers, and $[1 \ldots k] = \{i \in \mathbb{N} : 1 \leq i \leq k\}$. If Σ is an *alphabet* (finite set), then Σ^* denotes the free monoid generated by Σ. The elements of Σ^* are called *strings* or *words*; λ denotes the empty string. The morphism from the monoid Σ^* to $\mathbb{N}$ (with addition), defined by $a \mapsto 1$ for $a \in \Sigma$ is called *length* of a word; usually, we write $|w|$. $\Sigma^{\leq i}$ collects all words over Σ of length at most i. A word v is a subword of $x \in \Sigma^*$ if there are words u, w such that $x = uvw$. Let $sub(x) \subseteq \Sigma^*$ denote the set of all subwords of $x \in \Sigma^*$. We also use the *shuffle operation* $\sqcup\!\sqcup$ to describe the effect of insertions at a random position in the string. w^R denotes the reversal of $w \in \Sigma^*$. For the computational completeness results, we are using the fact that type-0 grammars in SGNF are known to characterize the class RE of recursively enumerable languages.

Definition 1 ([5]). *A type-0 grammar $G = (N, T, P, S)$ is said to be in* Special Geffert Normal Form, *or SGNF for short, if N decomposes as $N = N' \cup N''$, where $N'' = \{A, B, C, D\}$ and N' contains at least the two nonterminals S and S', the only non-context-free rules in P are the two erasing rules $AB \to \lambda$ and $CD \to \lambda$, the context-free rules are of the following forms:*

$$X \to Yb \text{ or } X \to bY, \text{ where } X, Y \in N', \ X \neq Y, \ b \in T \cup N'', \text{ or } S' \to \lambda.$$

The way the normal form is constructed is described in [5]. Also, the derivation of a string is done in two phases. In phase I, the context-free rules are applied repeatedly; this phase is completed by applying the rule $S' \to \lambda$ in the derivation. In phase II, only the non-context-free erasing rules are applied repeatedly until a terminal string is reached. From its invention, this normal form turned out to be a very tool for proving computational completeness results for (regulated) ins-del systems.

Definition 2 ([7,12]). *An* insertion-deletion *system, or ins-del system for short, is a construct $\gamma = (V, T, A, R)$, where V is an alphabet, $T \subseteq V$ is the terminal alphabet, A is a finite language over V, R is a finite set of triplets of the form $(u, \eta, v)_{ins}$ or $(u, \delta, v)_{del}$, where $(u, v) \in V^* \times V^*$, $\eta, \delta \in V^+$.*

The pair (u, v) is called the *context*, η is called the *insertion string*, δ is called the *deletion string* and $x \in A$ is called an *axiom*. If one of the u or v is λ for all the insertion (deletion) contexts, then we call the insertion (deletion) *one-sided*. If both $u, v = \lambda$ for every insertion (deletion) rule, then it means that the corresponding insertion (deletion) can be done freely anywhere in the string and is called *context-free* insertion (context-free deletion). The *descriptional complexity* of an ins-del system is measured by its *size* $s = (n, i', i''; m, j', j'')$, where the parameters represent resource bounds as given in Table 1.

Definition 3 ([6]). *A* semi-conditional insertion-deletion *system of degree (i, j), $i, j \geq 0$ is a construct $\Pi = (V, T, A, R)$, where V is a finite alphabet, $T \subseteq V$ is the terminal alphabet, $A \subseteq V^*$ is a finite set of axioms, R is a finite set of rules of the form $[(u, s, v)_t, \mathcal{P}, \mathcal{F}]$ where $u, s, v \in V^*$, $t \in \{ins, del\}$, $\mathcal{P}, \mathcal{F}$ are finite subsets of V^*.*

Table 1. Parameters in the size of ins-del system.

$n = \max\{\|\eta\| : (u, \eta, v)_{ins} \in R\}$	$m = \max\{\|\delta\| : (u, \delta, v)_{del} \in R\}$
$i' = \max\{\|u\| : (u, \eta, v)_{ins} \in R\}$	$j' = \max\{\|u\| : (u, \delta, v)_{del} \in R\}$
$i'' = \max\{\|v\| : (u, \eta, v)_{ins} \in R\}$	$j'' = max\{\|v\| : (u, \delta, v)_{del} \in R\}$

The set $\mathcal{P}$ is called the *permitting* set and $\mathcal{F}$ is called the *forbidden* set. For clarity, we often use unique labels for rules, even identifying a rule with its label, i.e., if $r \in R$ is a rule (label), then $r : [(u_r, s_r, v_r)_{t_r}, \mathcal{P}_r, \mathcal{F}_r]$. The ordered pair (i, j) is called the *degree* of the semi-conditional ins-del system Π where i is the smallest integer such that $\bigcup_{r \in R} \mathcal{P}_r \subseteq V^{\leq i}$ and j is the smallest integer such that $\bigcup_{r \in R} \mathcal{F}_r \subseteq V^{\leq j}$. We write $x \Rightarrow_r y$ if $\mathcal{P}_r \subseteq sub(x)$ and $\mathcal{F}_r \cap sub(x) = \emptyset$ and either

1. $t_r = ins$ and $x = x_1 u_r v_r x_2$, $y = x_1 u_r s_r v_r x_2$, for some $x_1, x_2 \in V^*$; or
2. $t_r = del$ and $x = x_1 u_r s_r v_r x_2$, $y = x_1 u_r v_r x_2$, for some $x_1, x_2 \in V^*$.

The language generated by a semi-conditional insertion-deletion system Π is

$$L(\Pi) = \{w \in T^* \mid x \Rightarrow^* w \text{ for some } x \in A\},$$

where $\Rightarrow^*$ is the reflexive and transitive closure of $\Rightarrow = \bigcup_{r \in R} \Rightarrow_r$. The families of languages generated by semi-conditional insertion-deletion systems of degree at most (i, j) having ID size at most $s = (n, i', i''; m, j', j'')$ is denoted as $SC_{i,j}ID(s)$. If, for each $r \in R$, either $\mathcal{P}_r = \emptyset$ or $\mathcal{F}_r = \emptyset$, then the semi-conditional ins-del system is said to be *simple*. The families of languages generated by such simple semi-conditional insertion-deletion (denoted in short as SSCID) systems of degree at most (i, j) and ID size at most s is denoted as $SSC_{i,j}ID(s)$.

Example 1. Consider the non context-free language $L_1 = \{a^n b^n c^n \mid n \geq 1\}$. We construct a simple semi-conditional ins-del system Π of degree $(1, 1)$ and ID size $(3, 1, 1; 1, 0, 0)$ describing L_1 as follows: $\Pi = (\{A, B, a, b, c\}, \{a, b, c\}, \{abc\}, R)$ where the set of rules of R are given in Table 2.

Table 2. SSCID rules describing $\{a^n b^n c^n \mid n \geq 1\}$.

$r1 : [(a, aAb, b)_{ins}, \emptyset, B]$	$r2 : [(b, Bc, c)_{ins}, A, \emptyset]$
$r3 : [(\lambda, A, \lambda)_{del}, B, \emptyset]$	$r4 : [(\lambda, B, \lambda)_{del}, \emptyset, A]$

We will now explain the working of the rules in Table 2. From the rules, we can see that $r1$ can be applied in the absence of B and $r2$ can be applied in the presence of A, thus, $r1$ has to be applied before $r2$ is applied. Note that in $r1$, as the contexts are a and b, once aAb is introduced between a and b, the rule $r1$ cannot (immediately) be applied again until A is deleted. Similarly, rule $r2$ cannot be applied for a second time unless B is deleted. Starting from the axiom abc, the only applicable rule is $r1$ which will results in $aaAbbc$. Now, $r3$

cannot be applied, as deleting A requires the presence of B and this symbol is not introduced yet. So, the only applicable rule is $r2$ which results in $aaAbbBcc$. Now, $r4$ cannot be applied as it requires the absence of A and A is still present in the derived string. The only applicable rule is hence $r3$ which deletes the A and then the only applicable rule is $r4$ which deletes the B and results to $aabbcc$. A sample derivation is given below for better understanding the system.

$$abc \Rightarrow_{r1} aaAbbc \Rightarrow_{r2} aaAbbBcc \Rightarrow_{r3} aabbBcc \Rightarrow_{r4} aabbcc = a^2b^2c^2.$$

The above process is repeated and as the rules are applied in a deterministic manner, it is easy to see that $L(\Pi) = L_1$.   □

Remark 1. The purpose of Example 1 is to explain how the system works and the size used in this example does not necessarily correspond to computational completeness results obtained in this paper. On the other hand, if a type-0 grammar (in SGNF) is given for L_1, then L_1 can be simulated by a simple semi-conditional ins-del system with the sizes that are shown in the computational completeness result.   □

The results of this paper and a sketch on how they complement the existing results of [6] are given in Table 3.

Table 3. Comparing the results of [6] and this paper.

S. No	Result of [6]	Complementing result(s) of this paper	Reference
1	$SC_{2,2}ID(1,0,0;1,0,0) = RE$	$SSC_{2,1}ID(2,0,0;2,0,0) = RE$	Theorem 2
2	$SC_{1,1}ID(1,1,0;2,0,0) \subsetneq RE$	$SSC_{2,1}ID(1,1,0;2,0,0) = RE$	Theorem 3
3	$SC_{1,1}ID(1,1,0;1,1,1) \subsetneq RE$	$SSC_{2,1}ID(1,1,0;1,1,1) = RE$	Theorem 4
4.	$SC_{1,1}ID(2,0,0;1,1,0) = RE$	$SSC_{2,1}ID(2,0,0;2,0,0) = RE$	Theorem 2
		$SSC_{3,1}ID(1,1,0;1,1,0) = RE$	Theorem 5
		$SSC_{3,1}ID(1,0,1;1,1,0) = RE$	Theorem 6

3   Main Results

In order to make some of our results simple, we claim the following, similar to other regulation mechanisms, as for example in [4].

Theorem 1. *If $s = (n, i', i''; m, j', j'')$ is some ID size and (i, j) is some degree, then $SSC_{i,j}ID(s) = [SSC_{i,j}ID(s')]^R$, with $s' = (n, i'', i'; m, j'', j')$, and moreover, $SSC_{i,j}ID(s) = RE$ if and only if $SSC_{i,j}ID(s') = RE$.*

In order to show that simple semi-conditional ins-del systems of certain sizes describe RE, we make use of the fact that RE languages can be generated by grammars in Special Geffert Normal Form where the rules are of the type (i) $p : X \to bY$ (ii) $q : X \to Yb$ (iii) $f : AB \to \lambda$ (iv) $g : CD \to \lambda$ and (v)

$h : S' \to \lambda$, where $p, q, f, g, h \in [1 \ldots |P|]$ are labels associated with each type of rule of SGNF. We provide a simulation of these rules by rules of simple semi-conditional ins-del system. The simulation of type $g : CD \to \lambda$ rules is similar to the simulation of f-type rules. Also, we always simulate the h type rule by $[(\lambda, S', \lambda)_{del}, \emptyset, \mathcal{M}]$, with $\mathcal{M} \in \{\mathcal{M}'', \mathcal{M}'''\}$ as defined below. Therefore, in the following proofs we mostly discuss the simulations of rules of type p, q, f and we let

$$
\begin{aligned}
M &= \{m \mid m \in [1 \ldots |P|]\}, & M' &= \{m' \mid m \in [1 \ldots |P|]\}, \\
M'' &= \{m'' \mid m \in [1 \ldots |P|]\}, & M''' &= \{m''' \mid m \in [1 \ldots |P|]\}, \\
\mathcal{M}'' &= M \cup M' \cup M'', & \mathcal{M}''' &= M \cup M' \cup M'' \cup M'''.
\end{aligned}
$$

We first recall from [6] that $SC_{2,2}ID(1, 0, 0; 1, 0, 0) = RE$. In the following we decrease the degree to $(2, 1)$ and further make the system simple but at the cost of increasing the insertion and deletion lengths from one to two. The computational completeness of $SSC_{0,2}ID(2, 0, 0; 2, 0, 0)$ is under study.

Theorem 2. $SSC_{2,1}ID(2, 0, 0; 2, 0, 0) = RE$.

Proof. Consider a type-0 grammar $G = (N, T, P, S)$ in SGNF in which the rules of P are labelled uniquely by numbers $[1 \ldots |P|]$. We construct an SSCID system $\Pi = (V, T, \{S\}, R)$ of degree $(2, 1)$ and ID size $(2, 0, 0; 2, 0, 0)$ as follows such that $L(\Pi) = L(G)$. The alphabet of Π is $V \subset N \cup T \cup \mathcal{M}'''$. The set of rules of R in Π is given as follows. (i) For every rule of type $p : X \to bY$ in G, the simulating rules are stated in Fig. 1(a). (ii) For every rule of type $q : X \to Yb$ in G, the simulating rules are stated in Fig. 1(b). (iii) Rules of type $f : AB \to \lambda$ are simulated by the (SSC)ID rule $f1 = [(\lambda, AB, \lambda)_{del}, \emptyset, \emptyset]$.

$p1 = [(\lambda, pp', \lambda)_{ins}, \emptyset, \mathcal{M}''']$	$q1 = [(\lambda, qq', \lambda)_{ins}, \emptyset, \mathcal{M}''']$
$p2 = [(\lambda, p'X, \lambda)_{del}, \{pp'\}, \emptyset]$	$q2 = [(\lambda, q'X, \lambda)_{del}, \{qq'\}, \emptyset]$
$p3 = [(\lambda, bp'', \lambda)_{ins}, \emptyset, N' \cup M' \cup M'' \cup M''']$	$q3 = [(\lambda, q''b, \lambda)_{ins}, \emptyset, N' \cup M' \cup M'' \cup M''']$
$p4 = [(\lambda, Yp''', \lambda)_{ins}, \emptyset, N' \cup M' \cup M''']$	$q4 = [(\lambda, q'''Y, \lambda)_{ins}, \emptyset, N' \cup M' \cup M''']$
$p5 = [(\lambda, p''', \lambda)_{del}, \{p'''p''\}, \emptyset]$	$q5 = [(\lambda, q''', \lambda)_{del}, \{q''q'''\}, \emptyset]$
$p6 = [(\lambda, p''p, \lambda)_{del}, \{bY\}, \emptyset]$	$q6 = [(\lambda, qq'', \lambda)_{del}, \{Yb\}, \emptyset]$
(a) Simulating $p : X \to bY$	(b) Simulating $q : X \to Yb$

Fig. 1. Simulating context-free rules of SGNF by $SSC_{2,1}ID(2, 0, 0; 2, 0, 0)$.

We now proceed to prove that $L(\Pi) = L(G)$. We initially prove that $L(G) \subseteq L(\Gamma)$ by showing that Π correctly simulates the application of the rules of the types p, q, f. We focus on the p rule simulation, as this is the most complicated one. The application of $p : X \to bY$ to $\alpha X \beta$ derives $\alpha bY \beta = w$, which is correctly simulated by Π as follows:

$$
\alpha X \beta \Rightarrow_{p1} \alpha pp'X\beta \Rightarrow_{p2} \alpha p\beta \Rightarrow_{p3} \alpha bp''p\beta \Rightarrow_{p4} \alpha bYp'''p''p\beta \Rightarrow_{p5} \alpha bYp''p\beta \Rightarrow_{p6} w.
$$

<u>Simulation idea</u>: We insert strings of length two in a random manner, such that one symbol of it acts as a marker to stitch to the correct position in the string. The correct position is verified with permitting strings or deletion strings of length two, which verifies that the previously introduced string has been inserted only at a particular correct position. For example, pp' is randomly inserted by rule $p1$ and the rule $p2$ demands that this insertion happens to the left of the only non-terminal X present in the string. Similarly, the permitting string in $p5$ demands to have the substring $p'''p''$ present in the string, thus Yp''' (see rule $p4$) is inserted between b and p'' and bp'' itself is inserted by rule $p3$. The forbidden strings in insertion rules prevent from using of the same rule again and also indirectly bring the order among the applications of the rules.

We now prove the converse inclusion $L(\Pi) \subseteq L(G)$ by showing that the rules stated in Fig. 1(a) can only be used in the intended way.

Consider a sentential form $w_0 = \alpha X \beta$ derivable in Π and G, where $X \in N'$ and $\alpha, \beta \in (N'' \cup T)^*$. Notice that, from the perspective of G, we are (still) in phase I. The only applicable rule is $p1$ (or any other insertion rule $r1$ where the left-hand side of rule r ix X) since other insertion rules like $p3$ or $p4$ forbid the presence of any non-terminal of N'. All deletion rules of Fig. 1 require the presence of rule markers (i.e. elements of $\mathcal{M}'''$), but $sub(w_0) \cap \mathcal{M}''' = \emptyset$. On applying the rule $p1$, pp' is inserted anywhere in the string thus yielding $w_1 \in pp' \sqcup (\alpha X \beta)$, with $pp' \in sub(w_1)$. We cannot apply any insertion rule $r1$, $r3$ or $r4$, as $p' \in \mathcal{F}_{r1} \cap \mathcal{F}_{r3} \cap \mathcal{F}_{r4}$. In particular, this rules out repeated applications of $p1$. Also, we cannot apply rule $h1$ now, as here (and also in any of the further steps discussed below) some rule marker is present in the string. Hence, we must apply a deletion rule of Fig. 1 to w_1. The application of any $r5$ or $r6$ requires r'' to appear, which is not the case for w_1. By the uniqueness of rule labels, the only applicable rule is $p2$ which actually fixes the position of pp' on the left of X, thereby deleting $p'X$. Hence, we obtain a unique string w_2 satisfying $w_1 \Rightarrow_{p2} w_2 = \alpha p \beta$. Now, there is a choice in applying $r3$ or $r4$ for some rule r. We focus on $r = p$ in the following, as this is the only possible fruitful continuation, as we will soon see. If $p4$ is applied to w_2, we get $w_2' \in Yp''' \sqcup \alpha p \beta$ and now $p3$ cannot be applied, as $p''' \in sub(w_2') \cap \mathcal{F}_{p3}$.

The derivation is stuck, as no other rule can be applied. In particular, $p5$ is not applicable, since $p'' \notin sub(w_2')$. Thus, the only applicable rule on w_2 is $p3$ which inserts bp'' randomly into w_2 yielding $w_3 \in bp'' \sqcup \alpha p \beta$, with $bp'' \in sub(w_3)$. The re-application of $p3$ on w_3 is stopped since p'' is a member of its forbidden set. On applying the only possible rule $p4$ on w_3,[1] Yp''' is randomly inserted, resulting in $w_4 \in Yp''' \sqcup bp'' \sqcup \alpha p \beta$, with $Yp''', bp'' \in sub(w_4)$. A careful case analysis reveals that now $p5$ is the only applicable rule.[2] Since $p5$ demands that $p'''p'' \in sub(w_4)$, this crucial rule application fixes several of our previous choices: (a) Recall that we could have applied any rule $r3$ (instead of $p3$) and any rule $\bar{r}4$ (instead of $p4$). But if we would have chosen $\bar{r} \neq r$, then the substring $r'''r''$ would not be present in w_4. We will see in the next step that only $r = p$ is

---

[1] Again, any $r4$ could be applied, but we will soon see that $r = p$ is enforced.

[2] Again, any $r5$ could be applied, but we will soon see that $r = p$ is enforced.

possible, which we will therefore use already in the following to avoid clumsy formulations. (b) Previously, we had the choice inserting Yp''', bp'' anywhere into w_2. However, $p'''p'' \in sub(w_4)$ ensures that Yp''' must have been inserted between b and p''. Hence, we know that $bYp'''p'' \in sub(w_4)$. Now, $w_4 \Rightarrow_{p5} w_5$ yields $bYp'' \in sub(w_5)$. With symbols from $M \cup M''$ being present in w_5, we understand that only rule $p6$ is applicable. Also, the deletion operation fixes that the right-hand side bY introduced with rules $r3$ and $r4$ corresponds to that of p, as this deletion is only possible if $r = p$. Similarly, bp'' must have been inserted to the left of p due to $p''p \in sub(w_5)$. Applying $p6$ on w_5 deletes the markers $p''p$, thus yielding $w_6 = \alpha bY\beta$. This series of rule applications that yields $w_6 = \alpha bY\beta$ from $w_0 = \alpha X\beta$ corresponds to the rewriting rule $X \to bY$ of G.

Consider now a sentential form w_0 derivable both in Π and in G, with $N' \cap sub(w_0) = \emptyset$. This means that the derivation of grammar G is in phase II. Hence, $w_0 = xyt$, where $x \in \{A, C\}^*$, $y \in \{B, D\}^*$, $t \in T^*$. Clearly, if $w_0 \in T^*$, no further derivation is possible. If AB or CD are substrings of w_0, we can (directly) apply $f1$ or $g1$, this way removing this substring as intended. Alternatively, we can apply $r1$ for some context-free rule r of G. As we have considered above, we would have to apply $r2$ next, but this is not possible due to the absence of symbols from N'. Hence, any such attempt will get stuck.

By induction, the previous arguments (that basically present the induction steps) show that $L(\Pi) \subseteq L(G)$, thus proving the theorem.   □

Next, we recall from [6] that $SC_{1,1}ID(1,1,0;2,0,0) \neq RE$. In the following we show that computational completeness can be achieved if we increase the degree of the system from $(1,1)$ to $(2,1)$, even when maintaining simplicity. The computational completeness of $SSC_{0,2}ID(1,1,0;2,0,0)$ is open for investigation.

Theorem 3. $SSC_{2,1}ID(1,1,0;2,0,0) = SSC_{2,1}ID(1,0,1;2,0,0) = RE$.

The reader might wonder why we could not deduce this result by sequentializing the construction of Theorem 2 or even by starting from a $SSC_{2,1}ID(2,0,0;2,0,0)$ system. In fact, as long as special symbols like rule labels are introduced as in rule $p1$ in Fig. 1(a), where a string of two rule labels is inserted (in this example pp') we might do the following. First, introduce the left one of them (in this example it is p) with the context conditions of the previous simulation (in this example it is M''), and then introduce the right one (in this example it is p') in the context of the left one (in this example it is p). One can avoid repetitions by having this newly introduced marker (in this example it is p') in the forbidden context. This trick can only work if we do not expect that this symbol (that we now check for not showing up in the string) may not already be present in the string. In our example we do not expect p' to be present before we introduced it, so we can sequentialize $p1$ in the described way. However, this expectation is not met, for instance, when trying to sequentialize rule $p3$ in Fig. 1(a) in a similar fashion. Here, we would need different ideas. In more general terms, this prevents us from starting out from a $SSC_{2,1}ID(2,0,0;2,0,0)$ system in our simulation for proving the claimed computational completeness result for $SSC_{2,1}ID(1,1,0;2,0,0)$. Hence, we now show a different simulation, starting from type-0 grammars in SGNF again.

Proof. Consider a type-0 grammar $G = (N, T, P, S)$ in SGNF. The rules of P are labelled uniquely by numbers $[1 \ldots |P|]$. We construct an SSCID system $\Pi = (V, T, \{S\}, R)$ of degree $(2, 1)$ and ID size $(1,1,0;2,0,0)$ as follows such that $L(\Pi) = L(G)$. The alphabet of Π is $V \subset N \cup T \cup \mathcal{M}''$. The set of rules R of Π is given as follows: (i) For every rule of type $p : X \to bY$ in G, the simulating rules are stated in Fig. 2(a), (ii) For every rule of type $q : X \to Yb$ in G, the simulating rules are stated in Fig. 2(b), (iii) Rules of type $f : AB \to \lambda$ is simulated by the SSCID rules $f1 = [(\lambda, AB, \lambda)_{del}, \emptyset, \emptyset]$.

$p1 = [(X, p, \lambda)_{ins}, \emptyset, \mathcal{M}'']$
$p2 = [(\lambda, X, \lambda)_{del}, \{p\}, \emptyset]$
$p3 = [(p, p', \lambda)_{ins}, \emptyset, N' \cup M' \cup M'']$
$p4 = [(p', p'', \lambda)_{ins}, \emptyset, N' \cup M'']$
$p5 = [(p', Y, \lambda)_{ins}, \{p'p''\}, \emptyset]$
$p6 = [(p, b, \lambda)_{ins}, \{pp'\}, \emptyset]$
$p7 = [(\lambda, p, \lambda)_{del}, \{bp', Yp''\}, \emptyset]$
$p8 = [(\lambda, p', \lambda)_{del}, \emptyset, M]$
$p9 = [(\lambda, p'', \lambda)_{del}, \emptyset, M \cup M']$

(a) Simulating $p : X \to bY$

$q1 = [(X, q, \lambda)_{ins}, \emptyset, \mathcal{M}'']$
$q2 = [(\lambda, X, \lambda)_{del}, \{q\}, \emptyset]$
$q3 = [(q, q', \lambda)_{ins}, \emptyset, N' \cup M' \cup M'']$
$q4 = [(q', q'', \lambda)_{ins}, \emptyset, N' \cup M'']$
$q5 = [(q', b, \lambda)_{ins}, \{q'q''\}, \emptyset]$
$q6 = [(q, Y, \lambda)_{ins}, \{qq'\}, \emptyset]$
$q7 = [(\lambda, q, \lambda)_{del}, \{Yq', bq''\}, \emptyset]$
$q8 = [(\lambda, q', \lambda)_{del}, \emptyset, M]$
$q9 = [(\lambda, q'', \lambda)_{del}, \emptyset, M \cup M']$

(b) Simulating $q : X \to Yb$

Fig. 2. Simulation of context-free rules of SGNF by $SSC_{2,1}ID(1,1,0;1,0,0)$.

We first explain the idea behind the construction of q rule simulation in Π as follows. We introduce three markers q, q', q'' in order to have $qq'q''$ present in the string. The X of N' is deleted before q' is introduced. So, the effect of executing $q1$ through $q4$ is the same as that of applying the rewriting rule $X \to qq'q''$. Then, Y is inserted in between q, q' and b is inserted in between q' and q''. Note that b cannot be introduced for a second time, as the string will be having $q'bq''$ and not $q'q''$ (see rule $q5$). On deleting the markers, first q is deleted in the presence of the Yq' and bq'' to ensure that Y and b are correctly introduced. Then, the markers q' and q'' are deleted in this order. The order of deletion is important since otherwise, the rules $q3$ and/or $q4$ can be applied again and a malicious string can be obtained by using the rules $q5$ and/or $q6$.

One can show that $L(G) \subseteq L(\Pi)$ by an inductive argument. The main point is to understand the simulation of a context-free rule, say, of type q:

$$\alpha X \beta \Rightarrow_{q1} \alpha Xq\beta \Rightarrow_{q2} \alpha q\beta \Rightarrow_{q3} \alpha qq'\beta \Rightarrow_{q4} \alpha qq'q''\beta \Rightarrow_{q5}$$
$$\alpha qq'bq''\beta \Rightarrow_{q6} \alpha qYq'bq''\beta \Rightarrow_{q7} \alpha Yq'bq''\beta \Rightarrow_{q8} \alpha Ybq''\beta \Rightarrow_{q9} \alpha Yb\beta.$$

To show the converse inclusion $L(G) \supseteq L(\Pi)$, consider a string w_0 derivable both in G and in Π. We discuss possible derivations for w_0 in Π and have to show that these either get stuck or correspond to derivation steps in G, which would then entail the claim by induction. Observe that any rules r_j for $j > 1$ require that $sub(w_0) \cap \mathcal{M}'' \neq \emptyset$, either by the permitting context, or because this is a requirement of the ins-del rules themselves. Hence, if $N' \cap sub(w_0) = \emptyset$, i.e., the SGNF grammar G would work in phase II, we have to apply one of $h1, f1, g1$, which directly corresponds to an erasing rule of G.

Therefore, we now consider a sentential form $w_0 = \alpha X \beta$ derivable in Π and G, where $X \in N'$ and $\alpha, \beta \in (N'' \cup T)^*$. The only applicable rules are some rules $q1$ that insert the marker q to the right of X, thus yielding $w_1 = \alpha X q \beta$. Notice that now (and also within the future discussions) always a marker from $\mathcal{M}''$ is present in the string, which disables applying rule $h1$ prematurely. No rule $r3$ is applicable, as $N' \cap sub(w_1) \neq \emptyset$. For any of the rules $r4, r5, r6, r7, r8$ to be applicable, $M' \cap sub(w_1) \neq \emptyset$ is necessary, which is not the case. Similarly, $r9$ is not applicable. Hence, the only applicable rule is $q2$ which deletes X yielding the string $w_2 = \alpha q \beta$. Again, none of the rules $r4, r5, r6, r7, r8$ is applicable, as $M' \cap sub(w_1) = \emptyset$. The presence of the marker q disables $r1$ and $r9$. As $N' \cap sub(w_1) = \emptyset$, no rule $r2$ is applicable. Due to the uniqueness of the rule labels, $q3$ is hence the only applicable rule, with $w_2 \Rightarrow_{q3} w_3 = \alpha q q' \beta$. As q, q' are present in w_3, any rule like $r1, r3, r8, r9$ is disabled. The absence of symbols from $N' \cup M''$ disables applying $r2, r4, r5, r7$. Label uniqueness leaves us with applying either $q4$ or $q6$. Hence, if $w_3 \Rightarrow w_4$ in Π, then $w_4 \in \{\alpha q q' q'' \beta, \alpha q Y q' \beta\}$. If $w_4 = \alpha q Y q' \beta$, a case analysis reveals that if $w_4 \Rightarrow w_5$ in Π, then this must be due to applying $q4$, i.e., $w_5 = \alpha q Y q' q'' \beta$. Now, $q5$ is the only applicable rule, so that $w_6 = \alpha q Y q' b q'' \beta$ is enforced. Alternatively, on $w_4 = \alpha q q' q'' \beta$, only rules $q5$ and $q6$ can apply. However, the order of application of $q5, q6$ does not matter, because if $q5$ is applied, then only $q6$ can be applied next, and vice versa. Hence, if $w_4 \Rightarrow w_5 \Rightarrow w_6$ in Π, $w_6 = \alpha q Y q' b q'' \beta$ is again enforced.

The presence of symbols from M, M', M'' and N' in the substring $q Y q' b q'$ within w_6 prevents applying any of the insertion rules, as well as of any $r8$ or $r9$. Because we can assume that $X \neq Y$ in any rule $q : X \to Y b$ or $p : X \to bY$ of G, no rule $r2$ can be applied at this point. The only applicable rule on w_6 is hence $q7$ which deletes the marker q, thus yielding $w_7 = \alpha Y q' b q'' \beta$. Let us stress that $q7$ could not have been applied at any earlier point, as it also checks that both $Y q'$ and $b q''$ are present within the sentential form. Following the application of $q7$, the rules $q8, q9$ are applied in a deterministic way which will delete the markers q', q'', respectively, from w_7 thus finally yielding $w_9 = \alpha Y b \beta$. A case-by-case analysis shows that no other rules are applicable within a derivation $w_7 \Rightarrow w_8 \Rightarrow w_9$ within Π. This series of rule applications yielding $w_9 = \alpha Y b \beta$ from $w_0 = \alpha X \beta$ corresponds to the rewriting rule $X \to Y b$. The second claim $SSC_{2,1}ID(1, 0, 1; 2, 0, 0) = RE$ follows now with Theorem 1.   □

It is shown in [6] that $SC_{1,1}ID(1, 1, 0; 1, 1, 1) \neq RE$. Analogous to the previous theorem, we show in the following that computational completeness of the system with ID $(1, 1, 0; 1, 1, 1)$ can be achieved if we increase the degree of the systems from $(1, 1)$ to $(2, 1)$. We prove the result even for simple semi-conditional ins-del systems. Thus, the size in the following result is optimal. The computational completeness of $SSC_{0,2}ID(1, 1, 0; 1, 1, 1)$ is under investigation.

Theorem 4. $SSC_{2,1}ID(1,1,0;1,1,1) = SSC_{2,1}ID(1,0,1;1,1,1) = RE$.

Proof. Consider a type-0 grammar $G = (N,T,P,S)$ in SGNF. The rules of P are labelled uniquely by numbers $[1\ldots|P|]$. We construct an SSCID system $\Pi = (V,T,\{S\},R)$ of degree $(2,1)$ and ID size $(1,1,0;1,1,1)$ as follows such that $L(\Pi) = L(G)$. The alphabet of Π is $V \subset N \cup T \cup \mathcal{M}''$. The set of rules R of Π is given as follows: (i) For every rule of type $p : X \to bY$ in G, the simulating rules are stated in Fig. 2(a). (ii) For every rule of type $q : X \to Yb$ in G, the simulating rules are stated in Fig. 2(b). (iii) Rules of type $f : AB \to \lambda$ in G are simulated by rules as stated in Fig. 3.

$$
\begin{aligned}
f1 &= [(\lambda, f, \lambda)_{ins}, \emptyset, N' \cup \mathcal{M}''] \\
f2 &= [(A, f', \lambda)_{ins}, \emptyset, N' \cup \mathcal{M}'' \setminus \{f\}] \\
f3 &= [(B, f'', \lambda)_{ins}, \emptyset, N' \cup \mathcal{M}'' \setminus \{f, f'\}] \\
f4 &= [(f, A, f')_{del}, \emptyset, N'] \\
f5 &= [(f', B, f'')_{del}, \emptyset, N'] \\
f6 &= [(f, f', f'')_{del}, \emptyset, \emptyset] \\
f7 &= [(f, f'', \lambda)_{del}, \emptyset, \{f'\}] \\
f8 &= [(\lambda, f, \lambda)_{del}, \emptyset, \{f', f''\}]
\end{aligned}
$$

Fig. 3. How to simulate $f : AB \to \lambda$ by $SSC_{0,1}ID(1,1,0;1,1,1)$

We now proceed to prove that $L(\Pi) = L(G)$. We initially prove that $L(G) \subseteq L(\Pi)$ by showing that Π correctly simulates the application of the rules of the types p, q, f. The working of the simulation rules for the cases p and q are already explained in Theorem 3. Hence, we now explain only the working of f.

The idea behind the construction of f rules is follows. We want to pin AB with the markers and to obtain a substring of the form $fAf'Bf''$. Though f is inserted at random, the correct position of f insertion is taken care with rule $f4$. Rule $f6$ is applicable only when A is deleted, since f' is inserted to the right of A and f cannot be present to the left of f' unless A is deleted. As only one f' is present in between A and B in the string (see rules $f4$ and $f5$) this makes sure that the A and B that are next to each other only gets deleted. Also, as $f4$ and $f5$ have both left and right context for deleting, we cannot delete more than one A and one B. To delete f' the presence of f'' is required which ensures the presence of B. Finally, the markers f', f'' and f are deleted. Note that the permitting sets for all the rules in the simulation of f rule are empty.

Simulation of $f : AB \to \lambda$: The rule $f : AB \to \lambda$ of G is simulated by rules of Π as stated in Fig. 3 as follows:

$$
\alpha AB\beta \Rightarrow_{f1} \alpha fAB\beta \Rightarrow_{f2} \alpha fAf'B\beta \Rightarrow_{f3} \alpha fAf'Bf''\beta \Rightarrow_{f4}
$$
$$
\alpha ff'Bf''\beta \Rightarrow_{f5} \alpha ff'f''\beta \Rightarrow_{f6} \alpha ff''\beta \Rightarrow_{f7} \alpha f\beta \Rightarrow_{f8} \alpha\beta.
$$

By induction, this shows that $L(G) \subseteq L(\Pi)$.

To show the reverse inclusion $L(G) \supseteq L(\Pi)$, assume that w_0 can be derived both in G and in Π. Hence, $w_0 \in (N'' \cup T)^*(N' \cup \{\lambda\})(N'' \cup T)^*$. If $N' \cap sub(w_0) \neq \emptyset$, from the perspective of G, we are still simulating phase I. We have to work through the explanations and case distinctions considered in Theorem 3 once more. A problem could arise if in a sentential form w_i considered in these discussions, $(\mathcal{M}'' \cup N') \cap sub(w_i) = \emptyset$, as then rules like $f1$ become applicable. However, this is never the case, so that there is no danger in starting a simulation of an f- or g-rule prematurely (i.e., when still simulating phase I).

Hence, $w_0 \in (N'' \cup T)^*$. If $w_0 \in T^*$, nothing remains to be shown. Hence, w.l.o.g., we consider a sentential form $w_0 = \alpha AB\beta$ in Π (and in G), where $A, B \in N''$ and $\alpha, \beta \in (N'' \cup T)^*$. At first glance, it may seem that we could start the simulation with one of the three rules $f1$ or $f2$ or $f3$. If we apply $f2$ and $f3$ (in this sequence, as first applying $f3$ would block $f2$, and actually any derivation starting with $f3$ on w_0 is immediately blocked), then the only applicable rule is $f5$ which will delete B between f' and f'', yielding $f'f''$ as a substring of some w''', with $w_0 \Rightarrow_{f2} w' \Rightarrow_{f3} w'' \Rightarrow_{f5} w'''$. Alternatively, this process yielding w''' can be described by applying the rewriting rule $B \to f'f''$ to w_0. The marker f has neither been introduced earlier nor could be inserted later, because its insertion rule $f1$ demands absence of f', f'' in particular. But, in the absence of f, it is impossible to delete the markers f', f'' using the rules $f6$ and $f7$, respectively.

Hence, in order to make a productive move, we have to begin by applying rule $f1$ to $w_0 = \alpha AB\beta$, which randomly inserts the marker f. So, if $w_0 \Rightarrow_{f1} w_1$, then $w_1 \in f \sqcup\!\sqcup (\alpha AB\beta)$. Notice that $f1$ cannot be applied again on w_1, nor can $g1$ be, as these rules require all rule marker symbols to be absent. This kind of reasoning reminds valid for the whole derivation that we are going to discuss, disabling unwanted premature starts of other simulations throughout. The only rules that are applicable on w_1 are $f2$, $f3$, or $f8$. As applying $f8$ simply deletes the f marker introduced in the previous derivation step, this gives no overall progress, so that we can ignore this as an unnecessary detour of the derivation process. Now we apply rules $f2$ and $f3$ to w_1 in order, as applying $f3$ first would lead to a blockage of the derivation. We remark here that it is possible that on applying $f2$, the marker f' may be placed after any occurrence of A in w_1. Similar is the case with the application of rule $f3$ with respect to B. Hence in general, if $w_0 \Rightarrow_{f1} w_1 \Rightarrow_{f2} w_2 \Rightarrow_{f3} w_3$, then $w_3 \in f \sqcup\!\sqcup f' \sqcup\!\sqcup f'' \sqcup\!\sqcup w_0$ with $Af', Bf'' \in sub(w_3)$. By the forbidden context conditions, none of the insertion rules are applicable to w_3. In order to apply $f4$, $fAf' \in sub(w_3)$ is necessary, and in order to apply $f5$, $f'Bf'' \in sub(w_3)$. The only way to get rid of the introduced markers again is to apply $f6$, $f7$ and $f8$ (in this order). But before being able to apply $f6$, the substrings fAf' and $f'Bf''$ of w_3 have to be transformed to ff' and $f'f''$, respectively, so that $f4$ and $f5$ have to be applied in any order. Hence, we find $w_3 \Rightarrow w_4 \Rightarrow w_5$, with w_5 could have been alternatively derived from w_0 by applying the rewriting rule $AB \to ff'f''$. Hence, $w_5 = \alpha ff'f''\beta$, because $w_0 = \alpha AB\beta$ was also derivable in G, and any such string contains the substring AB only in one place. It is not hard to see that $f6$ is the only applicable rule now. Application of the rules $f6, f7, f8$ in a deterministic manner (i.e., each time there is no other rule that applies, and there is only one location in the current string that may be transformed) finally yields $w_8 = \alpha\beta$. This series of rule applications, yielding w_8 from $w_0 = \alpha AB\beta$, corresponds to applying the rewriting rule $AB \to \lambda$ of G. By induction, the claim $L(\Pi) \subseteq L(G)$ follows.

Theorem 1 now entails $\mathrm{SSC}_{2,1}\mathrm{ID}(1,0,1;1,1,1) = \mathrm{RE}$.   □

In the previous theorem, the insertion had one-sided context and deletion had both the left and right contexts. In this case computational completeness was achieved with degree $(2,1)$. If we further wish to have one-sided context for deletion as well, then computational completeness is achieved with increasing the degree to $(3,1)$. These are the first RE results ever for degree $(3,1)$.

Theorem 5. $\mathrm{SSC}_{3,1}\mathrm{ID}(1,1,0;1,1,0) = \mathrm{SSC}_{3,1}\mathrm{ID}(1,0,1;1,0,1) = \mathrm{RE}$.

Proof. The proof is very similar to the previous one. We will first show that $\mathrm{SSC}_{3,1}\mathrm{ID}(1,1,0;1,1,0) = \mathrm{RE}$. The second part then follows from Theorem 1.

Consider a type-0 grammar $G = (N, T, P, S)$ in SGNF. The rules of P are labelled uniquely by numbers $[1 \ldots |P|]$. We construct an SSCID system $\Pi = (V, T, \{S\}, R)$ of degree $(3,1)$ and ID size $(1,1,0;1,1,0)$ as follows such that $L(\Pi) = L(G)$. The alphabet of Π is $V \subset N \cup T \cup \mathcal{M}''$. The set of rules R of Π is given as follows: (i) For every rule of type $p : X \to bY$ in G, the simulating rules are stated in Fig. 2(a). (ii) For every rule of type $q : X \to Yb$ in G, the simulating rules are stated in Fig. 2(b). (iii) Rules of type $f : AB \to \lambda$ in G are simulated as stated in Fig. 4(a). The idea behind the construction of f rules is very similar to the working of the rules in Fig. 3 and hence omitted. However we now highlight the difference in the two simulations (stated in Figs. 3 and 4(a)). Rules $f1, f2, f3, f7, f8$ in both the simulations are the same. If rules $f4, f5, f6$ of the former simulation deletes a symbol say α between the contexts c_1 and c_2 using the deletion rule $(c_1, \alpha, c_2)_{del}$, then the same is taken care by the rules $f4, f5, f6$ (respectively) of the latter simulation by their permitting string $c_1\alpha c_2$. Some formal arguments are presented below.

Simulation of $f : AB \to \lambda$: The intended derivation is the same as the one given in Theorem 4. This already shows that $L(G) \subseteq L(\Pi)$ by induction.

To show the reverse inclusion, we consider a sentential form $w_0 = \alpha AB\beta$ in Π, where $A, B \in N''$ and $\alpha, \beta \in (N'' \cup T)^*$. As in the proof of Theorem 4, we end up applying $f1, f2, f3$, in this order, to arrive at $w_3 = f \sqcup f' \sqcup f'' \sqcup w_0$ with $Af', Bf'' \in sub(w_3)$. The only way to continue is to apply rules $f4$ or $f5$ (in any order), with $f4$ guaranteeing that $fAf' \in sub(w_3)$ and with $f5$ guaranteeing that $f'Bf'' \in sub(w_3)$. Altogether, if $f4$ and $f5$ could have been applied, then $w_3 = \alpha fAf'Bf''\beta$, as there is only one position in w_0 where the substring AB could occur. Now, $w_3 \Rightarrow_{f4} w_4 \Rightarrow_{f5} w_5 = \alpha ff'f''\beta$, and the same result is obtained when first applying $f5$ and then $f4$. A simple case analysis shows that only $f6$ is applicable now, yielding $w_6 = \alpha ff''\beta$. From this point on, the argument continues again as in Theorem 3.   □

Theorem 6. $\mathrm{SSC}_{3,1}\mathrm{ID}(1,1,0;1,0,1) = \mathrm{SSC}_{3,1}\mathrm{ID}(1,0,1;1,1,0) = \mathrm{RE}$.

Proof. Along with the simulations presented in Figs. 2(a) and (b), we present a simulation of f rule in Fig. 4(b) which is a reflection of the simulation stated in Fig. 4(a) in order to prove that $SSC_{3,1}ID(1,1,0;1,0,1) = RE$ and hence we are not giving a formal proof. The claim $SSC_{3,1}ID(1,0,1;1,1,0) = RE$ again follows with Theorem 1.   □

$f1 = [(\lambda, f, \lambda)_{ins}, \emptyset, N' \cup \mathcal{M}'']$
$f2 = [(A, f', \lambda)_{ins}, \emptyset, N' \cup \mathcal{M}'' \setminus \{f\}]$
$f3 = [(B, f'', \lambda)_{ins}, \emptyset, N' \cup \mathcal{M}'' \setminus \{f, f'\}]$
$f4 = [(f, A, \lambda)_{del}, \{fAf'\}, \emptyset]$
$f5 = [(f', B, \lambda)_{del}, \{f'Bf''\}, \emptyset]$
$f6 = [(f, f', \lambda)_{del}, \{ff'f''\}, \emptyset]$
$f7 = [(f, f'', \lambda)_{del}, \emptyset, \{f'\}]$
$f8 = [(\lambda, f, \lambda)_{del}, \emptyset, \{f', f''\}]$

(a) $SSC_{3,1}ID(1,1,0;1,1,0)$

$f1 = [(\lambda, f, \lambda)_{ins}, \emptyset, N' \cup \mathcal{M}'']$
$f2 = [(A, f', \lambda)_{ins}, \emptyset, N' \cup \mathcal{M}'' \setminus \{f\}]$
$f3 = [(B, f'', \lambda)_{ins}, \emptyset, N' \cup \mathcal{M}'' \setminus \{f, f'\}]$
$f4 = [(\lambda, A, f')_{del}, \{fAf'\}, \emptyset]$
$f5 = [(\lambda, B, f'')_{del}, \{f'Bf''\}, \emptyset]$
$f6 = [(\lambda, f', f'')_{del}, \{ff'f''\}, \emptyset]$
$f7 = [(\lambda, f, f'')_{del}, \emptyset, \{f'\}]$
$f8 = [(\lambda, f'', \lambda)_{del}, \emptyset, \{f, f'\}]$

(b) $SSC_{3,1}ID(1,1,0;1,0,1)$

Fig. 4. Simulation of the rule $f : AB \to \lambda$

4   Conclusion and Future Work

In this paper, we introduced the mechanism of simple semi-conditional restrictions on the application of rules of ins-del systems. We described recursively enumerable languages with simple semi-conditional ins-del systems of degrees $(2,1)$ and $(3,1)$, as shown in Table 3, ignoring symmetric results obtainable from Theorem 1. We list below some most challenging problems in this area.

– While Ivanov and Verlan could prove that semi-conditional ins-del systems of degree $(2,2)$ and ID size $(1,0,0;1,0,0)$ are computationally complete, it is open if *simple* semi-conditional ins-del systems of degree $(2,2)$ and ID size $(1,0,0;1,0,0)$ characterize RE.
– Again, Ivanov and Verlan could prove that semi-conditional ins-del systems of degree $(1,1)$ and ID size $(2,0,0;1,1,0)$ are computationally complete, but even with degree $(2,1)$, it is unclear whether *simple* semi-conditional ins-del systems of this size characterize RE.
– With more limited resources, it seems to be difficult if not impossible to characterize RE. In such situations, it would be good to see if we can at least describe all context-free languages or nice sub-classes thereof, as attempted in similar situations in [1–3].

We also pose the following, a more general, open problem for further study: Given the degree (i,j) satisfying $i, j \geq 1$ and $3 \leq i + j \leq 4$, with what sizes does a simple semi-conditional ins-del system characterize RE?

References

1. Fernau, H., Kuppusamy, L., Raman, I.: Graph-controlled insertion-deletion systems generating language classes beyond linearity. In: Pighizzini, G., Câmpeanu, C. (eds.) DCFS 2017. LNCS, vol. 10316, pp. 128–139. Springer, Cham (2017). https://doi.org/10.1007/978-3-319-60252-3_10
2. Fernau, H., Kuppusamy, L., Raman, I.: Investigations on the power of matrix insertion-deletion systems with small sizes. Accepted with Natural Computing (2017)
3. Fernau, H., Kuppusamy, L., Raman, I.: On describing the regular closure of the linear languages with graph-controlled insertion-deletion systems. In: RAIRO Informatique théorique et Applications/Theoretical Informatics and Applications (2017, Submitted)
4. Fernau, H., Kuppusamy, L., Raman, I.: On path-controlled insertion-deletion systems. Accepted with Acta Informatica (2017)
5. Freund, R., Kogler, M., Rogozhin, Yu., Verlan, S.: Graph-controlled insertion-deletion systems. In: McQuillan, I., Pighizzini, G., (eds.) Proceedings Twelfth Annual Workshop on Descriptional Complexity of Formal Systems, DCFS, vol. 31. EPTCS, pp. 88–98 (2010)
6. Ivanov, S., Verlan, S.: Random context and semi-conditional insertion-deletion systems. Fundamenta Informaticae **138**, 127–144 (2015)
7. Kari, L., Thierrin, G.: Contextual insertions/deletions and computability. Inf. Comput. **131**(1), 47–61 (1996)
8. Krassovitskiy, A., Rogozhin, Yu., Verlan, S.: Computational power of insertion-deletion (P) systems with rules of size two. Nat. Comput. **10**, 835–852 (2011)
9. Krishna, S.N., Rama, R.: Insertion-deletion P systems. In: Jonoska, N., Seeman, N.C. (eds.) DNA 2001. LNCS, vol. 2340, pp. 360–370. Springer, Heidelberg (2002). https://doi.org/10.1007/3-540-48017-X_34
10. Kuppusamy, L., Rama, R.: On the power of tissue P systems with insertion and deletion rules. In: Pre-Proceedings of Workshop on Membrane Computing, vol. 28. Report RGML, pp. 304–318. University of Tarragona, Spain (2003)
11. Meduna, A., Svec, M.: Grammars with Context Conditions and Their Applications. Wiley-Interscience, New York (2005)
12. Păun, Gh., Rozenberg, G., Salomaa, A.: DNA Computing: New Computing Paradigms. Springer, Heidelberg (1998). https://doi.org/10.1007/978-3-662-03563-4
13. Takahara, A., Yokomori, T.: On the computational power of insertion-deletion systems. Nat. Comput. **2**(4), 321–336 (2003)
14. Verlan, S.: On minimal context-free insertion-deletion systems. J. Automata Lang. Comb. **12**(1–2), 317–328 (2007)
15. Verlan, S.: Recent developments on insertion-deletion systems. Comput. Sci. J. Moldova **18**(2), 210–245 (2010)

An FPGA Implementation
of a Distributed Virtual Machine

Lee A. Jensen and Lance R. Williams[✉]

Department of Computer Science, University of New Mexico,
Albuquerque, NM 87131, USA
williams@cs.unm.edu

Abstract. An expression in a functional programming language can
be compiled into a massively redundant, spatially distributed, concurrent computation called a *distributed virtual machine (DVM)*. A DVM
is comprised of bytecodes reified as actors undergoing diffusion on a
two-dimensional grid communicating via messages containing encapsulated virtual machine states *(continuations)*. Because the semantics of
expression evaluation are purely functional, DVMs can employ massive
redundancy in the representation of the heap to help ensure that computations complete even when large areas of the physical host substrate
have failed. Because they can be implemented as asynchronous circuits,
DVMs also address the well known problem affecting traditional machine
architectures implemented as integrated circuits, namely, clock networks
consuming increasingly large fractions of area as device size increases.
This paper describes the first hardware implementation of a DVM. This
was accomplished by compiling a VHDL specification of a special purpose
distributed memory multicomputer with a mesh interconnection network
into a *globally asynchronous, locally synchronous (GALS)* circuit in an
FPGA. Each independently clocked node combines a processor based
on a virtual machine for compiled Scheme language programs, with just
enough local memory to hold a single heap allocated object and a continuation.

1 Introduction

Research in *artificial life* often involves the construction of virtual worlds popu-
lated by artificial organisms reproducing and competing for resources. Whether
the artificial organisms are programs encoded in assembly language [3,23] or
cellular automata [19,29], concrete implementations make their resource use
explicit, which is necessary for meaningful competition. In contrast, in *genetic
programming*, programs are typically encoded in high-level languages, so that
mutation and crossover can more efficiently explore the space of computations
that solve a given problem [17,25]. Although this permits more rapid evolution,
the resource use of programs encoded in high-level languages can be difficult to
accurately gauge. Ideally, the two approaches could be combined: self-replicating

© Springer International Publishing AG, part of Springer Nature 2018
S. Stepney and S. Verlan (Eds.): UCNC 2018, LNCS 10867, pp. 101–116, 2018.
https://doi.org/10.1007/978-3-319-92435-9_8

programs written in a high-level language could be compiled into concrete implementations in a virtual world where they would efficiently evolve into more complex forms by competing for resources.

As a step in this direction, one of us (the second author) recently described a novel artificial organism based on a self-hosting compiler for a small subset of Scheme [31]. The gap between abstract self-description (faster evolution) and concrete implementation (transparent use of resources) was spanned by making the artificial organism an object program that replicates by compiling its own source code. Both object program (phenome) and source program (genome) were reified as a *distributed virtual machine (DVM)*, a spatially distributed, concurrent computation that can be implemented as an array of communicating finite state machines, or *asynchronous cellular automata*.

Unfortunately, simulation of the replication process on a laptop computer required nearly 8 h to finish. It goes without saying that without a huge speedup, the importance of self-replicating DVMs based on self-hosting compilers in evolutionary computation research will remain purely theoretical. The work described in the paper you are reading has, as its very practical goal, the design, implementation, and testing of a special purpose distributed memory multicomputer system able to host large numbers of self-replicating DVMs and speed up their execution by four orders of magnitude.

1.1   Emulation of SIMD by MIMD

At the present time, all of the world's fastest computers are *multicomputers* composed of a large number of general purpose processors with local memory *(nodes)* linked by a fast interconnection network. In Flynn's taxonomy [14], computers with this architecture are classified as distributed memory, multiple instruction, multiple data (MIMD) systems (see Fig. 1).

Given the potential of multicomputers to run different programs on different nodes (the first 'M' in MIMD), it's remarkable that this rarely happens. Indeed, this capability is not used when solving instances of the class of problems to which they are most commonly applied, *i.e.*, so-called *embarrassingly parallel* problems for which it is possible to achieve a speedup of up to n times on n nodes [5]. Most commonly, multicomputers function as globally asynchronous, locally synchronous (GALS) emulations of very large, single instruction, multiple data (SIMD) systems.[1] Although using a multicomputer like this might not fully exploit its capabilities, it is nevertheless useful because synchronous implementations of SIMD systems do not scale; a global clock signal cannot be transmitted to increasing numbers of spatially distributed nodes without a corresponding increase in transmission latency.

---

[1] This brings to mind the very interesting result concerning the ability of asynchronous cellular automata to emulate synchronous cellular automata with negligible slowdown [8].

1.2   Emulation of SISD by MIMD

Synchronous implementation also limits the scalability of more conventional single instruction, single data (SISD) systems. As the number of components in an integrated circuit implementation of a SISD system increases, the fraction of the circuit devoted to the distribution of the clock signal increases correspondingly. This ultimately limits the number of components a fully synchronous circuit can contain [12].

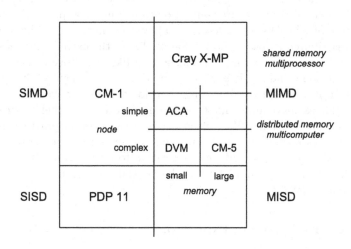

Fig. 1. Flynn's taxonomy [14] showing the relationship between SISD, SIMD and MIMD systems. The distributed virtual machine (DVM) implemented using VHDL and compiled to an FPGA is a distributed memory MIMD system where the nodes are processors based on Dybvig's virtual machine for Scheme [13] with a small amount of local memory (enough to hold a single heap allocated object and a continuation).

We have seen that multicomputers can host very large SIMD computations, and in doing so, overcome the scalability limitations of fully synchronous implementations. It is worth asking whether a multicomputer can likewise host very large SISD computations, *i.e.,* computations requiring address spaces significantly larger than the address space of any single node of the network, and in doing so, overcome the scalability limitations of synchronous implementations of SISD systems.

This question has been answered in the affirmative in prior work reported in this conference on *distributed virtual machines (DVMs)* [30]. The key insight underlying DVMs is that expression evaluation can be implemented as a spatially distributed, asynchronous, message passing computation. The program heap (including the bytecodes representing the compiled program itself) is reified as a set of *actors* that can be distributed across the nodes of a distributed memory MIMD system. Each node combines a general purpose processor with a small amount of local memory. Actors can send messages containing encapsulated virtual machine states, *i.e., continuations*, to actors hosted on adjacent nodes. They can also allocate new heap objects (also reified as actors) on adjacent nodes (if the nodes are empty). So that any actor can (in principle) communicate with any other actor, and in order to make space for new heap objects, all actors are subject to constant random motion *(diffusion)* which moves them between adjacent nodes of the network.

It is ironic that in the emulation of a SIMD system by a multicomputer, that a large part of the system's distributed memory is inefficiently used representing millions of identical copies of the same program (one copy per node), while in the emulation of a SISD system described above, a single copy of the program is efficiently distributed across all nodes. Sadly, due to the extreme slowness of the diffusion-based message passing, a DVM system like the above is unlikely to be built any time soon. Indeed, it is likely to be useful only when solving problems for which one is willing to wait a long time for the answer, yet also require a very large address space and cannot be decomposed into parallel subproblems.[2] Because this combination of factors is unlikely to occur in practice, it would seem that DVMs hosted on multicomputers are of purely theoretical interest. Happily, DVMs do have one advantage relative to conventional SISD systems, which is, they can use redundancy in the spatially distributed heap to solve problems more *robustly*.

1.3   Robust Evaluation of Expressions

Pure functional programming languages possess a property termed *referential transparency* that allows programs to be treated like expressions in mathematics [21]. In particular: (1) the value of an expression cannot depend on the order of evaluation of its subexpressions; and (2) functions must always return the same value when applied to the same arguments. Since side-effects would violate both properties, they are strictly forbidden. It follows that heap allocated objects in pure functional programming are *immutable, i.e.,* once created, they can never be changed.[3] The immutability of heap allocated objects has significant implications for DVMs since it means that multiple instances of each object (including bytecodes) can coexist in the same spatially distributed heap without inconsistency. Furthermore, multiple continuations representing parallel execution threads (each at a different point of progress) can also coexist in the same DVM. Because of referential transparency, objects created on one thread are completely interchangeable with objects created on other threads.

A DVM hosted on a modular substrate where each module represents a small fraction of the multicomputer nodes and interconnection network would possess some interesting features. First, hosted computations could survive the failure of

---

[2] Deep Thought from *The Hitch Hiker's Guide to the Galaxy* comes to mind.

[3] Despite this apparent limitation, functional programming languages are extremely expressive and modern compilers exploit referential transparency to perform powerful code optimizations.

a large fraction of the modules comprising the substrate. Second, modules could be added to the substrate either to replace modules that have failed or to extend it; hosted computations would proceed uninterrupted. Although this would not speed up a hosted computation, it would increase the likelihood that it will finish. Together, these two design features raise the possibility of computations with lifetimes longer than the hardware that hosts them.

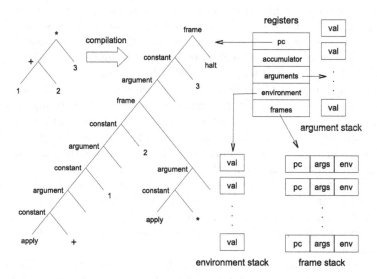

Fig. 2. Dybvig's *virtual machine* for evaluating compiled Scheme expressions showing its registers and associated heap-allocated data structures.

2 Virtual Machine

The process of evaluating expressions by compiling them into bytecodes which are executed on a VM was first described by Landin [18] for Lisp and was generalized for Scheme by Dybvig [13]. Because it plays an important role in our work, it is worth examining Dybvig's model for Scheme evaluation in some detail.

Expressions in Scheme can be numbers, booleans, primitive functions, closures, symbols, and pairs [26]. A closure is an expression with free variables together with a reference to the lexical environment; these two items suffice to describe a function in Scheme. Symbols can serve as names for other expressions and pairs are the basic building blocks of lists. As such, they are used to represent both Scheme source code and list-based data structures. All other types are self-evaluating, that is, they are simply constants.

Evaluating an expression which is not a constant or a symbol requires saving the current evaluation context onto a stack, then recursively evaluating subexpressions and pushing the resulting values onto a second stack. The second stack is then reduced by applying either a primitive function or a closure to the values it contains. Afterwards, the first stack is popped, restoring the prior evaluation context. Expressions in Scheme are compiled into trees of bytecodes which perform these operations when the bytecodes are interpreted. For book keeping during this process, Dybvig's VM requires five registers (see Fig. 2).

With the exception of the *accumulator*, which can point to an expression of any type, and the *program counter*, which points to a position in the tree of bytecodes, each of the registers in the VM points to a heap allocated data structure comprised of pairs; the *environment* register points to a stack representing the values of symbols in enclosing lexical scopes, the *arguments* register points to the stack of values which a function (or closure) is applied to, and the *frames* register points to a stack of suspended evaluation contexts.

Evaluation occurs as the contents of these registers are transformed by the interpretation of the bytecodes. For example, the *constant* bytecode loads the accumulator with a constant, while the *refer* bytecode loads it with a value from the environment stack. Other bytecodes push the frame and argument stacks (and allocate the pairs which comprise them). For example, the *frame* bytecode pushes an evaluation context onto the frame stack while the *argument* bytecode pushes the accumulator (which holds the value of an evaluated subexpression) onto the argument stack. Still other bytecodes pop these stacks. For example, the *apply* bytecode restores an evaluation context after applying a primitive function (or a closure) to the values found in the argument stack, leaving the result in the accumulator.

The most important of the remaining bytecodes in Dybvig's VM is *close* which constructs a *closure* and places a pointer to it in the accumulator. We have extended Dybvig's VM with a bytecode which is identical to his *close* bytecode except that the first value in the enclosed lexical environment of a closure created by our bytecode is a self-pointer. This device makes it possible to define recursive functions without the need for a mutable global environment. In this way, we preserve referential transparency without incurring the overhead associated with the use of the applicative order Y-combinator.

3   Distributed Virtual Machine

The actors comprising the distributed heap can represent any of the datatypes permissible in Scheme including numbers, booleans, primitive functions, closures, and pairs. Significantly, they can also represent the bytecodes of a compiled Scheme program. Like other heap-objects, a bytecode actor will respond to a *get* message by returning its value, but unlike actors representing other heap-objects, it can also send and receive encapsulated virtual machine states, or *continuations*. Upon receipt of a continuation, a bytecode actor transforms it in a manner specific to its type, then passes it on to the next bytecode in the program, and so on, until the continuation reaches a *halt* bytecode at which point the *accumulator* field of the continuation contains the result of evaluating the expression. In contrast to a conventional VM, where all control is centralized, control in a

DVM is distributed among the bytecodes which comprise it; instead of fetching bytecodes to one location where they update centralized virtual machine state, we encapsulate that state and pass it from one bytecode actor to the next (see Fig. 3).

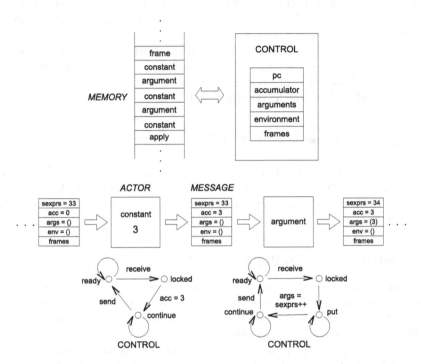

Fig. 3. Conventional *virtual machine* (top) and *distributed virtual machine* (bottom). In the DVM, the registers are encapsulated in a message called a *continuation* which is passed between bytecodes reified as actors. The *sexprs* register in the continuation holds the next free address on the execution thread. No program counter is needed since each bytecode actor knows the address of its children in the bytecode tree. Each actor is a finite state machine which transforms the continuation in manner specific to its type then passes it to the next bytecode in the program. Control is distributed not centralized.

Recall that applying a function requires the construction of a stack of evaluated subexpressions. In the simplest case, these subexpressions are constants, and the stack is constructed by executing the constant and argument bytecodes in alternation. We will use this two bytecode sequence to illustrate the operation of a DVM in more detail.

An actor of type constant bytecode in the *locked* state loads its accumulator with the address of its constant valued operand and enters the *continue* state. When a bytecode actor in the *continue* state sees its child in the bytecode tree in its neighborhood, it overwrites the child actor's registers with the contents of its own, sets the child actor's state to *locked*, and returns to the *ready* state.

The behavior of an actor of type argument bytecode in the *locked* state is more complicated. It must push its accumulator onto the argument stack, which is comprised of heap-allocated pairs. Since this requires allocating a new pair, it remains in the *put* state until it sees an adjacent empty site in its neighborhood. After creating the new pair actor on the adjacent empty site, it increments the register representing the last allocated heap address (for this execution thread) and enters the *continue* state.

For the most part, we have faithfully implemented the heap-based compiler for Scheme described by Dybvig [13] and have also respected the semantics of his VM in the implementation of the transformations performed on continuations by the bytecode actors which comprise our DVMs.

4   Four Implementation Models

In this section we describe four possible approaches to implementing DVMs, culminating in the approach which is the focus of this paper, a globally asynchronous, locally synchronous circuit implemented using a field programmable gate array (FPGA).

4.1   Shared Memory Multiprocessor

Erlang [6] is a functional programming language based on the *actor model* of concurrent computation [4, 7, 11]. Because communicating processes *(actors)* do not share state, all communication is by message passing. Actors can send messages to others if they possess their identifiers.

Given its support for the actor model, it would be straightforward to implement a DVM in Erlang; bytecodes and other heap allocated objects would be represented by actors and unique identifiers would be associated with heap addresses. A native code compiler would then compile the Erlang source code into one (or more) object programs which would then run on a uniprocessor (or a shared memory multiprocessor) system.

Sadly, the DVM implementation described above would have no advantages relative to a conventional SISD computer. Notably, it would not permit the simulation of SISD computations with address spaces larger than the memory of the shared memory multiprocessor. Furthermore, its lack of redundancy would give it no additional robustness.

4.2   Distributed Memory Multicomputer

This leads to a second possible DVM implementation. Erlang can (in principle) be compiled to set of programs distributed across the nodes of a multicomputer [33]. If the number of processors permitted, the addresses of heap allocated objects could be mapped to actors in one-to-one fashion, and actors (in turn) to nodes in many-to-one fashion using a static allocation strategy. The fact that the mapping is static would allow efficient routing of messages between communicating processes. Unlike the multiprocessor implementation sketched above, a multicomputer implementation would indeed be able to simulate a SISD computation with an address space larger than the memory contained in any single node. Furthermore, if the number of processors permitted redundancy in the representation of the distributed heap (the one-to-one address to actor mapping replaced by a one-to-many mapping), then the implementation would also be robust to node failure. However, the property which makes routing of messages relatively efficient, *i.e.*, static allocation, is incompatible with the design principle of *indefinite scalability*.

4.3 Movable Feast Machine

In recent work, Ackley et al. [1] introduced the idea of a distributed memory multicomputer system with an address space of *a priori* unknown size. Such an *indefinitely scalable* computer consists of independently clocked modules which tile space and only communicate with neighboring modules. Because information can propagate no faster than the speed of light, and because processing elements have finite size, processors and memory in an indefinitely scalable computer must be spatially distributed.

The multicomputer implementation described in the last section is not indefinitely scalable since the specifics of any static allocation strategy permitting efficient message routing would necessarily depend on the number of nodes in the network. This suggests a third possible DVM implementation, based on *reified actors*. Unlike actors in the classical actor model, which inhabit an absolute address space indexed by unique global identifiers, reified actors occupy locations on a 2D grid, and can only communicate with other actors in their neighborhoods [30]. This restriction, together with the fact that expression evaluation can potentially require a message to be sent from any object to any other object in the address space, necessitates the constant random motion of actors representing heap allocated objects on the grid.

In more recent work, Ackley, D.H. and Ackley, E.S. [2] describe a concurrent programming language for implementing reified actor models. In theory, *ulam* serves as a high-level interface to a low-level substrate consisting of an array of asynchronous cellular automata (ACA). In practice, it is a compiled language that targets an indefinitely scalable modular computer called the *Movable Feast Machine (MFM)*.

Like the multicomputer implementation, an MFM implementation of a DVM would be able to simulate a SISD computation with an address space larger than the memory contained in any single node. It would also be robust to failure of MFM modules. However, unlike the multicomputer implementation, it would (in fact) be indefinitely scalable, since modules could (in principle) be added to the machine and a running DVM computation could make effective use of them by increasing the redundancy of its heap representation.

Each module of the MFM contains a single processor with enough memory to simulate a small contiguous region of the (potentially) infinite 2D grid which forms the domain of a spatial computation. Although the size of this region is variable, in typical applications, modules simulate regions comprised of 48 × 48 sites, or 2304 sites per processor. A more direct and potentially much more efficient DVM implementation would allocate one processor per site, and these processors would implement the instruction set of the Dybvig virtual machine in hardware (as opposed to interpreting bytecodes in software).[4] These final refinements lead to a fourth possible implementation, the one we actually pursued.

4.4   Field Programmable Gate Array

Although they differ in significant respects, the three implementation models described thus far have one thing in common, namely, they all represent bytecodes and other heap allocated objects as communicating processes (actors). In the multiprocessor and multicomputer implementations, the actors existed in a non-physical, abstract identifier space. In the MFM implementation, the actors were reified by assigning them positions on a 2D grid and relying on diffusion for message passing. The fourth implementation is also actor-based, but the actors represent processors in a mesh-connected network, not heap allocated objects.

A *field programmable gate array (FPGA)* consists of an array of programmable logic blocks together with a configurable interconnection network [15]. By means of programming in the field, *i.e.,* after manufacture, FPGAs are capable of implementing a huge combinatorial space of application specific integrated circuits. VHDL is a concurrent programming language designed by the Dept. of Defense in the 1980s as a hardware description language for very high speed integrated circuits [22]. Used judiciously, a concurrent program written in VHDL can be automatically compiled to an FPGA implementation. The compilation *(synthesis)* process assigns VHDL constructs to individual logic blocks in specific locations in the device and configures the interconnection network to implement the specified functionality.

Although VHDL can (like Erlang) be used as a general purpose concurrent programming language, if it was merely used to implement a simulation of a DVM where bytecodes and heap allocated objects were represented as communicating processes (like the three other implementations), then there would be no reason to believe that the resulting concurrent program would be *synthesizeable, i.e.,* could be compiled to an FPGA implementation [9]. Furthermore, even if the program were synthesizeable, then there would be no reason to believe that its synthesized elements would operate with enough parallelism to produce a speedup relative to a sequential implementation; a concurrent program at a different level of abstraction is required to guarantee both of these properties. To ensure both synthesizeablity and effective parallelism, the communicating VHDL

---

[4] The first integrated circuit implementation of a processor customized for efficient execution of compiled Lisp programs was described by Steele and Sussman [16].

processes must represent the nodes of a distributed memory multicomputer hosting a DVM, not the heap allocated objects comprising the DVM itself.[5]

5   Technical Details

In our VHDL specification, the processes modeling multicomputer nodes are driven by independent local clocks implemented as ring oscillators [24]. A ring oscillator typically consists of an odd number of NOT gates connected in series with the last gate connected to the first gate in a feedback loop; see Fig. 4 (top). The odd number of gates insures that the output of the last gate is inverted compared to the input of the first gate. When power is applied, the circuit begins to oscillate spontaneously at a period of approximately twice the sum of the individual gate delays. The frequency of the oscillator can be decreased or increased by adding (or removing) an odd number of gates to (or from) the ring. Unfortunately, the use of ring oscillators in FPGA design is problematic since most design tools aggressively try to prevent these so-called *combinatorial loops* and aggressively optimize away what seem to be superfluous gates. These optimizations can be overcome using directives that allow for combinatorial loops and marking gates to be excluded from removal during optimization. We generate a ring oscillator at each node with a random length between 9 and 31 gates resulting in a clock frequency in the range 30 MHz–100 MHz.

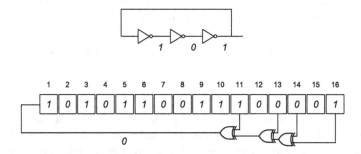

Fig. 4. Ring oscillator used to provide independent timing signals (top) and 16-bit Fibonacci linear feedback shift register (LFSR) used for pseudorandom number generation (bottom) at each node.

The globally asynchronous, locally synchronous circuit requires a source of randomness to implement the diffusion process that enables message passing. After exploring pseudorandom number generation using cellular automata, and true random number generation using ring oscillators, we settled on *linear feedback shift registers (LFSR)*, a simple and commonly used method of generating

---

[5] Others have used FPGAs to implement distributed memory multicomputers as arrays of soft processors [27,28].

pseudorandom numbers in hardware [20]. More specifically, we used a 16-bit Fibonacci LFSR in our implementation; see Fig. 4 (bottom). Each node contains a process implementing the LFSR that is clocked by a local ring oscillator. At each clock tick, the register shifts right 1 bit and the bit positions called *taps* are combined by XOR and fed back to the leftmost (input) bit. The output is the rightmost bit of the LFSR. A maximum-length period $(2^n - 1)$ is produced if the polynomial defined by the taps has an even number of terms and the tap indices are co-prime. In our implementation the seed and taps for each of the 16-bit LFSRs are randomly assigned by the code generator.

Communication and transfer of data between two nodes with independent clocks requires that the two nodes agree both that: (1) the transfer is going to occur; and (2) that the transfer has finished. If this agreement does not occur, multiple processes might simultaneously attempt to read or write data to a single node, resulting in an inconsistent device state. To avoid this problem, our design uses a *four phase handshake protocol* to ensure that data transfer between adjacent nodes is synchronized [10].

6   Experimental Results

We have implemented a DVM with an 8 bit address space on a Xilinx XC7A100 CSG324-2 FPGA [32]. The FPGA chip is manufactured using 28 nm technology and contains 101,440 logic blocks. The FPGA is hosted on a Trenz Electronics development board with a 100 MHz clock that communicates with the Xilinx Vivado Design Suite running on a Windows PC via a JTAG to USB adapter. We have been able to use this FPGA to implement DVMs with up to 40 nodes. To demonstrate the speedup due to parallelism in the implementation, we have conducted an experiment using the expression

$$(\texttt{pred (+ 2 3)})$$

where *pred* is the function that subtracts one. This expression compiles to 12 bytecodes. During evaluation, 5 additional actors representing heap allocated objects (2 numbers and 3 pairs) are created. It follows that there is enough room on a 4×5 grid to host the actors comprising the distributed heap at its maximum size of 17.

Density is grid size divided by redundancy. There is a complex relationship between density and expected evaluation time. Expected evaluation time is a function of both expected message passing latency and expected object allocation time. Expected message passing latency decreases with increasing density because senders of messages must wait less time before encountering the recipients of their messages. However, expected object allocation time increases because actors allocating objects must wait longer for empty sites to appear in their neighborhoods.[6] It follows that for a given expression and desired level of robustness, there is a density that minimizes expected evaluation time.

---

[6] Think of the so-called "8-puzzle" and its sliding plastic tiles.

The experiment was run with three different conditions: 4×5 ($\times 1$), 8×5($\times 1$) and 8×5 ($\times 1$) where $m \times n$ ($\times k$) indicates a grid of size $m \times n$ initialized with k copies of each bytecode actor. These conditions were chosen because the second and third have twice the number of nodes as the first, while the first and third have equal actor density. Equal density removes the confounding factors of different message passing latencies and different object allocation times. It consequently permits measurement of parallel speedup.

A code generator written in Java generates the VHDL code at the desired grid size and randomly populates the grid with the bytecode actors representing the compiled expression at the desired level of redundancy. The VHDL code is then synthesized by the design tool, which outputs a bitstream that is used to program the FPGA. We also insert the Integrated Logic Analyzer (ILA) core into the bitstream so we can capture data from the running device for our experimental results.

The implementation contains an additional process driven by the 100 MHz development board clock that increments a 32 bit counter on each clock pulse. This counter is used to get accurate timing at 10 ns intervals per counter increment. When a *halt* bytecode receives a continuation, the counter is stopped and the ILA is triggered to capture data. The counter value is the time required by the DVM to evaluate the compiled expression. Three different conditions were tested and each condition was run ten times. Evaluation times are shown in Table 1.

Table 1. Evaluation time in microseconds (μs)

	4×5 ($\times 1$)	8×5 ($\times 1$)	8×5 ($\times 2$)
Mean	1321.65	1953.48	1585.64
Standard deviation	471.46	603.38	391.80

The 8×5 ($\times 1$) condition is *slower* than the 4×5 ($\times 1$) condition because the lower actor density increases message passing latency. Actors must diffuse twice as long on average before bumping into the recipients of their messages. However, it is not twice as *slow*, and this is because of the *decreased* expected object allocation time of the 8×5 ($\times 1$) condition. A heap containing 17 objects barely fits on the 4×5 grid but there is plenty of room on the 8×5 grid.

Consistent with the fact that expected message passing latency decreases with increasing density, we observe that the 8×5 ($\times 2$) condition is *faster* than the 8×5 ($\times 1$) condition. However, it is not twice as *fast*, and this is because of the *increased* expected object allocation time of the 8×5 ($\times 2$) condition. A heap containing 34 objects barely fits on the 8×5 grid but a heap containing 17 objects fits quite easily.

Finally, the evaluation time for the 8×5 ($\times 2$) condition is only slightly longer than for the equal density 4×5 ($\times 1$) condition. This demonstrates that the FPGA implementation is an actual parallel circuit, solving a problem of twice the size in (essentially) the same amount of time. We believe that the evaluation time for the 8×5 ($\times 2$) condition is longer because the implementation of the DVM on the 8×5 grid very nearly fills the entire FPGA, resulting in less efficient component placement by the synthesis algorithm. We hypothesize that if the experiment were repeated using an FPGA with extra capacity, then the ratio of the times required to solve the different sized problems in the case of equal densities would be closer to one.

7   Conclusion

Recent work showed how an expression in a functional programming language can be compiled into a massively redundant asynchronous spatial computation called a distributed virtual machine (DVM). Because the semantics of expression evaluation are purely functional, DVMs can employ massive redundancy in the representation of the heap to help ensure that computations complete even when large areas of the physical host substrate have failed [30]. Because they can be implemented as asynchronous circuits, DVMs also address the well known problem affecting traditional machine architectures implemented as integrated circuits, namely, clock networks consuming increasingly large fractions of area as device size increases.

Although the use of self-replicating DVMs [31] in evolutionary computation research can potentially combine the advantages of the artificial life and genetic programming approaches, this cannot happen without a DVM implementation in hardware that is orders of magnitude faster than current software simulations. In this paper, we have described the first hardware implementation of a DVM. This was accomplished by synthesizing a globally asynchronous, locally synchronous circuit in an FPGA from a VHDL specification of a special purpose distributed memory multicomputer with a mesh interconnection network. The nodes of the multicomputer combine a processor based on Dybvig's virtual machine for executing compiled Scheme programs [13] with just enough local memory to hold a single heap allocated object and a continuation. Each node contains its own clock and pseudorandom number generator and synchronization between adjacent nodes is implemented using a four phase handshake protocol. A working implementation consisting of 40 nodes arranged in a 5×8 grid was used to evaluate a compiled Scheme expression. Significantly, the measured evaluation times were consistent with a parallel implementation. Use of FPGA devices with greater numbers of logic blocks will allow the implementation and testing of DVMs with larger grid sizes, capable of evaluating more complex expressions and with increased levels of redundancy.

References

1. Ackley, D.H., Cannon, D.C., Williams, L.R.: A movable architecture for robust spatial computing. Comput. J. **56**(12), 1450–1468 (2013)
2. Ackley, D.H., Ackley, E.S.: The ulam programming language for artificial life. Artif. Life **22**, 431–450 (2016)
3. Adami, C., Titus Brown, C., Kellogg, W.K.: Evolutionary learning in the 2D artificial life system "Avida". In: Artificial Life IV, pp. 377–381. MIT Press (1994)
4. Agha, G.: An overview of actor languages. ACM SIGPLAN Not. **21**(10), 58–67 (1986)
5. Amdahl, G.M.: Validity of the single processor approach to achieving large scale computing capabilities. In: Proceedings of the Spring Joint Computer Conference, pp. 483–485 (1967)
6. Armstrong, J.: Programming Erlang: Software for a Concurrent World. Pragmatic Bookshelf (2007)
7. Baker, H.: Actor Systems for Real-Time Computation. Ph.D. thesis. MIT, January 1978
8. Berman, P., Simon, J.: Investigations of fault-tolerant networks of computers. In: Proceedings of STOC, pp. 66–77 (1988)
9. Bezerra, E., Lettnin, D.V.: Synthesizable VHDL Design for FPGAs. Springer, Cham (2013)
10. Brand, D., Zafiropulo, P.: On communicating finite-state machines. J. ACM **30**(2), 323–342 (1983)
11. Clinger, W.: Foundations of Actor Semantics. Ph.D. thesis. MIT (1981)
12. Denning, P.J., Lewis, T.G.: Exponential laws of computing growth. Commun. ACM **60**(1), 54–65 (2017)
13. Dybvig, R.K.: Three Implementation Models for Scheme. Ph.D. thesis, University of North Carolina (1987)
14. Flynn, M.J.: Some computer organizations and their effectiveness. IEEE Trans. Comput. **C–21**(9), 948–960 (1972)
15. Hauck, S., DeHon, A.: Reconfigurable Computing: The Theory and Practice of FPGA-Based Computation. Morgan Kaufmann Publishers Inc., San Francisco (2007)
16. Steele Jr, G.L., Sussman, G.J.: Design of a LISP-based microprocessor. Commun. ACM **23**(11), 628–645 (1980)
17. Koza, J.R.: Genetic Programming: On the Programming of Computers by Means of Natural Selection. MIT Press, Cambridge (1992)
18. Landin, P.J.: The mechanical evaluation of expressions. Comput. J. **6**(4), 308–320 (1964)
19. Langton, C.G.: Self-reproduction in cellular automata. Phys. D Nonlinear Phenom. **10**(1), 135–144 (1984)
20. Lewis, T.G., Payne, W.H.: Generalized feedback shift register pseudorandom number algorithm. J. ACM **20**(3), 456–468 (1973)
21. Mitchell, J.C.: Concepts in Programming Languages. Cambridge University Press, New York (2002)
22. Pedroni, V.A.: Circuit Design with VHDL. MIT Press, Cambridge (2004)
23. Ray, T.S.: An evolutionary approach to synthetic biology, Zen and the art of creating life. Artif. Life **1**, 179–209 (1994)
24. Singh, M., Ranjan, S.M., Ali, Z.: A study of different oscillator structures. Int. J. Innovative Res. Sci. Eng. Technol. **3**(5), 12724–12734 (2014)

25. Spector, L., Robinson, A.: Genetic programming and auto-constructive evolution with the Push programming language. Genet. Programm. Evol. Mach. **3**(1), 7–40 (2002)

26. Sussman, G.J., Steele Jr., G.L.: Scheme: an interpreter for extended lambda calculus. High.-Order Symb. Comput. **11**(4), 405–439 (1998)

27. Vanderbauwhede, W., Benkrid, K.: High-Performance Computing Using FPGAs. Springer, New York (2013). https://doi.org/10.1007/978-1-4614-1791-0

28. Vassányi, I.: Implementing processor arrays on FPGAs. In: Hartenstein, R.W., Keevallik, A. (eds.) FPL 1998. LNCS, vol. 1482, pp. 446–450. Springer, Heidelberg (1998). https://doi.org/10.1007/BFb0055278

29. von Neumann, J.: Theory of Self-Replicating Automata. University of Illinois Press, Urbana (1966)

30. Williams, L.R.: Robust evaluation of expressions by distributed virtual machines. In: Durand-Lose, J., Jonoska, N. (eds.) UCNC 2012. LNCS, vol. 7445, pp. 222–233. Springer, Heidelberg (2012). https://doi.org/10.1007/978-3-642-32894-7_21

31. Williams, L.R.: Self-replicating distributed virtual machines. In: 14th International Conference on the Synthesis and Simulation of Living Systems (ALIFE 2014), New York, NY (2014)

32. Xilinx: 7 Series FPGAs Data Sheet: Overview, August 2017

33. Zuhdy, B., Fritzson, P., Engström, K.: Implementation of the real-time functional language Erlang on a massively parallel platform, with applications to telecommunications services. In: Hertzberger, B., Serazzi, G. (eds.) HPCN-Europe 1995. LNCS, vol. 919, pp. 886–891. Springer, Heidelberg (1995). https://doi.org/10.1007/BFb0046731

Algorithms for Inferring
Context-Sensitive L-Systems

Ian McQuillan[1]([⊠]), Jason Bernard[1], and Przemyslaw Prusinkiewicz[2]

[1] Department of Computer Science, University of Saskatchewan,
Saskatoon, SK, Canada
`mcquillan@cs.usask.ca`, `jason.bernard@usask.ca`
[2] Department of Computer Science, University of Calgary,
Calgary, AB, Canada
`pwp@ucalgary.ca`

Abstract. Lindenmayer systems (L-systems) are parallel string rewriting systems (grammars). By attaching a graphical interpretation to the symbols in the derived strings, they can be applied to create simulations of temporal processes, and have been especially successful in the modeling of plants. With the objective of automatically inferring L-system models in mind, here we study the inductive inference problem: the inference of models from observed strings. Exact algorithms are given for inferring L-systems that can generate input strings for both deterministic context-free and deterministic context-sensitive L-systems. The algorithms run in polynomial time assuming a fixed number of alphabet symbols and fixed context size. Furthermore, if a specific matrix calculated from the input words is invertible, then a context-sensitive L-system can be automatically created (if it exists) in polynomial time without assuming any fixed parameters.

1 Introduction

Lindenmayer systems (L-systems) are formal grammars that repeatedly rewrite strings. By definition, L-system rules are applied to each letter of a string in parallel to produce a new string, and the process is repeated on the new string. L-systems can be deterministic or non-deterministic, context-free or context-sensitive, and parameterized or non-parameterized. Theoretical properties of L-systems have been reviewed in [1,2].

By attaching a graphical interpretation to the symbols, L-systems can generate geometric objects (models). This is typically done via *turtle interpretation* wherein the turtle has a state consisting of its position and orientation, and specific symbols of the L-system provide instructions for moving, drawing, and turning in 2D [3] and 3D [2]. L-systems with turtle interpretation have been especially successful in the modelling of plants [2,4,5].

There has been relatively less work on methods for inferring L-systems. There are certain useful techniques for manually inferring models from images and real plants by experts [5], but existing approaches to automatically infer models from

© Springer International Publishing AG, part of Springer Nature 2018
S. Stepney and S. Verlan (Eds.): UCNC 2018, LNCS 10867, pp. 117–130, 2018.
https://doi.org/10.1007/978-3-319-92435-9_9

data have limitations; see survey [6]. One could imagine automatically inferring models from sequences of images over time, and this has been attempted in a preliminary fashion [7]. Acquiring such images digitally is now quite practical, from cameras in fields taking pictures periodically, to more complicated camera and sensor setups used in greenhouses, which can create point clouds representations of the plants [8]. Inference of models would be a useful step towards digitally characterizing plants, understanding the differences between them, and even breeding or designing new (real) plants from models. An intermediate step is to infer L-system models from strings that describe the plant structure. That is, given a sequence of strings produced by an unknown L-system, can the L-system itself be inferred? This problem is known as *inductive inference*. In [9], an algorithm was provided that used letter occurrence arithmetic and matrix inversion to infer a deterministic context-free L-system (D0L-system) from an initial sequence of strings. A related technique was implemented in [10], which infers D0L-systems for alphabets with at most two symbols, while calling the problem "immensely complicated" for alphabets of larger size. Inference of D0L-systems from branching structures was investigated in [11]. There has also been some investigation on inference where the given strings are non-consecutive [6,9,11,12]. In [13], an algorithm is given that infers hierarchical structure from a string by replacing repeated phrases with D0L-system rules.

In this paper, we review and extend selected algorithms for inductive inference of L-systems, and analyze their time complexity. Fixed-parameter-tractable algorithms are those that run in polynomial time if one assumes that a parameter is fixed [14]. We propose a fixed-parameter-tractable algorithm that can always infer a deterministic context-sensitive (or context-free) L-system from sequential data, if such a system exists. This algorithm runs in polynomial time for context-free systems, assuming the alphabet is of fixed size. For context-sensitive systems, it runs in polynomial time assuming that the context size is also fixed (ie. there are constants k and l such that each L-system rule only depends on at most k symbols of left context and l symbols of right context). Furthermore, a speedup to this algorithm is described by using letter occurrence arithmetic (similar to [9] for context-free systems). In particular, if a matrix defined using a generalization of the Parikh map from letters to subwords calculated on the input words is invertible, then a context-sensitive L-system can be inferred in polynomial time without fixing any parameters.

2   Preliminaries

This section provides definitions of the terms and symbols used throughout the paper.

The set of integers (positive integers, non-negative integers) is denoted by $\mathbb{Z}$ (respectively $\mathbb{N}$, $\mathbb{N}_0$). Given a vector $\boldsymbol{v}$, let $\boldsymbol{v}(i)$ be the ith component of $\boldsymbol{v}$. If M is a matrix, let $M_{*,j}$ be the column vector for the jth column of M. If X is a finite set, then $|X|$ is the number of elements in X.

An *alphabet* is a finite set of symbols. If V is an alphabet, then V^* is the set of all strings (or words) using letters from V. A *language* L is any subset of V^*. The *length* of a word w is denoted by $|w|$, and for any letter $a \in V$, $|w|_a$ is the number of occurrences of a's in w. Also, $V^i = \{w \mid w \in V^*, |w| = i\}$ and $V^{\leq i} = \{w \mid w \in V^*, |w| \leq i\}$. For a language L, $\mathrm{alph}(L) = \{a \in V \mid w \in L, |w|_a > 0\}$. Given a fixed ordering of the letters of V, $V = \{a_1, \ldots, a_k\}$, the *Parikh map* of w, $\psi(w)$, is the vector $(|w|_{a_1}, \ldots, |w|_{a_k})$. If $w \in V^*$, a *subword* of w is any y such that $w = xyz$, $x, z \in V^*$. If $w = yz$, then y is a *prefix* of w and z is a *suffix* of w. If $1 \leq i \leq j \leq |w|$, then $w[i, j]$ is the substring between positions i and j of w.

A *context-free L-system* (0L-system) is one in which productions are applied to symbols regardless of their context within the string. The 0L-system is denoted by $G = (V, \omega, P)$, where V is an alphabet, $\omega \in V^*$ is the *axiom*, and $P \subseteq V \times V^*$ is a finite set of *productions*. A production $(a, x) \in P$ is denoted by $a \to x$. The letter a is referred to as the production *predecessor*, and the word x as its *successor*. We assume that for each predecessor $a \in V$ there is at least one production $a \to x$ in P. The system 0L-system G is said to be deterministic (D0L-system) if for each $a \in V$ there is exactly one such production. Given a word $\mu = a_1 \ldots a_m \in V^*$, we write $\mu \Rightarrow \nu$ and say that μ directly derives ν if $\nu = x_1 \cdots x_m$, where $a_i \to x_i \in P$ for all $1 \leq i \leq m$. The (not necessarily direct) derivation $\Rightarrow^*$ is the reflexive and transitive closure of $\Rightarrow$ (the result of applying $\Rightarrow$ zero, one, or more times). The *language generated* by a 0L-system G is $L(G) = \{w \mid \omega \Rightarrow^* w\}$. The *developmental sequence* of length $n \in \mathbb{N}_0$ is the sequence of words $(w_1, w_2, \ldots, w_n)$, such that $\omega = w_1 \Rightarrow w_2 \cdots \Rightarrow w_n$. We call w_n the nth word generated by G.

In contrast to 0L-systems, the production chosen for each symbol in a context-sensitive L-system may depend on the surrounding symbols. Given $k, l \in \mathbb{N}_0$ such that $k + l > 0$, a deterministic (context-sensitive) (k, l)-system is a tuple $G = (V, \omega, P)$, where V and ω are the alphabet and axiom, respectively, and P is a finite set of productions of the form $u < a > v \to x$. We assume that $a \in V$, $u, v, x \in V^*, |u| \leq k$, and $|v| \leq l$. The letter a is called the *strict predecessor*, and the words u and v are the *left* and *right context*, respectively. If several context-sensitive productions could potentially be applied to the same symbol due to differently sized contexts, we assume that the production with the longest applicable left context, and then the longest applicable right context, will be chosen. In a deterministic (k, l)-system there is thus exactly one production that can be applied to any letter in any given context. If $\mu = a_1 \ldots a_m \in V^*$, we write $\mu \Rightarrow \nu$ if $\nu = x_1 \cdots x_m$ and for any $i = 1, \ldots, m$, the production $u_i < a_i > v_i \to x_i$ belongs to P, the left context u_i is the longest suffix of $a_1 \cdots a_{i-1}$, and the right context v_i is the longest prefix of $a_{i+1}a_{i+2} \cdots a_m$ among all the productions in P with the strict predecessor a_i.

3   Inferring L-Systems

In this section we study the problem of inferring an L-system from an initial sequence of words assumed to have been generated by it. We begin with the simplest case, the inference of D0L-systems, and use the resulting algorithms in the more complex case of context-sensitive L-systems.

3.1   Deterministic Context-Free L-Systems

We define the following problem:

> D0L **Inductive inference problem**: Given alphabet $V = \{a_1, \ldots, a_m\}$ and a sequence of n words over V, $\varrho = (w_1, \ldots, w_n)$, $n > 1$, determine a D0L-system G that generates ϱ as the developmental sequence of length n.

We say that G is *compatible* with ϱ if the developmental sequence of length n in G is ϱ. We also denote $S(\varrho)$ as the sum of the lengths of words in ϱ: $S(\varrho) = |w_1| + \cdots + |w_n|$. This is used when defining the time complexity of the algorithms in the paper. Before presenting the full algorithm for inductive inference, an intermediate algorithm is needed which is used within the full algorithm. The intermediate algorithm is provided with the lengths of the production successors for each letter of the alphabet as input, and it is able to determine whether the input words can produce a D0L-system with these successor lengths.

Proposition 1. *Given an alphabet* $V = \{a_1, \ldots, a_m\}$, *a sequence* $\varrho = (w_1, \ldots, w_n)$ *of* n *words over* V *such that* $V = \text{alph}(\{w_1, \ldots, w_{n-1}\})$ *and a set of integers* $j_1, \ldots, j_m \in \mathbb{N}_0$, *there exists at most one* D0L-*system* G *over* V *that is compatible with* ϱ *and satisfies condition* $j_i = |x_i|$ *for each production* $a_i \to x_i \in P$. *Furthermore,* G *can be determined in* $\text{O}(S(\varrho))$ *time.*

A constructive proof of this proposition is given by Algorithm 1. It scans the first letter of w_1, say a_i, and creates a production such that $a_i \to x_i$, where x_i consists of the first j_i letters of w_2. The algorithm continues with the second letter of w_1 and the subsequent letters of w_2. As each new letter is encountered, a production is added to the production set P. After processing all letters of w_1, the algorithm proceeds in the same way for all pairs of consecutive words $w_p, w_{p+1} \in \varrho$, $p \leq n-1$. Since $V = \text{alph}(\{w_1, \ldots, w_{n-1}\})$, every letter as well as its successor will be encountered, ensuring that every production has been determined. The result is a D0L-system G compatible with the developmental sequence ϱ. The algorithm will fail if a letter is encountered for which a production has already been found and the subsequent letters of the next word do not match the production successor. It can be seen that this algorithm runs in $\text{O}(S(\varrho))$ time.

Proposition 2. *Consider alphabet* $V = \{a_1, \ldots, a_m\}$ *and a sequence* $\varrho = (w_1, \ldots, w_n)$ *of* $n > 1$ *words over* V. *Let* k_i, $1 \leq i \leq m$ *be one plus the length of the first word in* ϱ *following the word in which* a_i *occurs for the first time. A* D0L-*system* G *compatible with* ϱ *can then be found or reported as non-existent in the worst-case time* $\text{O}((k_1 k_2 \cdots k_m) \cdot S(\varrho))$.

The constructive proof of this proposition consists of Algorithm 2 that uses a brute force approach to find a D0L-system compatible with the developmental sequence

Algorithm 1. Determines the unique D0L-system G compatible with ϱ, if it exists.

Input: Alphabet $V = \{a_1, \ldots, a_m\}$, sequence of words $\varrho = (w_1, \ldots, w_n)$ such that $V = \text{alph}(\{w_1, \ldots, w_{n-1}\})$, and the set $\beta = \{j_1 \ldots, j_m\}$ of the successor length for each letter a_i.

Output: The D0L-system G over V compatible with ϱ, if one exists, or $\emptyset$ otherwise,

```
 1: Let x₁,...,xₘ be string variables set to null
 2: for p from 1 to n − 1 do
 3:     Let r ← 1
 4:     for q from 1 to |wₚ| do
 5:         Let i be such that aᵢ is equal to wₚ[q]
 6:         if xᵢ is null then
 7:             xᵢ ← wₚ₊₁[r, r + jᵢ − 1]
 8:         else if xᵢ ≠ wₚ₊₁[r, r + jᵢ − 1] then
 9:             return ∅
10:         end if
11:         r = r + jᵢ
12:     end for
13: end for
14: return D0L-system with axiom w₁ and production set P = {aᵢ → xᵢ | 1 ≤ i ≤ m}.
```

ϱ by trying all possible combinations of successor lengths. The algorithm begins by determining, for each letter $a_i \in V$, the first word $w_p \in \varrho$ in which a_i occurs. This requires time $O(S(\varrho))$. Any D0L-system potentially compatible with ϱ has successor x_i of symbol a_i of length $|w_{p+1}|$ at most. There are $k_i = |w_{p+1}| + 1$ (including zero) possible values for the length $j_i = |x_i|$ of this successor, and $k_1 \cdot k_2 \cdots k_m$ possible combinations of the lengths $j_1, \ldots, j_m, 0 \leq j_i \leq k_i - 1$, overall. For each such combination, Algorithm 2 calls Algorithm 1 to find a D0L-system compatible with ϱ. If, in some iteration, such a D0L-system is found, it is reported as the output of Algorithm 2. In the opposite case, the algorithm reports that no D0L-system compatible with the given sequence ϱ exists. As each iteration of Algorithm 1 requires $O(S(\varrho))$ time, the overall complexity of Algorithm 2 is $O(k_1 \cdot k_2 \cdots k_m \cdot S(\varrho))$ (or $O(S(\varrho)^{m+1})$ as an upper bound). This time grows exponentially as m increases, but, if m is taken to be a fixed variable, the algorithm has polynomial time complexity with respect to $S(\varrho)$.

The construction presented in [15] with the goal of determining decidability of the D0L-system existence is very similar to the algorithm given here. We use Algorithm 2 as a subroutine within the context-sensitive algorithms later in the paper.

Different D0L-systems may generate the same sequence ϱ. For instance, the sequences generated by the systems $G_1 = (\{A, B, C\}, AB, \{A \rightarrow C, B \rightarrow AB, C \rightarrow C\})$ and $G_2 = (\{A, B, C\}, AB, \{A \rightarrow CA, B \rightarrow B, C \rightarrow C\})$ are the same. Algorithm 2 can be easily modified to determine every compatible D0L-system. Instead of returning a D0L-system G as soon as one is found, output G and continue the procedure.

Algorithm 2. Solves the DOL inference problem

Input: alphabet $V = \{a_1, \ldots, a_m\}$, sequence of words $\varrho = (w_1, \ldots, w_n)$,
Output: a DOL-system G over V that gives ϱ as the first n words generated, or $\emptyset$ if
  none exists
  1: Let $y_1, \ldots, y_m$ be integer variables set to -1
  2: **for** each letter position q of each word w_p where p is from 1 to $n-1$ **do**
  3:     Let i be such that a_i is equal to $w_p[q]$
  4:     **if** y_i is equal to -1 **then**
  5:         $y_i \leftarrow p$
  6:     **end if**
  7: **end for**
  8: **for** each vector $\beta = (j_1, \ldots, j_m)$, where $0 \le j_i \le |w_{y_i+1}|$ **do**
  9:     set G to the output of Algorithm 1 with ϱ and β
 10:     **if** $G \neq \emptyset$ **then**
 11:         **return** G
 12:     **end if**
 13: **end for**
 14: **return** $\emptyset$

Corollary 1. *For a fixed alphabet V, and sequence of words $\varrho = (w_1, \ldots, w_n)$, $n > 1$ such that $V = \mathrm{alph}(\{w_1, \ldots, w_{n-1}\})$, there is an algorithm to find every DOL-system over V that is compatible with ϱ in polynomial time $S(\varrho)$.*

3.2 Deterministic Context-Sensitive L-Systems

We now address the inductive inference problem for context-sensitive L-systems.

Deterministic context-sensitive inductive inference problem:
Given an alphabet $V = \{a_1, \ldots, a_m\}$, context lengths $k, l \in \mathbb{N}$, and a sequence $\varrho = (w_1, \ldots, w_n)$ of $n > 1$ words over V, find a deterministic (k, l)-system G that generates ϱ as the developmental sequence of length n.

Similarly to the case of DOL systems, we say that G is compatible with an input sequence $\varrho = (w_1, \ldots, w_n)$ if ϱ is the developmental sequence of length n in G.

Algorithm 1 can be extended to deterministic (k, l)-systems by replacing productions of the form $a \to x$ with productions of the form $u < a > v \to x$, for each substring uav of length $k + l + 1$ appearing in ϱ. The first k symbols then are the left context u, the next symbol is the strict predecessor a, and the last l symbols are the right context v. The inference process thus involves "sliding a window" of length $k+l+1$ over each word of $w_1, \ldots, w_{n-1}$. In addition, separate productions with shorter contexts are considered near the beginning and end of each word w_i. As discussed in Sect. 2, when applying rules for a context-sensitive L-system, the production with the longest applicable left context and then the longest applicable right context will be chosen. The left and right contexts can, however, be shorter than k and l when there are less than that many symbols of context in the letter a in w_i being rewritten, at which point, they are still the longest contexts possible. A deterministic (k,l)-system in which the context are always the longest possible up to the limit k,l is said to be of *maximal context*.

Formalizing these concepts, given a sequence of words $\varrho = (w_1, \ldots, w_n)$ over V we define the *set of (k,l)-predecessors in ϱ*, denoted by $\Delta_{k,l}(\varrho)$, as the set of all triplets $u < a > v$ such that:

- $a \in V$,
- uav is a subword of some $w \in \{w_1, \ldots, w_{n-1}\}$,
- either $|u| = k$ or $0 \le |u| < k$ and uav is a prefix of w, and
- either $|v| = l$ or $0 \le |v| < l$ and uav is a suffix of w.

We further define a $\Delta_{k,l}(\varrho)$-subset (k,l)-system to be a tuple $G = (V, \omega, P)$, where V is an alphabet, $\omega \in V^*$ is the axiom, and P is a finite set of productions $u < a > v \to x$ such that $u < a > v \in \Delta_{k,l}(\varrho)$. A $\Delta_{k,l}(\varrho)$-subset (k,l)-system is said to be compatible with ϱ if it can generate ϱ as the first sequence of words.

A $\Delta_{k,l}(\varrho)$-subset (k,l)-system may be incomplete, in the sense there may be words generated past w_{n-1} that have a subword uav such that $u < a > v \notin \Delta_{k,l}(\varrho)$. Nevertheless, by taking all remaining words $u < a > v \notin \Delta_{k,l}(\varrho)$ such that $|u| \le k$ and $|v| \le l$, and creating productions $u < a > v \to \chi$ where $\chi \in V^*$ is an arbitrary successor, results in a completely specified deterministic (k,l)-system. It is thus easy to extend any $\Delta_{k,l}(\varrho)$-subset (k,l)-system into a fully specified deterministic (k,l)-system.

Proposition 3. *Given an alphabet $V = \{a_1, \ldots, a_m\}$, context sizes k and l, a sequence of n words $\varrho = (w_1, \ldots, w_n)$ over V, and a function $f(u, a, v)$ into $\mathbb{N}_0$ defining the length of the successors for predecessors $u < a > v \in \Delta_{k,l}(\varrho)$, there exists at most one $\Delta_{k,l}(\varrho)$-subset (k,l)-system G such that:*

- *G is compatible with ϱ,*
- *$u < a > v \to x_{u,a,v}$ is a production with $f(u, a, v) = |x_{u,a,v}|$.*

Furthermore, G can be determined in $O((k + l) \cdot S(\varrho))$ time when data is stored in the form of a trie.

Proof. We construct Algorithm 3 that extends Algorithm 1 to the context-sensitive case. The goal is to take the sequence ϱ and a length associated with each predecessor string in $\Delta_{k,l}(\varrho)$ as input (these input length correspond to parameters $j \in \beta$ in Algorithm 1), and determine a $\Delta_{k,l}(\varrho)$-subset (k,l)-system compatible with these lengths. To this end, each predecessor string $u < a > v \in \Delta_{k,l}(\varrho)$ as well as the length of its successor, $f(u, a, v)$, is stored in a trie data structure. The trie enables the lookup of $u < a > v$ information in time linearly proportional to $|uav|$. The algorithm "slides a window" over each word, $w_1, \ldots, w_{n-1} \in \varrho$. As each new predecessor $u < a > v$ is encountered, the prescribed length of its successor, stored in the trie, is used to determine the letters from the next word that make up the successor (as done in Algorithm 1). The result is also stored in the trie. If a successor has previously been found, the algorithm compares it with the current candidate. If they do not match, the $\Delta_{k,l}(\varrho)$-subset (k,l)-system G sought does not exist. Alternatively, if no conflict occurs, the trie contains the inferred $\Delta_{k,l}(\varrho)$-subset (k,l)-system G, The time taken to slide such a window over ϱ is $O((k+l) \cdot S(\varrho))$.   □

Since each $\Delta_{k,l}(\varrho)$-subset (k,l)-system can be extended into a deterministic (k,l)-system by associating all elements not stored in the trie with identity productions, the following is true:

Corollary 2. *Given an alphabet* $V = \{a_1, \ldots, a_m\}$, *context sizes* k *and* l, *a sequence of* n *words* $\varrho = (w_1, \ldots, w_n)$ *over* V, *and a function* $f(u, a, v)$ *to* $\mathbb{N}_0$ *defining the length of the successors for predecessors* $u < a > v \in \Delta_{k,l}(\varrho)$, *a deterministic* (k,l)-*system* G *can be found, if it exists, such that:*

- G *is compatible with* ϱ,
- $u < a > v \to x_{u,a,v}$ *is a production with* $f(u, a, v) = |x_{u,a,v}|$.

Furthermore, one such system G, *if it exists, can be determined in* $O((k+l) \cdot S(\varrho))$ *time.*

It is also possible to use Algorithm 3 as a subprogram, similar to Algorithm 1, to consider all possible successor lengths.

Proposition 4. *Given an* m-*letter alphabet* V, *context sizes* k *and* l, *and a sequence of words* $\varrho = (w_1, \ldots, w_n)$ *where* q *is the longest word in* ϱ, *a* $\Delta_{k,l}(\varrho)$-*subset* (k,l)-*system compatible with* ϱ *can be found, if one exists, in worst case time* $O(q^{(m+1)^{k+l+1}} \cdot (k+l) \cdot S(\varrho))$.

Proof. We proceed by constructing Algorithm 4 that extends Algorithm 2 to the context-sensitive case. The algorithm starts by creating an empty trie. It then scans ϱ while sliding a window, such that when reading $u < a > v$, it stores this predecessor as well as the following information associated with it in the trie:

- the first word where $u < a > v$ occurs, denoted by $g(u, a, v)$ with $1 \le g(u, a, v) \le n - 1$,
- a unique natural number denoted by $h(u, a, v)$ such that the jth triple added to the trie is assigned j.

Both $g(u, a, v)$ and $h(u, a, v)$ can be determined as it is sliding the window. At the end, it can determine r such that $r = |\Delta_{k,l}(\varrho)|$ and each $h(u, a, v)$ is a unique number in $\{1, \ldots, r\}$. Next, it introduces two vectors α and β with r components. With a depth-first traversal of the trie, when scanning $u < a > v$, the algorithm stores one plus the length of the word following the occurrence of $u < a > v$, $1 + |w_{g(u,a,v)+1}|$, at position $h(u, a, v)$ of α; the length of the successor with predecessor $u < a > v$ is strictly less than this amount. The algorithm continues as with Algorithm 2 through all combinations of $\beta = (j_1, \ldots, j_r)$, where $0 \le j_i < \alpha(i)$, for $1 \le i \le r$. There are $\prod_{1 \le i \le r} \alpha(i)$ such combinations for β, and it calls Algorithm 3 for each. This is $O((k+l) \cdot S(\varrho) \cdot \prod_{1 \le i \le r} \alpha(i))$ time. Simplifying by letting q be the longest word in ϱ, we get $O(q^r \cdot (k+l) \cdot S(\varrho))$. Here, an upper bound for r is $(m+1)^{k+l+1}$ since there are m possibilities for a_i, $(m+1)^k$ for u (due to prefixes shorter than k), and similarly for v. Hence, the time is $O(q^{(m+1)^{k+l+1}} \cdot (k+l) \cdot S(\varrho))$.   □

This can be done in polynomial time if m, k, and l are fixed. For context-sensitive L-systems in the literature, k and l are often quite small (often only one). Therefore, for these systems, the time mainly depends on the alphabet size.

By associating any undefined elements in the trie with identity productions, the following is true:

Corollary 3. *Given an m-letter alphabet V, context sizes k and l, and a given sequence of words $\varrho = (w_1, \ldots, w_n)$ where q is the longest word in ϱ, a deterministic (k, l)-system compatible with ϱ can be found, if one exists, in worst case $O(q^{(m+1)^{k+l+1}} \cdot (k + l) \cdot S(\varrho))$ time.*

If the alphabet size and context sizes are fixed, the algorithm runs in polynomial time.

Corollary 4. *For a fixed size alphabet V, fixed k and l context sizes, and a given sequence of words ϱ, there is an algorithm to find a deterministic (k, l)-system compatible with ϱ in polynomial time, $S(\varrho)$.*

4 Speedups Using Letter Occurrence Arithmetic

4.1 Context-Free Case

This section will first present a mathematical approach to speeding up inductive inference of DOL-systems. The idea as applied to DOL systems is in fact already known [9], but we review it here as it helps understand the context-sensitive case. We then extend it to context-sensitive L-systems, for which it was not described before.

Let $G = (V, \omega, P)$ be a DOL system over alphabet $V = \{a_1, \ldots, a_m\}$, x_i the successor of production $a_i \rightarrow x_i \in P$, and $x_i^{(j)} = |x_i|_{a_j}$ the number of occurrences of letter a_j in this successor for $1 \leq i, j \leq m$. The *growth matrix* of G, denoted by $M(G)$, is then the $m \times m$ matrix such that position i, j contains $x_i^{(j)}$.

Given a sequence of words $\varrho = (w_1, \ldots, w_n)$ over $V = \{a_1, \ldots, a_m\}$, and $s, r \in \mathbb{N}$ such that $1 \leq s \leq s + r - 1 \leq n$, let $Y_{s,r}(\varrho)$ be the $r \times m$ matrix such that element i, j is $|w_{s+i-1}|_{a_j}$: the number of occurrences of letter a_j in word w_{s+i-1}. In other words, row i of $Y_{s,r}(\varrho)$ is the Parikh map of w_{s+i-1}. We then have:

$$\underbrace{\begin{bmatrix} y_1^{(1)} & y_1^{(2)} & \cdots & y_1^{(m)} \\ y_2^{(1)} & y_2^{(2)} & \cdots & y_2^{(m)} \\ \vdots & & \ddots & \vdots \\ y_m^{(1)} & y_m^{(2)} & \cdots & y_m^{(m)} \end{bmatrix}}_{Y_{1,m}(\varrho)} \underbrace{\begin{bmatrix} x_1^{(1)} & x_1^{(2)} & \cdots & x_1^{(m)} \\ x_2^{(1)} & x_2^{(2)} & \cdots & y_2^{(m)} \\ \vdots & & \ddots & \vdots \\ x_m^{(1)} & x_m^{(2)} & \cdots & x_m^{(m)} \end{bmatrix}}_{M(G)} = \underbrace{\begin{bmatrix} y_2^{(1)} & y_2^{(2)} & \cdots & y_2^{(m)} \\ y_3^{(1)} & y_3^{(2)} & \cdots & y_3^{(m)} \\ \vdots & & \ddots & \vdots \\ y_{m+1}^{(1)} & y_{m+1}^{(2)} & \cdots & y_{m+1}^{(m)} \end{bmatrix}}_{Y_{2,m}(\varrho)} \quad (1)$$

Now, suppose that we are given an initial sequence of words, $\varrho = (w_1, \ldots, w_{m+1})$, generated by an unknown DOL-system G over $V = \{a_1, \ldots, a_m\}$. The growth matrix M of G is a (not necessarily unique) solution to the equation

$$Y_{1,m}(\varrho)M = Y_{2,m}(\varrho). \quad (2)$$

The sum of the entries in row i of M is the length of the presumed successor x_i of a_i. Given this length for each $i = 1, \ldots, m$, we can use Algorithm 1 to infer the D0L-system compatible with ϱ, if it exists. As the word lengths are non-negative integers, only integer solutions to Eq. 2 are of interest, i.e., we consider Eq. 2 as a system of linear diophantine equations. The general solution to such a system can be calculated in polynomial time (Corollary 5.3c of [16]). The solution space of possible entries in M is further reduced to be finite, because each element $x_i^{(j)}$ must satisfy the inequality $0 \leq x_i^{(j)} \leq |w_{p+1}|_{a_j}$: the number of occurrences of letter a_j in the successor x_i of a_i cannot exceed the number of occurrences of a_j in the word w_{p+1} derived from a word w_p in which a_i occurs. Although we do not have a quantitative evaluation of the resulting speedup, the use of diophantine equations appears to significantly reduce the number of calls to Algorithm 1, compared to the brute-force Algorithm 2.

An important special case occurs when matrix $Y_{1,m}(\varrho)$ is invertible. The growth matrix $M = Y_{1,m}(\varrho)^{-1} Y_{2,m}(\varrho)$ is then unique. If it contains anything other than non-negative integers, a D0L-system compatible with the given sequence ϱ does not exist. If, in contrast, all elements of M are non-negative integers, Algorithm 1 can find the D0L-system compatible with ϱ (which is then unique) or determine that such a system does not exist, in $O(S(\varrho))$ time (Proposition 1). Since the inverse of an $m \times m$ matrix can be calculated in $O(m^{2.376})$ time ([17] combined with later result on faster matrix multiplication [18]), the following is immediate:

Proposition 5. *Given an m-letter alphabet V and a sequence of words $\varrho = (w_1, \ldots, w_{m+1})$ such that $Y_{1,m}(\varrho)$ is invertible, there is an algorithm that determines the unique D0L system compatible with ϱ, or reports that none exists, in time $O(S(\varrho) + m^{2.376})$. Furthermore, if m is fixed, then the algorithm runs in time $O(S(\varrho))$.*

Lastly, if more than $m + 1$ words are given as input, as long as there are m consecutive words starting at word i such that $Y_{i,m}$ is invertible, then this is enough to uniquely determine a D0L system if it exists.

4.2 Context-Sensitive Case

This procedure is extended next to work with deterministic (k, l)-systems.

Let $k, l \in \mathbb{N}$, and consider a deterministic (k, l)-system $G = (V, \omega, P)$ that is maximal context. Next, consider some fixed ordering (such as lexicographic) of all elements in $V^{\leq k} < V > V^{\leq l}$ (all possible windows including maximal contexts). Let r be the number of these words, and let z_i be the ith such word, for $1 \leq i \leq r$. Here, if $m = |V|$, then $r \leq (m + 1)^{k+l} m$.

Given a word $w \in V^*$, define the (k, l)-windowed Parikh vector of w as the r-coordinate vector $\psi_{k,l}(w)$, where for $1 \leq i \leq r$,

$$\psi_{k,l}(w)(i) = |\{q \mid z_i = u < a > v, w[q, s] = uav,$$
$$\text{and either } k = |u| \text{ or } |u| < k \text{ and } q = 1,$$
$$\text{and either } l = |v| \text{ or } |v| < l \text{ and } s = |w|\}|.$$

This can be explained as follows: Consider position i of the vector where $z_i = u < a > v$. Intuitively, position i would give the number of times a production with predecessor $u < a > v$ would get applied when rewriting w with maximal contexts. When $|u| = k$ and $|v| = l$, this is the number of times z_i occurs as a subword of w; when $|u| < k$ and $|v| = l$, this is 1 if uav is a prefix of w and 0 otherwise; when $|u| = k$ and $|v| < l$, this is 1 if uav is a suffix of w and 0 otherwise; when $|u| < k$ and $|v| < l$, this is 1 if $uav = w$ and 0 otherwise.

Let i satisfy $1 \le i \le r$, let x_i be the string such that $(z_i = u < a > v) \to x_i \in P$, and let $x_i^{(j)} = \psi(x_i)(j)$, for $1 \le j \le m$ ($\psi(x_i)$ is the normal Parikh vector). The growth matrix of G, denoted by $M(G)$, is the $r \times m$ matrix:

$$M(G) = \begin{bmatrix} x_1^{(1)} & x_1^{(2)} & \dots & x_1^{(m)} \\ x_2^{(1)} & x_2^{(2)} & \dots & y_2^{(m)} \\ \vdots & & \ddots & \vdots \\ x_r^{(1)} & x_r^{(2)} & \dots & x_r^{(m)} \end{bmatrix} \tag{3}$$

Let w_i be the ith word derived by G, for $1 \le i \le n$ (thus $\omega = w_1$). Furthermore, let $t_i^{(j)} = \psi_{k,l}(w_i)(j)$ for $1 \le i < n, 1 \le j \le r$. Let $s, r \in \mathbb{N}$ be such that $1 \le s \le s+r-1 \le n-1$, and let $T_{s,r}(\varrho)$ be the $r \times r$ matrix such that the element at position i, j is $t_{i+s-1}(j)$ (that is, the rows are $\psi_{k,l}(w_s), \dots, \psi_{k,l}(w_{s+r-1})$). Similar to Eq. 1, we have:

$$T_{1,r}(\varrho)M(G) = Y_{2,r}(\varrho). \tag{4}$$

Note $Y_{2,r}(\varrho)$ is an $r \times m$ matrix calculated using the normal Parikh map.

Now, suppose that we are given an initial sequence of words $\varrho = (w_1, \dots, w_n)$ over $V = \{a_1, \dots, a_m\}$ and context sizes k, l, and the goal is to determine if this sequence can be generated by an unknown deterministic (k, l)-system. Then, on input ϱ, an algorithm can scan one word at a time while sliding a window, and make a trie to hold $\Delta_{k,l}(\varrho)$ as with the proof of Proposition 4 (recall $\Delta_{k,l}(\varrho)$ is the set of all triplets $u < a > v$ that occur with maximal contexts in all but the last word of ϱ). Let $r = |\Delta_{k,l}(\varrho)|$. A vector α with r components is calculated. In the trie, when scanning $u < a > v$, the following are stored: the index of the first word where $u < a > v$ occurs, $g(u, a, v)$; and some unique number $h(u, a, v)$ from 1 to r giving a position of α. The length $1 + |w_{g(u,a,v)+1}|$ is stored in position $h(u, a, v)$ of α. Indeed, after all words $u < a > v$ are added to the trie based on ϱ, it is possible to calculate $r = |\Delta_{k,l}(\varrho)|$, and the $h(u, a, v)$ values then provides the fixed ordering of the elements in $\Delta_{k,l}(\varrho)$. This ordering can then be used for the calculation of $\psi_{k,l}(w_i)$.

Assume henceforth that $n \ge r + 1$. Then, as with DOL systems, an intermediate goal is instead to determine all integer matrices M such that

$$T_{1,r}(\varrho)M = Y_{2,r}(\varrho). \tag{5}$$

By Eq. 4, if M is the growth matrix of a (k, l)-system that is compatible with ϱ, then M is a solution to this equation. In this case, the sum of the entries of row

i gives the length of the successor of the production with predecessor $u < a > v$, where $h(u, a, v) = i$.

Instead of using brute force to try all possibilities of length combinations, the procedure instead calculates the inverse of $T_{1,r}(\varrho)$ if it exists. If the inverse does exist, it solves for M as $T_{1,r}(\varrho)^{-1} Y_{2,r}(\varrho)$. Indeed, if there is a (k,l)-system compatible with ϱ, then M must be the growth matrix of the maximal context (k,l)-system compatible with ϱ. From M, the length of each production is implied, and Proposition 3 then provides an algorithm to assess compatibility. In terms of complexity, the trie can be built in $O((k+l) \cdot S(\varrho))$ time. The inverse can be computed in $O(r^{2.376})$ if it exists and so $M = T_{1,r}(\varrho)^{-1} \cdot Y_{2,r}(\varrho)$ can again be computed in $O(r^{2.376})$ time. Then the row sums can be stored back in the trie, and by using Proposition 3, the unique maximal context $\Delta_{k,l}(\varrho)$-subset (k,l)-system, if it exists, can be computed in time $O((k+l) \cdot S(\varrho))$ time.

Proposition 6. *Given an m-letter alphabet V, context sizes k, l, and a sequence of words $\varrho = (w_1, \ldots, w_n)$ over V, with $r = |\Delta_{k,l}(\varrho)|$, $n \geq r + 1$, and such that $T_{1,r}(\varrho)$ is invertible, there is an algorithm that determines the unique maximal context $\Delta_{k,l}(\varrho)$-subset (k,l)-system compatible with ϱ, or reports that none exists, in time $O((k+l) \cdot S(\varrho) + r^{2.376})$.*

By setting all unused productions not in the trie to be identity productions, the following is implied:

Corollary 5. *Given an m-letter alphabet V, context sizes k, l, and a sequence of words $\varrho = (w_1, \ldots, w_n)$ over V, with $r = |\Delta_{k,l}(\varrho)|$, $n \geq r + 1$, and such that $T_{1,r}(\varrho)$ is invertible, there is an algorithm that determines a deterministic (k,l)-system compatible with ϱ, or reports that none exist, in time $O((k+l) \cdot S(\varrho) + r^{2.376})$.*

As with D0L-systems, more generally there can be more than one matrix that is a solution to Eq. 5. It is again possible to consider Eq. 5 as a system of linear diophantine equations. Then for each solution of M, Proposition 3 can be used to assess compatibility. Lastly, to use matrix inversion, if $n > r + 1$, then it is only necessary to have $T_{i,r}$ be an invertible matrix for some i in order to apply this approach.

5   Conclusions and Future Directions

In this paper, polynomial time algorithms are provided that solve the inductive inference problem, when the size of the alphabet and the context sizes are fixed. Then a speedup is provided using letter occurrence arithmetic. For context-sensitive L-systems, if a matrix defined by using a generalization of the Parikh map on the input words gives an invertible matrix, then the context-sensitive system can be inferred in polynomial time in the context lengths and the sum of the input word lengths. This technique can also be used when the matrix is not invertible by using solutions to linear diophantine equations.

Some immediate questions arise from this work. First, is there a complexity class such that inferring different types of L systems where the alphabet size is not fixed is hard for that class? Also, can any approaches presented here work for nondeterministic (or stochastic) L-systems? In addition, from a practical perspective, can these approaches be combined with a computer vision approach to automatically infer L-systems from sequences of images?

Acknowledgements. The research of all authors was supported in part by a grant from the Plant Phenotyping and Imaging Research Centre (P2IRC), and in part by grants from Natural Sciences and Engineering Research Council of Canada (I. McQuillan grant 2016–06172, J. Bernard scholarship, P. Prusinkiewicz grant 2014–05325).

References

1. Rozenberg, G., Salomaa, A.: The Mathematical Theory of L Systems. Academic Press Inc., New York (1980)
2. Prusinkiewicz, P., Lindenmayer, A.: The Algorithmic Beauty of Plants. Springer, New York (1990). https://doi.org/10.1007/978-1-4613-8476-2
3. Prusinkiewicz, P.: Graphical applications of L-systems. In: Proceedings of Graphics Interface 1986/Vision Interface 1986, pp. 247–253 (1986)
4. Prusinkiewicz, P.: Designing and growing virtual plants with L-systems. In: Proceedings of the XXVI International Horticultural Congress, vol. 630, pp. 15–28. Acta Horticulturae (2004)
5. Prusinkiewicz, P., Mündermann, L., Karwowski, R., Lane, B.: The use of positional information in the modeling of plants. In: Proceedings of the 28th Annual Conference on Computer Graphics and Interactive Techniques, SIGGRAPH 2001, pp. 289–300. ACM (2001)
6. Ben-Naoum, F.: A survey on L-system inference. INFOCOMP J. Comput. Sci. **8**(3), 29–39 (2009)
7. Runqiang, B., Chen, P., Burrage, K., Hanan, J., Room, P., Belward, J.: Derivation of L-system models from measurements of biological branching structures using genetic algorithms. In: Hendtlass, T., Ali, M. (eds.) IEA/AIE 2002. LNCS (LNAI), vol. 2358, pp. 514–524. Springer, Heidelberg (2002). https://doi.org/10.1007/3-540-48035-8_50
8. Sirault, X., Fripp, J., Paproki, A., Kuffner, P., Nguyen, C., Li, R., Daily, H., Guo, J., Furbank, R.: Plantscan[TM]: a three-dimensional phenotyping platform for capturing the structural dynamic of plant development and growth. In: 7th International Conference on Functional-Structural Plant Models, pp. 45–48 (2013)
9. Doucet, P.G.: The syntactic inference problem for d0l-sequences. In: Rozenberg, G., Salomaa, A. (eds.) L Systems. LNCS, vol. 15, pp. 146–161. Springer, Heidelberg (1974). https://doi.org/10.1007/3-540-06867-8_12
10. Nakano, R., Yamada, N.: Number theory-based induction of deterministic context-free L-system grammar. In: International Conference on Knowledge Discovery and Information Retrieval, SCITEPRESS, pp. 194–199 (2010)
11. Jürgensen, H., Lindenmayer, A.: Inference algorithms for developmental systems with cell lineages. Bull. Math. Biol. **49**(1), 93–123 (1987)
12. Feliciangeli, H., Herman, G.T.: Algorithms for producing grammars from sample derivations: a common problem of formal language theory and developmental biology. J. Comput. Syst. Sci. **7**(1), 97–118 (1973)

13. Nevill-Manning, C.G., Witten, I.H.: Identifying hierarchical structure in sequences: a linear-time algorithm. J. Artif. Intell. Res. **7**(1), 67–82 (1997)

14. Flum, J., Grohe, M.: Parameterized Complexity Theory. Texts in Theoretical Computer Science. An EATCS Series. Springer, Heidelberg (2006). https://doi.org/10.1007/3-540-29953-X

15. Herman, G.T., Rozenberg, G.: Developmental Systems and Languages. North-Holland Publishing Company, Oxford (1975)

16. Schrijver, A.: Theory of Linear and Integer Programming. Wiley, New York (1986)

17. Bunch, J.R., Hopcroft, J.E.: Triangular factorization and inversion by fast matrix multiplication. Math. Comput. **28**(125), 231–236 (1974)

18. Coppersmith, D., Winograd, S.: Matrix multiplication via arithmetic progressions. J. Symb. Comput. **9**(3), 251–280 (1990). Computational algebraic complexity editorial

Reaction Mining for Reaction Systems

Artur Męski[1,2(✉)], Maciej Koutny[3], and Wojciech Penczek[1,4]

[1] Institute of Computer Science, PAS, Jana Kazimierza 5, 01-248 Warsaw, Poland
{meski,penczek}@ipipan.waw.pl
[2] Vector GB Limited, London WC2N 4JF, UK
artur.meski@vector.com
[3] School of Computing, Newcastle University,
Newcastle upon Tyne NE1 7RU, UK
maciej.koutny@ncl.ac.uk
[4] Faculty of Science, Institute of Computer Science, Siedlce University,
3-Maja 54, 08-110 Siedlce, Poland

Abstract. Reaction systems are a formal model for specifying and analysing computational processes in which reactions operate on sets of entities (molecules), providing a framework for dealing with qualitative aspects of biochemical systems. This paper is concerned with reaction systems in which entities can have discrete concentrations and reactions operate on multisets of entities, providing a succinct framework for dealing with quantitative aspects of systems. This is facilitated by a dedicated linear-time temporal logic which allows one to express and verify a wide range of behavioural system properties.

In practical applications, a reaction system with discrete concentrations may only be partially specified, and effective calculation of the missing details would provide an attractive design approach. To develop such an approach, this paper introduces reaction systems with parameters representing the unknown parts of the reactions. The main result is a method which attempts to replace these parameters in such a way that the resulting reaction system operating in a given external environment satisfies a given temporal logic formula. We provide a suitable encoding of parametric reaction systems in SMT, and outline a synthesis procedure based on bounded model checking for solving the synthesis problem. We also provide preliminary experimental results demonstrating the feasibility of the new synthesis method.

The seminal paper [11] introduced a fundamental *reaction systems* model for computational processes inspired by the functioning of a living cell. The model can capture in a very simple way the basic mechanisms underpinning the dynamic behaviour of a living cell. A key feature of reaction systems is that the latter results from the interactions of biochemical reactions based on the mechanisms of facilitation and inhibition, i.e., the products of reactions may facilitate or inhibit each other. The basic model of reaction systems represents the reactions, states, and dynamic processes using (tuples of) finite sets, and so it directly captures the qualitative aspects of systems. Having said that, more involved concepts can be introduced using the basic ones.

© Springer International Publishing AG, part of Springer Nature 2018
S. Stepney and S. Verlan (Eds.): UCNC 2018, LNCS 10867, pp. 131–144, 2018.
https://doi.org/10.1007/978-3-319-92435-9_10

Reaction system related research topics have so far been motivated by biological issues or by a need to understand computations/processes underlying the dynamic behaviour of reaction systems (see, e.g., [9,10]). A number of extensions were also introduced, e.g., reaction systems with time [12], reaction systems with durations [5], and quantum and probabilistic reaction systems [16]. Mathematical properties of reaction systems were investigated in, e.g., [1,7,8,13–15,23–26].

Examples of applications of reaction systems to modelling of systems include, e.g., [4,6]. Verification of reaction systems was discussed in, e.g., [2,3,20]. The papers [19,22] introduced reaction systems with discrete concentrations of entities and reactions operating on multisets of entities, resulting in a model allowing direct quantitative modelling. Although there exist other approaches that support modelling of complex dependencies of concentration levels and their changes, e.g., chemical reaction networks theory based on [17], reaction systems provide much simpler framework and the processes of reaction systems take into account interactions with the external environment. Discrete concentrations can be simulated in the original qualitative reaction systems, but reaction systems with discrete concentrations provide much more succinct representations in terms of the number of entities being used, and allow for more efficient verification [19]. The properties being verified are expressed in rsLTL which is a version of the linear-time temporal logic defined specifically for reaction systems.

In practical applications, a reaction system with discrete concentrations may have only partially specified reactions, and a reaction mining i.e., an effective filling in the missing details would provide an attractive design approach. To develop such an approach, this paper introduces reaction systems with parameters representing the unknown parts of the reactions. The main result is a methodology which attempts to replace these parameters in such a way that the resulting reaction system satisfies a given rsLTL *formula* when operating in a given external *environment*. Intuitively, such a formula might correspond to a number of observations (runs) of the behaviour of a partially specified system. Moreover, the environment is specified using a *context automaton* which represents the influence of the bigger system in which the reaction system with discrete concentrations operates. We provide a suitable encoding of parametric reaction systems in SMT, and propose a synthesis procedure based on bounded model checking for solving the synthesis problem. We also provide preliminary successful experimental results demonstrating the scalability of the new synthesis method. The paper is organised in the following way. In the next section, we recall the basic notations and definitions used by reaction systems with discrete concentrations. Section 2 introduces parametric reaction systems, and the following section defines SMT-based encoding of such systems. Section 4 discusses experimental evaluation of the synthesis approach introduced in this paper, and Sect. 5 draws some concluding remarks.

1   Preliminaries

A *multiset* over a set X is a mapping $\mathbf{b} : X \rightarrow \{0, 1, \dots\}$, and its *carrier* is $carr(\mathbf{b}) = \{x \in X \mid \mathbf{b}(x) > 0\}$. The *empty* multiset $\varnothing_X$ is one with the empty carrier. $\mathcal{B}(X)$ denotes the set of all multisets over X. For a finite $\mathbf{B} \subset \mathcal{B}(X)$, $\mathbb{\wedge}(\mathbf{B})$ is the multiset over X such that $\mathbb{\wedge}(\mathbf{B})(x) = \max(\{0\} \cup \{\mathbf{b}(x) \mid \mathbf{b} \in \mathbf{B}\})$, for every $x \in X$. For $\mathbf{b}, \mathbf{b}' \in \mathcal{B}(X)$, $\mathbf{b} \le \mathbf{b}'$ if $\mathbf{b}(x) \le \mathbf{b}'(x)$, for every $x \in X$.

We use $x \mapsto i$ for denoting the multiplicity of x in multisets; e.g., $\{x \mapsto 1, y \mapsto 2\}$ is a multiset with one copy of x, two copies of y, and nothing else. If the multiplicity of an entity is 1, we may also simply omit the value, e.g., $\{x, y \mapsto 2\}$.

The syntax of *multiset expressions* $BE(X)$ is defined by the following grammar: $\mathfrak{a} :: = true \mid e \sim c \mid e \sim e \mid \neg \mathfrak{a} \mid \mathfrak{a} \vee \mathfrak{a}$, where $\sim \in \{<, \le, =, \ge, >\}$, $e \in X$, $c \in \mathbb{N}$. Then $\mathbf{b} \models_b \mathfrak{a}$ means that $\mathfrak{a}$ holds for $\mathbf{b} \in \mathcal{B}(X)$ assuming that:

$$\mathbf{b} \models_b true \quad \text{for every } \mathbf{b} \in \mathcal{B}(X),$$
$$\mathbf{b} \models_b e \sim c \quad \text{iff } \mathbf{b}(e) \sim c,$$
$$\mathbf{b} \models_b e \sim e' \quad \text{iff } \mathbf{b}(e) \sim \mathbf{b}(e'),$$
$$\mathbf{b} \models_b \neg \mathfrak{a} \quad \text{iff } \mathbf{b} \not\models_b \mathfrak{a},$$
$$\mathbf{b} \models_b \mathfrak{a} \vee \mathfrak{a}' \quad \text{iff } \mathbf{b} \models_b \mathfrak{a} \text{ or } \mathbf{b} \models_b \mathfrak{a}'.$$

Reaction Systems with Discrete Concentrations. The enabling of biochemical reactions may depend not only on the availability of reactants and the absence of inhibitors, but also on their concentration levels. We will now recall an extension of the basic reaction systems with explicit representation of the discrete concentration levels of entities (the k-th level of concentration of x is represented by a multiset containing k copies of x). The model uses multisets rather than sets of entities, but otherwise retains key features of the original framework.

A *reaction system with discrete concentrations* (rsc) is a pair $rsc = (S, A)$, where S is a finite *background* set (comprising *entities*) and A is a nonempty finite set of *reactions* over the background set. Each reaction is a triple $a = (\mathbf{r}, \mathbf{i}, \mathbf{p})$ such that $\mathbf{r}, \mathbf{i}, \mathbf{p}$ are nonempty multisets over S with $\mathbf{r}(e) < \mathbf{i}(e)$, for every $e \in carr(\mathbf{i})$. The multisets $\mathbf{r}, \mathbf{i}$, and $\mathbf{p}$ are respectively denoted by $\mathbf{r}_a, \mathbf{i}_a$, and $\mathbf{p}_a$ and called the *reactant*, *inhibitor*, and *product concentration levels* of reaction a. An entity e is an inhibitor of a whenever $e \in carr(\mathbf{i}_a)$.

A reaction $a \in A$ is *enabled* by $\mathbf{t} \in \mathcal{B}(S)$, denoted $en_a(\mathbf{t})$, if $\mathbf{r}_a \le \mathbf{t}$ and $\mathbf{t}(e) < \mathbf{i}_a(e)$, for every $e \in carr(\mathbf{i}_a)$. The *result* of a on $\mathbf{t}$ is given by $res_a(\mathbf{t}) = \mathbf{p}_a$ if $en_a(\mathbf{t})$, and by $res_a(\mathbf{t}) = \varnothing_S$ otherwise. Then the *result* of A on $\mathbf{t}$ is $res_A(\mathbf{t}) = \mathbb{\wedge}\{res_a(\mathbf{t}) \mid a \in A\}$.

Intuitively, $\mathbf{t}$ is a *state* of a biochemical system being modelled, and $\mathbf{t}(e)$ is the *concentration level* of each entity e (e.g., $\mathbf{t}(e) = 0$ indicates that e is not present in the current state while $\mathbf{t}(e) = 1$ indicates that e is present at its lowest concentration level). A reaction a is enabled by $\mathbf{t}$ and can take place if the current concentration levels of all its reactants are at least as high as those specified by $\mathbf{r}_a$, and the current concentration levels of all its inhibitors (i.e., entities in the carrier of $\mathbf{i}_a$) are below the thresholds specified by $\mathbf{i}_a$.

The above gives the behaviour of an rsc as a closed system. To define its operation as an open system, we need a suitable representation of the environment. A *context automaton* over a background set S is a triple $ca = (Q, q^{init}, R)$, where Q is a finite set of *states*, $q^{init} \in Q$ is the *initial state*, and $R \subseteq Q \times \mathcal{B}(S) \times Q$ is the *transition relation*. We assume that, for every $q \in Q$, there exist $\mathbf{c} \in \mathcal{B}(S)$ and $q' \in Q$ such that $(q, \mathbf{c}, q') \in R$. We also denote $(q, \mathbf{c}, q') \in R$ by $q \xrightarrow{\mathbf{c}} q'$.

A *context restricted reaction system with discrete concentrations* (crrsc) [22] is a pair $crrsc = (rsc, ca)$ such that $rsc = (S, A)$ is an rsc, and $ca = (Q, q^{init}, R)$ is a context automaton over S. The dynamic behaviour of *crrsc* is captured by the state sequences of its interactive processes, where an *interactive process* in *crrsc* is a triple $\pi = (\zeta, \gamma, \delta)$ such that:

- $\zeta = (z_0, z_1, \ldots, z_n)$, $\gamma = (\mathbf{c}_0, \mathbf{c}_1, \ldots, \mathbf{c}_n)$, and $\delta = (\mathbf{d}_0, \mathbf{d}_1, \ldots, \mathbf{d}_n)$
- $z_0, z_1, \ldots, z_n \in Q$ with $z_0 = q^{init}$
- $\mathbf{c}_0, \mathbf{c}_1, \ldots, \mathbf{c}_n, \mathbf{d}_0, \mathbf{d}_1, \ldots, \mathbf{d}_n \in \mathcal{B}(S)$ with $\mathbf{d}_0 = \varnothing_S$
- $(z_i, \mathbf{c}_i, z_{i+1}) \in R$, for every $i \in \{0, \ldots, n-1\}$
- $\mathbf{d}_i = res_A(\bigwedge\{\mathbf{d}_{i-1}, \mathbf{c}_{i-1}\})$, for every $i \in \{1, \ldots, n\}$.

The sequence γ is the context sequence of π and δ is the *result* sequence, while ζ is simply the sequence of states of ca. The *state sequence* of π is $\tau = (\mathbf{w}_0, \ldots, \mathbf{w}_n) = (\bigwedge\{\mathbf{c}_0, \mathbf{d}_0\}, \ldots, \bigwedge\{\mathbf{c}_n, \mathbf{d}_n\})$.

Reaction Systems Linear-Time Temporal Logic. Here we recall the logic (rsLTL) introduced in [22], which captures requirements imposed on paths of crrsc.

The *model* of a crrsc given by $crrsc = (rsc, ca)$ with $rsc = (S, A)$ and $ca = (Q, q_{init}, R)$ is the triple $\mathcal{M}(crrsc) = (\mathbb{W}, \mathbf{w}^{init}, \longrightarrow, L)$, where: $\mathbb{W} = \mathcal{B}(S) \times Q$ is the set of states; $\mathbf{w}^{init} = (\varnothing, q^{init})$ is the initial state; and $\longrightarrow \subseteq \mathbb{W} \times \mathcal{B}(S) \times \mathbb{W}$ is the transition relation such that, for all $\mathbf{w}, \mathbf{w}', \alpha \in \mathcal{B}(S)$ and $q, q' \in Q$, we have $((\mathbf{w}, q), \alpha, (\mathbf{w}', q')) \in \longrightarrow$ if $(q, \alpha, q') \in R$ and $\mathbf{w}' = res_A(\bigwedge\{\mathbf{w}, \alpha\})$.

We write $\mathcal{M}$ instead of $\mathcal{M}(crrsc)$ when *crrsc* is understood. We also denote $(\mathbf{w}, \alpha, \mathbf{w}') \in \longrightarrow$ by $\mathbf{w} \xrightarrow{\alpha} \mathbf{w}'$.

A *path* of $\mathcal{M}$ is an infinite sequence $\sigma = (\mathbf{w}_0, \alpha_0, \mathbf{w}_1, \alpha_1, \ldots)$ of states and actions (context multisets) such that $\mathbf{w}_i \xrightarrow{\alpha_i} \mathbf{w}_{i+1}$, for every $i \geq 0$. For every $i \geq 0$, we denote $\sigma_s(i) = \mathbf{w}_i = (\sigma_b(i), \sigma_{ca}(i))$ and $\sigma_a(i) = \alpha_i$. Moreover, $\sigma^i = (\mathbf{w}_i, \alpha_i, \mathbf{w}_{i+1}, \alpha_{i+1}, \ldots)$ is a suffix of σ. By $\Pi_\mathcal{M}(\mathbf{w})$ we denote the set of all the paths that start in $\mathbf{w} \in \mathbb{W}$ and $\Pi_\mathcal{M} = \bigcup_{\mathbf{w} \in \mathbb{W}} \Pi_\mathcal{M}(\mathbf{w})$ is the set of all paths of $\mathcal{M}$.

The syntax of rsLTL is given by the following grammar:

$$\phi ::= \mathfrak{a} \mid \phi \wedge \phi \mid \phi \vee \phi \mid \mathbf{X}_\mathfrak{a} \phi \mid \phi \mathbf{U}_\mathfrak{a} \phi \mid \phi \mathbf{R}_\mathfrak{a} \phi,$$

where $\mathfrak{a} \in BE(S)$. Intuitively, $\mathbf{X}_\mathfrak{a}\phi$ means 'following an action satisfying $\mathfrak{a}$, ϕ holds in the next state', $\phi \mathbf{U}_\mathfrak{a} \phi'$ means 'ϕ' holds eventually, and ϕ must hold at every preceding state, following only actions satisfying $\mathfrak{a}$', and $\phi \mathbf{R}_\mathfrak{a} \phi'$ means 'following only actions satisfying $\mathfrak{a}$, ϕ' holds up to and including the first state where ϕ holds'.

Let $\mathcal{M} = (\mathbb{W}, \mathbf{w}^{init}, \longrightarrow, L)$ be a crrsc model and $\sigma \in \Pi_\mathcal{M}$. The fact that ϕ holds over σ is denoted by $\mathcal{M}, \sigma \models \phi$ (or $\sigma \models \phi$ if $\mathcal{M}$ is understood), where $\models$ is defined as follows:

$$\sigma \models \mathfrak{a} \quad \text{if } \sigma_b(0) \models_b \mathfrak{a}$$
$$\sigma \models \phi \vee \phi' \quad \text{if } \sigma \models \phi \text{ or } \sigma \models \phi'$$
$$\sigma \models \phi \wedge \phi' \quad \text{if } \sigma \models \phi \text{ and } \sigma \models \phi'$$
$$\sigma \models \mathbf{X}_\mathfrak{a}\phi \quad \text{if } \sigma_a(0) \models_b \mathfrak{a} \text{ and } \sigma^1 \models \phi$$
$$\sigma \models \phi \mathbf{U}_\mathfrak{a}\phi' \quad \text{if } (\exists j \geq 0)(\sigma^j \models \phi' \text{ and } (\forall 0 \leq l < j)(\sigma^l \models \phi \text{ and } \sigma_a(l) \models_b \mathfrak{a}))$$
$$\sigma \models \phi \mathbf{R}_\mathfrak{a}\phi' \quad \text{if } (\forall j \geq 0)(\sigma^j \models \phi')$$
$$\text{or } (\exists 0 \leq l < j)(\sigma^l \models \phi \text{ and } (\forall 0 \leq m < l)(\sigma_a(m) \models_b \mathfrak{a}))).$$

Moreover, $\mathfrak{a} \Rightarrow \phi$ stands for $\neg \mathfrak{a} \vee \phi$, $\mathbf{G}_\mathfrak{a}\phi$ for $false\mathbf{R}_\mathfrak{a}\phi$, $\mathbf{F}_\mathfrak{a}\phi$ for $true\mathbf{U}_\mathfrak{a}\phi$, and $\mathbf{F}\phi$ is the same as $\mathbf{F}_{true}\phi$, for every rsLTL operator $\mathbf{F}$. Thus, $\phi\mathbf{U}\phi'$ means that 'ϕ' holds eventually, and ϕ must hold at every preceding state', and $\phi\mathbf{R}\phi'$ means that 'ϕ' holds up to and including the first state where ϕ holds'.

An rsLTL formula ϕ holds in a model $\mathcal{M}$ if it holds in all the paths starting in its initial state, i.e., $\mathcal{M} \models \phi$ if $\sigma \models \phi$ for all $\sigma \in \Pi_\mathcal{M}(\mathbf{w}^{init})$. A formula ϕ may also hold existentially in $\mathcal{M}$, i.e., $\mathcal{M} \models_\exists \phi$ if $\sigma \models \phi$ for some $\sigma \in \Pi_\mathcal{M}(\mathbf{w}^{init})$.

Bounded Semantics for rsLTL. We use the bounded model checking approach which requires us to specify when a given formula holds while considering only a finite number of states and actions of the prefix of the path being considered.

A path $\sigma = (\mathbf{w}_0, \alpha_0, \mathbf{w}_1, \alpha_1, \dots)$ is a (k,l)-*loop* (or k-*loop*) if there exist $k \geq l > 0$ such that $\sigma = (\mathbf{w}_0, \alpha_0, \dots, \alpha_{l-2}, \mathbf{w}_{l-1})(\alpha_l, \mathbf{w}_{l+1}, \alpha_{l+1}, \dots, \alpha_{k-1}, \mathbf{w}_k)^\omega$ and $\mathbf{w}_{l-1} = \mathbf{w}_k$. The bounded semantics for rsLTL is defined for finite path prefixes. We define a satisfiability relation that for a given path considers its first k states and $k-1$ actions only. The fact that a formula ϕ holds in a path σ with a bound $k \in \mathbb{N}$ is denoted by $\sigma \models^k \phi$ and defined as follows:

- σ is a (k,l)-loop for some $0 < l \leq k$ and $\sigma \models \phi$,
  or
- $\sigma \models_{nl} \phi$, where:

$\sigma \models_{nl} \mathfrak{a}$ if $\sigma_b(0) \models_b \mathfrak{a}$

$\sigma \models_{nl} \phi \wedge \phi'$ if $\sigma \models_{nl} \phi$ and $\sigma \models_{nl} \phi'$

$\sigma \models_{nl} \phi \vee \phi'$ if $\sigma \models_{nl} \phi$ or $\sigma \models_{nl} \phi'$

$\sigma \models_{nl} \mathbf{X}_\mathfrak{a}\phi$ if $k > 0$, $\sigma_a(0) \models_b \mathfrak{a}$, and $\sigma^1 \models_{nl} \phi$

$\sigma \models_{nl} \phi\mathbf{U}_\mathfrak{a}\phi'$ if $(\exists 0 \leq j \leq k)(\sigma^j \models_{nl} \phi'$ and $(\forall 0 \leq l < j)(\sigma^l \models_{nl} \phi$
                   and $\sigma_a(l) \models_b \mathfrak{a}))$

$\sigma \models_{nl} \phi\mathbf{R}_\mathfrak{a}\phi'$ if $(\exists 0 \leq j \leq k)(\sigma^j \models_{nl} \phi$ and $((\forall 0 \leq l \leq j)(\sigma^l \models_{nl} \phi')$
                   and $(\forall 0 \leq l < j)(\sigma_a(l) \models_b \mathfrak{a})))$

For a bound $k \in \mathbb{N}$ and a crrsc model $\mathcal{M}$, $\mathcal{M} \models_\exists^k \phi$ if there exists $\sigma \in \Pi_\mathcal{M}(\mathbf{w}^{init})$ such that $\sigma \models^k \phi$. The *bounded model checking problem* for rsLTL is the decision problem of checking if $\mathcal{M} \models_\exists^k \phi$, for a given $k \in \mathbb{N}$ and $\mathcal{M}$.

Theorem 1 ([22]). *Let ϕ be an rsLTL formula and $\mathcal{M}$ be a crrsc model. Then, $\mathcal{M} \models_\exists \phi$ if and only if there exists $k \in \mathbb{N}$ such that $\mathcal{M} \models_\exists^k \phi$.*

2 Parametric Reaction Systems

We introduce parametric reaction systems which allow for defining also incomplete reactions by using parameters in place of reactant, inhibitor, and product sets.

A *parametric reaction system* (prs) is a triple $prs = (S, P, A)$, where S is a finite *background* set, P is a finite set of elements called *parameters*, and A is a nonempty finite set of *parametric reactions* over the background set. Each parametric reaction in A is a triple $a = (\mathfrak{r}, \mathfrak{i}, \mathfrak{p})$ such that $\mathfrak{r}, \mathfrak{i}, \mathfrak{p} \in \mathcal{B}(S) \cup P$.

The elements $\mathfrak{r}$, $\mathfrak{i}$, and $\mathfrak{p}$ are respectively denoted by $\mathfrak{r}_a$, $\mathfrak{i}_a$, and $\mathfrak{p}_a$ and called the *reactants*, *inhibitors*, and *products* of parametric reaction a. A *parameter valuation* of prs is a function $\mathsf{v} : P \cup \mathcal{B}(S) \to \mathcal{B}(S)$ such that $\mathsf{v}(\mathfrak{b}) = \mathfrak{b}$ if $\mathfrak{b} \in \mathcal{B}(S)$. We also write $\mathfrak{b}^{\leftarrow\mathsf{v}}$ for $\mathsf{v}(\mathfrak{b})$. The set of all the parameter valuations for prs is denoted by PV_{prs}. Let $\mathsf{v} \in \mathrm{PV}_{prs}$. For $X \subseteq A$ we define $X^{\leftarrow\mathsf{v}} = \{(a_{\mathfrak{r}}^{\leftarrow\mathsf{v}}, a_{\mathfrak{i}}^{\leftarrow\mathsf{v}}, a_{\mathfrak{p}}^{\leftarrow\mathsf{v}}) \mid a \in X\}$. Then, by $prs^{\leftarrow\mathsf{v}}$ we denote the structure $(S, A^{\leftarrow\mathsf{v}})$ where all the parameters in A are substituted according to the parameter valuation v. We say that $\mathsf{v} \in \mathrm{PV}_{prs}$ is a *valid parameter valuation* if $prs^{\leftarrow\mathsf{v}}$ yields an rsc.

A *context-restricted parametric reaction system* (crprs) is a pair $crprs = (prs, ca)$ such that $prs = (S, P, A)$ is a prs and $ca = (Q, q^{init}, R)$ is a context automaton over S. For $\mathsf{v} \in \mathrm{PV}_{prs}$ we define $crprs^{\leftarrow\mathsf{v}} = (prs^{\leftarrow\mathsf{v}}, ca)$.

Example 1. We consider a simple prs for a simplified abstract genetic regulatory system based on [9]. The system contains two (abstract) genes x and y expressing proteins X and Y, respectively, and a protein complex Q formed by X and Y. The background set is defined as $S = \{x, \widehat{x}, X, y, \widehat{y}, Y, h, Q\}$, where $\widehat{x}$ and $\widehat{y}$ denote RNA polymerase attached to the promoter of genes x and y, respectively. Here h is used as an abstract inhibitor. Finally, the set of parametric reactions consists of the following subsets: $A_x = \{(\{x\}, \{h\}, \{x\}), (\{x\}, \{h\}, \{\widehat{x}\}), (\{x, \widehat{x}\}, \{h\}, \{X\})\}$, $A_y = \{(\{y\}, \{h\}, \lambda_1), (\lambda_2, \{h\}, \{\widehat{y}\}), (\{y, \widehat{y}\}, \{h\}, \lambda_3)\}$, $A_Q = \{(\{X, Y\}, \{h\}, \{Q\})\}$. Notice that the reactions of A_y use parameters $\lambda_1, \lambda_2, \lambda_3$ to define expression of the protein Y. Suppose that we investigate the processes starting from the states that already contain x and y. This leads to the following definition of the context automaton: $ca = (\{0, 1\}, 0, R)$, where: $R = \{0 \xrightarrow{\{x,y\}} 1, 1 \xrightarrow{\varnothing} 1, 1 \xrightarrow{\{h\}} 0)\}$. When the context set contains the entity h, ca reverts back to the initial state, while for the empty context set the ca remains in the state 1. Then, crprs is defined as $crprs = ((S, P, A), ca)$, where: $P = \{\lambda_1, \lambda_2, \lambda_3\}$ and $A = A_x \cup A_y \cup A_Q$.   ◇

In this paper, our focus is on the synthesis of a parameter valuation given some observations expressed with rsLTL formulae. Let $crprs = (prs, ca)$ be a crprs, and $F = \{\phi_1, \ldots, \phi_n\}$ be a set of rsLTL formulae. The aim of *parameter synthesis* for crprs is to find a valid parameter valuation v of $crprs$ such that $(\mathcal{M}(crprs^{\leftarrow\mathsf{v}}) \models_\exists \phi_1) \wedge \cdots \wedge (\mathcal{M}(crprs^{\leftarrow\mathsf{v}}) \models_\exists \phi_n)$. Each formula of F corresponds to an interactive process observed in the analysed system via, e.g., experiments or simulations. Therefore, for each such process we expect an individual path in $\mathcal{M}(crprs^{\leftarrow\mathsf{v}})$ and we solve n the model checking problems for rsLTL in one instance. However, the parameter valuation v is shared among all instances, which allows us to calculate v such that all properties of F are satisfied.

Example 2. Let us assume we performed an experiment on the system of Example 1 where protein Y was expressed. We have the following observations related to the expression of the protein Y:

- whenever the current state contains y, then y and $\widehat{y}$ are found in the next state: $\phi_1^c = \mathbf{G}_{\neg h}(y \Rightarrow \mathbf{X}(y \wedge \widehat{y}))$;

- when y and $\widehat{y}$ are present, then Y is finally produced: $\phi_2^c = \mathbf{G}_{\neg h}((y \wedge \widehat{y}) \Rightarrow \mathbf{F}Y)$;
- the entities y, $\widehat{y}$, and Y are eventually produced: $\phi^r = (\mathbf{F}_{\neg h} y) \wedge (\mathbf{F}_{\neg h} \widehat{y}) \wedge (\mathbf{F}_{\neg h} Y)$.

These observations are made assuming h is not provided in the context set. Additionally, we observe that the protein Q is not present in the first three steps of the execution and then, after an arbitrary number of steps it is finally produced: $\phi^d = \neg Q \wedge \mathbf{X}(\neg Q \wedge \mathbf{X}(\neg Q \wedge \mathbf{F}Q))$. The observations are related to a single interactive process (experiment), therefore we constrain the problem using the conjunction of all the observations. Finally, the observations are expressed using the rsLTL formula $\phi = \phi^r \wedge \phi_1^c \wedge \phi_2^c \wedge \phi^d$. Next, we perform parameter synthesis for $F = \{\phi\}$, that is, we obtain a valid parameter valuation v such that $\mathcal{M}(crprs^{\leftarrow v}) \models_\exists \phi$. A parameter valuation v such that $\lambda_1^{\leftarrow v} = \{y\}$, $\lambda_2^{\leftarrow v} = \{y\}$, $\lambda_3^{\leftarrow v} = \{Y\}$ is valid and satisfies the requirements of our observations.   ◇

Parameter Constraints. In some cases restricting parameter valuations using only rsLTL formulae may prove to be less efficient than constraining the valuation using specialised constraints for the parameters of a prs.

For $prs = (S, P, A)$ the *parameter constraints* $PC(prs)$ are defined using the following grammar:

$$\mathfrak{c} ::= true \mid \lambda[e] \sim c \mid \lambda[e] \sim \lambda[e] \mid \neg \mathfrak{c} \mid \mathfrak{c} \vee \mathfrak{c},$$

where $\lambda \in P$, $e \in S$, $c \in \mathbb{N}$, and $\sim \in \{<, \leq, =, \geq, >\}$. Intuitively, $\lambda[e]$ can be used to refer to the concentration of $e \in S$ in the multisets corresponding to the valuations of λ.

Let v be a parameter valuation of prs. The fact that $\mathfrak{c}$ holds in v is denoted by $\text{v} \models_p \mathfrak{c}$ and defined as follows:

$$
\begin{array}{ll}
\text{v} \models_p true & \text{for every v,} \\
\text{v} \models_p \lambda[e] \sim c & \text{if } \lambda^{\leftarrow v}(e) \sim c, \\
\text{v} \models_p \lambda_1[e_1] \sim \lambda_2[e_2] & \text{if } \lambda_1^{\leftarrow v}(e_1) \sim \lambda_2^{\leftarrow v}(e_2), \\
\text{v} \models_p \neg\mathfrak{c} & \text{if } \text{v} \not\models_p \mathfrak{c}, \\
\text{v} \models_p \mathfrak{c}_1 \vee \mathfrak{c}_2 & \text{if } \text{v} \models_p \mathfrak{c}_1 \text{ or } \text{v} \models_p \mathfrak{c}_2.
\end{array}
$$

A *constrained parametric reaction system* (cprs) is a tuple $cprs = (S, P, A, \mathfrak{c})$ such that (S, P, A) is a prs and $\mathfrak{c} \in PC(prs)$. For $\text{v} \in \text{PV}_{prs}$, we then define $cprs^{\leftarrow v} = prs^{\leftarrow v}$. A parameter valuation $\text{v} \in \text{PV}_{prs}$ is *valid* in $cprs$ if it is valid in prs and $\text{v} \models_p \mathfrak{c}$. A *context-restricted cprs* (cr-cprs) is a pair $cr\text{-}cprs = (cprs, ca)$ such that $cprs = (S, P, A, \mathfrak{c})$ is a cprs and ca is a context automaton over S. We also denote $cr\text{-}cprs^{\leftarrow v} = (cprs^{\leftarrow v}, ca)$.

The proposed language of parameter constraints allows for specifying constraints on multisets corresponding to parameters and relationships between them, which is demonstrated in the following example.

Example 3. Suppose $\lambda_1, \lambda_2, \lambda_3 \in P$. To constrain $\lambda_1^{\leftarrow v}$ to be a sub-multiset of $\lambda_2^{\leftarrow v}$ (i.e., $\lambda_1^{\leftarrow v} \subseteq \lambda_2^{\leftarrow v}$, for all v), we define $submset(\lambda_1, \lambda_2) = \bigwedge_{e \in S}(\lambda_1[e] \leq$

$\lambda_2[e]$). To constrain $\lambda_3^{\leftarrow v}$ to be the intersection of $\lambda_1^{\leftarrow v}$ and $\lambda_2^{\leftarrow v}$ (i.e., $\lambda_1^{\leftarrow v} \cap \lambda_2^{\leftarrow v} = \lambda_3^{\leftarrow v}$, for all v), we define $intersect(\lambda_1, \lambda_2, \lambda_3)$ as

$$\bigwedge_{e \in S} (((\lambda_1[e] > \lambda_2[e]) \wedge (\lambda_3[e] = \lambda_2[e])) \vee ((\lambda_1[e] \leq \lambda_2[e]) \wedge (\lambda_3[e] = \lambda_1[e]))).$$
$\diamond$

The parameter synthesis problem for cr-cprs is defined similarly as for crprs. Let $cr\text{-}cprs = (cprs, ca)$, $F = \{\phi_1, \ldots, \phi_n\}$ be a rsLTL formulae, and $\mathfrak{c}$ be a parameter constraint. The aim is to calculate a valid parameter valuation v of $cr\text{-}cprs$ such that $(\mathcal{M}(cr\text{-}cprs^{\leftarrow v}) \models_\exists \phi_1) \wedge \cdots \wedge (\mathcal{M}(cr\text{-}cprs^{\leftarrow v}) \models_\exists \phi_n)$. In the next section, we show how this problem can be solved using an incremental approach, which amounts to checking $(\mathcal{M}(cr\text{-}cprs^{\leftarrow v}) \models_\exists^k \phi_1) \wedge \cdots \wedge (\mathcal{M}(cr\text{-}cprs^{\leftarrow v}) \models_\exists^k \phi_n)$ for $k \geq 0$, by increasing the value of k until a valid parameter valuation is found.

3   SMT-Based Encoding

In this section we provide a translation of the parameter synthesis problem for cr-cprs and rsLTL into the satisfiability modulo theory (SMT) [18] with the integer arithmetic theory. The SMT problem is a generalisation of the Boolean satisfiability problem, where some functions and predicate symbols have interpretations from the underlying theory.

Let $cr\text{-}cprs = ((S, P, A, \mathfrak{c}), (Q, q^{init}, R))$ and $F = \{\phi_1, \ldots, \phi_n\}$ be a set of rsLTL formulae. Then, we encode the model $\mathcal{M}(cr\text{-}cprs^{\leftarrow v})$, where v is a valid parameter valuation of $cr\text{-}cprs$. Let $k \geq 0$ be an integer, then for each $f \in \{1, \ldots, n\}$ we encode any possible path of $\mathcal{M}(cr\text{-}cprs^{\leftarrow v})$ bounded with k. That is, for each formula ϕ_f we encode a separate bounded path representing its witness. The entities of S are denoted by $e_1, \ldots, e_m$, where $m = |S|$. For each $\phi_f \in F$ and $i \in \{0, \ldots, k\}$ we introduce sets of positive integer variables:

▶ $\mathbf{P}_{f,i} = \{\mathsf{p}_{f,i,1}, \ldots, \mathsf{p}_{f,i,m}\}$, $\mathbf{P}_{f,i}^{\mathcal{E}} = \{\mathsf{p}_{f,i,1}^{\mathcal{E}}, \ldots, \mathsf{p}_{f,i,m}^{\mathcal{E}}\}$, $\mathbf{Q}_f = \{\mathsf{q}_{f,0}, \ldots, \mathsf{q}_{f,k}\}$.

Let $\mathsf{ta} : A \to \{1, \ldots, |A|\}$ be a bijection mapping all the reactions to integers. Then, for each $a \in A$ we also introduce a set of variables encoding products:

▶ $\mathbf{P}_{f,i,a}^p = \{\mathsf{p}_{f,i,\mathsf{ta}(a),1}^p, \ldots, \mathsf{p}_{f,i,\mathsf{ta}(a),m}^p\}$.

Let $\sigma.f$ be a path of $\mathcal{M}(cr\text{-}cprs^{\leftarrow v})$. Then

▶ $\overline{\mathbf{P}}_{f,i} = (\mathsf{p}_{f,i,1}, \ldots, \mathsf{p}_{f,i,m})$ and $\overline{\mathbf{P}}_{f,i}^{\mathcal{E}} = (\mathsf{p}_{f,i,1}^{\mathcal{E}}, \ldots, \mathsf{p}_{f,i,m}^{\mathcal{E}})$

are used to encode $(\sigma.f)_b(i)$ and $(\sigma.f)_a(i)$, respectively. With $\overline{\mathbf{P}}_{f,i}[j]$ and $\overline{\mathbf{P}}_{f,i}^{\mathcal{E}}[j]$ we denote, respectively, $\mathsf{p}_{f,i,j}$ and $\mathsf{p}_{f,i,j}^{\mathcal{E}}$. If $i \geq 1$, we define, for all $a \in A$:

▶ $\overline{\mathbf{P}}_{f,i}^p = (\mathsf{p}_{f,i,1,1}^p, \ldots, \mathsf{p}_{f,i,1,m}^p, \ldots, \mathsf{p}_{f,i,|A|,1}^p, \ldots, \mathsf{p}_{f,i,|A|,m}^p)$.

The following functions map the background set entities to the corresponding variables of the encoding: for all $i \in \{0, \ldots, k\}$ we define $\mathsf{t}_{f,i} : S \to \mathbf{P}_{f,i}$ and $\mathsf{t}_{f,i}^{\mathcal{E}} : S \to \mathbf{P}_{f,i}^{\mathcal{E}}$ such that

▶ $t_{f,i}(e_j) = p_{f,i,j}$ and $t^{\mathcal{E}}_{f,i}(e_j) = p^{\mathcal{E}}_{f,i,j}$ for all $j \in \{1, \ldots, m\}$.

For all $i \in \{0, \ldots, k\}$ and $a \in A$ we define $t^p_{f,i,a} : S \rightarrow \mathbf{P}^p_{f,i,a}$ such that:

▶ $t^p_{f,i,a}(e_j) = p^p_{f,i,\mathsf{ta}(a),j}$ for all $j \in \{1, \ldots, m\}$.

The bijection $\mathbf{e} : Q \rightarrow \{1, \ldots, |Q|\}$ maps states of the context automaton to the values used in the encoding. Let $\mathsf{tp} : P \rightarrow \{1, \ldots, |P|\}$ be a bijection mapping all the parameters to their corresponding integers. Then we introduce the tuple of parameters:

▶ $\overline{\mathbf{p}}^{par} = (p^{par}_{1,1}, \ldots, p^{par}_{1,m}, \ldots, p^{par}_{|P|,1}, \ldots, p^{par}_{P,m})$.

For each parameter $\lambda \in P$ we define

▶ $\mathbf{P}^{par}_{\lambda} = \{p^{par}_{\mathsf{tp}(\lambda),1}, \ldots, p^{par}_{\mathsf{tp}(\lambda),m}\}$

and $\mathsf{pm}_{\lambda} : S \rightarrow \mathbf{P}^{par}_{\lambda}$ such that $\mathsf{pm}_{\lambda}(e_j) = p^{par}_{\mathsf{tp}(\lambda),j}$. Let $a \in A$ and $\mathfrak{s} \in \{\mathfrak{r}_a, \mathfrak{i}_a, \mathfrak{p}_a\}$. Then, $re^{\mathfrak{s}}(e_j)$ denotes $\mathsf{pm}_{\mathfrak{s}}(e_j)$ if $\mathfrak{s} \in P$, and $\mathfrak{s}(e_j)$ otherwise. To define the SMT encoding of the paths we need auxiliary functions that correspond to elements of the encoding.

Initial state: To encode the initial state of the model for $\phi_f \in F$ we define

▶ $\mathsf{Init}(\overline{\mathbf{p}}_{f,i}, \mathsf{q}_{f,i}) = (\bigwedge_{e \in S} t_{f,i}(e) = 0) \wedge \mathsf{q}_{f,i} = \mathbf{e}(q^{init})$,

where all the concentration levels are set to zero, and the context automaton is in its initial state.

Context: To encode a multiset $\mathbf{c} \in \mathcal{B}(S)$ of context entities we define:

▶ $\mathsf{Ct}_{\mathbf{c}}(\overline{\mathbf{p}}^{\mathcal{E}}_{f,i}) = \bigwedge_{e \in S} t^{\mathcal{E}}_{f,i}(e) = \mathbf{c}(e)$

Parameter correctness: With $\mathsf{PC}(\overline{\mathbf{p}}^{par})$ we encode the parameter constraints, require that the concentration levels of the reactants are always lower than the concentration levels of the inhibitors, and ensure that all the multisets corresponding to the parameters are non-empty, i.e., for each parameter at least one entity must have positive concentration level:

▶ $\mathsf{PC}(\overline{\mathbf{p}}^{par}) = enc^{par}(\mathfrak{c}) \wedge (\bigwedge_{a \in A} \bigwedge_{e \in S} re^{\mathfrak{i}_a}(e) > 0$
$\Rightarrow (re^{\mathfrak{r}_a}(e) < re^{\mathfrak{i}_a}(e))) \wedge (\bigwedge_{\lambda \in P} \bigvee_{e \in S} \mathsf{pm}_{\lambda}(e) > 0)$

where $enc^{par}(\mathfrak{c})$ is the encoding of $\mathfrak{c}$ which follows directly from the semantics of parameter constraints.

Parametric reaction: The parametric reactions $a \in A$ are encoded with

▶ $\mathsf{Rct}_a(\overline{\mathbf{p}}_{f,i}, \overline{\mathbf{p}}^{\mathcal{E}}_{f,i}, \overline{\mathbf{p}}^p_{f,i+1}, \overline{\mathbf{p}}^{par}) = \bigwedge_{e \in S}((t_{f,i}(e) \geq re^{\mathfrak{r}_a}(e) \vee t^{\mathcal{E}}_{f,i}(e) \geq re^{\mathfrak{r}_a}(e))$
$\wedge (t_{f,i}(e) < re^{\mathfrak{i}_a}(e) \wedge t^{\mathcal{E}}_{f,i}(e) < re^{\mathfrak{i}_a}(e)) \wedge (t^p_{f,a,i+1}(e) = re^{\mathfrak{p}_a}(e)))$.

The encoding for parametric reactions specifies the required concentration levels for $a \in A$ to be enabled, as well as encodes the concentration levels for the produced entities. The encoding for the produced entities uses the variables specific to the encoded reaction.

Transitions of cprs: Then, we encode the local state changes of *cprs* with

▶ $\mathsf{Tr}_{cprs}(\overline{\mathbf{P}}_{f,i}, \overline{\mathbf{P}}^{\mathcal{E}}_{f,i}, \overline{\mathbf{P}}^{p}_{f,i+1}, \overline{\mathbf{P}}_{f,i+1}, \overline{\mathbf{P}}^{par}) = (\bigwedge_{a \in A} \mathsf{Rct}_a(\overline{\mathbf{P}}_{f,i}, \overline{\mathbf{P}}^{\mathcal{E}}_{f,i}, \overline{\mathbf{P}}^{p}_{f,i}, \overline{\mathbf{P}}^{par}))$
$\wedge (\bigwedge_{e \in S} \mathsf{t}_{f,i+1}(e) = max(\{0\} \cup \bigcup_{a \in A} \{\mathsf{t}^{p}_{f,a,i+1}(e)\})).$

In this function, we encode the concentration levels for all the entities in the successor state using the individual concentration levels encoded for all $a \in A$ in Rct_a.

Transitions of context automaton: The encoding of the transition relation of the context automaton is a disjunction of the encoded transitions:

▶ $\mathsf{Tr}_{ca}(\mathsf{q}_{f,i}, \overline{\mathbf{P}}^{\mathcal{E}}_{f,i}, \mathsf{q}_{f,i+1}) = \bigvee_{(q,c,q') \in R}(\mathsf{q}_{f,i} = \mathsf{e}(q) \wedge \mathsf{Ct}_c(\overline{\mathbf{P}}^{\mathcal{E}}_{f,i}) \wedge \mathsf{q}_{f,i+1} = \mathsf{e}(q')).$

Transition relation: The transition relation of the model for *cr-cprs* is a conjunction of the transition relations for *cprs* and *ca*:

▶ $\mathsf{Tr}_{cr\text{-}cprs}(\overline{\mathbf{P}}_{f,i}, \mathsf{q}_{f,i}, \overline{\mathbf{P}}^{\mathcal{E}}_{f,i}, \overline{\mathbf{P}}^{p}_{f,i+1}, \overline{\mathbf{P}}_{f,i+1}, \overline{\mathbf{P}}^{par})$
$= \mathsf{Tr}_{cprs}(\overline{\mathbf{P}}_{f,i}, \overline{\mathbf{P}}^{\mathcal{E}}_{f,i}, \overline{\mathbf{P}}^{p}_{f,i+1}, \overline{\mathbf{P}}_{f,i+1}, \overline{\mathbf{P}}^{par}) \wedge \mathsf{Tr}_{ca}(\mathsf{q}_{f,i}, \overline{\mathbf{P}}^{\mathcal{E}}_{f,i}, \mathsf{q}_{f,i+1}).$

Paths: Finally, to encode the paths of $\mathcal{M}(cr\text{-}cprs^{\leftarrow \mathbf{v}})$ that are bounded with k we unroll the transition relation up to k and combine it with the encoding of the initial state of the model:

▶ $\mathsf{Paths}^{k}_{f} = \mathsf{Init}(\overline{\mathbf{P}}_{f,0}, \mathsf{q}_{f,0}) \wedge (\bigwedge_{i=0}^{k-1} \mathsf{Tr}_{cr\text{-}cprs}(\overline{\mathbf{P}}_{f,i}, \mathsf{q}_{f,i}, \overline{\mathbf{P}}^{\mathcal{E}}_{f,i}, \overline{\mathbf{P}}^{p}_{f,i+1}, \overline{\mathbf{P}}_{f,i+1}, \overline{\mathbf{P}}^{par})).$

The encoded rsLTL formula ϕ_f at the position $i \in \{0, \ldots, k\}$ is denoted by $[\![\phi_f]\!]^k_i$. To encode the formula $[\![\phi_f]\!]^k_i$ we use our translation presented in Sect. 5 of [22]. However, for each formula $\phi_f \in F$, we use independent sets of variables corresponding to its path, i.e., the variables indexed with f. The encoding Loops^k_f for the loop positions is defined for each formula $\phi_f \in F$.

Calculation of Parameter Valuation. We perform the synthesis of the parameter valuation v by testing the satisfiability of the formula:

$$\left(\bigwedge_{\phi_f \in F} \mathsf{Paths}^k_f \wedge \mathsf{Loops}^k_f \wedge [\![\phi_f]\!]^k_0 \right) \wedge \mathsf{PC}(\overline{\mathbf{P}}^{par}).$$

Therefore, in the first step we test the satisfiability of the formula and then we extract the valuation of the parameters of P when the formula is satisfiable. That is, for the satisfied formula we obtain its model, i.e., the satisfying valuations of the variables used in the formula. Let $V(\mathbf{p})$ be the valuation of a variable p used in our encoding. Then, the parameter valuations are defined as follows: $\lambda^{\leftarrow \mathbf{v}}(e) = V(\mathsf{pm}_\lambda(e))$ for each $e \in S$ and $\lambda \in P$.

4   Experimental Evaluation

In this section we present the results of an experimental evaluation of the translation presented in Sect. 3. We test our method on the reaction system model for the mutual exclusion protocol (Mutex) introduced in [20]. The system consists of $n \geq 2$ processes competing for exclusive access to the critical section. The background set of crrsc modelling the mutual exclusion protocol is defined as $S = \bigcup_{i=1}^{n} S_i$, where the set of background entities corresponding to the i-th process is defined as $S_i = \{out_i, req_i, in_i, act_i, lock, done, s\}$, where the entities $lock$, $done$, and s are shared amongst all the processes. The set of reactions is defined as $A = \bigcup_{i=1}^{n} A_i \cup \{(\{lock\}, \{done\}, \{lock\})\}$, where A_i is the set of reactions associated with the i-th process. The complete description of the system may be found in [20]. The context automaton ca provides the initial context set and provides context sets such that only at most two simultaneously active processes are allowed. We define the crrsc modelling Mutex as $crrsc_M = ((S, A), ca)$.

Next, we assume here that the system is open and we allow for introducing new processes that participate in the communication to gain access to the critical section. Let us assume we are allowed to modify the behaviour of the additional process (here, the n-th process) only by introducing an additional reaction. Such an assumption could be justified by a mechanism that accepts new processes to participate in the protocol only if they contain the reactions of A_i for any $i \in \{1, \ldots, n\}$, while the remaining reactions could be performing some computation outside of the critical section.

Our aim is to violate the property of mutual exclusion by making the first and the n-th process enter their critical sections simultaneously. The additional (malicious) reaction uses the parameters of $P = \{\lambda_r, \lambda_i, \lambda_p\}$. Then, we define the extended model $cr\text{-}cprs_M = ((S, P, A \cup \{(\lambda_r, \lambda_i, \lambda_p)\}, \mathfrak{c}), ca)$, where $\mathfrak{c} = \neg\lambda_p[in_n] \wedge \bigwedge_{\lambda \in P, e \in S \setminus S_n} \neg\lambda[e]$ constrains the additional reaction by requiring that it may produce only entities related to the n-th process and it cannot produce in_n, to avoid trivial solutions. Then, we need to synthesise a parameter valuation $\mathbf{v}$ of $cr\text{-}cprs_M$ which gives the rsLTL property $\phi = \mathbf{F}(in_1 \wedge in_n)$, i.e., $\mathcal{M}(cr\text{-}cprs_M^{\leftarrow \mathbf{v}}) \models_\exists \phi$.

The verification tool was implemented in Python and uses Z3 4.5.0 [21] for SMT-solving. We implement an incremental approach, i.e., in a single SMT instance we increase the length of the encoded interactive processes by unrolling their encoding until witnesses for all the verified formulae are found. Then, the corresponding parameter valuation is extracted. The verification results[1] presented in Figs. 1 and 2 compare four approaches: the implementation of the encoding from Sect. 3 ($cr\text{-}cprs$) and its extension ($cr\text{-}cprs_{opt}$) that optimises the obtained parameter valuations by using OptSMT provided with Z3. Then, we also use the same encoding for verification of the rsLTL property ($crrsc$), i.e., we replace all the parameters with the obtained parameter valuations and test the formula ϕ in the same way as in [22]. Next, we compare our results with the ones obtained using the non-parametric method ($crrsc_{np}$) of [22]. The results presented are attained from averaging three executions of the benchmark. Our experimental implementation provides a valuation $\mathbf{v}$ which allows to violate the mutual exclution property, where $\lambda_r^{\leftarrow \mathbf{v}} = \{out_n\}$, $\lambda_i^{\leftarrow \mathbf{v}} = \{s\}$, and

---

[1] The experimental results were obtained using a system equipped with 3.7 GHz Intel Xeon (E5-1620 v2) processor and 12 GB of memory, running Mac OS X 10.13.2.

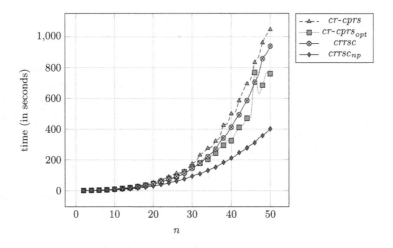

Fig. 1. Synthesis results for Mutex (time)

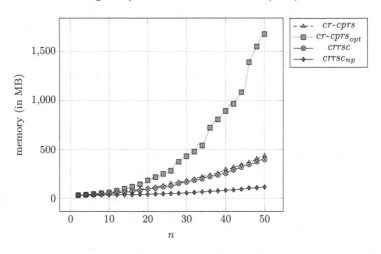

Fig. 2. Synthesis results for Mutex (memory)

$\lambda_p^{\leftarrow \mathbf{v}} = \{req_n, done\}$ for all the tested values $n \geq 2$. This valuation was obtained using $cr\text{-}cprs_{opt}$.

When using $cr\text{-}cprs_{opt}$, the memory consumption increases. However, the method might require less time to calculate the result than $cr\text{-}cprs$. The difference in time and memory consumption between the parametric ($cr\text{-}cprs$) and the non-parametric ($crrsc$) approach is minor. However, $crrsc_{np}$ is the most efficient of all the approaches tested. This suggests that our parameter synthesis method might possibly be improved by optimising the encoding used. However, this is merely a preliminary experimental evaluation and in the future we are going to test our method on a larger number of systems.

5   Concluding Remarks

We have presented a method for reaction mining which allows for calculating parameter valuations for partially defined reactions of reaction systems. We also demonstrated how the presented method can be used for synthesis of an attack in which we inject an additional instruction represented by a reaction, where we use rsLTL to express the goal of the attack.

Assuming there is a finite set of allowed concentration levels for the parameters, the presented method also allows for enumerating all the possible parameter valuations for fixed-length processes. This can be achieved by adding an additional constraint blocking the parameter valuation obtained in the previous step.

Our method focuses only on existential observations which can be obtained from simulations or experiments performed on the system. However, when we consider some widely accepted laws governing the system under investigation, those should be formulated as universal observations.

Since we use the bounded model checking approach, if no valid parameter valuation exists and no bound on k is assumed, then our method does not terminate.

In our future work we are going to focus on complexity considerations of the parameter synthesis, tackle the problem of universal observations, as well as optimise the SMT encoding.

Acknowledgements. W. Penczek acknowledges the support of the National Centre for Research and Development (NCBR), Poland, under the PolLux project VoteVerif (POL-LUX-IV/1/2016).

References

1. Alhazov, A., Aman, B., Freund, R., Ivanov, S.: Simulating R systems by P systems. In: Leporati, A., Rozenberg, G., Salomaa, A., Zandron, C. (eds.) CMC 2016. LNCS, vol. 10105, pp. 51–66. Springer, Cham (2017). https://doi.org/10.1007/978-3-319-54072-6_4
2. Azimi, S., Gratie, C., Ivanov, S., Manzoni, L., Petre, I., Porreca, A.E.: Complexity of model checking for reaction systems. Theor. Comput. Sci. **623**, 103–113 (2016)
3. Azimi, S., Gratie, C., Ivanov, S., Petre, I.: Dependency graphs and mass conservation in reaction systems. Theor. Comput. Sci. **598**, 23–39 (2015)
4. Azimi, S., Iancu, B., Petre, I.: Reaction system models for the heat shock response. Fundamenta Informaticae **131**(3–4), 299–312 (2014)
5. Brijder, R., Ehrenfeucht, A., Rozenberg, G.: Reaction systems with duration. In: Kelemen, J., Kelemenová, A. (eds.) Computation, Cooperation, and Life. LNCS, vol. 6610, pp. 191–202. Springer, Heidelberg (2011). https://doi.org/10.1007/978-3-642-20000-7_16
6. Corolli, L., Maj, C., Marini, F., Besozzi, D., Mauri, G.: An excursion in reaction systems: from computer science to biology. Theor. Comput. Sci. **454**, 95–108 (2012)
7. Dennunzio, A., Formenti, E., Manzoni, L.: Reaction systems and extremal combinatorics properties. Theor. Comput. Sci. **598**, 138–149 (2015)
8. Dennunzio, A., Formenti, E., Manzoni, L., Porreca, A.E.: Ancestors, descendants, and gardens of eden in reaction systems. Theor. Comput. Sci. **608**, 16–26 (2015)

9. Ehrenfeucht, A., Kleijn, J., Koutny, M., Rozenberg, G.: Reaction systems: a natural computing approach to the functioning of living cells. In: A Computable Universe, Understanding and Exploring Nature as Computation, pp. 189–208 (2012)
10. Ehrenfeucht, A., Kleijn, J., Koutny, M., Rozenberg, G.: Evolving reaction systems. Theor. Comput. Sci. **682**, 79–99 (2017)
11. Ehrenfeucht, A., Rozenberg, G.: Reaction systems. Fundamenta Informaticae **75**(1–4), 263–280 (2007)
12. Ehrenfeucht, A., Rozenberg, G.: Introducing time in reaction systems. Theor. Comput. Sci. **410**(4–5), 310–322 (2009)
13. Formenti, E., Manzoni, L., Porreca, A.E.: Cycles and global attractors of reaction systems. In: Jürgensen, H., Karhumäki, J., Okhotin, A. (eds.) DCFS 2014. LNCS, vol. 8614, pp. 114–125. Springer, Cham (2014). https://doi.org/10.1007/978-3-319-09704-6_11
14. Formenti, E., Manzoni, L., Porreca, A.E.: Fixed points and attractors of reaction systems. In: Beckmann, A., Csuhaj-Varjú, E., Meer, K. (eds.) CiE 2014. LNCS, vol. 8493, pp. 194–203. Springer, Cham (2014). https://doi.org/10.1007/978-3-319-08019-2_20
15. Formenti, E., Manzoni, L., Porreca, A.E.: On the complexity of occurrence and convergence problems in reaction systems. Nat. Comput. **14**, 1–7 (2014)
16. Hirvensalo, M.: On probabilistic and quantum reaction systems. Theor. Comput. Sci. **429**, 134–143 (2012)
17. Horn, F., Jackson, R.: General mass action kinetics. Arch. Ration. Mech. Anal. **47**(2), 81–116 (1972)
18. Kroening, D., Strichman, O.: Decision Procedures - An Algorithmic Point of View. Texts in Theoretical Computer Science. An EATCS Series, 2nd edn. Springer, Heidelberg (2016). https://doi.org/10.1007/978-3-662-50497-0
19. Męski, A., Koutny, M., Penczek, W.: Towards quantitative verification of reaction systems. In: Amos, M., Condon, A. (eds.) UCNC 2016. LNCS, vol. 9726, pp. 142–154. Springer, Cham (2016). https://doi.org/10.1007/978-3-319-41312-9_12
20. Męski, A., Penczek, W., Rozenberg, G.: Model checking temporal properties of reaction systems. Inf. Sci. **313**, 22–42 (2015)
21. de Moura, L., Bjørner, N.: Z3: an efficient SMT solver. In: Ramakrishnan, C.R., Rehof, J. (eds.) TACAS 2008. LNCS, vol. 4963, pp. 337–340. Springer, Heidelberg (2008). https://doi.org/10.1007/978-3-540-78800-3_24
22. Męski, A., Koutny, M., Penczek, W.: Verification of linear-time temporal properties for reaction systems with discrete concentrations. Fundam. Inform. **154**(1–4), 289–306 (2017)
23. Salomaa, A.: Functions and sequences generated by reaction systems. Theor. Comput. Sci. **466**, 87–96 (2012)
24. Salomaa, A.: On state sequences defined by reaction systems. In: Constable, R.L., Silva, A. (eds.) Logic and Program Semantics. LNCS, vol. 7230, pp. 271–282. Springer, Heidelberg (2012). https://doi.org/10.1007/978-3-642-29485-3_17
25. Salomaa, A.: Functional constructions between reaction systems and propositional logic. Int. J. Found. Comput. Sci. **24**(1), 147–160 (2013)
26. Salomaa, A.: Minimal and almost minimal reaction systems. Nat. Comput. **12**(3), 369–376 (2013)

Analyzing Execution Time of Card-Based Protocols

Daiki Miyahara[1(✉)], Itaru Ueda[1], Yu-ichi Hayashi[2], Takaaki Mizuki[3], and Hideaki Sone[3]

[1] Graduate School of Information Sciences, Tohoku University,
6–3–09 Aramaki-Aza-Aoba, Aoba, Sendai 980–8579, Japan
`daiki.miyahara.q4@dc.tohoku.ac.jp`
[2] Graduate School of Information Science,
Nara Institute of Science and Technology,
8916–5 Takayama, Ikoma, Nara 630–0192, Japan
[3] Cyberscience Center, Tohoku University,
6–3 Aramaki-Aza-Aoba, Aoba, Sendai 980–8578, Japan
`tm-paper+cardtime@g-mail.tohoku-university.jp`

Abstract. Card-based cryptography is an attractive and unconventional computation model; it provides secure computing methods using a deck of physical cards. It is noteworthy that a card-based protocol can be easily executed by non-experts such as high school students without the use of any electric device. One of the main goals in this discipline is to develop efficient protocols. The efficiency has been evaluated by the number of required cards, the number of colors, and the average number of protocol trials. Although these evaluation metrics are simple and reasonable, it is difficult to estimate the total number of operations or execution time of protocols based only on these three metrics. Therefore, in this paper, we consider adding other metrics to estimate the execution time of protocols more precisely. Furthermore, we actually evaluate some of the important existing protocols using our new criteria.

Keywords: Cryptography · Card-based protocols
Real-life hands-on cryptography · Secure multi-party computations

1 Introduction

Card-based protocols are unconventional computing methods using a deck of physical cards; their advantage is that they can be executed by humans practically (e.g. [4,6,13]). To illustrate this, let us explain how to manipulate Boolean values based on a two-colored deck of cards. Given a black card ♣ and a red card ♡, a Boolean value can be expressed as:

$$\boxed{♣}\,\boxed{♡} = 0\,,\ \boxed{♡}\,\boxed{♣} = 1\,.$$

© Springer International Publishing AG, part of Springer Nature 2018
S. Stepney and S. Verlan (Eds.): UCNC 2018, LNCS 10867, pp. 145–158, 2018.
https://doi.org/10.1007/978-3-319-92435-9_11

Following this encoding, for example, two players, Alice and Bob, can each put two cards face down on a table representing their private bits a and b, respectively:

$$\boxed{?}\boxed{?} \quad \boxed{?}\boxed{?} \ . \tag{1}$$
$$\quad\ \underbrace{\quad}_{a} \qquad \underbrace{\quad}_{b}$$

Here, we assume that the backs $\boxed{?}$ of all cards are indistinguishable and that the fronts $\boxed{\clubsuit}$ or $\boxed{\heartsuit}$ are also indistinguishable if the cards have the same color. We call the left pair of two face-down cards in (1) a *commitment* to a. Similarly, the right pair of two face-down cards are a commitment to b.

Typically, given two input commitments to $a, b \in \{0, 1\}$, as in (1), a card-based protocol should generate a commitment to the value of a predetermined function $f(a, b)$. For instance, we can get a commitment to $a \wedge b$ without leaking any information about a and b, if we execute an AND protocol:

$$\underbrace{\boxed{?}\boxed{?}}_{a} \ \underbrace{\boxed{?}\boxed{?}}_{b} \ \rightarrow \ \cdots \ \rightarrow \ \underbrace{\boxed{?}\boxed{?}}_{a \wedge b} \ .$$

As shown in Table 1, there are many existing AND protocols (in committed format[1]). This table implies that the design of "efficient" protocols is one of the goals of card-based protocols; so far, the efficiency has been evaluated in terms of three metrics: (i) the number of required cards, (ii) the number of colors, and (iii) the average number of required trials. These evaluation metrics are simple and reasonable. However, if we are going to actually execute a card-based protocol, these three metrics are insufficient to accurately estimate the number of operations that need to be done during the protocol and the overall execution time of the protocol.

Therefore, in this paper, we introduce new metrics to evaluate protocol efficiency more precisely. That is, we determine all the operations during a protocol, and then analyze the execution time of each operation. Furthermore, we actually evaluate all the AND protocols[2] shown in Table 1, based on our new criteria by counting the number of operations thoroughly. We also make a comparison of the AND protocols and discuss which protocol is the most efficient and practical. It should be noted that card-based protocols are outside the Turing model [8,9].

The rest of this paper is organized as follows. In Sect. 2, we introduce the AND protocol invented by Stiglic [15] as an example, and then give a formalization of the operations in card-based protocols [8]. In Sect. 3, we give new metrics of efficiency, which directly indicate the execution time of a protocol. In Sect. 4, we evaluate the existing AND protocols based on our proposed metrics. We conclude this study in Sect. 5.

---

[1] There are also "non-committed-format" AND protocols [1,7].

[2] This paper addresses only AND computation because the other important primitive, XOR, can be done with only four cards and one trial [10].

Table 1. The existing AND protocols (in committed format)

	Year	#Colors	#Cards	Avg. #Trials
Crépeau and Kilian [2]	1993	4	10	6
Niemi and Renvall [11]	1998	2	12	2.5
Stiglic [15]	2001	2	8	2
Mizuki and Sone [10]	2009	2	6	1
Five-card KWH [5]	2015	2	5	1
Four-card KWH [5]	2015	2	4	3

2   Preliminaries: A Protocol with Operations

In this section, we introduce Stiglic's AND protocol [15] as an example to demonstrate the possible operations in card-based protocols. As already seen in Table 1, this protocol requires a two-colored deck of eight cards and two average trials. Given input commitments to a and b along with four additional cards ♣ ♣ ♡ ♡, the protocol proceeds as follows.

1. Arrange the sequence as:

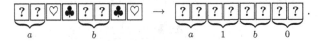

2. Apply a *random cut* to the sequence of eight cards:

$$\langle \boxed{?}\boxed{?}\boxed{?}\boxed{?}\boxed{?}\boxed{?}\boxed{?}\boxed{?} \rangle \rightarrow \boxed{?}\boxed{?}\boxed{?}\boxed{?}\boxed{?}\boxed{?}\boxed{?}\boxed{?}.$$

The term random cut means a cyclic shuffle. If we attach numbers to the cards for the sake of convenience:

$$\begin{array}{cccccccc} 1 & 2 & 3 & 4 & 5 & 6 & 7 & 8 \\ \boxed{?}&\boxed{?}&\boxed{?}&\boxed{?}&\boxed{?}&\boxed{?}&\boxed{?}&\boxed{?} \end{array},$$

then a random cut results in one of the following eight sequences (with a probability of 1/8):

$$\begin{array}{cccccccc} 1 & 2 & 3 & 4 & 5 & 6 & 7 & 8 \\ \boxed{?}&\boxed{?}&\boxed{?}&\boxed{?}&\boxed{?}&\boxed{?}&\boxed{?}&\boxed{?} \end{array},$$

$$\begin{array}{cccccccc} 2 & 3 & 4 & 5 & 6 & 7 & 8 & 1 \\ \boxed{?}&\boxed{?}&\boxed{?}&\boxed{?}&\boxed{?}&\boxed{?}&\boxed{?}&\boxed{?} \end{array},$$

$$\vdots$$

$$\begin{array}{cccccccc} 8 & 1 & 2 & 3 & 4 & 5 & 6 & 7 \\ \boxed{?}&\boxed{?}&\boxed{?}&\boxed{?}&\boxed{?}&\boxed{?}&\boxed{?}&\boxed{?} \end{array}.$$

Note that a random cut is known to be easily implemented by humans securely via the Hindu cut [16] (as shown in Fig. 1).

Fig. 1. The Hindu cut

3. Turn over the first two cards (from the left).
   (a) If the revealed cards are ♡ ♡, we obtain a commitment to $a \wedge b$ as follows:

   (b) If the revealed cards are ♣ ♣, we obtain

   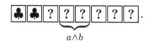

   (c) If the revealed cards are ♣ ♡ or ♡ ♣, turn over the third card.
      i. If the three face-up cards are ♡ ♣ ♣, we have

      ii. If the three face-up cards are ♣ ♡ ♡, we have

      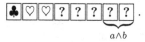

      iii. If the three face-up cards are ♣ ♡ ♣ or ♡ ♣ ♡, turn them over and go back to Step 2.

This is Stiglic's AND protocol, which we denote by $\mathcal{P}_{\text{Sti}}$ hereinafter. A shuffling operation called a random cut is used in Step 2 of $\mathcal{P}_{\text{Sti}}$. The average number of trials is two, because the probability that Step 3–(c)–iii occurs and we go back to Step 2 is 1/2. As seen partially in the description of $\mathcal{P}_{\text{Sti}}$, the possible operations used in card-based protocols (not just Stiglic's but others that have not been described thus far) are turning-over, rearrangement, and shuffling operations, which can be formalized as follows [8]. Below, we assume a sequence of d cards $\Gamma = (\alpha_1, \alpha_2, \ldots, \alpha_d)$.

1. **Turning-over operation:** (turn, i)
   A turn operation involves turning over the i-th card α_i, as shown in Fig. 2. The resulting sequence is $(\alpha_1, \ldots, \alpha_{i-1}, \beta_i, \alpha_{i+1}, \ldots, \alpha_d)$, where β_i is obtained by turning over α_i.

Fig. 2. Turning-over operation

2. **Rearrangement operation:** (perm, π)

   A perm operation involves the application of a permutation $\pi \in S_d$ (where S_d represents the symmetric group of degree d) to the sequence, as illustrated in Fig. 3. The resulting sequence is $(\alpha_{\pi^{-1}(1)}, \alpha_{\pi^{-1}(2)}, \ldots, \alpha_{\pi^{-1}(d)})$.

Fig. 3. Rearrangement operation

3. **Shuffling operation:** (shuffle, Π, $\mathcal{F}$)

   A shuffle operation involves the application of a permutation $\pi \in \Pi$ chosen from a permutation set $\Pi \subseteq S_d$ according to a probability distribution $\mathcal{F}$, as shown in Fig. 4. Note that a set Π along with a distribution $\mathcal{F}$ specifies a shuffle.

Fig. 4. Shuffling operation

3   New Metrics and Execution Time of Protocols

As mentioned in Sect. 2, turn, perm, and shuffle operations are used in card-based protocols. We need to take these operations into account to analyze the "execution time" of protocols. In other words, the efficiency evaluation metrics shown in Table 1, i.e., the number of required cards, the number of colors, and the average number of trials, are insufficient to estimate the overall execution time.

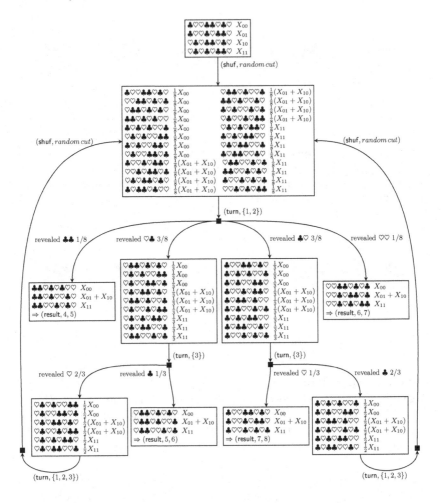

Fig. 5. $\mathcal{P}_{\mathrm{Sti}}$'s KWH-tree

In Sect. 3.1, we clarify all the operations that need to be considered. In Sect. 3.2, we count the number of occurrences of each operation for every AND protocol. In Sect. 3.3, we provide new metrics to estimate the execution time of protocols.

3.1 Operations to Consider

In addition to the three kinds of operations, i.e., turn, perm, and shuffle, introduced in Sect. 2, we define another operation, named place. The place operation involves the addition of a card to the sequence with its face up (in order for play-

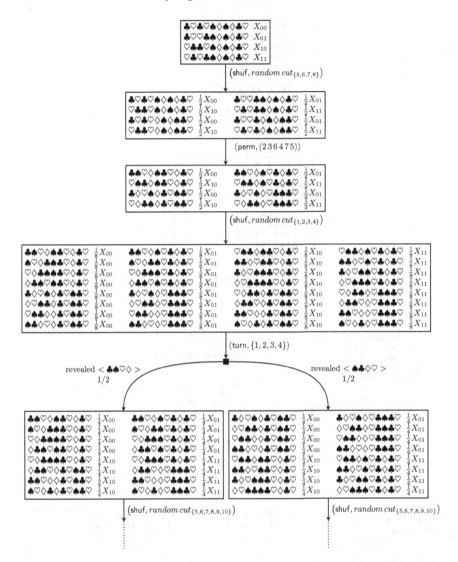

Fig. 6. The first part of $\mathcal{P}_{\mathrm{CK}}$'s KWH-tree. The expression $<\clubsuit\spadesuit\heartsuit\diamondsuit>$ means $\clubsuit\spadesuit\heartsuit\diamondsuit$, $\spadesuit\heartsuit\diamondsuit\clubsuit$, $\heartsuit\diamondsuit\clubsuit\spadesuit$, or $\diamondsuit\clubsuit\spadesuit\heartsuit$.

ers to be able to confirm the color), as shown in Fig. 8. When actually executing a protocol that requires additional cards, this place operation is necessary.

Therefore, altogether, the actual execution of a card-based protocol invokes four kinds of operations: place, turn, perm, and shuffle.

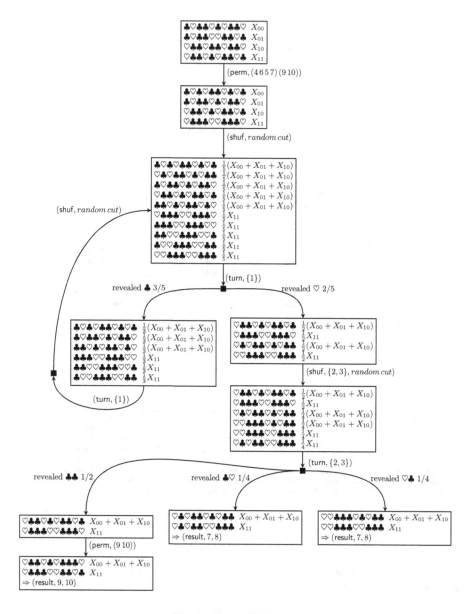

Fig. 7. $\mathcal{P}_{\mathrm{NR}}$'s KWH-tree

Fig. 8. Place operation: adding two cards

3.2   Analysis of the Number of Operations in Each Protocol

In this subsection, we analyze the number of operations in each of the six existing AND protocols shown in Table 1. To this end, we use the *KWH-tree* [5] developed by Koch, Walzer, and Härtel, which is a diagram showing the state transition.

We first analyze $\mathcal{P}_{\mathrm{Sti}}$ in detail. The KWH-tree of $\mathcal{P}_{\mathrm{Sti}}$ is shown in Fig. 5. This figure enables us to count all the operations appearing in $\mathcal{P}_{\mathrm{Sti}}$, as follows.

1. **The number of place (adding a card) operations in $\mathcal{P}_{\mathrm{Sti}}$**
   The number of place operations in $\mathcal{P}_{\mathrm{Sti}}$ is four, because we add four cards to execute the protocol.
2. **The number of turn (turning over a card) operations in $\mathcal{P}_{\mathrm{Sti}}$**
   Firstly, we execute the turn operation four times, because we need to turn over the four added cards after checking their colors. Secondly, we require the turn operation twice because of (turn, $\{1,2\}$) after applying the first random cut. At this time, the probability that ♣♣ or ♡♡ appears and the protocol terminates is $\frac{1}{8} \times 2$. On the other hand, the probability that the protocol terminates by (turn, $\{3\}$) is $\frac{3}{8} \times \frac{1}{3} \times 2$. If the protocol does not terminate by (turn, $\{3\}$), we have to turn over the three face-up cards and execute (turn, $\{1,2\}$) again after applying a random cut. Consequently, the expected number of turn operations in $\mathcal{P}_{\mathrm{Sti}}$ is

$$4 + \sum_{n=1}^{\infty} \left\{ (12n - 7) \times \frac{1}{4} \times \left(\frac{1}{2} \right)^{n-1} \right\} = 12.5.$$

3. **The number of perm (rearranging a sequence of cards) operations in $\mathcal{P}_{\mathrm{Sti}}$**
   We use no perm operation in $\mathcal{P}_{\mathrm{Sti}}$, and hence the number of utilizations of the perm operation is 0.
4. **The number of shuffle (shuffling a sequence of cards) operations in $\mathcal{P}_{\mathrm{Sti}}$**
   As seen in the calculation for turn, the probability that $\mathcal{P}_{\mathrm{Sti}}$ terminates by (turn, $\{1,2\}$) is $\frac{1}{4}$. The probability that $\mathcal{P}_{\mathrm{Sti}}$ terminates by (turn, $\{3\}$) is $\frac{1}{4}$, and the probability that $\mathcal{P}_{\mathrm{Sti}}$ does not terminate and gets into a loop is $\frac{1}{2}$. Therefore, the expected number of shuffle operations is

$$\sum_{n=1}^{\infty} \left\{ n \times \frac{1}{2} \times \left(\frac{1}{2} \right)^{n-1} \right\} = 2.$$

Thus, the numbers of place, turn, perm, and shuffle operations are 4, 12.5, 0, and 2, respectively. See the line of $\mathcal{P}_{\mathrm{Sti}}$ in Table 2.

Similarly, we also create the KWH-trees of $\mathcal{P}_{\mathrm{CK}}$ (Crépeau and Kilian's protocol [2]) and $\mathcal{P}_{\mathrm{NR}}$ (Niemi and Renvall's protocol [11]), as shown in Figs. 6 and 7, respectively; the KWH-tree of $\mathcal{P}_{\mathrm{MS}}$ (Mizuki and Sone's protocol [10]) has been given in some existing literatures (e.g. [9]). Utilizing these KWH-trees, we are able to count each operation in $\mathcal{P}_{\mathrm{CK}}$, $\mathcal{P}_{\mathrm{NR}}$, and $\mathcal{P}_{\mathrm{MS}}$. Table 2 summarizes the results.

In addition, we conducted the same calculation for the two KWH protocols [5]. Table 3 shows the number of operations in the protocols. These protocols need shuffles which have non-uniform probability distributions, and hence, they need special indistinguishable boxes or envelopes [12] to be implemented. Therefore, we have judged that these two protocols are more time-consuming than the other four protocols. Therefore, in the sequel, we focus on the four protocols in Table 2, which we call "practical" AND protocols.

Table 2. The number of operations in the practical AND protocols

	#place	#turn	#perm	#shuffle
$\mathcal{P}_{\text{CK}}$ [2]	6	21	1	8
$\mathcal{P}_{\text{NR}}$ [11]	8	28	4.5	7.5
$\mathcal{P}_{\text{Sti}}$ [15]	4	12.5	0	2
$\mathcal{P}_{\text{MS}}$ [10]	2	4	2	1

Table 3. The number of operations in the KWH protocols [5]

	#place	#turn	#perm	#shuffle
Five-card KWH [5]	1	11/3	7/6	14/3
Four-card KWH [5]	0	7	2	8

3.3 Execution Time of Protocols

Here, we present an expression for the execution time of each protocol based on four metrics. First, we denote the execution time of place, turn, perm, and shuffle by t_{place}, t_{turn}, t_{perm}, and t_{shuf}, respectively. In addition, Time($\mathcal{P}$) denotes the overall execution time of a protocol $\mathcal{P}$. Then, the execution time of the protocols in Table 2 can be easily expressed as follows.

1. Crépeau & Kilian's protocol ($\mathcal{P}_{\text{CK}}$).
   Time($\mathcal{P}_{\text{CK}}$) $= 6t_{\text{place}} + 21t_{\text{turn}} + t_{\text{perm}} + 8t_{\text{shuf}}$.
2. Niemi & Renvall's protocol ($\mathcal{P}_{\text{NR}}$).
   Time($\mathcal{P}_{\text{NR}}$) $= 8t_{\text{place}} + 28t_{\text{turn}} + 4.5t_{\text{perm}} + 7.5t_{\text{shuf}}$.
3. Stiglic's protocol ($\mathcal{P}_{\text{Sti}}$).
   Time($\mathcal{P}_{\text{Sti}}$) $= 4t_{\text{place}} + 12.5t_{\text{turn}} + 2t_{\text{shuf}}$.
4. Mizuki & Sone's protocol ($\mathcal{P}_{\text{MS}}$).
   Time($\mathcal{P}_{\text{MS}}$) $= 2t_{\text{place}} + 4t_{\text{turn}} + 2t_{\text{perm}} + t_{\text{shuf}}$.

In the next section, we make a comparison to determine the most efficient and practical protocol.

4   Comparison of the Protocols

In this section, we evaluate the efficiency of the four practical AND protocols in Table 2 and discuss which protocol is the most efficient.

4.1   Efficiency Comparison Based on the Execution Time

In this subsection, we compare the execution times of the protocols.

First, we compare each coefficient of equation shown in Sect. 3.3 or Table 2. Obviously, we obtain the following inequalities:

$$\text{Time}(\mathcal{P}_{\text{Sti}}) < \text{Time}(\mathcal{P}_{\text{CK}}),$$

$$\text{Time}(\mathcal{P}_{\text{Sti}}) < \text{Time}(\mathcal{P}_{\text{NR}}).$$

Therefore, $\mathcal{P}_{\text{Sti}}$ is superior to $\mathcal{P}_{\text{CK}}$ and $\mathcal{P}_{\text{NR}}$. Hence, it suffices to compare $\mathcal{P}_{\text{Sti}}$ with $\mathcal{P}_{\text{MS}}$.

At first glance, the coefficients might give us an impression that $\mathcal{P}_{\text{MS}}$ would be better than $\mathcal{P}_{\text{Sti}}$. However, we cannot immediately come to a conclusion because $\text{Time}(\mathcal{P}_{\text{MS}})$ has $2t_{\text{perm}}$ while $\text{Time}(\mathcal{P}_{\text{Sti}})$ has no t_{perm}. Therefore, we actually measured the duration of each operation by manipulating real cards. As a result, our measurement provides us the following relationship:

$$t_{\text{place}} = t_{\text{turn}} \text{ and } 0.1t_{\text{perm}} < t_{\text{turn}}.$$

Moreover, it is reasonable to assume that

$$t_{\text{perm}} < t_{\text{shuf}}$$

because the shuffling operation generally takes more time than the rearrangement operation. From these findings, we have

$$\begin{aligned}
\text{Time}(\mathcal{P}_{\text{MS}}) &= 2t_{\text{place}} + 4t_{\text{turn}} + 2t_{\text{perm}} + t_{\text{shuf}} \\
&< 2t_{\text{place}} + 14t_{\text{turn}} + t_{\text{perm}} + t_{\text{shuf}} \\
&< 4t_{\text{place}} + 12.5t_{\text{turn}} + 2t_{\text{shuf}} = \text{Time}(\mathcal{P}_{\text{Sti}}).
\end{aligned}$$

Therefore, we have $\text{Time}(\mathcal{P}_{\text{MS}}) < \text{Time}(\mathcal{P}_{\text{Sti}})$. This implies that $\mathcal{P}_{\text{MS}}$ is the protocol with the least execution time.

4.2   Impact of the Execution Time of Shuffling

In the previous subsection, we assumed that $t_{\text{perm}} < t_{\text{shuf}}$ holds. In this subsection, we further investigate how the difference between t_{perm} and t_{shuf} affects the overall execution time of a protocol. To this end, we regard t_{shuf} as a variable and other metrics t_{place}, t_{turn}, and t_{perm} as constants. Specifically, based on our measurement of the actual execution time, we fix

$$t_{\text{place}} = t_{\text{turn}} = 0.8 \text{ (s)}, \quad t_{\text{perm}} = 7t_{\text{turn}}.$$

Then, we vary the value t_{shuf} from three seconds to sixty seconds; Fig. 9 shows the result. According to this figure, $\mathcal{P}_{\text{Sti}}$ and $\mathcal{P}_{\text{MS}}$ are considered to be more efficient.

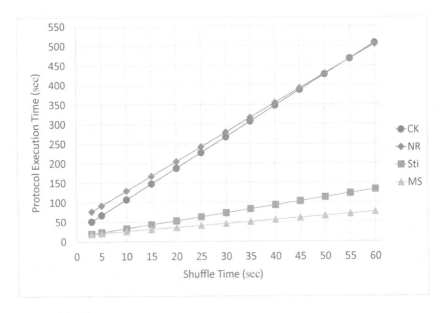

Fig. 9. The total execution time of each protocol for different shuffle times

5   Conclusion

The widely-used efficiency evaluation metrics of card-based protocols do not capture the number of operations fully, and hence, it is difficult to estimate their execution time accurately. Therefore, we considered all kinds of possible operations so that we have four metrics, and focused on counting the number of operations comprehensively to estimate the execution time of protocols. Our new criteria allows us to evaluate the efficiency of protocols. Thus, we were able to compare the execution time of the protocols. We concluded that the Mizuki–Sone AND protocol [10] is the most efficient and practical as an AND protocol in terms of the execution time.

To count the number of operations, we created KWH-trees for $\mathcal{P}_{CK}$, $\mathcal{P}_{NR}$, and $\mathcal{P}_{Sti}$, as shown in Figs. 7, 6 and 5, respectively. This is the first attempt to describe KWH-trees for these previous protocols, and we believe that Figs. 7, 6 and 5 themselves form one of the major contributions of this paper.

Our future work involves (i) applying our new criteria to the other existing protocols (e.g. [3,14]) and (ii) clarifying the variables that affect the execution time of a shuffle (e.g., the number of cards) and other operations.

Acknowledgments. We thank the anonymous referees, whose comments have helped us to improve the presentation of the paper. This work was supported by JSPS KAK-ENHI Grant Number JP17K00001.

References

1. Boer, B.: More efficient match-making and satisfiability *The Five Card Trick*. In: Quisquater, J.-J., Vandewalle, J. (eds.) EUROCRYPT 1989. LNCS, vol. 434, pp. 208–217. Springer, Heidelberg (1990). https://doi.org/10.1007/3-540-46885-4_23

2. Crépeau, C., Kilian, J.: Discreet solitary games. In: Stinson, D.R. (ed.) CRYPTO 1993. LNCS, vol. 773, pp. 319–330. Springer, Heidelberg (1994). https://doi.org/10.1007/3-540-48329-2_27

3. Hashimoto, Y., Shinagawa, K., Nuida, K., Inamura, M., Hanaoka, G.: Secure grouping protocol using a deck of cards. In: Shikata, J. (ed.) ICITS 2017. LNCS, vol. 10681, pp. 135–152. Springer, Cham (2017). https://doi.org/10.1007/978-3-319-72089-0_8

4. Ishikawa, R., Chida, E., Mizuki, T.: Efficient card-based protocols for generating a hidden random permutation without fixed points. In: Calude, C.S., Dinneen, M.J. (eds.) UCNC 2015. LNCS, vol. 9252, pp. 215–226. Springer, Cham (2015). https://doi.org/10.1007/978-3-319-21819-9_16

5. Koch, A., Walzer, S., Härtel, K.: Card-based cryptographic protocols using a minimal number of cards. In: Iwata, T., Cheon, J.H. (eds.) ASIACRYPT 2015. LNCS, vol. 9452, pp. 783–807. Springer, Heidelberg (2015). https://doi.org/10.1007/978-3-662-48797-6_32

6. Mizuki, T., Asiedu, I.K., Sone, H.: Voting with a logarithmic number of cards. In: Mauri, G., Dennunzio, A., Manzoni, L., Porreca, A.E. (eds.) UCNC 2013. LNCS, vol. 7956, pp. 162–173. Springer, Heidelberg (2013). https://doi.org/10.1007/978-3-642-39074-6_16

7. Mizuki, T., Kumamoto, M., Sone, H.: The five-card trick can be done with four cards. In: Wang, X., Sako, K. (eds.) ASIACRYPT 2012. LNCS, vol. 7658, pp. 598–606. Springer, Heidelberg (2012). https://doi.org/10.1007/978-3-642-34961-4_36

8. Mizuki, T., Shizuya, H.: A formalization of card-based cryptographic protocols via abstract machine. Int. J. Inf. Secur. **13**(1), 15–23 (2014)

9. Mizuki, T., Shizuya, H.: Computational model of card-based cryptographic protocols and its applications. IEICE TRANS. Fundam. Electron. Commun. Comput. Sci. **100**(1), 3–11 (2017)

10. Mizuki, T., Sone, H.: Six-card secure AND and four-card secure XOR. In: Deng, X., Hopcroft, J.E., Xue, J. (eds.) FAW 2009. LNCS, vol. 5598, pp. 358–369. Springer, Heidelberg (2009). https://doi.org/10.1007/978-3-642-02270-8_36

11. Niemi, V., Renvall, A.: Secure multiparty computations without computers. Theor. Comput. Sci. **191**(1–2), 173–183 (1998)

12. Nishimura, A., Hayashi, Y.I., Mizuki, T., Sone, H.: An implementation of non-uniform shuffle for secure multi-party computation. In: Proceedings of the 3rd ACM International Workshop on ASIA Public-Key Cryptography, AsiaPKC 2016, pp. 49–55. ACM, New York (2016)

13. Nishimura, A., Nishida, T., Hayashi, Y.I., Mizuki, T., Sone, H.: Card-based protocols using unequal division shuffles. Soft Comput. **22**(2), 361–371 (2018). https://doi.org/10.1007/s00500-017-2858-2

14. Shinagawa, K., et al.: Multi-party computation with small shuffle complexity using regular polygon cards. In: Au, M.-H., Miyaji, A. (eds.) ProvSec 2015. LNCS, vol. 9451, pp. 127–146. Springer, Cham (2015). https://doi.org/10.1007/978-3-319-26059-4_7

15. Stiglic, A.: Computations with a deck of cards. Theor. Comput. Sci. **259**(1–2), 671–678 (2001)
16. Ueda, I., Nishimura, A., Hayashi, Y., Mizuki, T., Sone, H.: How to implement a random bisection cut. In: Martín-Vide, C., Mizuki, T., Vega-Rodríguez, M.A. (eds.) TPNC 2016. LNCS, vol. 10071, pp. 58–69. Springer, Cham (2016). https://doi.org/10.1007/978-3-319-49001-4_5

Algorithmic Design of Cotranscriptionally Folding 2D RNA Origami Structures

Abdulmelik Mohammed[✉], Pekka Orponen, and Sachith Pai

Department of Computer Science, Aalto University, 00076 Aalto, Finland
{abdulmelik.mohammed,pekka.orponen,sachith.pai}@aalto.fi

Abstract. We address a biochemical folding obstacle of "polymerase trapping" that arises in the remarkable RNA origami tile design framework of Geary, Rothemund and Andersen (Science 2014). We present a combinatorial formulation of this obstacle, together with an optimisation procedure that yields designs minimising the risk of encountering the corresponding topological trap in the tile folding phase. The procedure has been embedded in an automated software pipeline, and we provide examples of designs produced by the software, including an optimised version of the RNA smiley-face tile proposed by Geary and Andersen (DNA 2014).

Keywords: RNA origami · RNA tiles · RNA nanotechnology
Rational design · Cotranscriptional folding · Grid graphs
Spanning trees

1 Introduction

Following the introduction of Paul Rothemund's DNA origami technique in 2006 [14], the research area of DNA nanotechnology [15] has made rapid progress in the rational design of highly complex 2D and 3D DNA nanostructures and their applications [10,12,13,16,18]. In the past few years, there has also been increasing interest in using RNA, rather than DNA, as the fundamental construction material for similar purposes [5,7–9]. One great appeal of this alternative is that while the production of designed DNA nanostructures typically proceeds by a multi-stage laboratory protocol that involves synthesising the requisite nucleic acid strands and hybridising them together in a thermally controlled process, RNA nanostructures can in principle be produced in quantity by the natural process of polymerase transcription from a representative DNA template, isothermally at room temperature, *in vitro* and eventually *in vivo*.

The challenge in this approach, however, is that in contrast to DNA, RNA characteristically exists in single-stranded form, and the varied 3D conformations of RNA molecules are the result of a given strand folding upon itself in tertiary

Research supported by Academy of Finland grant 311639, "Algorithmic Designs for Biomolecular Nanostructures (ALBION)".

structures whose formation is quite difficult to predict and control algorithmi-cally. Nevertheless, in the emerging field of RNA nanotechnology, there have also been several approaches to the rational design of RNA nanostructures [7,9]. For instance, in "RNA tectonics" [1,3,17], well-characterised elementary structural modules are linked together by connector motifs to form intricate 2D and 3D complexes.

On the other hand, the approach of *de novo* algorithmic structure design, which has been so successful in the case of DNA origami, has been less explored in the context of RNA, most likely because of the higher complexity of RNA's single-stranded folding kinetics. One notable exception has been the work of Geary, Rothemund and Andersen [5], which presents an approach to designing 2D "RNA origami tiles" by a systematic scheme of intra-structure couplings of collinear helical stem segments by crossover and kissing-loop motifs.

Fig. 1. Cotranscriptional folding of a 2D RNA origami tile from a DNA template, mediated by an RNA polymerase enzyme. Reprinted with permission from [4].

Geary et al. [5] also demonstrate experimentally that the designed tiles can be folded in the laboratory both by a heat-annealing protocol from prefabricated RNA strands, and by a cotranscriptional protocol, whereby the RNA strand folds into its 2D conformation concurrently to being transcribed from its DNA template by an RNA polymerase enzyme (Fig. 1).

While such cotranscriptional folding of *de novo* designed RNA nanostructures is a remarkable achievement, there appear to be some challenges in extending the methodology of [5] to bigger and more complex structures, related in particular to risks of kinetic and topological traps in the folding process. We shall discuss in this paper a systematic design approach that addresses one potentially signif-icant topological obstacle which we call *polymerase trapping*. This involves the cotranscriptional folding of the RNA strand proceeding in such a way that the design's intra-structure kissing-loop interactions block its downstream helices from forming while the structure is still coupled to its large polymerase-DNA template complex.

In the following, Sect. 2 discusses the basic structure of the RNA origami tiles from [5] and introduces the polymerase trapping problem. Section 3 then presents a more abstract view of origami tiles as renderings of 2D grid graphs, and how minimising the risk of polymerase trapping can be formulated as a combinatorial optimisation task in this general framework. Section 4 discusses a branch-and-bound solution method for this task, which requires a somewhat nontrivial search in the very large space of spanning trees of a given grid graph.

Section 5 outlines our software pipeline that leads from a bitmap design of a targeted 2D pattern to a secondary-structure description of an RNA strand that would fold to render that pattern as a generalised tile, with minimal risk of polymerase trapping.[1] This Section also contains some examples of (almost) completely trap-free designs, including a smiley-face design embedded on 14 × 6-grid, similar to the one presented in article [6]. Section 6 concludes with some general observations and further challenges.

2   RNA Tiles, Cotranscriptional Folding and Polymerase Trapping

We start our discussion by considering the structure of the 2H-AE tile, the simplest design from article [5]. Figure 2a presents a helix-level diagram of the 3D structure of this molecule. The 5' end of the RNA strand, marked here with a black dot, is located in the middle of the lower helix. From there the strand winds towards the right end of the diagram, creates a hairpin loop (marked in red), crosses to the upper helix, creates another hairpin loop etc. The most interesting part of the design is the kissing-loop motif (marked in blue) in the middle of the upper helix. This is a naturally occurring (dimerization initiation site of HIV-1 RNA) arrangement of two antiparallel RNA hairpin loops that hybridise together trans-helically to form a very precise 180° coupling between their respective

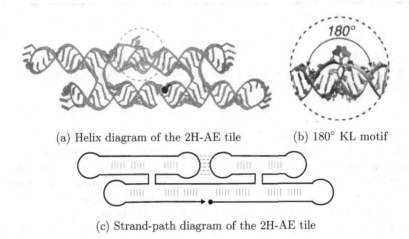

(a) Helix diagram of the 2H-AE tile   (b) 180° KL motif

(c) Strand-path diagram of the 2H-AE tile

Fig. 2. (a) A helix-level diagram of the 2H-AE RNA origami tile from [5]. (b) The 180° kissing loop motif used as intra-structure connector. (c) A strand-path schematic of the tile. Figures (a) and (b) adapted with permission from [5]. (Color figure online)

---

[1] We are currently working on the challenge of transforming the secondary-structure descriptions to actual RNA sequences, but lab-proof sequence design is a nontrivial task, and validating that the generated sequences really fold as intended requires experimental work.

hairpins: geometrically this is almost as if the helix constituting the stem of one hairpin continued into the other, even though there is no continuity in the strand. Figure 2b displays a slightly expanded view of this motif.

Figure 2c exhibits a more abstract strand-path diagram of the structure. Here the vertical dotted lines indicate the intra-helical stem pairings, and the dashed horizontal lines the trans-helical kissing-loop interactions. The 5' end of the strand is marked with a black dot and the 3' end with an arrowhead.

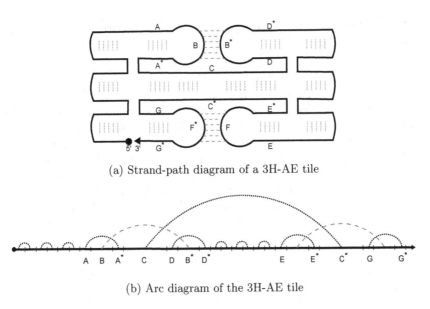

(a) Strand-path diagram of a 3H-AE tile

(b) Arc diagram of the 3H-AE tile

Fig. 3. (a) Strand path diagram of a 3H-AE tile. (b) A domain-level arc diagram of the 3H-AE tile.

Let us then consider the design of a 3H-AE tile, an extension of the 2H-AE tile with a third helical layer, and using the specific strand-path routing outlined in Fig. 3a. One could also route the strand and arrange the kissing-loop connections differently for the same high-level 3 × 2 tile scheme (3 horizontal helices, 2 vertical cross-over seams), and we will return to this issue in Sect. 3. But for now let us focus on the specific H-like design shown in Fig. 3a.

In Fig. 3a, each main domain of the strand constituting the tile is labelled with a capital letter, and its complementary domain with the same letter followed by an asterisk. Figure 3b presents an arc diagram that outlines the pairings between these domains: the intervals between tick marks correspond to the respective strand segments, stem domain pairings are indicated with dotted arcs and kissing loop interactions with dashed arcs. Note that compared to the 2H-AE tile from [5], our 3H-AE design has been simplified so that the perimeter kissing loops (denoted by red in Fig. 2a), which are used to connect tiles to each other in [5], have been replaced by simple nonpairing tetraloop "caps".

Let us then consider how a cotranscriptional folding process for the 3H-AE tile structure presented in Fig. 3 might proceed. Instead of thinking of the RNA strand being spooled out of the polymerase starting at the 5' end and folding as the appropriate base pairings become available, it may be easier to visualise the large polymerase-DNA template complex as traversing the 5'-3' strand route outlined in Fig. 3a and generating the bases as it goes. Generating the A and B strand segments is uneventful, and the RNA strand stays linear until sometime after the A* segment has been generated. (In reality of course several transient nonspecific pairings will arise during the folding process, but we are ignoring these in this simplified discussion.) Then segment A gets paired to segment A*, D to D*, the kissing loop B–B* closes etc.

Consider now what happens when the polymerase reaches domain C* which should constitute a double-strand helix with domain C by winding strand segment C* around C. If kissing loop B–B* has already closed, the strand with the big polymerase-DNA complex coupled to it cannot achieve this, since the kissing-loop pairing is blocking the pathway.

This topological folding obstacle of "polymerase trapping" is briefly addressed by Geary and Andersen in article [6] (Sect. 4.4), which discusses the technical design principles of RNA origami tiles. However, this article does not explain the background of this design constraint in any detail or formulate it in a general way. (The authors kindly explained these issues in a personal discussion.)

Viewed more closely, the significance of the polymerase trapping obstacle depends on the relative timescales of kissing loop formation and the speed of polymerase transcription. (In a purely combinatorial sense, the problem arises already in the 2H-AE tile design of Fig. 2a, but there the time from kissing loop formation to the completion of the transcription is apparently so short that the issue does not significantly affect the experimental results.) This can be understood more clearly by considering the situation in the representative arc diagram: in the case of the 3H-AE tile, the problem is created by the long forward stem pairing C–C* that emerges from inside the kissing loop pairing B–B*. The longer the arc, the more time the enclosing kissing loop has to close, and the higher the likelihood that the folding process gets trapped by this obstacle.

In Sect. 3, we formulate the goal of minimising the risk of polymerase trapping as a design objective for tile design, and in Sect. 4 we discuss a computational approach to optimising this objective.

3   Tiles, Grids and Spanning Trees

In this Section, we introduce a combinatorial model for designing 2D RNA shapes, presented here for rectangular shapes and discussed in a more general framework in Sect. 4.

In our combinatorial model, we represent an M-helix tall, $(N \times u)$-turn wide rectangular shape (tile) by an $M \times N$ grid. We assume the vertical dimension of the target shape to be a multiple of the diameter of an RNA A-helix (~ 2.3 nm) and the horizontal dimension to be approximately a multiple u of A-helical turns

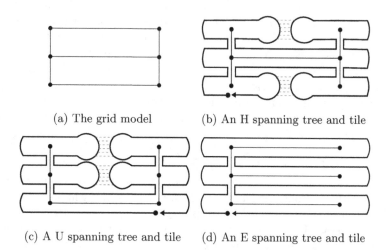

(a) The grid model   (b) An H spanning tree and tile

(c) A U spanning tree and tile   (d) An E spanning tree and tile

Fig. 4. (a) 3×2 grid model for a 3-helix tall, $\sim$2-turn wide RNA rectangular shape, and (b)–(d) three tiles derived from three different spanning trees of the grid. The tiles are formed by routing the RNA strands around the spanning tree and bulging out kissing hairpin loops in towards non-spanning tree edges. In (b)–(d), the thick outer paths indicate the tiles' strand routings, the thin internal schematics outline the spanning trees of the grid, and the dashed horizontal lines in between the loops indicate kissing loop interactions.

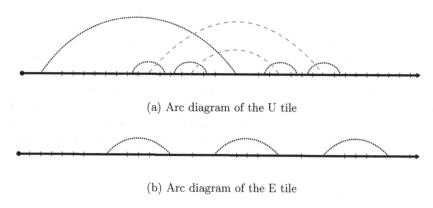

(a) Arc diagram of the U tile

(b) Arc diagram of the E tile

Fig. 5. Arc diagrams of the U and E tiles from Fig. 4. Dotted arcs indicate stem pairings while dashed arcs show kissing loop pairings. The arc diagram in (a) reveals that the horizontal spanning tree edge of the U tile has no cost since the corresponding long stem pairing only crosses the kissing loops in the backward direction. Hence, the U tile only has a trivial cost due to the second hairpins of the kissing loops. The arc diagram in (b) shows that the E tile has a zero cost since it has no kissing loops. For clarity, the stem pairing arcs of the perimeter stem loops have been left out in both (a) and (b).

($\sim$3.2 nm), where $u \geq 1$ is the minimum number of full-turns needed to implement an HIV-1 DIS type 180° kissing loop complex. For instance, the 3H-AE tile sketched in Fig. 3 implements a rectangular shape derived from the 3 × 2 grid illustrated in Fig. 4a. Correspondingly, the 2H-AE tile design by Geary et al. [5] in Fig. 2a could be rendered from a 2 × 2 grid model; the four perimeter hairpin domains flanking the crossovers would then constitute an approximation error in the horizontal dimension.

Having employed a grid to model a rectangular shape, we aim to render the horizontal edges of the grid as either continuous A-helical stem domains, or as kissing-loop complexes, and a selected set of vertical edges as crossover locations. Note that since the vertical edges correspond to potential crossover locations, they essentially have zero length, even though they are presented, for the sake of clarity, with non-zero length in the schematics. The set of edges corresponding to the helical domains and the crossover locations are selected based on a spanning tree of the grid graph.[2]

Accordingly, in order to design an RNA tile corresponding to the input shape, a spanning tree of the grid model is first computed and the single stranded RNA strand is routed twice around this tree.[3] Such a routing pairs distal segments of the RNA strand in an antiparallel fashion on the spanning tree edges, thus making it suitable for rendering horizontal spanning tree edges as A-helical domains and the vertical spanning tree edges as crossovers. Next, at every non-spanning tree horizontal edge, two hairpins are spliced into the strand routing at the edge's endpoints such that the hairpin loops kiss at the centre of the edge. To ensure every crossover is flanked by helical arms, short stems capped with inactive tetraloops are finally spliced to the routing at perimeter vertices, with the tetraloops facing horizontally outward. Three different tiles derived in such a manner from three different spanning trees of the 3 × 2 grid in Fig. 4a are shown in Figs. 4b, c and d. We refer to these three tiles as the "H", "U" and "E" tiles based on the resemblance of their associated spanning trees to the respective Latin letters. (The H tile is the 3H-AE example from Sect. 2.)

After generating a tile from a spanning tree, we can linearise its strand routing to an arc diagram and investigate it for cotranscriptional polymerase trapping. Note that the pairings in the tile, and correspondingly the arcs in the arc diagram, are determined by the strand routing; in particular, we place short arcs corresponding to the stems of the tetraloop capped perimeter hairpins, long-range stem arcs corresponding to the long-range A-helix stem pairings on the spanning tree edges, and long-range kissing loop arcs corresponding to the kissing loop complexes on the non-spanning tree edges. The arc diagram of the H tile is shown in Fig. 3b, while those of the U and E tiles are shown in Fig. 5.

Recall that cotranscriptional polymerase trapping is a risk if there is a stem-pairing arc crossing a kissing-loop arc in the forward direction. Moreover, the trapping is more likely if the later segment of the stem pairing (e.g. segment C* in

---

[2] A *spanning tree* of a graph is a cycle-free subset of the graph that includes all the vertices of the graph [2, Chap. 23].

[3] This standard graph algorithm technique is discussed e.g. in [2, Sect. 35.2].

Fig. 3b) is transcribed much later than the second hairpin loop of the kissing loop (e.g. segment B* in Fig. 3b.) Hence, in case a stem pairing crosses a kissing loop in the forward direction, we associate a cost to the stem pairing proportional to the strand-distance between the second hairpin loop of the kissing loop and the stem pairing's second segment. If a stem pairing crosses multiple kissing loops, we associate with it the maximum cost over all the kissing loops it crosses. In this formulation, a stem pairing which does not cross any kissing-loop arc in the forward direction will have zero cost. For instance, the central stem pairing of the H tile (Fig. 4b) has non-zero cost because it crosses the top kissing loop in the forward direction (cf. Fig. 3b), but the bottom stem pairing of the U tile (Fig. 4c) has zero cost since it crosses neither kissing loop in the forward direction (cf. Fig. 5a). Also note that the stems of tetraloop capped perimeter stem loops have zero cost since they cross no kissing loops.

We set the cost of a tile to be the maximum over all costs of its stem pairings. Note that since the stem of the second hairpin of every kissing loop complex (e.g. stem D–D* in Fig. 3b) crosses the kissing loop (e.g. KL B–B* in Fig. 3b), every tile with a kissing loop has this trivial non-zero cost. In this regard, only the E tile (Fig. 4d) has zero polymerase trapping cost (compare its arc diagram in Fig. 5b with the other tiles' arc diagrams). Nevertheless, the U tile has a cost no more than the trivial hairpin stem cost since the only long range stem pairing, which corresponds to the horizontal spanning tree edge, has zero cost (cf. Fig. 5a). In contrast, the H tile has non-trivial cost because the stem pairing on the spanning tree edge crosses the upper kissing loop (cf. Fig. 3b). Even though the U tile thus technically has slightly larger cost than the E tile, it is more likely to stay well-formed than the E tile, due to its two-crossovers-per-row design that limits rotational flexibility compared to the single crossovers of the E tile. Hence our tile design scheme always imposes this constraint.

Note that the cost of a stem pairing depends on the 5' to 3' routing direction since the cost definition involves the crossing of a kissing-loop arc in the forward direction. In this regard, the main stem pairing of the U tile would have had a non-zero cost if the routing direction was reversed. Indeed, if the transcription direction was reversed in the arc diagram of Fig. 5a, the stem pairing would have crossed both kissing-loop arcs in the forward direction. Furthermore note that, given a fixed spanning tree, the cost of a routing depends also on the starting point of the routing. For instance, starting a clockwise routing at the lowest left vertex of the U spanning tree (Fig. 4c) would have yielded a non-trivial cost in the resulting tile because the spanning-tree-edge stem pairing would then have had a non-trivial cost. In particular, since the upper segment of the stem pairing would have preceded the complementary lower segment in the linearisation to an arc diagram, the stem-pairing arc would have crossed both kissing-loop arcs in the forward direction. Since there are an infinite number of possible starting points, we limit routings to only start at vertices. Given the above two considerations, we associate with a spanning tree the minimum cost among all the possible combinations of starting points and directions (clockwise or counterclockwise).

4 Search Algorithm

In principle, we can develop the search for good spanning trees on arbitrary finite connected subgraphs of the infinite rectangular grid. To model reasonable 2D RNA shapes, we however limit our attention to subgraphs corresponding to bitmap shapes carved from the infinite grid (see Fig. 6c). In particular, we shall consider the input to our algorithm to be a finite subgraph derived from a finite set of connected pixels (faces) of the infinite grid; we consider two pixels to be connected if there is a common vertex bounding both pixels. The input is then the set of vertices and edges bounding the selected pixels. To build RNA tiles out of such partial grids, we follow the same procedure as in the case of rectangular shapes (cf. Sect. 3), except that in this case, every vertex in the partial grid which only has one horizontal edge incident to it will be considered a perimeter/boundary vertex and will be flanked with a tetraloop capped stem loop in the missing horizontal edge (see e.g. the vertices bounding the eyes of the smiley-face in Fig. 7).

Finding a good strand routing, i.e. one that is least likely to cause cotranscriptional polymerase trapping, entails searching through a large number of possible spanning trees of the input grid. For instance, even in the relatively small 6×6 complete grid, the number of spanning trees is approximately $3.2 * 10^{15}$ [11].

Algorithm 1. Find a spanning tree that minimises risk of polymerase trapping

---

Input: A grid graph G modelling a 2D shape
Output: A minimum cost spanning tree
1: $best\_tree \leftarrow$ Randomly generated spanning tree of G
2: $min\_cost \leftarrow$ Cost($best\_tree$)
3: RECURSIVE SEARCH($G, G,$ some vertex v of G)
4: **return** $best\_tree$
5:
6: **procedure** RECURSIVE SEARCH($G, residual, tree$)
7:     **if** $tree$ is a valid spanning tree of G **then**
8:         **if** Cost($tree$) $< best\_cost$ **then**
9:             $min\_cost \leftarrow$ Cost($tree$)
10:            $best\_tree \leftarrow tree$
11:            **return**
12:        **end if**
13:    **end if**
14:    $new\_edge \leftarrow$ Select from $residual$ a random edge which is adjacent to $tree$ but does not create a cycle when added to $tree$.
15:    **if** Cost($tree \cup new\_edge$) $< min\_cost$ **then**
16:        Recursive search($G, residual - new\_edge, tree \cup new\_edge$)
17:    **end if**
18:    **if** new_edge is not a cut edge in $residual$ **then**
19:        Recursive search($G, residual - new\_edge, tree$)
20:    **end if**
21: **end procedure**

To effectively manage such a large search space, we developed a search procedure (Algorithm 1) that applies a branch-and-bound search on the spanning tree space of the underlying grid graph of the given shape. The branch-and-bound process conceptually performs an exhaustive search of all spanning trees, but prunes the search paths based on lower bounds evaluated from partial solutions, which in this case, correspond to trees spanning an incomplete set of vertices.

The algorithm's branch-and-bound search tree is based on binary choices for edges. At each step, the algorithm selects an edge and decides whether to include or exclude this edge (Lines 15 and 18); two branches corresponding to this decision are generated in the search tree. The choice edge is selected at random from the list of edges adjacent to the current spanning tree, i.e. to the current partial solution (Line 14 of Algorithm 1). To bound the search tree effectively, we use the cost of this spanning tree as the lower bound for all spanning trees which can be extended from it in the current search path. Note that the search process here evolves a single partial spanning tree to eventually find a tree that spans the complete target shape. This structuring of the search tree, combined with the bounding mechanism, makes it possible to find minimum-cost spanning trees for large designs such as the smiley-face in Fig. 7. Alternatively, one could have decided on arbitrary edges instead of edges adjacent to the current tree. However, this entails growing forests of trees as partial solutions, and leads to several difficulties in obtaining a lower-bounding function for the search process.

Efficient search through branch-and-bound search is possible because of the monotonically increasing cost function. Recall that the cost is incurred by stem-pairing arcs crossing kissing-loop arcs in the forward direction in the arc diagram representing the routing. When an edge is selected to extend the tree, it only adds a small segment to be spliced into the arc diagram of a routing around the tree. Clearly, this can never decrease the strand-distance of the forward crossing arcs. Therefore, adding edges to any tree can only increase the cost of the tree. The algorithm also prevents the possibility of a vertex from not being spanned through a connectivity check before the exclusion of an edge (lines 18–20). This connectivity check ensures the graph does not become disconnected as the result of an edge exclusion.

5   Design Pipeline and Examples

We have integrated our spanning tree search algorithm into a software design pipeline for generating RNA tiles from 2D meshes. The pipeline, along with a representative example, is presented in Fig. 6. The design process starts in a custom 2D mesh design tool we developed, whereby the user first sets the dimensions of the grid and henceforth selects a set of pixels constituting the target shape. After exporting the mesh as a bitmap, the user can run a script to generate an RNA secondary structure, including the kissing loop interactions, in the standard dot-bracket notation.

The pipeline, as shown in Fig. 6a, consists of three modules. The first module, framed in the "Bitmap to grid graph" box in Fig. 6a, is used to manually design

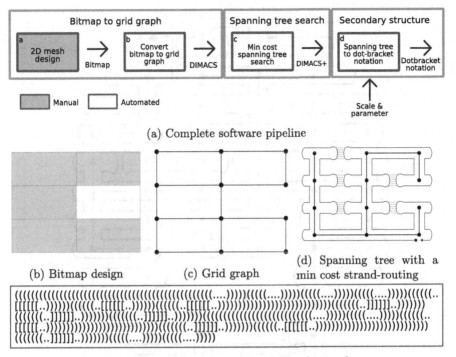

(a) Complete software pipeline

(b) Bitmap design   (c) Grid graph   (d) Spanning tree with a min cost strand-routing

(e) The final secondary structure including kissing loops

Fig. 6. Our software pipeline for designing 2D RNA shapes.

a 2D pattern as a bitmap image and convert it to a grid graph representation in the standard DIMACS format. For the current example, the input and output of this module are shown in Figs. 6b and c, respectively. Note that the edges and vertices bounding the selected pixels define the grid graph. Hence, the right vertical edge bounding the unselected pixel is not part of the output grid graph. The second module reads the input grid graph and searches, using Algorithm 1, for a minimum cost spanning tree. The output spanning tree for the running example is shown in Fig. 6d. The module outputs the spanning tree in DIMACS format with additional comments on the starting position and direction of the minimum cost strand routing. The final module performs a twice around the tree traversal and generates a secondary structure in dot-bracket notation, augmented with information about the kissing-loop interactions. In our example, the resulting secondary structure is shown in Fig. 6e, where the matching square brackets indicate the kissing-loop pairings. This module also allows one to input secondary structure parameters and other design choices such as the number of turns per one horizontal edge, size and structure of the perimeter caps, kissing loop design, etc.

We demonstrate the capability of our software pipeline to produce polymerase-untrapped designs by running it on our grid representation of the

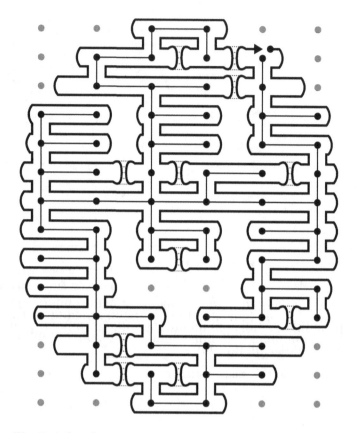

Fig. 7. A (near) zero cost strand routing of a smiley-face shape.

smiley-face shape from [6]. We carved the smiley-face from a 14 by 6 canvas by deleting pixels corresponding to the two eyes, the mouth and the background. Our algorithm produced a spanning tree and routing, as shown in Fig. 7, which only has the trivial cost. In the figure, black vertices correspond to the input grid graph, while grey vertices are only placed to hint at the canvas from which the shape was carved. The fact that our pipeline found a (near) zero cost solution illustrates the utility of our algorithmic approach for finding designs that avoid polymerase trapping even in relatively large shapes. Nevertheless, we note, for instance, that our supplementary two-crossover-per-row constraint is insufficient to overcome flexibility in partial grids and further modelling is required to fully capture other constraints of RNA design of complex shapes.

6   Conclusions and Future Work

In the framework of RNA origami tile design, we have identified the topological folding obstacle of polymerase trapping, formulated it as a combinatorial problem, and designed an optimisation procedure and operational software to minimise the risk of encountering this obstacle. The software pipeline still needs to be extended to include sequence generation, but this involves several further considerations that we are currently investigating.

In the process, we have observed that in fact zero-cost routings (according to our present cost measure) are quite prevalent, and are planning another paper on a combinatorial characterisation of those.

In the actual biochemical setting, our present cost measure and design constraints are certainly too simplistic, and other considerations need to be taken into account. However the optimisation framework should be able to accommodate such changes quite conveniently.

Acknowledgments. We thank Ebbe Andersen and Cody Geary for introducing us to the problem of polymerase trapping in RNA origami tile design, and their encouragement to proceed with the solution approach discussed in this paper.

References

1. Chworos, A., Severcan, I., Koyfman, A.Y., Weinkam, P., Oroudjev, E., Hansma, H.G., Jaeger, L.: Building programmable jigsaw puzzles with RNA. Science **306**(5704), 2068–2072 (2004). https://doi.org/10.1126/science.1104686
2. Cormen, T.H., Leiserson, C.E., Rivest, R.L., Stein, C.: Introduction to Algorithms. MIT Press, Cambridge (2009)
3. Geary, C., Chworos, A., Verzemnieks, E., Voss, N.R., Jaeger, L.: Composing RNA nanostructures from a syntax of RNA structural modules. Nano Lett. **17**(11), 7095–7101 (2017). https://doi.org/10.1021/acs.nanolett.7b03842
4. Geary, C., Meunier, P.E., Schabanel, N., Seki, S.: Programming biomolecules than fold greedily during transcription. In: Proceedings, 41st International Conference on Mathematical Foundations of Computer Science (MFCS 2016). LIPIcs, vol. 58, pp. 43:1–43:14. Dagstuhl Publishing (2016). https://doi.org/10.4230/LIPIcs.MFCS.2016.43
5. Geary, C., Rothemund, P.W.K., Andersen, E.S.: A single-stranded architecture for cotranscriptional folding of RNA nanostructures. Science **345**(6198), 799 (2014). https://doi.org/10.1126/science.1253920
6. Geary, C.W., Andersen, E.S.: Design principles for single-stranded RNA origami structures. In: Murata, S., Kobayashi, S. (eds.) DNA 2014. LNCS, vol. 8727, pp. 1–19. Springer, Cham (2014). https://doi.org/10.1007/978-3-319-11295-4_1
7. Guo, P.: The emerging field of RNA nanotechnology. Nat. Nanotech. **5**, 833–842 (2010). https://doi.org/10.1038/nnano.2010.231
8. Han, D., Qi, W., Myhrvold, C., Wang, B., Dai, M., Jiang, S., Bates, M., Liu, Y., An, B., Zhang, F., Yan, H., Yin, P.: Single-stranded DNA and RNA origami. Science **358**(6369), eaao2648 (2017). https://doi.org/10.1126/science.aao2648
9. Jasinski, D., Haque, F., Binzel, D.W., Guo, P.: Advancement of the emerging field of RNA nanotechnology. ACS Nano **11**(2), 1142–1164 (2017). https://doi.org/10.1021/acsnano.6b05737
10. Kohman, R., Kunjapur, A.M., Hysolli, E., Wang, Y., Church, G.M.: From designing the molecules of life to designing life: future applications derived from advances in DNA technologies. Angew. Chem. Int. Ed. **57**, 4313–4328 (2018). https://doi.org/10.1002/anie.201707976

11. Kreweras, G.: Complexité et circuits eulériens dans les sommes tensorielles de graphes. J. Comb. Theory Ser. B **24**(2), 202–212 (1978). https://doi.org/10.1016/0095-8956(78)90021-7
12. Li, Y., Mao, C., Deng, Z.: Supramolecular wireframe DNA polyhedra: assembly and applications. Chin. J. Chem. **35**(6), 801–810 (2017). https://doi.org/10.1002/cjoc.201600789
13. Orponen, P.: Design methods for DNA nanostructures. Nat. Comput. **17**(1), 147–160 (2018). https://doi.org/10.1007/s11047-017-9647-9
14. Rothemund, P.W.K.: Folding DNA to create nanoscale shapes and patterns. Nature **440**(7082), 297–302 (2006). https://doi.org/10.1038/nature04586
15. Seeman, N.C.: Structural DNA Nanotechnology. Cambridge University Press, Cambridge (2015)
16. Seeman, N.C., Sleiman, H.F.: DNA nanotechnology. Nat. Rev. Mater. **3**, 17068 (2017). https://doi.org/10.1038/natrevmats.2017.68
17. Westhof, E., Masquida, B., Jaeger, L.: RNA tectonics: towards RNA design. Fold. Des. **1**(4), R78–R88 (1996). https://doi.org/10.1016/S1359-0278(96)00037-5
18. Zhang, F., Nangreave, J., Liu, Y., Yan, H.: Structural DNA nanotechnology: state of the art and future perspective. J. Am. Chem. Soc. **136**(32), 11198–11211 (2014). https://doi.org/10.1021/ja505101a

Deterministic Sensing $5' \to 3'$ Watson-Crick Automata Without Sensing Parameter

Shaghayegh Parchami and Benedek Nagy[(✉)]

Department of Mathematics, Faculty of Arts and Sciences,
Eastern Mediterranean University,
Famagusta, North Cyprus, via Mersin-10, Turkey
shaghayegh.parchami@gmail.com, nbenedek.inf@gmail.com

Abstract. Watson-Crick (WK) finite automata are working on double stranded DNA molecule that is also called Watson-Crick tape. Subsequently, these automata have two reading heads, one for each strand. While in traditional WK automata both heads read the whole input in the same physical direction, in $5' \to 3'$ WK automata the heads start from the two extremes (say $5'$ end of the strands) and read the input in opposite direction. In sensing $5' \to 3'$ WK automata the process on the input is finished when the heads meet. Since the heads of a WK automaton may read longer strings in a transition, in previous models a so-called sensing parameter took care for the proper meeting of the heads (not allowing to read the same positions of the input in the last step). Recently a new model is investigated, which works without the sensing parameter. In this paper, the deterministic counterpart is studied and proved to be accept the language class 2detLIN, i.e., the same class that is accepted by the deterministic variant of the earlier version. However, using some of restricted variants, e.g., all-final automata, the classes of the accepted languages are changed showing a more finer hierarchy inside the class of linear context-free languages.

Keywords: Deterministic Watson-Crick automata
$5' \to 3'$ WK automata · Finite automata
Linear context-free languages · Hierarchy · Deterministic languages

1 Introduction

From the end of last century, DNA computing has appeared as a relatively new computational paradigm [1,11]. In contrast, automata theory is from the middle of the last century and it is one of the bases of computer science. An interesting combination of these two fields, the theory of Watson-Crick automata (abbreviated as WK automata), was introduced in [3] as a branch of DNA computing. They have important relations to formal language and automata theory. To read more about these automata the book [11] and the survey [2] are recommended.

© Springer International Publishing AG, part of Springer Nature 2018
S. Stepney and S. Verlan (Eds.): UCNC 2018, LNCS 10867, pp. 173–187, 2018.
https://doi.org/10.1007/978-3-319-92435-9_13

A WK automaton works on a double-stranded tape called Watson-Crick tape (i.e., DNA molecule), whose strands are scanned separately by read only heads. The symbols in the corresponding cells of the double-stranded tapes are related by (the Watson-Crick) complementarity relation. Restricted classes having either or both restrictions on the states, e.g., all states are final, or on the transitions, e.g., only one of the heads can read in a transition, are analysed. The relationships between various classes of the Watson-Crick automata are investigated in [3,5,11]. The two strands of a DNA molecule have opposite $5' \rightarrow 3'$ orientation. Considering the reverse and the $5' \rightarrow 3'$ variants, they are more realistic in the sense, that both heads use the same biochemical direction (that is opposite physical directions) [3,6,7]. A WK automaton is sensing if it has the information whether the heads are at the same position. Some variants of the $5' \rightarrow 3'$ Watson-Crick automaton with sensing parameter, i.e., with a feature which tells whether the upper and the lower heads are within a fixed small distance (or meet at the same position) are discussed in [7–9]. The heads of these automata start from the opposite ends from the input, assuming the complementarity relation to be bijective (as it is in the nature), the automaton already has information about the whole input at the point where the heads meet. Consequently, the automaton makes the decision on acceptance at that point and the process on the input is finished. It was shown that the linear context-free languages and some of their subclasses (e.g., the class of even linear languages) can be characterised by these models. Since the heads of a WK automaton may read longer strings in a transition, in these models the sensing parameter took care of the proper meeting of the heads sensing if the heads are close enough to meet in the next transition. This parameter could also be used to deny acceptance of some strings, e.g., by not allowing to read the last letter(s) to finish the process in that way. This idea leaded to the fact that there were no difference of the language classes accepted by arbitrary and all-final automata. The motivation of the new model, recently introduced in [10], is to erase the rather artificial term of sensing parameter from the model. Here, continuing the work started there with the new model, its deterministic counterpart is investigated. As one of the main results, we show that the new deterministic model accepts exactly the same class of languages, namely 2detLIN, that is accepted by the deterministic variant of the model with sensing parameter. The class 2detLIN was investigated in [9] as a language class obtained by a two head deterministic finite automata model, i.e., the class accepted by deterministic sensing $5' \rightarrow 3'$ WK automata with sensing parameter. The class of deterministic linear languages (characterised by deterministic one-turn pushdown automata) and the class 2detLIN are incomparable sets of languages. This latter is an interesting class of languages containing, e.g., all even linear languages. The accepted language classes of various restricted classes and their relations are also analyzed here showing a more finer hierarchy than the previous model has provided.

2 Definitions, Preliminaries

We assume that the reader is familiar with the basic concepts of formal languages and automata, otherwise she or he is referred, e.g., to [4, 12]. We denote the empty word by λ. The set of non-negative integers is denoted by $\mathbb{N}$.

The two strands of the DNA molecule have opposite $5' \to 3'$ orientations. This proposes taking into account a variant of Watson-Crick finite automata that parse two strands of a Watson-Crick tape in opposite directions. Figure 1 indicates the initial configuration of such an automaton on the left. (We note here that the abbreviation WK fits well specially to these automata, since WK comes from the initial of the name Watson and the last letter of the name Crick.) The $5' \to 3'$ WK automaton is sensing, if the heads sense that they meet. We are working with models that finishes the computing process at that phase. In Fig. 1, this moment can be seen on the right. We note that there are also models which continuing the process and they can accept even some non-context-free languages [9].

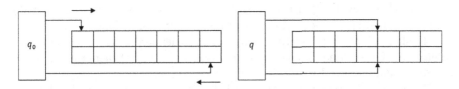

Fig. 1. A sensing $5' \to 3'$ WK automaton in the initial configuration and in an accepting configuration (with a final state q).

Here, we follow the definition and description from [10]. (Later on we will also recall the earlier concept using sensing parameter from, e.g., [9] to show some results connecting the two models.)

Formally, a Watson-Crick automaton is a 6-tuple $M = (V, \rho, Q, q_0, F, \delta)$, where: V is the (input) alphabet, $\rho \subseteq V \times V$ denotes a symmetric binary relation that is called the complementarity relation, Q represents a finite set of states, $q_0 \in Q$ is the initial state, $F \subseteq Q$ is the set of final (or accepting) states and δ is called transition mapping, it is of the form $\delta : Q \times \binom{V^*}{V^*} \to 2^Q$, such that it is nonempty only for finitely many triplets $(q, u, v), q \in Q, u, v \in V^*$.

In sensing $5' \to 3'$ WK automata every pair of positions in the Watson-Crick tape is read by exactly one of the heads in an accepting computation, and therefore the complementarity relation cannot play importance, instead, for simplicity, we assume that it is the identity relation. Thus, it is more convenient to consider the input as a normal word instead the double stranded form. Note here that complementarity can be excluded from the traditional models as well, see [5] for details.

Since δ is not empty only for a finite set of triplets, there is/are a/some word(s) with maximal length that can be read in a transition by a given automaton. Consequently, let us define the radius r of an automaton by the maximum length of the substrings of the input that can be read by the automaton in a transition.

Further, a configuration of a Watson-Crick automaton is a pair (q, w) where q is the current state of the automaton and w is the part of the input word which has not been processed (read) yet. For $w', x, y \in V^*, q, q' \in Q$, we write a transition between two configurations as: $(q, xw'y) \Rightarrow (q', w')$ if and only if $q' \in \delta(q, x, y)$. We denote the reflexive and transitive closure of the relation $\Rightarrow$ (one step of a computation, that is, a transition) by $\Rightarrow^*$ (computation). Therefore, for a given $w \in V^*$, an accepting computation is a sequence of transitions $(q_0, w) \Rightarrow^* (q_F, \lambda)$, starting from the initial state and ending in a final state with no input left.

The language accepted by a WK automaton M is:

$$L(M) = \{w \in V^* | (q_0, w) \Rightarrow^* (q_F, \lambda), q_F \in F\}.$$

It was shown in [10] that the class of sensing $5' \to 3'$ WK automata that we have recalled accepts exactly the class of linear context-free languages.

The shortest nonempty word accepted by M is denoted by w_s, if it is uniquely determined. Otherwise we may use the notation w_s for any of them (in case there are more than one word with this condition).

There are some restricted variants of WK automata which are widely known:

F: all-final, i.e., with only final states: if $Q = F$;

N: stateless, i.e., with only one state: if $Q = F = \{q_0\}$;

S: simple (at most one head moves in a step) $\delta : (Q \times ((\lambda, V^*) \cup (V^*, \lambda))) \to 2^Q$.

1: 1-limited (exactly one letter is being read in each step) $\delta : (Q \times ((\lambda, V) \cup (V, \lambda))) \to 2^Q$.

Clearly, all **N** WK automata are **F** WK automata at the same time. Also, by definition, all **1** WK automata are, in fact, **S** WK automata also. However, since the restrictions **N** and **F** are about the states, and the restrictions **S** and **1** are about the length of the words that can be read in a transition (step of a computation), additional variants are also understood by using mixed constrains such as **F1, N1, FS, NS** WK automata.

We start our studies by the following simple observation.

It is clear that an input with at most length r can be processed in one step, that is, for longer inputs the automaton must make more steps of computation before accepting them.

Now, we formally state and prove a statement about some classes of languages accepted by restricted variants.

Lemma 1. *Let M be an **F1** sensing $5' \to 3'$ WK automaton and let the word $w \in V^+$ that is in $L(M)$. Let $|w| = n$, then for each m, where $0 \le m \le n$, there is at least one word $uv \in L(M)$ such that $|uv| = m$, $w = uxv$ and $u, x, v \in V^*$.*

Proof. By considering the definition of **F1** sensing $5' \to 3'$ WK automaton, w can be accepted in n steps such that in each step, the automaton can read exactly one letter. Moreover, each state is final, therefore by considering the first m steps of the n steps, the word uv is accepted by M, where u is read by the left head and v is read by the right head during these m steps, respectively.   □

Although this lemma is more general and works also for nondeterministic WK automata, it will also be very helpful studying the deterministic variants. Remember, that all **N1** WK automata are also **F1** WK automata at the same type.

So far, we have not given anything about determinism. We are using the following definition. If at each possible configuration at most one transition step is possible, then a WK automaton is deterministic. It means that a WK automaton is deterministic if and only if $\forall w \in V^*$ and $\forall q \in Q$ there exists at most one $w' \in V^*$ and $q' \in Q$ such that $(q, w) \Rightarrow (q', w')$.

We note that for the traditional WK automata reading both strands completely, there are various definitions of determinism (allowing also to play with the complementarity relation), but for our automata there is only one type of determinism.

Determinism is a feature that is orthogonal to the earlier special restrictions, thus we will study here, deterministic sensing $5' \to 3'$ WK automata (without any further restriction), deterministic sensing **F** $5' \to 3'$ WK automata, deterministic sensing **N** $5' \to 3'$ WK automata, deterministic sensing **S** $5' \to 3'$ WK automata, ..., deterministic sensing **F1** $5' \to 3'$ WK automata, ...

Since in this paper we are working only with deterministic sensing $5' \to 3'$ WK automata, usually we abbreviate this term, and write shortly only 'WK automata'.

3   Results on Deterministic Sensing $5' \to 3'$ WK Automata

In this section, we consider the deterministic variants of these automata; and our focus is to establish hierarchy results among the classes of accepted languages.

Allowing long strings to read with both heads may confuse the users to immediately see whether an automaton, in fact, is deterministic. Therefore, we start with a characterisation of the deterministic WK automata.

Proposition 1. *The automaton is not deterministic $5' \to 3'$ WK automaton if and only if $\exists q, q_1, q_2 \in Q$ and $w_L, w_R, u_1^L, u_2^L, u_1^R, u_2^R \in V^*$ such that $q_1 \in \delta(q, w_L u_1^L, u_1^R w_R)$ and $q_2 \in \delta(q, w_L u_2^L, u_2^R w_R)$ where either*

- *$|u_1^i| + |u_2^i| = \max\{|u_1^i|, |u_2^i|\}$ for $i \in \{L, R\}$ and $\exists u_j^i \neq \lambda$, $j \in \{1, 2\}$.*
  or
- *$u_1^L u_1^R u_2^L u_2^R = \lambda$ and $q_1 \neq q_2$.*

The first case of the condition of the theorem allows the cases when exactly one of the strings $u_1^L, u_2^L, u_1^R, u_2^R$ is not empty, and cases, when exactly two of them are nonempty, especially, when $u_1^L \neq \lambda$, $u_2^R \neq \lambda$ and when $u_2^L \neq \lambda$, $u_1^R \neq \lambda$. In the second case of the condition all four of these words are empty.

Next, we start from the smallest classes of languages showing some proper hierarchy results in the next subsection, then some incomparability results are shown to complete the picture among these classes of languages accepted by restricted classes. Finally, we show that some of the restrictions are not real restrictions, but more like normal forms. We also show that our deterministic WK automata accepts exactly the class 2detLIN defined by the deterministic counterpart of the model working with sensing parameter.

3.1   Proper Hierarchy Results

Now, we are focusing on the most restricted classes to obtain our first hierarchy results.

Theorem 1. *The language class that can be accepted by deterministic **N1** sensing $5' \to 3'$ WK automata is properly included in the language class accepted by deterministic **NS** sensing $5' \to 3'$ WK automata.*

Proof. Let us consider the language $L = \{(ab)^n | n \in \mathbb{N}\}$. The shortest nonempty word of L is $w_s = ab$ and in **NS** sensing $5' \to 3'$ WK automaton it can be accepted by one of the transitions: (λ, ab) or (ab, λ). By Lemma 1, w_s cannot be the shortest nonempty word accepted by an **N1** sensing $5' \to 3'$ WK automaton. In the other hand, the language L, as shown in Fig. 2, can be accepted by an **NS** sensing $5' \to 3'$ WK automaton.   □

(ab, λ)

Fig. 2. A deterministic sensing $5' \to 3'$ WK automaton of type **NS** accepting the language $\{(ab)^n | n \in \mathbb{N}\}$.

Theorem 2. *The class of languages that can be accepted by deterministic **NS** sensing $5' \to 3'$ WK automata is properly included in the language class accepted by deterministic **N** sensing $5' \to 3'$ WK automata.*

Proof. Let us consider the language $\{a^{2n}b^{2n} | n \in \mathbb{N}\}$. For this language, the shortest nonempty word w_s is $aabb$. Let us assume that this language is accepted by deterministic **NS** sensing $5' \to 3'$ WK automaton. Then, w_s is accepted by one of the transitions: $(aabb, \lambda)$ or $(\lambda, aabb)$. However, having any of these transitions the accepted language will be different from the language $\{a^{2n}b^{2n} | n \in \mathbb{N}\}$.

For instance, consider the transition $(aabb, \lambda)$. Since the automaton has exactly one state, this transition returns to the same state and by repeating the transition, the language $\{(aabb)^n | n \in \mathbb{N}\}$ can be accepted which language is not a subset of the language we have assumed the automaton accept. This reasoning works also for the transition $(\lambda, aabb)$. Hence, it is impossible to accept the considered language by deterministic **NS** sensing $5' \to 3'$ WK automaton. What is remained to prove is that the language L, as it is shown in Fig. 3, can be accepted by an **N** sensing $5' \to 3'$ WK automaton.   □

Fig. 3. A deterministic sensing $5' \to 3'$ WK automaton of type **N** accepting the language $\{a^{2n}b^{2n} | n \in \mathbb{N}\}$.

The next results highlight the difference between the new model (without sensing parameter) and the old model [9], since deterministic **F1** sensing $5' \to 3'$ WK automata with sensing parameter were so powerful as deterministic sensing $5' \to 3'$ WK automata with sensing parameter without any additional restrictions. In the new model, opposite to this, we have a finer hierarchy:

Theorem 3. *The language class that can be accepted by deterministic **F1** sensing $5' \to 3'$ WK automata is properly included in the language class accepted by deterministic **FS** sensing $5' \to 3'$ WK automata.*

Proof. Let us consider the language $L = \{(ab)^n c^{2m} | n \in \mathbb{N}, m \in \{0, 1\}\}$. The word w_s of this language is ab or cc which can be accepted by (λ, ab), (ab, λ), (cc, λ) or (λ, cc) in an **FS** sensing $5' \to 3'$ WK automaton. According to Lemma 1, w_s cannot be the shortest nonempty accepted word in any **F1** sensing $5' \to 3'$ WK automaton. But L can be accepted by an **FS** sensing $5' \to 3'$ WK automaton (see Fig. 4).   □

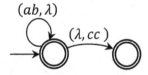

Fig. 4. A deterministic sensing $5' \to 3'$ WK automaton of type **FS** accepting the language $\{(ab)^n c^{2m} | n \in \mathbb{N}, m \in \{0, 1\}\}$.

Theorem 4. *The class of languages that can be accepted by deterministic **FS** sensing $5' \to 3'$ WK automata is properly included in the language class of deterministic **F** sensing $5' \to 3'$ WK automata.*

Proof. Now, we present the language $L = \{a^{2n}c^{5q}b^{2n}|n \in \mathbb{N}, q \in \{0,1\}\}$. Let us assume, contrary that L is accepted by a deterministic **FS** sensing $5' \to 3'$ WK automaton. Let the radius of this automaton be r. Let $w = a^{2m}b^{2m} \in L$ with $m > \frac{r}{4}$. Then the word w cannot be accepted by using only one of the transitions from initial state q_0, i.e., $\delta(q_0, a^{2m}b^{2m}, \lambda)$ or $\delta(q_0, \lambda, a^{2m}b^{2m})$ is not possible. Since, all states are final and every word of L have the same number of a's and b's then neither prefix nor suffix of w can be accepted by a transition from q_0. This fact contradicts to our assumption, hence L cannot be accepted by any deterministic **FS** sensing $5' \to 3'$ WK automata. However, the language L can be accepted by a deterministic **F** sensing $5' \to 3'$ WK automaton (see Fig. 5).   □

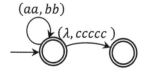

Fig. 5. A deterministic sensing $5' \to 3'$ WK automaton of type **F** accepting the language $\{a^{2n}c^{5q}b^{2n}|n \in \mathbb{N}, q \in \{0,1\}\}$.

Theorem 5. *The class of languages that can be accepted by deterministic **F** sensing $5' \to 3'$ WK automata is properly included in the accepted language class of deterministic sensing $5' \to 3'$ WK automata.*

Proof. Consider the language $L = \{a^n db^n c|n \geq 1\}$ that can be accepted by a deterministic sensing $5' \to 3'$ WK automaton (without restrictions) as it is shown in Fig. 6. In the proof of Theorem 6 in [10], we showed that language L cannot be accepted by any nondeterministic **F** sensing $5' \to 3'$ WK automata. Hence, there is no deterministic **F** sensing $5' \to 3'$ WK automaton that can accept language L and the theorem is proven.   □

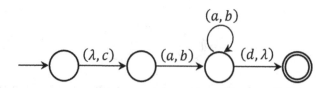

Fig. 6. A deterministic sensing $5' \to 3'$ WK automaton accepts the language $\{a^n db^n c|n \geq 1\}$.

Theorem 6. *The class of languages accepted by deterministic **N/NS/N1** sensing $5' \to 3'$ WK automata is properly included in the class of languages that can be accepted by deterministic **F/FS/F1** sensing $5' \to 3'$ WK automata (respectively).*

Proof. All the three inclusions trivially hold by definition. Let us consider the regular language a^*b^*. This language can easily be accepted even by a deterministic **F1** sensing $5' \to 3'$ WK automaton similarly as by deterministic finite automata using only the left head. Let the automaton have 2 states q and p, where q is the initial. Both states are final (as we use all final automaton). Let it be a loop transition by (a, λ) at q and a loop transition (b, λ) at p. Further let one more transition from q to p by (b, λ). Obviously this is a deterministic **F1**, and thus, also **FS** and **F** sensing $5' \to 3'$ WK automaton accepting the given language.

On the other side it can easily be shown that a^*b^* cannot be accepted by any deterministic **N** (and thus, neither **NS**, nor **N1**) sensing $5' \to 3'$ WK automata. Since both a and b is in the language, the automaton must have loop transition by reading any of these letters. Having these transitions by using the same head leads to accept any word of $\{a, b\}^*$ including, e.g., $baba$ that is clearly not in the language. Using different heads in these transitions, e.g., reading a by the left head while the right head reads nothing and reading b with the right head while the left head reads nothing (even accepting the desired language), however, leads to a not deterministic automaton (by Proposition 1).   □

3.2   Incomparability Results

In this subsection we present some results concerning incomparability of some of the analysed language classes under set theoretical inclusion.

Theorem 7. *The class of languages that can be accepted by deterministic **N** sensing $5' \to 3'$ WK automata is incomparable with the class of languages that can be accepted by deterministic **FS** and deterministic **F1** sensing $5' \to 3'$ WK automata.*

Proof. We present the language $L = \{a^{2n}b^{2n}|n \in \mathbb{N}\}$ that can be accepted by deterministic **N** sensing $5' \to 3'$ WK automaton (Fig. 3). Let us assume that L is accepted by a deterministic **FS** sensing $5' \to 3'$ WK automaton. Let the radius of this automaton be r. Let $w = a^{2m}b^{2m} \in L$ with $m > \frac{r}{4}$. Then the word w cannot be accepted by using only one of the transitions from initial state q_0, i.e., $\delta(q_0, a^{2m}b^{2m}, \lambda)$ or $\delta(q_0, \lambda, a^{2m}b^{2m})$ is not possible. Since, all states are final and every word of L have the same number of a's and b's then neither prefix nor suffix of w can be accepted by a transition from q_0. This fact contradicts to our assumption, hence this language cannot be accepted by any deterministic **FS** sensing $5' \to 3'$ WK automata and obviously by **F1** sensing $5' \to 3'$ WK automata. Thus, it is shown that the language class accepted by deterministic **N** sensing $5' \to 3'$ WK automaton is not included in the language class accepted by deterministic **FS** and **F1** sensing $5' \to 3'$ WK automata.

Now consider language $L = \{a^n b^m | n \in \mathbb{N}, m \in \{0,1\}\}$. This language can be accepted by deterministic **FS** and **F1** sensing $5' \rightarrow 3'$ WK automata (Fig. 7), however, it is not accepted by any deterministic **N** sensing $5' \rightarrow 3'$ WK automata since a deterministic **N** sensing $5' \rightarrow 3'$ WK automaton has one state. The word b is in L. Also if a word contain a letter b, then the automaton needs a transition (b, λ) or (λ, b) and it should appear as a loop. It means that, by using this loop, the automaton can accept the language that contains some words with more than one letter b which is not subset of L. Hence, the language classes accepted by deterministic **FS** and **F1** sensing $5' \rightarrow 3'$ WK automata are not included in the language class accepted by deterministic **N** sensing $5' \rightarrow 3'$ WK automaton.   □

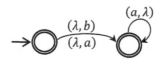

Fig. 7. A sensing $5' \rightarrow 3'$ WK automaton of type **FS** and **F1** accepting the language $L = \{a^n b^m | n \in \mathbb{N}, m \in \{0,1\}\}$.

Theorem 8. *The language class accepted by deterministic **NS** sensing $5' \rightarrow 3'$ WK automata is incomparable with the language class accepted by deterministic **F1** sensing $5' \rightarrow 3'$ WK automata.*

Proof. The language $L = \{(ab)^n | n \in \mathbb{N}\}$ can be accepted by deterministic **NS** sensing $5' \rightarrow 3'$ WK automaton as it was shown in Fig. 2. By using Lemma 1 this language cannot be accepted by any deterministic **F1** sensing $5' \rightarrow 3'$ WK automata. Thus, the language class accepted by deterministic **NS** sensing $5' \rightarrow 3'$ WK automata is not included in the language class accepted by deterministic **F1** sensing $5' \rightarrow 3'$ WK automata.

Now, let us consider the language $L = \{a^n b^m | n \in \mathbb{N}, m \in \{0,1\}\}$. This language can be accepted by the deterministic **F1** sensing $5' \rightarrow 3'$ WK automaton shown in Fig. 7. In the proof of Theorem 7, it was shown the language L cannot be accepted by a deterministic **N** sensing $5' \rightarrow 3'$ WK automaton. Therefore it cannot be accepted by a deterministic **NS** sensing $5' \rightarrow 3'$ WK automaton. Hence the language class accepted by deterministic **F1** sensing $5' \rightarrow 3'$ WK automaton is not included in the language class accepted by deterministic **NS** sensing $5' \rightarrow 3'$ WK automaton.   □

3.3   Some Equivalent Classes (To 2detLIN)

In this subsection first we show that the restricted version not analysed yet, namely deterministic **S** and **1** WK automata accept the same class of languages as the unrestricted deterministic WK automata. Then we recall the concept of sensing $5' \rightarrow 3'$ WK finite automata with sensing parameter. Further, as one of our main results we claim that the new model has the same accepting power as the one with sensing parameter regarding their deterministic counterpart.

As we have already seen in Proposition 1 that deterministic WK-automata may have some not obvious transitions. Consider, e.g., transitions reading pairs of strings $(aa, babab)$ and $(aaac, bbab)$ in a state. It is easy to see that to divide each of those transitions to two allowing only to read the same strings head by head one after the other, we receive an automaton that is not deterministic any more. Thus, we cannot use the technique which can easily be used in the nondeterministic case, we need to work out a more careful technique. However, with a long technical construction the following theorem can be proven.

Theorem 9. *The accepted language classes of deterministic S and 1 sensing $5' \rightarrow 3'$ WK finite automata are equal to the language class that can be accepted by deterministic sensing $5' \rightarrow 3'$ WK finite automata (without restrictions).*

Remark 1. Notice that in deterministic sensing S, and so in deterministic sensing 1 $5' \rightarrow 3'$ WK automata, in each state at most one of the heads is allowed to read. Consequently, the states can be partitioned to two subsets depending on whether the first (left) head is allowed to move or not.

Now the concept of sensing $5' \rightarrow 3'$ WK automaton with sensing parameter is recalled from [8,9]. A 6-tuple $M = (V, \rho, Q, q_0, F, \delta_s)$ is a sensing $5' \rightarrow 3'$ WK automaton with sensing parameter, where, V, ρ, Q, q_0 and F are exactly the same as in our model and δ_s is the transition mapping. It is defined using the sensing condition in the following way:

$\delta_s : \left(Q \times \binom{V^*}{V^*} \times D \right) \rightarrow 2^Q$, where the sensing distance set is defined by

$D = \{0, 1, \ldots, r, +\infty\}$ where r is the radius of the automaton. The set D gives the distance between two heads from 0 to r, and gives $+\infty$, when the distance of the two heads is more than r. On the other hand, by the set D, the automaton controls the appropriate meeting of the heads. Some transitions are allowed or denied depending on the actual distance of the positions of the heads (if it is not more than r) taking care of reading only string(s) having their length not more than the distance of the heads. In a sensing $5' \rightarrow 3'$ WK automaton with sensing parameter a configuration $\binom{w_1}{w_2} (q, s) \binom{w'_1}{w'_2}$ contains the state $q \in Q$, the sensing distance $s \in D$, where the input is $\binom{w_1 w'_1}{w_2 w'_2}$ with the condition $w_1 w'_1 = w_2 w'_2$. The part w_1 has been already processed by the left head (upper strand) and the part w'_2 has been processed by the right head (lower strand). A transition between two configurations can be written as:

$\binom{w_1}{w_2 y} (q, +\infty) \binom{x w'_1}{w'_2} \Rightarrow \binom{w_1 x}{w_2} (q', s) \binom{w'_1}{y w'_2}$ for $w_1, w_2, w'_1, w'_2, x, y \in V^*$

with $|w_2 y| - |w_1| > r, q, q' \in Q$ if and only if $w_1 x w'_1 = w_2 y w'_2$ and $q' \in$

$\delta_s \left(q, \binom{x}{y}, +\infty \right)$, further $s = \begin{cases} |w_2| - |w_1 x|, & \text{if } |w_2| - |w_1 x| \le r, \\ +\infty, & \text{otherwise,} \end{cases}$ and

$$\begin{pmatrix} w_1 \\ w_2y \end{pmatrix} (q, s_1) \begin{pmatrix} xw_1' \\ w_2' \end{pmatrix} \Rightarrow \begin{pmatrix} w_1x \\ w_2 \end{pmatrix} (q', s) \begin{pmatrix} w_1' \\ yw_2' \end{pmatrix} \text{ for } w_1, w_2, w_1', w_2', x, y \in V^*$$

with $0 \leq |w_2y| - |w_1| = s_1 \leq r$, and $q, q' \in Q$ if and only if $w_1xw_1' = w_2yw_2'$ and $q' \in \delta_s\left(q, \begin{pmatrix} x \\ y \end{pmatrix}, s_1\right)$, further $s = |w_2| - |w_1x|$.

A sensing $5' \to 3'$ WK automaton M with sensing parameter accepts a string w if and only if $\begin{pmatrix} \lambda \\ w \end{pmatrix} (q_0, s_0) \begin{pmatrix} w \\ \lambda \end{pmatrix} \Rightarrow^* \begin{pmatrix} w_1' \\ w_1' \end{pmatrix} (q_f, 0) \begin{pmatrix} w_2'' \\ w_2'' \end{pmatrix}$ for $q_f \in F$ where s_0 is $+\infty$ if $|w| > r$, otherwise $|w|$. The automaton M accepts the language $L(M)$ consisting of all such strings. The deterministic sensing $5' \to 3'$ WK automata with sensing parameter were also defined. If there is at most one transition step allowed in each configuration, then the automaton is deterministic. The language class that can be accepted by deterministic $5' \to 3'$ WK automata with sensing parameter is denoted by 2detLin, as these are exactly those languages that are accepted by the deterministic counterpart of a 2-head machine model capable to accept the linear context-free languages. It is known that 2detLin is incomparable with the class of deterministic linear languages accepted by deterministic one-turn pushdown automata [9].

Even we have deterministic sensing $5' \to 3'$ WK automata, in this old model, the possible transitions are depending on the distance of the heads. It is an important difference between the models that Remark 1 does not hold for deterministic sensing **S**, and so 1 $5' \to 3'$ WK automata with sensing parameter. In any state, the transitions should be uniquely defined only for every fixed sensing parameter. Thus, it may happen that a transition reading an a with the left head is allowed with sensing parameter $+\infty$, but the right head may read an a when the sensing distance is 1 such that the automaton is still deterministic. Thus, it is not evident at all if our weaker model (without the additional tool, the parameter) is able to accept the same language class.

However, we can establish the following important result.

Theorem 10. *The language class accepted by deterministic sensing $5' \to 3'$ WK automata without sensing parameter equals to the class of languages that can be accepted by deterministic sensing $5' \to 3'$ WK automata with sensing parameter.*

Proof. By Theorem 4 in [9] and our Theorem 9, it is enough to show that the language class accepted by deterministic 1 sensing $5' \to 3'$ WK automaton without sensing parameter equals to the to the class of languages that can be accepted by a deterministic 1 sensing $5' \to 3'$ WK automaton with sensing parameter. It is obvious that in these latter automata the sensing parameter set D could include only values ∞ and 1. The proof is constructive in both directions.

Let us consider, first, the direction to show that the language class accepted by deterministic 1 sensing $5' \to 3'$ WK automaton without sensing parameter is included in the language class accepted by deterministic 1 sensing $5' \to 3'$ WK automaton with sensing parameter.

Let $A' = (V, id, Q, q_0, F, \delta')$ be the sensing $5' \to 3'$ WK automaton without sensing parameter. The language $L(A')$ can be accepted by this automaton. Let $A = (V, id, Q, q_0, F, \delta_s)$ be the sensing $5' \to 3'$ WK automaton with sensing parameter. For each transition $q' \in \delta'(q, a, \lambda)$ where $a \in V$, let $q' \in \delta_s \left(q, \begin{pmatrix} a \\ \lambda \end{pmatrix}, +\infty \right)$ be the transition in automaton sensing $5' \to 3'$ WK automaton with sensing parameter when $q' \notin F$, otherwise if $q' \in F$ then both $q' \in \delta_s \left(q, \begin{pmatrix} a \\ \lambda \end{pmatrix}, 1 \right)$ and $q' \in \delta_s \left(q, \begin{pmatrix} a \\ \lambda \end{pmatrix}, +\infty \right)$. Similarly this can be done for transition $q' \in \delta'(q, \lambda, a)$. It is clear that the automaton A accepts exactly $L(A')$ having essentially the same accepting computation.

Technical details of the other direction are omitted here due to the page limit. □

We close our results by showing how the new model is applicable to know more about the language class 2detLIN. Note that some closure properties of 2detLIN was already established in [9]. It was shown that this family is not closed under union, concatenation, Kleene-closure. We complement those results by showing the closure under complementation.

Proposition 2. *The language class 2detLIN is closed under the operation set theoretic complement.*

Proof. The idea of the proof is as follows. Based on a deterministic **1** $5' \to 3'$ WK automaton without sensing parameter in which the transitions for each letter is defined, one may complement the set of accepting states. □

4   Conclusions

It was known about sensing $5' \to 3'$ Watson-Crick automata that the general nondeterministic variants (the automata without using any restrictions) of the new model without sensing parameter and the old model with sensing parameter have the same accepting power, i.e., exactly the linear context-free languages [7,9,10] are accepted by them. In this paper we have shown that this is also true for their deterministic counterparts, both of them characterise the class 2detLin. This result was not straightforward, since the sensing parameter gave more freedom in the old model allowing different set of transitions when the heads are close to the meeting point and when they are not. However, the original automata can be efficiently simulated with the new model keeping it deterministic. In this way, by our results, the class 2detLIN can be further analysed using these newer and simpler automata without the very technical sensing parameter.

A summary of our hierarchy results is shown in Fig. 8. We note that the deterministic hierarchy of languages investigated in this paper is very similar to the hierarchy shown for the nondeterministic model in [10], even the classes are different. Already nondeterministic **N1** automata are more powerful than their deterministic variants. We should also recall that, in the nondeterministic case, it was trivial to simulate the string reading feature of the automata by having the restriction to read exactly 1 letter in each transition. This is more technical in the deterministic case (Theorem 9). On the other side, the hierarchy presented here is finer (containing 7 classes) than the hierarchy obtained by the model with sensing parameter (containing only 4 classes including 2detLin, [9]).

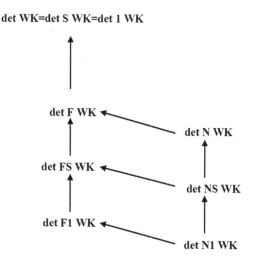

det WK=det S WK=det 1 WK

Fig. 8. Hierarchy of classes of languages accepted by deterministic sensing $5' \rightarrow 3'$ WK finite automata in a Hasse diagram. The language classes are accepted by various types of deterministic sensing $5' \rightarrow 3'$ WK finite automata, the types of the automata are displayed in the figure with the abbreviations: **N:** stateless, **F:** all-final, **S:** simple, **1:** 1-limited. The class on the top of the hierarchy is exactly the formerly known class 2detLin. The language classes for which the containment is not shown are incomparable.

Further comparisons of related language classes and properties of the language classes defined by the new model are left to the future.

References

1. Adleman, L.M.: Molecular computation of solutions to combinational problems. Science **226**, 1021–1024 (1994)
2. Czeizler, E.: A short survey on Watson-Crick automata. Bull. EATCS **88**, 104–119 (2006)
3. Freund, R., Păun, Gh., Rozenberg, G., Salomaa, A.: Watson-Crick finite automata. In: 3rd DIMACS Symposium on DNA Based Computers, Philadelphia, pp. 305–317 (1997)
4. Hopcroft, J.E., Ullman, J.D.: Introduction to Automata Theory: Languages and Computation. Addison-Wesley Publishing Company, Reading (1979)
5. Kuske, D., Weigel, P.: The role of the complementarity relation in Watson-Crick automata and sticker systems. In: Calude, C.S., Calude, E., Dinneen, M.J. (eds.) DLT 2004. LNCS, vol. 3340, pp. 272–283. Springer, Heidelberg (2004). https://doi.org/10.1007/978-3-540-30550-7_23

6. Leupold, P., Nagy, B.: $5' \rightarrow 3'$ Watson-Crick automata with several runs. Fundamenta Informaticae **104**, 71–91 (2010)
7. Nagy, B.: On $5' \rightarrow 3'$ sensing Watson-Crick finite automata. In: Garzon, M.H., Yan, H. (eds.) DNA 2007. LNCS, vol. 4848, pp. 256–262. Springer, Heidelberg (2008). https://doi.org/10.1007/978-3-540-77962-9_27
8. Nagy, B.: On a hierarchy of $5' \rightarrow 3'$ sensing WK finite automata languages. In: CiE 2009, Abstract Booklet, pp. 266–275 (2009)
9. Nagy, B.: On a hierarchy of $5' \rightarrow 3'$ sensing Watson-Crick finite automata languages. J. Log. Comput. **23**(4), 855–872 (2013)
10. Nagy, B., Parchami, S., Mir-Mohammad-Sadeghi, H.: A new sensing $5' \rightarrow 3'$ Watson-Crick automata concept. In: AFL 2017, EPTCS, vol. 252, pp. 195–204 (2017)
11. Păun, Gh., Rozenberg, G., Salomaa, A.: DNA Computing – New Computing Paradigms. Texts in Theoretical Computer Science. An EATCS Series, p. IX, 400. Springer, Heidelberg (1998). https://doi.org/10.1007/978-3-662-03563-4. ISBN 978-3-540-64196-4
12. Rozenberg, G., Salomaa, A.: The Handbook of Formal Languages: Volume 1 Word, Language, Grammar. Springer, Heidelberg (1997). https://doi.org/10.1007/978-3-642-59136-5

Collaborative Computation
in Self-organizing Particle Systems

Alexandra Porter[1]([✉]) and Andrea Richa[2]

[1] Stanford University, Stanford, USA
amporter@stanford.edu
[2] Arizona State University, Tempe, USA
aricha@asu.edu

Abstract. Many forms of programmable matter have been proposed for various tasks. We use an abstract model of self-organizing particle systems for programmable matter which could be used for a variety of applications, including smart paint and coating materials for engineering or programmable cells for medical uses. Previous research using this model has focused on shape formation and other spatial configuration problems (e.g., coating and compression). In this work we study foundational computational tasks that exceed the capabilities of the individual constant size memory of a particle, such as implementing a counter and matrix-vector multiplication. These tasks represent new ways to use these self-organizing systems, which, in conjunction with previous shape and configuration work, make the systems useful for a wider variety of tasks. They can also leverage the distributed and dynamic nature of the self-organizing system to be more efficient and adaptable than on traditional linear computing hardware. Finally, we demonstrate applications of similar types of computations with self-organizing systems to image processing, with implementations of image color transformation and edge detection algorithms.

1 Introduction

The concept of *programmable matter* was first defined by Toffoli and Margolus as a computing medium which can be used dynamically and in arbitrary amounts, controlled by both internal and external events [20]. Examples of programmable matter exist in nature, such as proteins closing wounds, bacteria building colonies, and the construction of coral reefs. These examples indicate potential applications of programmable matter, such as smart paint or coating materials for engineering, programmable cells for medical purposes, or adaptable and recyclable building blocks for everyday objects. These applications require tasks for which programmable matter is uniquely capable, such as shape formation and coating. However, they also require computations resembling those

This work was supported in part by NSF under Awards CCF-1353089 and CCF-1422603, and matching NSF REU awards; this work was conducted while the first author was an undergraduate student at ASU.

S. Stepney and S. Verlan (Eds.): UCNC 2018, LNCS 10867, pp. 188–203, 2018.
https://doi.org/10.1007/978-3-319-92435-9_14

done by traditional computers to process information and make decisions. Work so far using the geometric amoebot model for self-organizing particle systems has focused on spatial configuration, including demonstrating efficient programmable matter algorithms for shape formation, coating, and compression (e.g., [2,8,9]).

We introduce solutions using the amoebot model for basic computational tasks exceeding the capabilities of a single particle, including counting or number storage, and matrix-vector multiplication. Basic constructions for computational tasks can then be used as building blocks to solve more complex problems. Self-organizing particle systems have the potential to increase efficiency of algorithms by using dynamic spatial configurations of these computational building blocks to minimize communication costs. We describe and analyze a binary counter algorithm and a matrix-vector multiplication algorithm using the amoebot model. In order to illustrate how our algorithms can be used as part of more complex systems, we discuss concrete applications of our matrix-vector multiplication approach to the image processing tasks of color transformations and edge detection.

1.1 Amoebot Model

In the amoebot model, we represent the particle system as a subset of an infinite, undirected graph $G = (V, E)$, where V is the set of all possible positions a particle can occupy, and E is the set of all possible transitions between positions in V [7]. In the *geometric amoebot model* we impose an underlying geometric structure for G in the form of the *equilateral triangular grid*, as shown in Fig. 1(a). Each particle occupies either a single node (i.e., it is *contracted*) or a pair of two adjacent nodes (i.e., it is *expanded*) on the graph, and each node can be occupied by at most one particle at any point in time, as shown in Fig. 1(b). Two distinct particles occupying adjacent nodes are connected by a *bond* and we refer to such particles as *neighbors*. The bonds ensure the particle system forms a connected structure and are used for exchanging information.

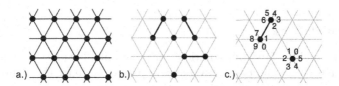

Fig. 1. (a) A section of G, where nodes of G are shown as black circles; (b) five particles on G; the underlying graph G is depicted as a gray mesh; a contracted particle is depicted as a single black circle and an expanded particle is depicted as two black circles connected by an edge; (c) labeling of bonds for an expanded particle and a contracted particle.

Each particle is *anonymous*, meaning it has no globally unique identifier. Particles may communicate with each neighbor by reading and writing to their shared constant sized memory, which can equivalently be considered as the ability to pass a limited number of bounded-size tokens to adjacent particles.[1] Particles move by asynchronously executing a series of *expansions* and *contractions*. If a particle occupies only one node, it is contracted and can expand to an unoccupied adjacent node. An expanded particle can then contract to occupy only one of the two nodes it occupied while expanded.

We assume a compass-free model, meaning there is no global sense of orientation shared by the particles, and we assume that the particles do not share any underlying coordinate system in G. In the case of the triangular grid, each particle p fixes an arbitrary head direction, which specifies an adjacent edge e_{head} to p. We assume particles have shared *chirality* (sense of clockwise direction) and so they can label their ports in a consistent direction (note that in the presence of gravity, chirality follows naturally). Ports are labeled from 0 to 5 or from 0 to 9 depending on if the particle is expanded. Possible labelings for two nodes are shown in Fig. 1(c).

We assume an asynchronous, concurrent system of particles, where conflicts of movement (e.g., two particles trying to expand into the same empty node location) or shared memory (e.g., two adjacent particles trying to write concurrently onto their shared memory) are resolved arbitrarily so that at most one of the particles involved in the conflict "wins". Thus we can rely on the seminal results for the classical asynchronous model in distributed computing (see, e.g., [14]) that state that any asynchronous execution of the system, where conflicts are resolved arbitrarily, produces an equivalent outcome as a sequence of *atomic particle activations*. Hence, we can assume, without loss of generality, that at most one particle is active at any point in time. Under this model, we define:

Definition 1. *An* asynchronous round *is given by the elapsed time until each particle has been activated at least once.*

In our context, when a particle is activated it can perform an arbitrary bounded amount of computation using its local memory and the shared memory of its neighbors, and at most one movement.

1.2   Related Work

There are a number of existing solutions for programmable matter, which can be categorized as active and passive systems. In passive systems, the computational units have no ability to control their motion, so they move and bond only based on their structure and environmental conditions. Passive systems include DNA computing and tile assembly models, in which computation occurs as a result of tiles bonding together in ways controlled by the tile attributes (see, e.g. [16,22]. Work on tile assembly considers computational problems similar to those we study, including demonstration of a binary counter [18]. However, the specifications of those systems (passive motion, unlimited supply of tiles of any type, etc.) differ considerably from ours. Active systems consist of computational units

---

[1] For more details on our message sharing model, please refer to [7].

that control their actions, motions, and communications to accomplish specific tasks. Applications of active systems, including shape formation, coating, and compression, have been explored using robotic implementations (see, e.g. [13]). These applications have also been explored using abstract models (see, e.g. [5]), including the amoebot model (see [8] and the referencestherein), which is an active system. The amoebot system has also been used for the application of building convex hulls [6], which requires a binary counter or similar computational primitive.

Classical algorithms for distributed matrix multiplication include Fox's [10] and Cannon's [1]. These divide matrices into consecutive blocks to perform multiplication. More recent algorithms, including the Scalable Universal Matrix Multiplication Algorithm (SUMMA) [21] and Distribution-Independent Matrix Multiplication Algorithm (DIMMA) [4], further reduce the number of necessary operations. In SUMMA, the matrix is divided into rows and columns of blocks, and values are then broadcast down columns and across rows. DIMMA improves on this by adding pipelining to communication and taking advantage of a Least-Common Multiple strategy to reduce computation requirements. Our simpler algorithm for matrix-vector multiplication broadcasts values down columns of the matrix in a way similar to how values are broadcast in SUMMA and DIMMA.

In the field of computer vision and image processing, matrix multiplication is used to apply operators for fundamental tasks including determining gradient (see, e.g. [19]) and measuring color invariants such as luminance [11]. Basic color transformations operators, such as adjustments to brightness, saturation, and hue are also often used in image editing [12].

An application of these image operators is edge detection, which is an important problem due to its applications in feature extraction and recognition. The edge detection algorithm introduced by Canny uses a series of steps including smoothing, filtering, and thresholding to extract edges from an image [3]. Research has been done into how to implement this method efficiently, including a distributed GPU implementation [15].

1.3   Our Contributions

We address the very basic and general problems of *counting* and *matrix-vector multiplication*. We describe the image processing applications of *edge detection* and *color transformations*, as examples of applications that can use and benefit from our matrix-vector and matrix-matrix multiplication setup and algorithms. We assume each instance of these problems is fed into our particle system as a sequence of values passed through a seed particle. Results are stored distributed across the system, and can be output by each particle individually or passed to the seed to output the result as a data stream.

We present an algorithm for a basic *binary counter* using the amoebot model, and show that it counts to a value v in $O(v)$ *asynchronous rounds*. We also present a two-part algorithm for *matrix-vector multiplication* using the amoebot model. The first part of the algorithm is to self-organize particles to set up the input matrix and vector and the resulting vector entries. The second part of the algorithm distributedly performs the actual multiplication (note that these two algorithmic components run concurrently and there is no need for synchronization). Let h and w denote the number of rows and columns of the matrix (unknown to the set of particles). We show that the *number of asynchronous rounds* it takes to *set up* the matrix and vector entries is $O(hw)$ and the *number of rounds required for matrix-vector multiplication* is $O(h + w)$. Extending this result by executing a sequence of matrix-vector multiplications, the *number of rounds required for matrix-matrix multiplication* is $O(y(h + w))$ with a second matrix of height w and width y, for a total of $O(hw + y(h+w))$ rounds including setup.

As an example of an application of our approach, we describe and analyze a simple implementation of *Canny edge detection* in image processing, which utilizes the setup algorithm introduced for matrix-vector multiplication. We show this implementation requires $O(1)$ *rounds to complete edge detection* after the $O(hw)$ setup is completed (again no synchronization between these two algorithmic phases is needed). Another sample application of our approach in image processing is that of *color transformation*, which is setup in the same way with $O(hw)$ rounds and then requires $O(y(h + w))$ rounds for multiplication. We also provide experimental results on actual implementations of the Canny edge detection algorithm and the color transformation algorithm we consider.

2   Preliminaries

In each of the problems considered here, we categorized particles as being either in the *structure* built for the operation or as *free* particles.

Definition 2. *At any point during the execution of the algorithm the* structure *refers to the set of particles recruited for use in some operations and assigned a specific role and position for that operation. They are in one of the states {seed, matrix, vector, counter, prestop, result}.*

Definition 3. *At any point during the execution of the algorithm, the set of free particles consists of those particles that are not yet assigned a specific purpose. They are in one of the states {leader, follower, inactive}.*

Free particles may eventually become part of the structure or remain available for other uses. As free particles they actively move to make themselves available to extend the structure if needed, but may continue moving indefinitely if they are not recruited. Particle states are defined as the corresponding algorithms are presented in Sects. 3, 4, and 5.

Tokens are small structures (of constant size) of data which are held by exactly one particle at a time during their existence. Tokens are treated as units or allowed to carry a value within the constant range determined by their storage size, depending on the algorithm. Respecting the particles' memory constraints, each particle holds at most a constant number of tokens at any time. Configurations and schedules are defined for a set of particles and will be used to analyze the progress of the entire system toward the final goal.

Definition 4. *A configuration of the particle system at a point in time consists of the set of state variables P_j for each particle j, including position, current state, and tokens held.*

We use $p_C(t)$ to describe the position of token t at configuration C: If particle j holds t in configuration C, then $p_C(t) = j$ (ownership of t is indicated in P_j). Tokens travel through a predefined sequence of nodes, regardless of which particles occupy those nodes during the execution of the algorithm.

Definition 5. *A token path of length m is a set of particles $P_{k_1}, P_{k_2}, ..., P_{k_m}$ such that P_{k_l} is adjacent to $P_{k_{l+1}}$ and one or more tokens travel from P_{k_x} to P_{k_y} passing through only particles in the path for some x, y with $1 \leq x < y \leq m$.*

We consider a configuration C to be valid if the system is connected (including both the structure and free particle set) and each particle is either contracted or expanded into adjacent positions with no single position occupied by two particles. When clear from context, we will refer to the particle j and P_j indistinctly.

In an asynchronous execution, the system progresses through a sequence of *asynchronous rounds* (Definition 1). When a particle P_j is activated during an asynchronous round, if it holds a token t it can pass t to any neighbor which has available token capacity at the time of the current activation of P_j.

3   Binary Particle Counter Algorithm

The first computational application of the amoebot model we analyze is a binary counter. The binary counter we describe here will also be used as a primitive for the matrix-vector multiplication algorithm presented in Sect. 4. In this implementation, the system contains only the seed particle and a set of initially inactive particles, already forming a line with the seed at the end at round 0.[2]

We denote the non-seed particles $P_0, ..., P_{n-1}$ such that P_0 is a neighbor of the seed particle, denoted S, and labeling follows the line of particles moving away from the seed. Each non-seed particle represents a digit of the counter, with the particle in line closest to the seed representing the least significant bit of the counter. Each P_j with $j < n-1$ receives counting tokens (treated as units) only from P_{j-1} (or S if $j = 0$). When P_j reaches its token capacity, here defined as two, it discards one token and attempts to send the other, representing a carryover, to P_{j+1}. The value of the system as a whole can then be calculated using the state of each digit particle to determine the value it represents.

The seed behaves as an interface to the counter. It receives activations from an external source to increment the counter, upon which it constructs new tokens and sends those to P_0 if there is space in the shared memory with P_0. Due to space limitations, the pseudocode describing this procedure appears in the full arXiv paper [17].

---

[2] If a line of particles is not readily available, one can easily build one following the algorithm presented in [9] concurrently with the binary counting procedure – i.e., there is no need for synchronization of the phases.

3.1   Runtime Analysis

All of our algorithms, presented in Sects. 3, 4, and 5, follow an asynchronous execution. However, for the analyses of these algorithms, we considered executions according to parallel schedules, since those are easier to handle and will provide a worst-case scenario in terms of number of rounds for asynchronous schedules. In a parallel execution, the system progresses through a sequence of *parallel rounds*.

Definition 6. *During one* parallel round *starting with configuration C and resulting in configuration C^*, one of the following is true for each particle p:*

1. *p occupies the same node(s) in C and C^*,*
2. *p occupies one node in C and expands to an additional adjacent node during the round,*
3. *p occupies two adjacent nodes in C and contracts to a single node during the round, leaving the other node empty in C^*, or*
4. *p occupies two adjacent nodes in C and contracts in a handover such that in C^* a different particle has expanded into one of the nodes p occupied in C.*

Additionally, for each token t, let P_k be such that $k = p_C(t)$. Then at the end of the parallel round one of the following is true:

1. *$p_{C^*}(t) = p_C(t)$,*
2. *if a particle $P_{k'}$ adjacent to P_k is below capacity in C, $p_{C^*}(t) = k'$, or*
3. *if there is a token path length d (labeled as particles $P_{k_1}, ..., P_{k_d}$), for each $1 \leq l \leq d - 1$ the particle P_{k_l} in the path has a token t_l (such that $t = t_l$ for some l) which needs to move to $P_{k_{l+1}}$, and P_{k_l} has available token capacity, then $p_{C^*}(t_l) = p_C(t_l) + 1$ for each $1 \leq l \leq d - 1$.*

Definition 7. *A movement schedule $(C_0, C_1, ...C_f)$ is a* parallel schedule *if each C_i is a valid configuration and for each $i \geq 0$, C_{i+1} is reached from C_i in exactly one parallel round.*

In asynchronous execution, the system progresses through a sequence of *particle activations*, meaning only one particle is active at a time. When activated, a particle can perform an arbitrary bounded amount of computation (including passing tokens) and make at most one movement. An *asynchronous round* is the elapsed time until each particle has been activated at least once. When a particle P is activated, if it holds a token t it can pass t to any neighbor which has available token capacity at the time of the current activation of P.

Definition 8. *A movement schedule $(C_0, C_1, ...C_f)$ is an* asynchronous schedule *if each C_i is a valid configuration and for each $i \geq 0$, C_{i+1} is reached from C_i by execution of one asynchronous round.*

We now provide a brief, high-level sketch of the proof that shows that a counter with n particles can count to v (where $v \leq 2^n - 1$) in $\Theta(v)$ asynchronous rounds (the proofs and more details can be found in our full arXiv paper [17]).

Lemma 1. *For any asynchronous particle activation sequence A, there exists a parallel schedule P such that the number of asynchronous rounds needed by the binary counter algorithm according to A is at most equal to the number of parallel rounds required by the algorithm following P.*

We can then count the total number of bit flips that occur in the counter to get the result:

Lemma 2. *The parallel binary counter algorithm counts to the value v in $O(v)$ parallel rounds.*

Combining these two results, we get:

Theorem 1. *The asynchronous binary counter counts to the value v in $\Theta(v)$ asynchronous rounds.*

4   Particle Matrix Multiplication Algorithm

The next computational problem we solve using the amoebot model is matrix-vector multiplication. As before, the seed acts as a source of external input into the system. We suppose the system is initially unaware of the dimensions or values of the matrix and vector to be multiplied, so they will enter the system through the seed particle. The stream of information entering the system from the seed can contain values of matrix or vector entries (we assume each fits on a single particle), end of column markers, and end of vector markers. The seed particle at no point computes the dimensions of the problem since it receives values online in sequence from an external source. The seed then passes values, encapsulated in tokens, into the system as the algorithm proceeds. As these values are passed, the system "recruits" particles to represent the different matrix, vector, and result entries, by having the particles occupy the respective position in the system. We describe how the necessary matrix-vector result structure is built in Sect. 4.1. Below we give an abstract description of how the matrix-vector multiplication proceeds, assuming we have the necessary particles in place to perform the respective operations.

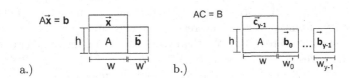

Fig. 2. (a) General matrix-vector multiplication $A\boldsymbol{x}$ setup for $h \times w$ matrix A and $w \times 1$ vector $\boldsymbol{x}$; (b) general matrix-matrix multiplication AC for $h \times w$ matrix A and $w \times y$ matrix C. Shown during final matrix-vector multiplication $A\boldsymbol{c}_{y-1}$.

Let A be a $h \times w$ matrix and $\boldsymbol{x}$ be a $w \times 1$ vector for some nonzero integers h and w. The result of the matrix vector multiplication $A\boldsymbol{x}$ is then $\boldsymbol{b}$, which is stored using a set of the binary counters described in Sect. 3. The problem is streamed into the system in the order: values for each matrix column from top to bottom, left to right, followed by the values of x ordered from top to bottom. As vector values reach their final positions, vector particles also generate result counter tokens, which are passed along to determine how many particles should position themselves to store the results of the multiplication.

As shown in Fig. 2(a), particles assigned to represent values of x are positioned across the top of those representing matrix A, such that the line of matrix particles directly below a vector particle is the corresponding matrix column. The vector value is then passed down the column and used by each matrix particle it reaches to produce an individual product. Products are then passed across the row of matrix columns to where the set of result particles are positioned to store the product totals.

This algorithm can also be extended to complete matrix-matrix multiplication. To multiply matrices A and C, the setup is the same as before but with the first column of C, c_0 replacing the vector x. If C has a width of y, after each column c_i is multiplied by A, for $i < y$, we add a new set of results particles to store the vector b_i. Thus the entire result matrix B can be stored as series of vectors $b_0, b_1, ..., b_{y-1}$, as shown in Fig. 2(b).

The matrix, vector, and result particles do not know their indices relative to the whole system but can orient themselves such that they know which direction is across the matrix row and which direction is down the matrix column. To multiply a matrix by multiple vectors in a stream, this setup only needs to be executed once. If a finished notification is sent to the seed after each matrix-vector multiplication completes, an additional vector can be used without any changes to the matrix.

4.1   The Algorithm

We refine the notation of a configuration from Sect. 2 to specify the particles' functions in the final system. Let $C_i = (M_{0,0}, M_{0,1}...M_{0,w-1}, M_{1,0}...M_{h-1,w-1},$ $R_{0,0}, R_{0,1}, ..., R_{0,w'}, ...R_{1,0}...R_{h,w'}, V_0, V_1...V_{w-1})$ be the configuration at round i where $M_{u,v}$ is the configuration of the particle which will eventually be the matrix particle at position (u, v), $R_{u,q}$ will be a result particle at position (u, q) in the results matrix, and V_v is the vector particle at index v in vector x. Let c be the token capacity of matrix, vector and result particles, and let m be the maximum value of a matrix or vector entry. We then use w' to denote the number of columns of results particles constructed, so $0 \leq u < h$, $0 \leq v < w$, and $0 \leq q < w'$. Enough result columns are constructed to hold the maximum possible number of tokens generated, so $w' = \lceil \log_c(m^2 w) \rceil$. Finally, we denote the minimum number of particles necessary to complete setup as n', so $n' = hw + w + hw'$. Since particles are given tasks on a first-come, first-serve basis, particles that remain free particles throughout execution do not have any effect on the correctness of the system.

Particles are categorized in configurations based on their final location, but are all initially free particles (except for the seed particle). At the start of execution, the spanning forest algorithm in [9] is used to organize the connected system of free particles into trees rooted on the seed particle (for completeness, we present the full spanning forest algorithm in [17] as well). Free particles adjacent to the seed are called *leaders* and all other free particles are *followers*, so each leader is the root of a tree of followers. Leader particles move along the surface of the structure (initially consisting of just the seed particle) until they are assigned a role and position in the structure. As leader particles move, they pull along their attached trees of follower particles. When follower particles become adjacent to the structure, they also become leaders and begin moving along the surface.

Flags are set from the seed, vector, and matrix particles to point to where a new particle needs to be added to the structure. As a free particle moves along the surface, it will stop and become part of the structure when one of these flags points to it. Result particles are similarly recruited by setting flags to point to where a particle may be needed based on the maximum possible values of the matrix and vector, but result particles have the option to leave the structure after multiplication has completed if they are not needed to represent the result.

Tokens travel in a predetermined direction in the set of matrix, vector, and result particles. For clarity, we extend the range of the position function $p(t)$ for token t to be ordered pairs representing position in a two-dimensional arrangement of system particles. Input matrix and vector entries are bounded such that an individual token can carry an input vector or matrix value.

Figure 3(a) conceptually shows a system in the process of executing the setup algorithm. Note that any notions of "up/down" and "left/right" are relative to the orientation passed to the system from the seed particle, and do not assume any absolute orientation of the system. At the depicted point in time, each of the matrix values $m_{0,0}, m_{1,0} \ldots m_{h,0}, m_{0,1}, \ldots m_{u-4,v}$ has been streamed into the system through the seed, and assigned to a corresponding particle. For example, the value $m_{0,0}$ is assigned to particle $M_{0,0}$ at the upper left corner of the matrix. Additional matrix tokens (squares labeled t) hold the next three matrix values to be assigned positions.

The next value to be assigned to a token, $m_{u,v}$ is shown at the head of the stream of values entering the seed particle. A token holding $m_{u,v}$ will follow the same path as the other tokens depicted, across the row of vector particles $(V_0, \ldots V_v)$ to the furthest particle, V_v, that has been recruited so far, and then down the corresponding matrix column. The most recently added matrix particle, $M_{u-4,v}$, will be responsible for recruiting a new matrix particle from the set of free particles (not shown) to be $M_{u-3,v}$ and hold the value $m_{u-3,v}$. This process will continue until the last column is completed.

The last part of the value stream, shown in the left half of the stream entering the seed in Fig. 3(a), is the set of vector values. Vector values are assigned to the first vector particle they reach which does not yet have a value. As each vector value is assigned, a result counter token (treated as a unit) is generated and passed down the vector away from the seed. In Fig. 3(b) these are

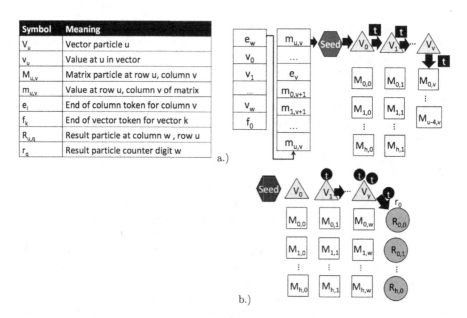

Fig. 3. Diagram of system setup and notation used. Shapes labeled $V_v, M_{u,v}$, or $R_{u,q}$ are particles and small squares/circles labeled t are tokens. In (a) the square tokens hold the matrix values $m_{u-3,v}$, $m_{u-2,v}$, and $m_{u-1,v}$ while in (b) the circular tokens are unit tokens without values. Free particles are not shown.

the circular tokens which are passed from V_{w-1} to $R_{0,0}$ such that $R_{0,0}, R_{1,0}, \ldots$ acts as a counter. When the farthest vector particle receives or generates result counter tokens it begins to recruit particles to start forming the result segment of the structure. When using multiple matrix-vector multiplications to perform a matrix-matrix multiplication, the existing result particles at the end of each matrix-vector product stop performing operations other than passing tokens. Then new sets of result particles are recruited for each matrix-vector multiplication in the sequence. Note that all phases of the algorithm are running *concurrently*, and there is *no synchronization between phases*. In order to prove the correctness and runtime of our algorithm, we will show that the different phases of our algorithm eventually correctly terminate in order.

Once the first end of vector marker, f_0, is received by the seed, setup will be completed and the multiplication can be executed, as summarized by the following steps:

1. each vector particle V_u passes its value v_u in a token to matrix particle $M_{u,0}$,
2. each matrix particle $M_{u,v}$ with value $m_{u,v}$ computes the product $m_{u,v} \cdot v_u$,
3. $M_{u,v}$ passes the vector value v_u to $M_{u+1,v}$ (if $M_{u+1,v}$ exists) so the vector value continues to move down the column,
4. $M_{u,v}$ passes a total of $m_{u,v} \cdot v_u$ result counter tokens to $M_{u,v+1}$ (or $R_{u,0}$ if $M_{u,v+1}$ does not exist), i.e. to the right across the row, and

5. each result particle $R_{u,v}$ accepts result counter tokens until at capacity, and then clears its counter and passes a carry over token to $R_{u+1,v}$ (executing the binary counter algorithm relative to its row of result particles).

Once multiplication has completed, the excess particles recruited to be result particles can be released back to being free, so that the final system configuration is minimal. Detailed pseudocode descriptions of the algorithms can be found in [17].

4.2   Correctness and Runtime Analysis

Similarly to the binary counter case, in order to show bounds on the runtime of the matrix multiplication system, we show bounds for a parallel schedule (Definition 7) and show that such a parallel schedule is dominated by the asynchronous schedule. For comparisons of progress in a system, we look at how close particles and tokens are to their final position nodes of the graph G. We give a high-level sketch of the proof here; please see [17] for the full proof.

Each matrix value token's final position is at the particle in the input matrix structure corresponding to the value. Each vector value token's final position is at the bottom matrix particle in the column under the vector particle corresponding to their value. Each product token's final position is in the counter representing the value of the result vector corresponding to the matrix row in which the product token originated. By comparing progress of tokens and particles toward their final destinations, we show:

Lemma 3. *For any asynchronous particle activation sequence A, there exists a parallel schedule $\mathcal{P}$ such that the number of asynchronous rounds needed by the matrix-vector multiplication algorithm according to A is at most equal to the number of parallel rounds required by the algorithm following $\mathcal{P}$.*

We first consider the setup phase, which includes particles moving into the structure configuration of *matrix*, *vector*, and *result* particles and the passing of tokens corresponding to inputted matrix and vector values. To show that system setup completes in $O(n')$ parallel rounds, we first show that our modified spanning tree primitive supplies particles to construction as necessary, so that:

Lemma 4. *Each matrix and result particle column takes $O(h)$ rounds to fill with particles in the parallel execution.*

Since $w + w' = O(w)$ columns need to be filled, we get:

Lemma 5. *The parallel matrix system setup completes in $O(n')$ rounds.*

Lemma 5, together with Lemma 3, implies:

Theorem 2. *The streaming matrix system setup completes in $\Theta(n')$ rounds.*

We next consider the actual matrix-vector multiplication process. Multiplication is initiated by each vector particle sending a token representing the value corresponding to its position down the column of the matrix, such that it is seen by the matrix particle at each position which directly multiplies with that vector value. The amount of computation for the multiplication step is bounded by the time for tokens to travel down matrix columns and across matrix and result rows, so we have:

Lemma 6. *The parallel matrix-vector multiplier completes in $O(h + w)$ rounds.*

Theorem 3. *The asynchronous matrix-vector multiplier completes calculations in $\Theta(h + w)$ rounds.*

We can extend the result of Theorem 3 for matrix-matrix multiplications, namely:

Theorem 4. *The asynchronous matrix-matrix multiplier for matrices of dimensions $h \times w$ and $w \times y$ completes calculations in $\Theta(y(h + w))$ rounds.*

5   Image Processing Applications

Both the setup and multiplication steps of the matrix-vector multiplication algorithm can be used in image processing applications. Individual particles can be assigned to store individual pixels or small grids of pixels of an image, and their proximity to particles holding the corresponding adjacent pixels makes a number of localized image processing algorithms highly efficient.

We first discuss using the amoebot model to execute the Canny edge detection algorithm on a single channel image, meaning with a single scalar value for each pixel. Pixel values are streamed into the system as matrix values and a grid is established in the same way as in matrix-vector multiplication setup (Sect. 4.1), but without the requirement of result particles. Thus matrix particles store the image and can independently start to execute the algorithm as soon as they receive a value. The Canny edge detection algorithm includes local comparisons between pixel values and a matrix convolution operation to identify pixels most likely to be on the edges (see [17] for the full algorithm). Since these operations do not require information to travel between particles further than a constant distance, we have that:

Theorem 5. *Edge detection will complete in constant time after image setup.*

We next discuss how to use the amoebot model to execute image color transformations that use matrix-matrix multiplications. In this application, the input matrix has a row corresponding to each pixel of the original image and three columns corresponding to red, green, and blue. The transformation matrix is then streamed into the system as a sequence of vectors, each of which is multiplied by the matrix. The values in the transformation matrix determine the operation, such as filtering or saturation changes.

6   Simulation Results

As expected, Fig. 4(a) shows that the number of rounds required for the binary counter to reach a value v increases linearly with v. The results shown are each for a set of 10 particles arranged in a line before the system begins to execute. Value counted is the number of distinct counter tokens fed into the system by the seed particle.

For matrix-vector multiplication, the experiments in Fig. 4(b) show an approximately linear increase in the number of rounds for system setup and execution as the number of particles for the matrix-vector structure, n', increases.

In Fig. 4(c) we show two examples of edge detection on small images. The implementation discards an outer boundary at each step rather than using an inference method to fill in nonexistent values around edge pixels, so the images are padded with borders of zero-value pixels before inputted into the system. Results of edge detection are shown for a simple 10×10 shape and a more complex 16×16 image of a coin.

Figure 4(d) shows the results of color transformations by multiplying an image matrix by a 3×3 operator. The upper right example shows increased saturation, the bottom left shows conversion to grayscale, and the lower right shows color filtering.

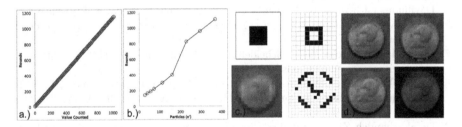

Fig. 4. (a) Asynchronous rounds per value of v counted in the binary counter; (b) asynchronous rounds per vector dimension in matrix-vector multiplication; (c) edge detection results (using red component of RGB); (d) color transformation results. (Color figure online)

7   Discussion

We have described basic computational algorithms that can be used in much larger computing applications, such as image processing tasks or building convex hulls [6]. Due to the limitations of the system receiving input through a seed particle, the binary counter requires $\Theta(v)$ asynchronous rounds to count to a value of v. The setup of the matrix-vector multiplication system is similarly limited by the input and time to assemble the structure of particles, so it requires $\Theta(n')$ rounds to setup the n' particles used to represent the matrix, vector, and the vector of the product. However, the actual matrix-vector multiplication operations benefit from the parallelism of the system and each matrix-vector multiplication requires only $\Theta(h + w)$ asynchronous rounds (recall that h is the matrix height and w is the matrix width). This is especially beneficial for a matrix-matrix multiplication which requires only one execution of the setup algorithm (excluding the setup of additional results particles) to multiply an input matrix by each column of the other input matrix.

References

1. Cannon, L.E.: A cellular computer to implement the Kalman Filter Algorithm. Technical report, DTIC Document (1969)
2. Cannon, S., Daymude, J.J., Randall, D., Richa, A.W.: A Markov chain algorithm for compression in self-organizing particle systems. In: ACM PODC, pp. 279–288 (2016)
3. Canny, J.: A computational approach to edge detection. IEEE Trans. Pattern Anal. Mach. Intell. **6**, 679–698 (1986)
4. Choi, J.: A new parallel matrix multiplication algorithm on distributed-memory concurrent computers. In: HPC Asia 1997, pp. 224–229. IEEE (1997)
5. Das, S., Flocchini, P., Santoro, N., Yamashita, M.: On the computational power of oblivious robots: forming a series of geometric patterns. In: SIGACT-SIGOPS, pp. 267–276. ACM (2010)
6. Daymude, J.J., Gmyr, R., Hinnenthal, K., Kostitsyna, I., Richa, A.W., Scheideler, C.: Convex hull formation in self-organizing particle systems (2018). Manuscript in preparation
7. Daymude, J.J., Richa, A.W., Scheideler, C.: The Amoebot model (2017). https://sops.engineering.asu.edu/sops/
8. Derakhshandeh, Z., Gmyr, R., Richa, A.W., Scheideler, C., Strothmann, T.: Universal shape formation for programmable matter. In: ACM SPAA, pp. 289–299 (2016)
9. Derakhshandeh, Z., Gmyr, R., Strothmann, T., Bazzi, R.A., Richa, A.W., Scheideler, C.: Leader election and shape formation with self-organizing programmable matter. DNA **21**, 117–132 (2015)
10. Fox, G.C., Otto, S.W., Hey, A.J.: Matrix algorithms on a hypercube I: matrix multiplication. Parallel Comput. **4**(1), 17–31 (1987)
11. Geusebroek, J.M., Van den Boomgaard, R., Smeulders, A.W.M., Geerts, H.: Color invariance. IEEE Trans. Pattern Anal. Mach. Intell. **23**(12), 1338–1350 (2001)
12. Haeberli, P.: Matrix operations for image processing (1993). http://www.sgi.com/graca/matrix/index.html
13. Kernbach, S.: Handbook of Collective Robotics: Fundamentals and Challenges. CRC Press, Boca Raton (2013)
14. Lynch, N.A.: Distributed Algorithms. Morgan Kaufmann, San Francisco (1996)
15. Ogawa, K., Ito, Y., Nakano, K.: Efficient canny edge detection using a GPU. In: ICNC, pp. 279–280. IEEE (2010)
16. Patitz, M.J.: An introduction to tile-based self-assembly and a survey of recent results. Nat. Comput. **13**(2), 195–224 (2014)
17. Porter, A., Richa, A.W.: Collaborative computation in self-organizing particle systems. arXiv preprint arXiv:1710.07866 (2017)

18. Rothemund, P.W., Winfree, E.: The program-size complexity of self-assembled squares. In: ACMSTOC, pp. 459–468. ACM (2000)
19. Sobel, I.: An Isotropic 3 × 3 Image Gradient Operator. Machine Vision for Three-dimensional Scenes, pp. 376–379 (1990)
20. Toffoli, T., Margolus, N.: Programmable matter: concepts and realization. Physica D **47**, 263–272 (1991)
21. Van De Geijn, R.A., Watts, J.: SUMMA: scalable universal matrix multiplication algorithm. Concurrency Pract. Experience **9**(4), 255–274 (1997)
22. Woods, D.: Intrinsic universality and the computational power of self-assembly. Phil. Trans. R. Soc. A **373**(2046), 20140214 (2015)

Phase Transitions in Swarm Optimization Algorithms

Tomáš Vantuch[1(✉)], Ivan Zelinka[1], Andrew Adamatzky[2],
and Norbert Marwan[3]

[1] Department of Computer science, Technical University of Ostrava,
Ostrava, Czech Republic
tomas.vantuch@vsb.cz
[2] Unconventional Computing Lab, UWE, Bristol, UK
[3] Transdisciplinary Concepts and Methods,
Potsdam Institute for Climate Impact Research (PIK),
Potsdam, Germany

Abstract. Natural systems often exhibit chaotic behavior in their space-time evolution. Systems transiting between chaos and order manifest a potential to compute, as shown with cellular automata and artificial neural networks. We demonstrate that swarms optimisation algorithms also exhibit transitions from chaos, analogous to motion of gas molecules, when particles explore solution space disorderly, to order, when particles follow a leader, similar to molecules propagating along diffusion gradients in liquid solutions of reagents. We analyse these 'phase-like' transitions in swarm optimization algorithms using recurrence quantification analysis and Lempel-Ziv complexity estimation. We demonstrate that converging and non-converging iterations of the optimization algorithms are statistically different in a view of applied chaos, complexity and predictability estimating indicators.

Keywords: Chaos · Recurrence · Complexity · Swarm · Convergence

1 Introduction

Natural systems not rarely undergo phase transition when performing a computation (as interpreted by humans), e.g. reaction-diffusion chemical systems produce a solid precipitate representing geometrical structures [10], slime mould transits from a disorderly network of 'random scouting' to a prolonger filaments of protoplasmic tube connecting source of nutrients [2], 'hot ice' computer crystallizes [1]. Computation at the phase transition between chaos and order was firstly studied by Crutchfield and Young [12], who proposed measures of complexity characterising the transition. The ideas were applied to cellular automata by Langton [19]: a computation at the edge of chaos occurs due to gliders. Phase transitions were also demonstrated for a genetic algorithm which fall into a chaotic regime for some initial conditions [24, 31] and network traffic models [25].

© Springer International Publishing AG, part of Springer Nature 2018
S. Stepney and S. Verlan (Eds.): UCNC 2018, LNCS 10867, pp. 204–216, 2018.
https://doi.org/10.1007/978-3-319-92435-9_15

Algorithmic models of evolutionary based optimization, AI and ALife possess comparable features of the systems with a higher complexity, they simulate [14, 36]. We focus on the behavioral modes: the presence of a random or pseudo-random cycling (analogous to gaseous phase state), ordered or a stable states (analogous to solid state), or the chaotic oscillations (transitive states). Each of the modes could imply different level of a computational complexity or an algorithm performance as it was revealed on different algorithms [6,7,15]. By detecting such modes we can control and dynamically tune performance of the computational systems.

A swarm-like behavior has been extensively examined in studies of Zelinka et al. [35] where the changing dynamics of an observed algorithm was modeled by a network structure. The relevance between network features and algorithm behavior supported the control mechanism that was able to increase the algorithm performance [30]. An extensive empirical review of existing swarm based algorithms has been brought by Schut [28] where approaches like collective intelligence, self-organization, complex adaptive systems, multi-agent systems, swarm intelligence were empirically examined and confronted with their real models which reflected several criteria for development and verification.

We aim to evaluate the dynamics of optimization algorithms, inspired by evolution and swarm-like behavior. We evaluate the dynamical modes of algorithms based on predictability, complexity and chaos features. At the end, we statistically examine the difference between estimated modes, they possessed. In case of successful detection of statistically different modes and their transitions during the optimization process, the edge of chaos may be examined as well as controlling tools may be designed. Having these tools may increase the ability to control the optimization process being on maximal convergence level.

2 Theoretical Background

2.1 Swarm Based Optimization

The optimization algorithms examined in our study are representatives of bio-inspired single-objective optimization algorithms. They iteratively maintain the population of candidates migrating through the searched space. Their current position represents the solution vector X of the optimized problem.

Particle Swarm Optimization implies that the combined particle's aim towards the global leader and its previous best position [17]. The composition of these two stochastically altered directions modifies its current position in order to find a better optimum of the given function. Several reviewing studies are available as extensive descriptions of the algorithm and they are also surveying proposed extensions and variations [4,13].

Differential Evolution (DE) was developed by Storn and Price [29] and it possesses the features of a self-organizing search as well as an evolutionary based optimization. This interconnection is deserved due to its three main stages. DE offers several strategies driving the computation of new positions for its candidates. One of them takes three random candidates to calculate an intermediate candidate which creates a new position by binary crossover with an optimized candidate x_i. It takes this new position only if it is better than the current one.

Self-organizing migrating algorithm (SOMA) is a stochastic evolutionary algorithm was proposed by Zelinka [34]. Ideologically, this algorithms stands right between purely swarm optimization driven PSO and evolutionary-like DE. The entire nature of migrating individuals across the search-space is represented by steps in the defined path length and a stochastic nature of a perturbation parameter that represents specific version of the mutation. The perturbation creates binary vector by the adjusted PRT parameter and the given formula

$$v_j^{prt} = \begin{cases} 1, & \text{if } r_j < PRT \\ 0, & \text{otherwise} \end{cases}, (j = 1, 2, \cdots, d) \tag{1}$$

Applying V^{prt}, the path is perturbed towards new solution using current particle's and leaders position.

$$x_i^{t+1} = x_i^t + (x_L^t - x_i^t) v_i^{prt} \tag{2}$$

During each migration loop, each particle performs n steps according to the adjusted step size and the path length. If the path length is higher than one, particle will travel longer distance, than is his distance towards the leader.

2.2 Lemplel-Ziv Complexity

According to the Kolmogorov's definition of complexity, the complexity of an examined sequence X is the size of a smallest binary program that produces such sequence [11]. Because this definition is way too general and any direct computation is not guaranteed within the finite time [11], approximative techniques are frequently employed.

Lempel and Ziv designed a complexity estimation in a sense of Kolmogorov's definition, but limiting the estimated program only to two operations: recursive copy and paste [21]. The entire sequence based on an alphabet $\aleph$ is split into a set of unique words of unequal lengths, which is called a vocabulary. The approximated binary program making use of copy and paste operations on the vocabulary, is able to reconstruct the entire sequence. Based on the size of vocabulary $(c(X))$, the complexity is estimated as $C_{LZ}(X) = c(X)(\log_k c(X) + 1) \cdot N^{-1}$, where k means the size of the alphabet and N is the length of the input sequence. A natural extension for multi-dimensional LZ complexity was proposed in [37]. In case of a set of l symbolic sequences $X^i (i = 1, \cdots, l)$, Lempel and Ziv's definitions remain valid if one extends the alphabet from scalar values x_k to l-tuples elements $(x_k^1, \cdots, x_k^l)$. The joined-LZC is than calculated as $C_{LZ}(X^1, \cdots, X^l) = c(X^1, \cdots, X^l)(\log_{k^2} c(X^1, \cdots, X^l) + 1) \cdot N^{-1}$.

2.3 Recurrence Quantification Analysis

The recurrence plot (RP) is the visualization of the recurrence matrix of m-dimensional system states $x \in \mathbb{R}^m$ [23]. The closeness of these states for a given trajectory $\boldsymbol{x}_i$ ($i = 1, 2, ..., N$) where N is the trajectory length, is thresholded in the Heaviside step function $\Theta(\cdot)$ which results in the binary matrix of recurrence $R_{i,j}(\epsilon) = \Theta(\epsilon - \|\boldsymbol{x}_i - \boldsymbol{x}_j\|)$. The Euclidean norm is the most frequently applied distance metric $\|\cdot\|$ and the threshold value ϵ can be chosen according to several techniques [18, 23, 27, 32, 33].

If only one-dimensional time series is given, the phase space trajectory has to be reconstructed from the time series $\{u_i\}_{i=1}^N$, e.g., by using the time-delay embedding $\boldsymbol{x}_i = (u_i, u_{i+\tau}, ..., u_{i+(m-1)\tau})$, where m is the embedding dimension and τ is the embedding delay [26]. The parameters m and τ may be found using methods based on false nearest neighbors and auto-correlation [16].

The RQA measures applied in this experiment describe the predictability and level of chaos in the observed system. Determinism is defined as the percentage of points that form diagonal lines (Eq. 3)

$$DET = \sum_{l=2}^{N} lP(l) \left[\sum_{l=1}^{N} lP(l) \right]^{-1} \tag{3}$$

where $P(l)$ is the histogram of the lengths l of the diagonal lines [23]. Its values, ranging between zero and one, estimate the predictability of the system.

Divergence is related to the sum of the positive Lyapunov exponents, naturally computing the amount of chaos in the system, and it is defined as follows

$$DIV = L_{\max}^{-1}, \qquad L_{\max} = \max(\{l_i; i = 1, \cdots, N_l\}) \tag{4}$$

where $L_{\max}$ is the longest diagonal line in the RP (excluding the main diagonal line) [23].

3   Experiment Design

Data Preparation. All three examined algorithms attempted to optimize one common fitness-function, the Rastrigin function, because of its frequent application with similar manners and its dimensional scalability that satisfies our testing purposes: $f(x) = A \cdot n + \sum_{i=1}^{n} (x_i^2 - A \cdot \cos(2\pi x_i))$, where $A = 10$ and $x_i \in [-5.12, 5.12]$. The function has a global minimum at $x = 0$ where $f(x) = 0$.

The adjustment of the optimization algorithms was tuned by random search hyper-parameter optimization [5] in order to find the optimal adjustment to perform the best possible convergence. The only fixed hyper-parameters were the dimension of the optimized function (it also affected the dimension of the particles, $D = 10$) and the population size of the algorithm ($NP = 40, 60, 100$- it varied in order to see the affect of population size on the appearing dynamics). The rest of the hyper-parameters were optimized in the ranges according to Table 1.

The behavior of the optimization algorithms is represented by the positions ($X_{t_1} = \{x_{t_1,1}, x_{t_1,2}, \cdots, x_{t_1,D}\}$) taken by their population members ($P = p_1, p_2, \cdots, p_N$) during their migrations/iterations ($p_1 = X_{t_1,1}, X_{t_2,1}, \cdots, X_{t_m,1}$). All of them are stored for the further examination. The time windows w of iterations are taken and transfered into matrices of particles positions where columns are particle's coordinates and rows are ordered particles by their population number and time.

$$(P_{w_i} = \{x_{t_i,1}, x_{t_i,2}, \cdots, x_{t_i,N}, x_{t_{i+1},1}, x_{t_{i+1},2} \cdots, x_{t_{i+1},N}, \cdots x_{t_{i+w},N}\}).$$

Table 1. The value ranges of hyper-parameters of optimization algorithms to be adjusted with their meaning.

Parameter	Algorithm	Meaning	Value
c_1	PSO	global best position multiplier	$\langle 0.5, 1.5 \rangle$
c_2	PSO	local best position multiplier	$\langle 0.5, 1.5 \rangle$
w	PSO	inertia weight	$\langle 0.5, 0.95 \rangle$
F	DE	differential weight	$\langle 0.1, 1.0 \rangle$
Cr	DE	crossover probability	$\langle 0.1, 1.0 \rangle$
prt	SOMA	pertubation probability	$\langle 0.1, 1.0 \rangle$
step size	SOMA	size of the performed step	$\langle 0.1, 1.0 \rangle$

Convergence. Applying the before-mentioned algorithms' hyper-parameters, the optimization converged towards an optimum. In case of our experiment, the exclusive finding of a global optimum does not play such an important role as the fact that algorithms converge towards a fixed point performing various changes and interactions inside of their swarm. Various visualization settings (window size, population size) were tested in order to plot the most kinds of phase shifting behaviors. Figures, depicted as follows (Figs. 2, 3, 4), performed visually the representatives of the most common kinds.

The changes and interactions inside of their migrating populations are not usually visible in convergence plots, however changes during the convergence may be estimated using recurrence plots. For this purpose, three selected windows of algorithms' iterations were visualized to spot the differences among them. Figure 1 illustrates how phases of the algorithm convergences are reflected in recurrence plots.

Complexity Estimation. The obtained matrix P_{w_i} served as input for a joint Lempel-Ziv complexity (LZC) estimation and RQA. For the purpose of joint LZC estimation, the input matrix was discretized into adjustable number of letters n_l of an alphabet by the given formula. Let $p_{\min} = \min\{p_j | 1 \leq j \leq w\}$, $p_{\max} = \max\{p_j | 1 \leq j \leq w\}$ and $p_d = p_{max} - p_{min}$ then each element p_j is assigned value $p_j \leftarrow \lfloor n_l \frac{p_j - p_{min}}{p_d} \rfloor$. The joint-LZC therefore stands, in our case, for the complexity of time ordered n dimensional tuples (populations).

In case of RQA, there is a possibility to directly use the spatial data representation [22], therefore we did not apply the Takens' embedding theorem and we directly calculated the thresholded similarity matrix from our source data. The RQA features like determinism and divergence were calculated.

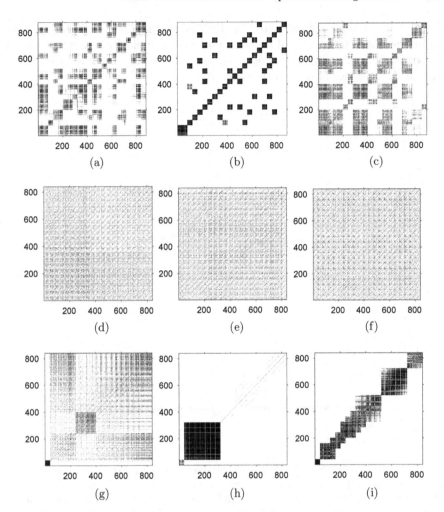

Fig. 1. Recurrence plots of the PSO (abc), DE (def), and SOMA (ghi) behavior calculated as similarities among the particles' positions X_t grouped into the windows of populations P_{w_i} during their (adg) "post-initial" (10th migration), (beh) "top-converging"
(60th migration) and (cfi) "post-converging" (400th migration) phase.

Based on the obtained visualizations (Figs. 2, 3 and 4) we are able to confirm
the visible differences in cases of PSO and SOMA algorithm. These two optimizations are performing similarities when the population is migrating the same
direction. Once the optimum is reached, the similarities decrease. We are not able
to confirm the same in case of DE. Due to the randomly performed crossover
and additional mutation, this algorithm seems to contain more randomness and
evolution-like behavior.

Further examinations calculated the DET, DIV and LZC values during all of the migrations. The statistical difference of these complexity indicators among the converging and non-converging iterations will be examined by ANOVA to confirm the presence of state transitions [20].

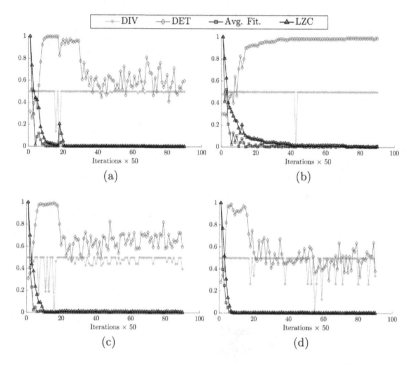

Fig. 2. Progress of the PSO algorithms executed several times with varying populations and window sizes. Horizontal axis represents the migrations while the vertical line holds values of average fitness-function of the population (Avg. Fit.) and obtained indicators. (a) population size 40, window 20, (b) population size 70, window 20, (c) population size 100, window 30, (d) population size 100, window 40

4 Results

Levels of complexity and the RQA indicators may posses different values based on a given window size as well as the size of the population, therefore we tried several combinations of these parameters (3 per each, therefore nine combinations for each algorithm). Only each tenth value of each time set was plotted in the charts (see Figs. 2, 3 and 4). The values of fitness-function and LZ complexity were normalized into the range between 0 and 1. The determinism returns such normalized values originally, therefore there was no need for an additional normalization. In case of the divergence, its values were very low ($\times E10^{-3}$), so it was necessary to multiply them in order to keep the similar visual scale in charts.

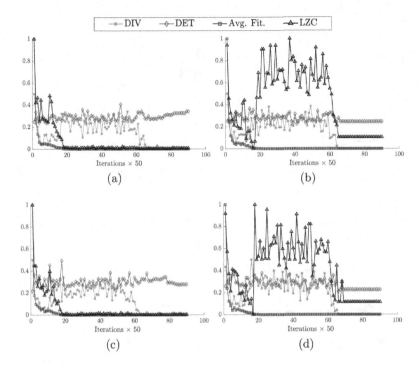

Fig. 3. Progress of the DE algorithms executed several times with varying populations and window sizes. Horizontal axis represents the migrations while the vertical line holds values of average fitness-function of the population (Avg. Fit.) and obtained indicators. (a) population size 40, window 20, (b) population size 70, window 20, (c) population size 70, window 30, (d) population size 70, window 40

Particle Swarm Optimization. The progress of PSO (Fig. 2) possess quickly decreasing LZC as the population converges towards an optimum and looses diversity. This behavior is expected as well as some appearing pulses in times when population probably left a local optimum, which was also reflected by an additional converges towards some better solution.

The progress of the population was very much predictable as it was evaluated by DET which possesed values close to 1 when the convergence of the population was the highest. Once a found optimum was reached by the majority of the population, DET dropped and evaluated the population's progress as unpredictable.

Higher values of DIV imply the presence of chaotic behavior in the system. All of the evaluations returned only very small values of this indicator therefore the only small amount of chaos can be confirmed. In the available visual evaluation, the DIV appears to possess the smallest relation to the progress of the algorithm.

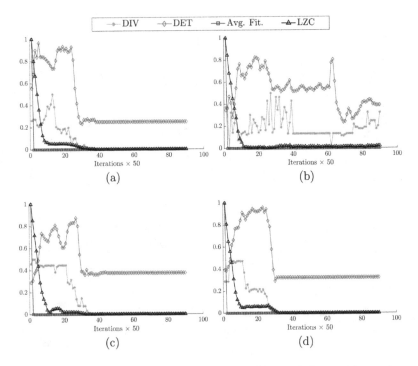

Fig. 4. Progress of the SOMA algorithms executed several times with varying populations and window sizes. Horizontal axis represents the migrations while the vertical line holds values of average fitness-function of the population (Avg. Fit.) and obtained indicators. (a) population size 40, window 20, (b) population size 40, window 30, (c) population size 40, window 40, (d) population size 100, window 20

Differential Evolution. DE performs elitism during its operation which can be the reason of an absolute flat progress of all its indicators during last iterations. The significant increase of LZC values in some cases remains unclear and can be connected with situation when the population found several optimums of the same quality and the population randomly switched among them (see Fig. 3). The values of DET only evaluate the entire progress of DE as unpredictable almost the same way as the DIV which marked the behavior as chaotic until the found optimum was reached by the population and any other better solution was found.

Self-Organizing Migration Algorithm. The progress of the SOMA algorithm has similarities with both previous algorithms. All indicators are very flat during its last migrations, because particles remains on their positions in cases when better solution was not found. The pertubet following of the leader is similarly reflected by DET as it was in case of PSO, when the behavior of the algorithm was marked as predictable until the majority of the population reached the found optimum. The appearance of the chaos is very low the same way as it was in previous cases (DIV). The LZC as well as the Fitness dropped very quickly because of the nature of SOMA. Each particle performed multiple trials (steps as the path length divided by the step size) and the each population's individual migrated towards its best trial. This is the nature of the algorithm and the reason why it appears as the algorithm with the highest performance in the frame of our experiments.

4.1   ANOVA Testing

The DET, DIV and LZC values were split into values obtained in different phases of the optimization. Six groups, marked from 1 to 6, were defined by visual estimation as follows.

- **1** as progress of PSO algorithm during its converging migrations [10, 60]
- **2** as progress of DE algorithm during its converging migrations [10, 60]
- **3** as progress of SOMA algorithm during its converging migrations [10, 60]
- **4** as progress of PSO algorithm during its non-converging migrations [300, 350]
- **5** as progress of DE algorithm during its non-converging migrations [300, 350]
- **6** as progress of SOMA algorithm during its non-converging migrations [300, 350]

The presence of statistically significant differences among the means of these groups will confirm the state transitions. Especially we are interested whether the groups of the same algorithms are different and in which indicators.

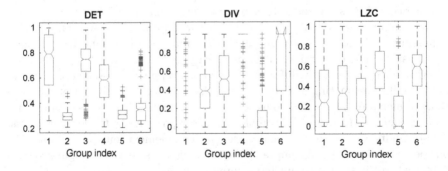

Fig. 5. Means with standard deviations obtained by ANOVA testing on six defined groups of data.

ANOVA testing rejected the null hypothesis that says about similarity of the means across the examined groups of the data (see Fig. 5). Obtained p-values are 0 for $ANOVA_{DET}$ and $ANOVA_{DIV}$, and $2.657e - 94$ for $ANOVA_{LZC}$. The performed additional post-hoc analysis revealed the specific differences among the groups according to their means and it is as follows. The means of Determinism results were able to differentiate the groups 1 and 3 from the rest of the groups, while the means of second group were not significantly different from others (5, 6). The separability performance of the means of Divergence were able to significantly exclude the groups 2 and three from the rest while the means of the first group were similar to the fourth group. Both of them differed from the rest significantly. In case of LZC, the groups 1 and 3 are have means significantly different from the rest of the groups while group 2 possesses this difference against all of the groups.

These results mean that optimization phases are distinguishable by means of this complexity measure. From the above mentioned differences of the means, it is clearly visible that the convergence phases of PSO are separable by the means of Determinism and LZC while in case of Divergence we are not able to distinguish among them. In case of DE, its LZC and Divergence means possessed significant differences between DEs' convergence phases while Determinism was not applicable for this task. And finally the case of SOMA. All of the applied complexity criteria returned significantly different means among the SOMA convergence phases, therefore they are able to be distinguished by these values.

5   Discussion

In contrast to conventional computers, natural systems never stop to function, therefore by simply observing a physical, chemical or living computer we might never know when its completed the task and produced result. This phenomenon was formalized in a framework of inductive Turing machines [8] and advanced in structural machines [9], however still there is a lack of a definite measure. Some measures of spatio-temporal dynamics of a computing system are necessary to infer weather consider its current state as representing a final solution or wait longer.

In computer experiments with particle swarm optimization we found that it is possible to detect the convergence of algorithm using RQA and LZ complexity measures. The converging and non-converging iterations of the optimization algorithms are statistically different in the view of applied chaos, complexity and predictability estimating indicators. Typically, the degree of RQA Determinism sharply increases, as if undergoing a phase transition, when fitness approaches its maximum. Dynamics of LZ complexity follows, in general, the level of fitness. These results are well in line, and somewhat complement, our previous studies on the use of dynamics of compressibility of a system's spatial configurations to detect when the system completed computation [3].

Our findings may lead to the future work which is related to the estimation of the edge of chaos in the swarm-like optimization algorithms. It may be applied in a design of adaptive approaches aiming to control their progress in order to sustain the best possible performance.

Acknowledgment. The following grants are acknowledged for the financial support provided for this research: Grant of SGS No. SGS 2018/177, VSB-Technical University of Ostrava and German Research Foundation (DFG projects no. MA 4759/9-1 and MA4759/8).

References

1. Adamatzky, A.: Hot ice computer. Phys. Lett. A **374**(2), 264–271 (2009)
2. Adamatzky, A.: Advances in Physarum Machines: Sensing and Computing with Slime Mould., vol. 21. Springer, Switzerland (2016). https://doi.org/10.1007/978-3-319-26662-6
3. Adamatzky, A., Jones, J.: On using compressibility to detect when slime mould completed computation. Complexity **21**(5), 162–175 (2016)
4. Banks, A., Vincent, J., Anyakoha, C.: A review of particle swarm optimization. part i: background and development. Nat. Comput. **6**(4), 467–484 (2007)
5. Bergstra, J., Bengio, Y.: Random search for hyper-parameter optimization. J. Mach. Learn. Res. **13**, 281–305 (2012)
6. Bertschinger, N., Natschläger, T.: Real-time computation at the edge of chaos in recurrent neural networks. Neural Comput. **16**(7), 1413–1436 (2004)
7. Boedecker, J., Obst, O., Lizier, J.T., Mayer, N.M., Asada, M.: Information processing in echo state networks at the edge of chaos. Theory Biosci. **131**(3), 205–213 (2012)
8. Burgin, M.: Inductive turing machines with a multiple head and kolmogorov algorithms. Sov. Math. Dokl. **29**, 189–193 (1984)
9. Burgin, M., Adamatzky, A.: Structural machines and slime mould computation. Int. J. Gen. Syst. **42**, 1–24 (2017)
10. Costello, B.D.L., Adamatzky, A.: Calculating voronoi diagrams using chemical reactions. In: Advances in Unconventional Computing, pp. 167–198. Springer, Switzerland (2017). https://doi.org/10.1007/978-3-319-33921-4
11. Cover, T.M., Thomas, J.A.: Elements of Information Theory. Wiley, Hoboken (2012)
12. Crutchfield, J.P., Young, K.: Computation at the onset of chaos. In: The Santa Fe Institute, Westview, Citeseer (1988)
13. Del Valle, Y., Venayagamoorthy, G.K., Mohagheghi, S., Hernandez, J.C., Harley, R.G.: Particle swarm optimization: basic concepts, variants and applications in power systems. IEEE Trans. Evol. Comput. **12**(2), 171–195 (2008)
14. Detrain, C., Deneubourg, J.L.: Self-organized structures in a superorganism: do ants "behave" like molecules? Phys. Life Rev. **3**(3), 162–187 (2006)
15. Kadmon, J., Sompolinsky, H.: Transition to chaos in random neuronal networks. Phys. Rev. X **5**(4), 041030 (2015)
16. Kantz, H., Schreiber, T.: Nonlinear Time Series Analysis. University Press, Cambridge (1997)
17. Kennedy, J., Eberhart, R.C.: Particle swarm optimization. In: Proceedings of the IEEE International Conference on Neural Networks, pp. 1942–1948 (1995)
18. Koebbe, M., Mayer-Kress, G.: Use of recurrence plots in the analysis of time-series data. In: SFI Studies in the Sciences of Complexity, vol. 12, pp. 361–361. Addison-Wesley Publishing (1992)
19. Langton, C.G.: Computation at the edge of chaos: phase transitions and emergent computation. Physica D **42**(1–3), 12–37 (1990)
20. Larson, M.G.: Analysis of variance. Circulation **117**(1), 115–121 (2008)
21. Lempel, A., Ziv, J.: On the complexity of finite sequences. IEEE Trans. Inf. Theory **22**(1), 75–81 (1976)
22. Marwan, N., Kurths, J., Saparin, P.: Generalised recurrence plot analysis for spatial data. Phys. Lett. A **360**(4), 545–551 (2007)

23. Marwan, N., Romano, M.C., Thiel, M., Kurths, J.: Recurrence plots for the analysis of complex systems. Phys. Rep. **438**(5), 237–329 (2007)
24. Mitchell, M., Hraber, P., Crutchfield, J.P.: Revisiting the edge of chaos: evolving cellular automata to perform computations. arXiv preprint adap-org/9303003 (1993)
25. Ohira, T., Sawatari, R.: Phase transition in a computer network traffic model. Phys. Rev. E **58**(1), 193 (1998)
26. Packard, N.H., Crutchfield, J.P., Farmer, J.D., Shaw, R.S.: Geometry from a time series. Phys. Rev. Lett. **45**(9), 712 (1980)
27. Schinkel, S., Dimigen, O., Marwan, N.: Selection of recurrence threshold for signal detection. Eur. Phys. J. Spec. Top. **164**(1), 45–53 (2008)
28. Schut, M.C.: On model design for simulation of collective intelligence. Inf. Sci. **180**(1), 132–155 (2010)
29. Storn, R., Price, K.: Differential evolution-a simple and efficient heuristic for global optimization over continuous spaces. J. Global Optim. **11**(4), 341–359 (1997)
30. Tomaszek, L., Zelinka, I.: On performance improvement of the soma swarm based algorithm and its complex network duality. In: 2016 IEEE Congress on Evolutionary Computation (CEC), pp. 4494–4500. IEEE (2016)
31. Wright, A.H., Agapie, A.: Cyclic and chaotic behavior in genetic algorithms. In: Proceedings of the 3rd Annual Conference on Genetic and Evolutionary Computation, pp. 718–724. Morgan Kaufmann Publishers Inc. (2001)
32. Zbilut, J.P., Webber, C.L.: Embeddings and delays as derived from quantification of recurrence plots. Phys. Lett. A **171**(3–4), 199–203 (1992)
33. Zbilut, J.P., Zaldivar-Comenges, J.M., Strozzi, F.: Recurrence quantification based liapunov exponents for monitoring divergence in experimental data. Phys. Lett. A **297**(3), 173–181 (2002)
34. Zelinka, I.: Soma–self-organizing migrating algorithm. In: New optimization Techniques in Engineering, vol. 141, pp. 167–217. Springer, Heidelberg (2004). https://doi.org/10.1007/978-3-540-39930-8_7
35. Zelinka, I., Tomaszek, L., Vasant, P., Dao, T.T., Hoang, D.V.: A novel approach on evolutionary dynamics analysis-a progress report. J. Comput. Sci. **37**(5), 739–749 (2017)
36. Zenil, H., Gauvrit, N.: Algorithmic cognition and the computational nature of the mind. In: Encyclopedia of Complexity and Systems Science, pp. 1–9 (2017)
37. Zozor, S., Ravier, P., Buttelli, O.: On lempel-ziv complexity for multidimensional data analysis. Phys. A **345**(1), 285–302 (2005)

Author Index

Printed in the United States
By Bookmasters